FIGHTING
FOR
AIR

FIGHTING FOR AIR

In the Trenches with Television News

LIZ TROTTA

UNIVERSITY OF MISSOURI PRESS
COLUMBIA AND LONDON

Copyright © 1991, 1994 by Liz Trotta
Originally published by Simon & Schuster
First University of Missouri Press paperback printing 1994
University of Missouri Press, Columbia, Missouri 65201
Printed and bound in the United States of America
5 4 3 2 1   98 97 96 95 94

Library of Congress Cataloging-in-Publication Data
Trotta, Liz.
    Fighting for air : in the trenches with television news / Liz
Trotta
       p.   cm.
    Includes index.
    ISBN 0-8262-0952-1
    1. Television broadcasting of news—United States.   2. Trotta,
Liz.   3. War correspondents—United States—Biography.
4. Vietnamese Conflict, 1961-1965—Journalists—Biography.   5. Women
journalists—United States—Biography.   I. Title.
PN4888.T4T7   1994
070'.95—dc20   93-40369
                                                              CIP

⊗™ This paper meets the requirements of the American National Standard
for Permanence of Paper for Printed Library Materials, Z39.48, 1984.

To the memory

of George Barrett

"Much have I seen and known; cities of men
    And manners, climates, councils, governments,
    Myself not least, but honor'd of them all;
    And drunk delight of battle with my peers,
    Far on the ringing plains of windy Troy.
    I am part of all that I have met;
    Yet all experience is an arch wherethrough
    Gleams that untravel'd world."

                        "Ulysses"
                        Alfred, Lord Tennyson

CONTENTS

PROLOGUE   9

1 "FIND ME A GIRL REPORTER"   13

2 "BUT I DON'T DO WEDDINGS"   32

3 CARTHAGE BURNING   61

4 SOME ENCHANTED EVENINGS   80

5 RAW FOOTAGE   107

6 ARMY WITHOUT BANNERS   129

7 THROUGH THE SIFTER   147

8 THE FORGETTING OF MARY JO   168

9 KNIGHTS AND KNAVES   191

10 OUTPOSTS OF EMPIRE   218

11 OCEANS APART   240

12 THE LADY IN THE IRON MASK   266

8

13 ON BOARD THE ROLLS-ROYCE *285*

14 SEND IN THE CLOWNS *311*

15 ENEMIES: OLD AND NEW *333*

16 GHOSTS *354*

AFTERWORD *376*
to the paperback edition

ACKNOWLEDGMENTS *381*

INDEX *383*

PROLOGUE

I always knew I would go back to Vietnam. Not because I believed that my career in television news made it likely. And not because I thought the mud and elephant grass would one day bloom into a tourist paradise. It was a compulsion, a resolve to return to the place where I had endured the worst—and some of the best—moments of my life. Perhaps I thought that one more glance would give me some focus beyond what I could see through a television camera. Perhaps it was time to clean up unfinished business.

My country and I were in step that spring of 1985. Vietnam had become a scar in the national consciousness, not even a place anymore, but a code word for a country's catharsis. Memories haunted both sides except that, as I would find, Vietnam remained a constant—

it knew where it was going—while America was still in analysis. Television news had realized its power in bringing home the war's harrowing images. It could hardly escape the force that had so altered our politics and our values. And it, too, would never be the same.

Some very practical reasons also urged me upon this journey: my career was in trouble. Nobody said as much, but since a new breed of management had taken over CBS News, there was no mistaking it. In the past six years I had been assigned to overseas stories often enough, but for the tenth anniversary of the fall of Saigon the networks were sending in their big guns. I was not among them, at least not at first. Given my many years in TV news—which included two tours of duty covering the war—there were clearly other influences at work. It looked hopeless until the foreign desk ran into trouble getting the necessary visas and discovered that I could help smooth the way. For my efforts I was rewarded with a spot on the team.

So here was the chance for a comeback, and the reassuring signs of spring were telling me that I couldn't miss. After all, hadn't I made my name in Vietnam? A "pioneering newswoman," boasted the press releases, the first female TV journalist to cover combat in that bloody war, or for that matter, any war.

I had grown up with TV news, trained originally like so many correspondents in those days as a newspaper reporter who had "made the switch." The years that followed were a feast for anyone in the business: war in Southeast Asia, the civil rights struggle, the assassination of Robert Kennedy, the antiwar protests, Chappaquiddick, the emergence of the women's movement, a walk on the moon, the hostages in Iran, and the election of Ronald Reagan. It was a world in transition, and as it changed so did the way television covered it.

Vietnam saw the Model-T days of TV news, a test under fire for reporters and camera crews struggling with erratic film technology. Soon new kinds of electronic magic would transmit news pictures from anywhere in the world in a blink. But there was no reason to suspect that the basic rules of news, its precepts and habits, would change anymore than the journalistic skills required to cover and air it. As a correspondent dashing from Timbuktu to İzmir by way of Paris, I took it for granted that being a journalist was enough. This was an innocent premise. There were personal assumptions, too, namely that the parade of people who drifted in and out of my life witnessing and reporting these events would somehow remain untouched, just as I would. All you had to do was stand outside the story, report it, and not look back. A shortsighted appraisal.

My career, I suppose, was a first of sorts. Even apart from being a woman in a profession dominated by men and a conservative in the generally liberal climate of the media, I had worked a far-flung beat, reporting great events and small, recording the words of the important, self-important, and forgotten people of this world. I had covered conflict from the streets of the South Bronx to the sands of the Sinai, and along the way fought many private battles of my own. All in the name of television news. Forget the glamour. It was often gritty, exhausting, lonely—and exhilarating—work. And I have never regretted choosing it.

After twenty years in the business, I had gained a wider perspective on broadcast news and those who reported it—then and now, past ideals eroded by present realities. Mine was not the view from an anchor desk, an air-conditioned office, or the hushed hallways of the corporate brass. It was the view of a line correspondent, the grunt of TV news, closer to events than anyone else, and close enough to the people and the pressures that had so inexorably altered the craft and intent of television journalism.

That was why, at this particular moment in my life, it seemed altogether appropriate that I was going back to Vietnam. It was the crucible in which television news—and my own career—had been forged. It would be an opportunity to rekindle old fires, sharpen dull edges, do my job the way I still thought it should be done. And, sure enough, three weeks after my return from that journey into the past, I learned that CBS was, at last, ready to talk about renewing my recently expired contract. My tour in Vietnam appeared to have nudged management into deciding I was worth keeping around. Curious, I thought, that no one put it in writing, but I dismissed the unworthy thought and waited for the payoff. Within days I signed for another four years, admittedly at a salary hardly commensurate with what the stars of TV news were drawing; but, hell, for better or worse, it was my chosen calling. There were plenty of kind words to go around about my trip and even some good press reaction. One effusive columnist referred to me as the Diogenes of the media. Over lunch, a vice-president handed me a copy of this piece, saying, "He's right. You were the only reporter there who told the truth." I was elated.

The weeks of summer melted away before I saw him again. And when I did, he fired me.

1

"FIND ME A GIRL REPORTER"

A low murmur of voices yielded to silence under the no-nonsense tone of the floor manager.

"All right everybody," he ordered. "Stand by."

I heard a throat clear, a shuffle of footsteps. The floor man's hands, shining white in the darkness below the camera lens, fixed my attention like a falling star, fingers disappearing one by one as he counted.

"Three, two, one." Silence. He thrust his hand downward. It could only mean go.

I began to read, unevenly at first, my voice strangled by fright. After a minute or so I began to get the hang of it and found a lower range as my throat opened, dividing my attention between the lens and the script, not quite certain what the proportion should be. This wasn't quite as easy as it looked.

Slowly, back arched, reaching for breath, I had entered into the forbidding rites of behind-the-scenes television broadcasting: the casual chatter of the world-weary makeup artists and hairdressers who turn men from Boise into sleek pundits and girls from New Haven into sloe-eyed vamps; the wisecracking studio crew with their "show me" body language; the floor manager's fingers that count you down into the open while your stomach tightens and your lips dry out; the black hoods of the ceiling lights in the studio's chill darkness, menacing down like so many stalactites in an ancient cave.

As I look back, subliminal images flash into my mind, scenes from the movie *Coma*—a hospital where demented doctors kept "dead" people alive by suspending them in space and connecting their bodies with a series of cables to various machines. The bodies hung motionless, waiting, lying still in the overhead light, apart from the world of mortals, utterly alone. That's what it felt like sitting in that bright circle of light, connected yet set apart—a cocoon, helpless, at the mercy of the hands in the darkness and the reactions of the invisible people who watched and listened to me through the black lens.

I could never understand why a lady from *The Washington Post*, who once dabbled in TV news, wrote that her on-air confusion stemmed from ignorance of what the red light meant. What could she have thought it was? A traffic light? Perhaps a devil's eye—that would be closer to the mark—a silent siren calling you to order, demanding that blood-quickening, adrenaline-pumping, gut-churning response that is the only way to survive its glance.

When the red glow appeared that April morning, it was only a test, a closed-circuit exercise in seeing what would happen between the camera and me. Still, parallel to my terror of this strange apparatus lurked the more sickening thought that I would fail. Who was I supposed to be talking to anyway? The newsroom? The executive suite? Last night's date? A little old lady in Omaha? The answer, I learned, was yes to all of the above. This was, indeed, the dangerous side of the camera. And it was where I wanted to be.

After an agonizing wait of three weeks, Dick Kutzleb, the WNBC news director who had read a series I wrote as a reporter for *Newsday*, called me up: "Why don't you come to work?" The audition had gone well, but it was the writing test—a five-minute broadcast derived from the latest news on the wires that had to be finished in forty-five minutes—and my newspaper and wire service background that had given me the edge. The competition had narrowed down to me and a fair-haired beauty from Chicago—the first and last time in my career that I would win over a blonde.

REACHING for the gold ring had begun early, with the usual small-town yearnings and dreams of the big city, but I took the first shaky steps on what guidance counselors like to call "a career path" when I applied to journalism's boot camp, the Graduate School of Journalism at Columbia University. Unlike today, most newspaper editors then looked upon journalism schools as irrelevant, if not downright sacrilegious, that is except for Columbia, which from its commanding position on Morningside Heights exerted a traditional influence on the newspaper elite of the East. A degree from the Columbia J-school meant prestige and acceptance into the fraternity.

The first time I applied I was turned down and advised to get a year of print experience. So after striking out at several interviews "because women leave and have babies," I found a job as an editorial assistant at Hillman Periodicals, writing copy for four confession magazines. Blurb writing became my specialty. "They called me the town tramp— until I finally found love, and lost." Captions, too. " 'Oh Jean, Jean,' he moaned, his hands trembling with desire." Heavy stuff for a convent-bred newcomer to New York.

Finally, one day between blurbs, the long-awaited acceptance letter arrived, and bidding farewell to that hotbed of eroticism, I became part of the class of '61, ready to be tutored and trained by the best in the business—not just academics but working newsmen. At last, I had made it to the first rung. The Columbia J-school had its pick of thousands but took in only about seventy-five students, many of whom were already working press. Under an acknowledged quota system, about a dozen women could be admitted. By sheer persistence I was one of the anointed that year—at the beginning of a decade that would resound harshly in the annals of American history and completely transform the perception and practice of journalism.

It was a time of great events: Nikita Khrushchev banged his shoe on the desk at the United Nations; John Kennedy won the presidency as the Age of Camelot began; the U.S.-supported Bay of Pigs invasion floundered in a Cuban swamp; and two commercial jetliners collided over Brooklyn. The latter qualified as "a corking yarn" in the cavernous newsroom where we learned our trade.

To most in 1960, journalism meant writing, and writing meant print. There was little mention of TV news in our classes, even though most of us had already spent part of our youth before the flickering black-and-white pictures of John Cameron Swayze and the "Camel News Caravan." We saw Mao Tse-tung's Red Army swallowing China; the Army-McCarthy hearings draw the nation to the tiny screens of its few television sets; the North Koreans get ready to drive south. But for the most part TV news had the look and feel of movie newsreels. It was something that had already happened. And TV commentary was something we had already read. Words, not pictures, were what journalism was all about.

I scurried all over town with my "press pass," losing my way on the subways, sitting in the back rows at news conferences, getting elbowed by the "real" press and learning how to stand in the rain on a stakeout. The afternoon I cornered Nelson Rockefeller for an interview, it seemed certain the Pulitzer Prize was in my reach. I ambushed him as he got off an elevator, and, never one to ignore a young lady, the governor spent the next fifteen minutes answering my questions and looking deep into my eyes. It was the first of many interviews with "Rocky," and even though it would appear only in the J-school newspaper, I treasured it more than all others, even when they led the evening news.

Three evenings a week I earned pocket money and practiced my still-anemic writing skills by working three jobs. One, at the Inter-Catholic Press Agency, entailed editing a newsletter with dispatches from Poland. A former Polish prince ran the dingy office in a battered walk-up on Fourteenth Street, an elegant man who, in heavily accented English, recounted cold-war tales of horror behind the Iron Curtain. His aide—and my partner in editing—was a diminutive Catholic priest, Father Raphael, who had survived five years in Dachau.

For contrast, I taught journalism to young women at the Stern College of Yeshiva University. And for a trip into what was then a solid male bastion, I wrote sports for *The Long Island Press*. "Wrote" is rather an overstatement, as the job simply meant taking scores from the local high school correspondents—basketball, hockey, wrestling, and the like—and making a short piece out of them. My periodic panic about who scored what was usually relieved by a co-worker and classmate at Columbia, Christopher Wren, now a distinguished correspondent for *The New York Times*. Chris nicknamed me "Scoopie"— an obvious salute to my cool aproach to the labyrinthine world of high school gladiators.

Our classes at Columbia were taught by a prestigious group of resident or "uptown" professors, and a glamorous group from "downtown"—a casual euphemism for the real working press who taught part-time. The *Times* had the strongest representation; among them, George Barrett, a veteran reporter of two wars, easily became the class favorite. Dapper, sophisticated, with a neat mustache and wavy silver hair, Barrett was a dead ringer for William Faulkner. He had the ability to size up a person or a situation in seconds, and so it was natural for him to be dubbed dean of rewrite men at the *Times*, that band of quick-thinking pros who could pull it all together—a downed plane, a mass murder, a profile—on top of a deadline without a wasted motion.

Legends abounded about Barrett. His Rolls-Royce, his mystery women, his lifelong love affair with Europe. He had covered the stuff of reporters' dreams: Paris, when the lights went on at the close of World War II; the front lines in the Korean War; the South at the dawn of the civil rights movement.

"Being a reporter means leaving airports with no one to say 'Good-bye,' and arriving at airports with no one to say 'Hello.' " That was how Barrett summed up what my life was to be. At the time it sounded brave. It had a lone wolf quality that appealed to my sense of the reporter as a voyager and witness. From the start of the school term and throughout my career, Barrett was to be the touchstone, the journalistic measure by which I would weigh the tough decisions. He committed me to the open road of the working journalist, and when it got lonely in so many of those airports, I would recall it was a bargain struck in these formative years.

Newspapering was what we trained for that year. And while I wrestled with the intricacies of writing about second-strike nuclear capability and truth as a defense in libel law, television news muddled along on its primitive black-and-white small-screen stage, improving but still held within the confines of fifteen-minute evening broadcasts and the old habits of radio.

A course listed as News Broadcasting had a cartoon flavor sandwiched in a no-nonsense curriculum aimed at working in print. It was the school's one concession to what would become known as electronic journalism, a throwaway course that a few students took if they had a spare hour. Dallas Townsend, the famous and respected voice of CBS News, was the instructor.

One day he pulled me aside: "Liz, have you ever considered going into broadcasting? I think you're a natural for it."

I was flattered—but also taken aback. "Me, oh no," I said, trying to stave off this frivolity. "I'm going to be a newspaper woman, not a performer."

Townsend didn't forget that answer, and years later chided me about it as we went to and from our offices on the same floor at CBS.

A bevy of canonized liberal thinkers paraded before us that year: A. A. Berle, Averell Harriman, Anthony Lewis, among others, newsmakers and newsmen of no mean accomplishment. One faculty member in particular, Penn Kimball, a former press secretary to Harriman, once a writer for *Time* and *The New Republic,* lashed himself to the mast of left-thinking and could scarcely contain his joy when Kennedy was elected President. Kimball, who liked to give the impression of the rumpled Ivy League freethinker, was appointed my advisor. His task included supervision of my major paper, a kind of journalism thesis every student produced as a prerequisite for graduation. We were an ill-matched pair—he a WASP liberal, I an Italian-Catholic conservative (and a woman to boot)—and from the outset he specialized in needling me, mocking my suggestions for a theme, and offering little guidance. The deadline began to loom and I appealed to him for help. He seemed to lick his chops as he spoke: "The trouble with you is that you're Catholic," he said, "and Catholics can't write." It was the inevitable outcome of "all that parochial training."

Like so many professed liberals, Kimball took it for granted that Catholics, and especially Catholic conservatives—a hopelessly priest-ridden and unquestioning breed—had no ideas beyond giving up sweets for Lent. The Kennedys, however, were an exception. They were rich and international, and for these two attributes even calcified minds like that of the good professor would unbend.

It was a classic case of cherishing certain bigotries under the guise of sound liberal postures. Kimball epitomized the hypocrisy of those counting themselves among the well-educated, tightly connected, upper-middle-class liberal establishment, who issued their pronouncements ex cathedra from beneath the shade trees of Martha's Vineyard. While I eventually completed my thesis, which he meanly marked down because of my false start, I had learned a valuable lesson about American political thought.

IF TV journalism was still in the dark ages, network entertainment was in trouble on a different front, drawing fire from the Federal Communications Commission for its jejune programming. FCC chairman

Newton Minow that very year delivered his famous summation of television: "a vast wasteland." Game shows and westerns were making big money for the networks, and while there was little about television to attract young reporters set on the established goals of journalism, one sober broadcast—the Kennedy-Nixon debate—dramatized how powerful television could be, capturing the sharp differences between two men and in the end making the news, not just reporting it.

Kennedy's election heralded what is now considered a seminal period in American history. As eastern intellectuals saw it, significant social change would accompany this new venture into enlightened liberalism. They were right about change, but wrong about its direction. Out of the literary and peaceful Beat Generation movement of the 1950s a new shift in the wind was felt, a turbulence that would culminate in nothing less than a social revolution. First came the young people who carried the narcissistic extremes of the Beats even further—jeans, joints, hair, rock 'n' roll, love and peace. Then the civil rights marches, race riots, the feminist movement, and finally, tragically, a crescendo of adolescent anger against the war in Vietnam. Perhaps the metaphor of the Kennedy White House as Camelot was more apt than it first appeared. For during these years of the early sixties American society, like King Arthur's realm, was coming apart at the seams.

Revolutionaries laid part of their groundwork in Greenwich Village, where I lived. A strong Italian flavor still enveloped those narrow streets, not the precious pasta hangouts of later years offering boutique food but spaghetti joints with boccie courts in the back, Mamma yelling from the kitchen, and old ladies in black leaning out of tenement windows. It reminded me of growing up in New Haven, especially since my mother, as a young immigrant, had lived on Bleecker Street, steps away from Our Lady of Pompeii, where the eleven o'clock sermon was still delivered in Italian.

An old college pal, Jeannie, and I shared a cramped apartment on Cornelia Street, which evolved into a way station for a rather varied circle of friends: clean-shaven interns from Columbia studying to be rich doctors; revolutionaries such as World Citizen movement founder Gary Davis, who lived upstairs; Beat Generation poets; wild-eyed conservatives from Young Americans for Freedom (which I joined in its first week of existence that very year, 1960); reporters from the *Times*; stockbrokers from Wall Street; glamorous debs looking for husbands. Democracy in action.

One night, this coterie included more than the usual number of guitar players, among them my friend Maxine from New Haven who was a student at Barnard College and played at hootenannies in the Village. A "hoot" meant a group of people singing folk songs to guitar strums. Who could have guessed that as the concept grew and the number of string-pickers multiplied, the staid hoots of the fifties would one day culminate in the raucous howls of Woodstock.

Maxine pulled me aside midst the confusion of that two-room apartment and pointed to a gaunt young man with an aquiline nose. "He hasn't had any food in some time," she said. "And he's too shy to ask for something to eat."

"No problem," I said, and went over to introduce myself and ask him into the cramped kitchen.

I made him a peanut butter and jelly sandwich and poured a glass of milk. He wolfed down the Wonder Bread, and although basically monosyllabic in the style of the Beats, told me he was a musician and composer. Until 3 A.M., the no-longer-hungry young man with the stooped shoulders played the guitar in my bedroom to a circle of admirers, singing, clapping, carrying on. I looked in once or twice—but heard very little of the music that would later haunt the most vivid years of my career. I was too busy flirting with the medical students. When the party broke up, I caught his name during the good-byes. It was Bob Dylan.

In the newspaper business, no town claims more legends than Chicago, so after graduation I headed west. Jean left for Spain, pursuing a lifetime dream to become an expatriate. She drank the wine, ran with the bulls, and even joined up with the Hemingway crowd. The wide-eyed convent girl took to the flamenco and matador circuit like one of Papa's characters, a young Lady Brett who ran from whatever furies she thought pursued her. Soon, the letters stopped coming, and it would be years before I heard of her again.

I started in Chicago as a reporter for the *Tribune* on the metro or suburban section of the newspaper, covering town meetings, school boards and, the worst of all, zoning hearings, the litmus test for cub reporters. George Barrett, as usual, extended his invisible hand. The morning I arrived at the majestic Tribune Building overlooking the Chicago River, a letter appeared on my empty desk: "Welcome to Chicago . . . The main thing, of course, is to be yourself, and if you're scared, say so, and get help, and don't hesitate ever ever ever to ask questions, even of the guy (particularly of the guy) next to you."

And so it continued that most of what I had learned—and was about to learn—was from men.

Weekly section reporting soon paled and I began to lobby for a daily reporting slot in the main newsroom—a masterpiece of mahogany grandeur, solid and enduring beneath the flutter of a huge American flag. Colonel McCormick's legacy lived on, but getting into that newsroom was something else. There were only two woman reporters: one wrote features, the other stories about pets. Both had jobs because there hadn't been enough men to go around during World War II. My immediate editors held out little hope for promotion, so when I heard about an opening in the *Tribune* syndication office in New York, I went straight to the executive city editor of the paper, Clayton Kirkpatrick, a taciturn man given to dressing like a riverboat gambler, waving a cigarette holder to underline his remarks. He politely said no. "It's not a job for a woman."

I had heard that before. When I was sixteen and raring to go, I had raced over to the *New Haven Register,* my hometown newspaper. It didn't seem at all audacious to walk into the offices on Orange Street and ask the man in charge for a summer job in the newsroom. My inquiries prompted a patronizing smile—the kind of half-smug, bemused expression women who stepped out of character were so used to they didn't notice anymore. I did. "Why?" I asked, when he said it was impossible. "You hire copy boys, don't you?"

"Yes," he replied, still in half-smile, "but they're not girls."

He then suggested I try a job in classified for the summer. Adding up columns of figures and general clerical stuff. Swallowing hard, I took it. Just to be near the newsroom was reason enough—even though classified was on a different floor. During lunch hours, I would sneak away, position myself in view of the city desk, and burn with longing as I watched what I thought was the most wondrous process in the world: reporting and writing the news.

I was still trying to batter my way into a newsroom. Rebuffed again by Kirkpatrick, I left the *Tribune,* and after a long job hunt, listening to a dozen more guys announcing they didn't hire women, I landed a job in the Miami bureau of the Associated Press. It was the kind of basic training that looked good on my résumé, and by 1963, *Newsday* offered me a job. It was an aggressive, expanding tabloid started in a Hempstead, Long Island, garage in 1940 by Alicia Patterson, member of a newspaper dynasty that included the owners of the *Tribune* and *The New York News.* Over her father's objections that it would never work, this strong-willed woman created a journalistic bonanza. She also planted the idea that hiring a woman for a bona fide reporting job was not in the same category as taking on rejects from a leper colony.

The paper, small and daring, drew young reporters who relished the chance to learn it all: politics, sports, entertainment, rewrite, copyediting. The night rewrite bank consisted of a dirty dozen of us who spent every spare hour either angling for a better beat or hoping to land a job on one of the big dailies in Manhattan. Television news was still remote as far as I was concerned, even though there were now daily network and local news broadcasts from the Big Three.

The entertainment beat, basically chasing celebrities, was amusing for a while, the kind of chatty canned stuff where you sat in the Russian Tea Room or a Broadway dressing room interviewing Liza Minnelli, who couldn't stop talking about "Momma"; John Huston, who felt there were no more big stars because there was no more "spiritual ease"; Carol Burnett, Edward Albee, Franco Corelli, Lillian Gish, Agnes Moorehead, Ben Gazzara, Alan Arkin—and the list chattered on. The beat rankled me, but it was still practice and every now and then it was actually fun. Sean Connery was fun.

Agent 007 answered the door himself the day I pushed his room bell at the St. Regis Hotel in New York. He was barefoot. This couldn't be the devastatingly suave superspy. Or could it?

His eyes took my measurements in a flash.

"So you're the lady from Newsday. Please forgive my appearance, but I've been having a nap. Come in, come in."

There was no missing his charm or his sex appeal, slender and muscled in a short-sleeved polo shirt and chinos. He flopped onto a beige satin sofa, motioned me to a bergère chair across from him and waited. I found myself ill at ease, thrown off my guard by his informality. I also had the distinct feeling he was up for anything.

He offered me a scotch, which is what he was drinking, not the very dry martini with just the right graze of gin favored by Commander Bond.

"Do you really think I have a playboy image?" he asked.

Rather mock-ingenuous, I thought, considering that Connery was in New York to launch the first James Bond movie, Dr. No. He was thirty-two and still unknown, a Hollywood discovery being packaged as the superspy equally fast with his fists and the ladies—every man's Walter Mitty dream, every woman's Sheikh of Araby. Reinforcing this image, United Artists selected three beautiful young models, dressed them in furs and gowns, and assigned them to accompany Connery wherever he went. He was photographed at every fashionable boîte and bistro in Manhattan, culminating, of course, in a grand entrance at the movie premiere with his trio of lovelies. Old-fashioned Hollywood press-agentry was still alive in the early sixties. Connery played the role like a champ.

"I admit I identify with Bond," he said. "I, too, enjoy drinking, women, eating, the physical pleasures—smells and tastes, living by my senses, being alive. And, as far as Bond is concerned, he has no past."

Somewhere deep in my reporter's computer I knew I was listening to the regurgitation of press flackery. I mean, after all, here was a guy who got a medical discharge from the Royal Navy with ulcers. Agent 007 with ulcers? Still, the soft Scottish burr, the chiseled face, and a rough-hewn charm softened my cynicism. That was my first mistake.

Lolling on the couch, stopping only to order dinner and ask if I would join him (I declined), Connery continued to do what all actors do best—talk about themselves. I scribbled away, even when he reported with gusto that he liked to take baths, "lots of baths." Was there no end to this sexual imagery? Not yet.

Suddenly, he interrupted himself, lifted his head from the couch, and with a leering charm right out of the 007 handbook, said, "Has anyone ever told you—you have a perfectly wicked mouth?"

My composure collapsed as I felt a flush starting somewhere around my neck and working up through my scalp. The aforementioned mouth mumbled something about "Thank you, no, no one has ever said that" and I tried valiantly to reassume the reportorial mask. I didn't fool him. He knew he had scored. My second mistake.

Secure that he had, indeed, made a rapier hit, the man who would become a surrogate to millions of male fantasies about seductions on satin sheets and spies slain with a silent stroke continued: "I don't mind being called an epicurean. I see life as birth, life and death. Like a flower or an ear of corn that is born, lives and dies . . ." His voice trailed off into a whisper.

It was shameless, and I recorded every word and wrote the most lopsided story of my career, a pure valentine, a clinical example of show biz puffery. I even included the part about the baths. It happens to every reporter, at least once, to be taken down the garden path, suspending your critical sense because you've been flattered or brainwashed. I'm glad it happened with Sean Connery. As they used to say in Hollywood, what a way to go.

One afternoon, in a fit of boredom, I began hounding Lou Schwartz, then the entertainment editor at *Newsday*, for a chance to do something different. Schwartz, a man of sharp wit, didn't miss a beat. "Go get yourself a job in a dime-a-dance hall in Times Square," he dared.

So that's what I did—and wrote a series on how it feels to be in a rented sequin gown stuffed with Kleenex, selling dance tickets to the kind of customer Doris Day described when she sang "Ten Cents a Dance": "Fighters and sailors and bowlegged tailors can pay for their tickets and rent me! Butchers and barbers and rats from the harbors are sweethearts my good luck has sent me."

It was at the "sweethearts" where I drew the line. And when the mob moved in with offers of prostitution, the paper pulled me off and I had a whale of a story. The city raided and closed down three of the Times Square joints, and I had proved a point. That was at least one story no male reporter could have written.

The star of New York local television news at the time was Gabe Pressman, a former *New York World-Telegram* reporter who embodied the spirit of the tough print reporter. On the rounds for WNBC-TV, Gabe was greeted by every cabdriver, ward heeler, Mafia don, and call girl from the Bronx to Staten Island. If there was a pioneer in TV news, it was "Mr. New York." A squat cannonball of a man, he would barge into an all-print news conference with his oversize microphone, trailed by thick cables and a ragtag crew, staggering under the weight of film, cameras, and sound equipment, to transform the New York world of news into an electronic event. Despite the built-in drama of the "presence of a TV crew," and the hostility it aroused among his colleagues, Gabe usually asked the question no one had thought of, or simply got the answer that looked and sounded better than it read in the morning paper. To a child kidnapper and murderer just after he was caught in a three-state manhunt, he demanded: "Are you sorry?" The man's expression was indelible. Every politician in the five boroughs courted and trusted him.

One day Gabe was late in meeting Governor Rockefeller's private plane at La Guardia. Rockefeller had to leave, so the cameraman asked the question, which had to do with a bill stuck in the legislature. The camera went on, and talking into the wind Rockefeller said, "Well, Gabe . . ." It made air. That's clout.

Politicians such as Rockefeller were early in catching on to the impact of TV news. What the *Times* reported each morning was still of prime importance for the record, but as the number of city newspapers began to dwindle, so too did the unchallenged power of the written word. There were no media schools for a pol to learn about polishing his half-truths, styling his hair, or picking the right power tie. The most any of them knew was to wear a blue and not a white shirt, to avoid "kick" or glare from the high-intensity lights. Much of the interviewing was done on the fly—a street corner, outside an elevator, on the steps of an office, even outside men's rooms, wherever you could catch them. The rough-and-tumble charm of it all, the lack of orchestration, fostered a high excitement level. Even the ubiquitous press aides, and there were very few, could not control slips of the tongue, beads of perspiration, dandruff, or tempers beginning to fray on camera. The people on both sides of the camera—politicians and correspondents—merely tried to avoid trapdoors. In short, there were so many ways to make a fool of yourself, you *had* to be good.

Newsmakers caught on more quickly to the damage they could do themselves or the glory they might gain through TV than did the members of the Fourth Estate. "A picture may be worth a thousand words," huffed one irate *News* staffer as he pushed past a TV crew in front of the mayor's office, "but at least *we* write those words."

Harmony would be slow in coming for the upstart TV reporters and the "inkstained wretches" who were their stepbrethren. Routine acts of sabotage were committed against these interlopers from the world of electronics: pulling out plugs at news conferences, stepping in front of the lens at a critical point in a statement, even cutting cables. What's more, these TV types were making twice as much money for their efforts. As far as the print establishment was concerned, the words of Mark Twain prevailed: "There are only two forces that can carry light to all corners of the globe—the sun in the heavens and the Associated Press."

Another rivalry, even more intense, pitted the network giants against one another. It was led by their standard-bearers, men who had come to be known as "anchors," presumably because their mere presence prevented the broadcasts from drifting out to sea. While the personality of Edward R. Murrow had certainly set a tone for the early days of CBS-TV news after World War II, by the late 1950s the anchor strength had shifted to NBC with, notably, Chet Huntley, David Brinkley, Frank McGee, Edwin Newman, Sander Vanocur, and John Chancellor. Meanwhile, the perception had been building that the "bench strength" belonged to CBS, that if Walter Cronkite— NBC's only real competition—ever got hit by falling scenery, there would always be ten ready-trained substitutes to take his place. The argument held for correspondents, too, as CBS liked to boast about its depth and breadth, an arguable point and very much a part of the propaganda, masquerading as lore, that the networks contrived. In

any case, perception notwithstanding, it was reason enough to hammer the competition on the playing fields of news. While CBS and
NBC would play this game for almost three decades, ABC, the network in search of itself, was plodding along a distant third.

Even physically, the networks were markedly individual. NBC
had embedded itself in the marble of 30 Rockefeller Plaza, shielded by
the corporate might of RCA, guarded by a gilded statue of Prometheus,
hard by Radio City Music Hall—perhaps the most famous address in
America—dignified, soft-spoken, solid. CBS lay cramped in an old
dairy barn a block from the Hudson River, labyrinthine, dark, hard-
edged, not unlike an old newspaper city room from the legendary days
when men yelled "copy" and a boy would grovel to carry some lumi-
nary's precious words to the desk. ABC inhabited a colorless, unfinished, lackluster building with the look of temporary housing, self-
consciously sandwiched in a slum between the area about to become
the cultural oasis of Lincoln Center and the soothing green of Central
Park West.

Although television as entertainment was firmly established in the
American psyche by the 1960s, the ascendancy of TV news began
with the death of John Kennedy. This avalanche of searing images—
an assassination, a presidential succession, a murder, a funeral, a
widow in black clutching a child's hand as he saluted his father's
casket—established television news as a medium unparalleled in its
capacity to tell a story. An entire generation of Americans marked
that day as a watershed in their own lives. "Where were you?" they
still ask.

I was on my way to work at *Newsday*, swerving dangerously to the
side of the road as the news came over the car radio. People stood
looking dazed in front of the Garden City building. Inside, the newsroom had dissolved into pandemonium, not the kind of upbeat frenzy
that takes over when the big stories break, but an unsmiling, almost
desperate mood of disbelief. We ground out a special edition on the
assassination and then went to work on the aftermath during those
four memorable days. My modest contributions included a wrapup of
eulogies from Long Island religious leaders and a sidebar on the eight
geldings drawing the caisson that bore the President's body to Arlington National Cemetery.

How the paper—or, indeed, even the front page of the *Times*—
looked that weekend I cannot remember, but the impact of the television coverage would remain indelible. This relatively new medium,
never really tested on a major breaking story, had clearly galvanized

the nation. Newspaper reporters and editors vainly struggled to capture the event with the same intensity, but words could not equal the pictures. Television had seized the future of news coverage, although at the time I couldn't bring myself to admit it.

As the number and size of sets increased and color television made pictures even more compelling, reporters armed with microphones and oversize cameras began to take on a glamour of their own. While the anchors sat somberly behind desks in TV studios, reporters covered breaking stories "on the scene," their pictures flashing on the screen. Print journalists with pens and pencils could hardly compete with that. Television crews were still a long way from their folk-hero standing of the wild years to come, but the seeds of a "media" world had been scattered. The day would soon come when a television crew arriving in the midst of a hostage-taking standoff would inspire applause from the crowds.

NBC was the premier network in news, with a lock on number one in the ratings since 1960. While the folks over at CBS were still intoning the legacy of the sainted Murrow, NBC was cleaning their clocks on a daily basis and at the nominating conventions with the team of Huntley and Brinkley. It was also perceived as the gentleman among the Big Three, a place where people didn't throw tantrums, as did their unpolished brethren over at CBS or the funny folk with the almost-news department at ABC.

Women remained virtually invisible in network news. At NBC, the most progressive at the time, Pauline Frederick covered the United Nations and Nancy Dickerson worked the White House. Barbara Walters had not yet arrived to cohost the "Today" show, which in any event was not considered "news." There was no female general assignment reporter—a reporter on call to cover whatever the desk ordered anywhere in the world. Most perceived this as men's work; women weren't tough enough, and besides, after you train them, they go off and have babies. Behind the cameras, too, editorial and technical staffers were with one or two exceptions—or flukes—solidly male and white.

Arguably, there weren't many women around who could qualify by meeting the standards demanded by the networks. At NBC, before you could even be considered for an editorial job—even before you were granted an interview with management—you had to pass the "five years in a major market" test; that is, you had to have at least five years' experience on a medium-size newspaper or wire service. This was a philosophy that an NBC executive had explained very carefully to me when I applied for a job fresh out of college. So I set a goal for myself while working on the *Tribune* and *Newsday*: experience, experience, experience. The Horatio Alger ethic was still alive.

Every now and then as I pursued my goal, I would hear a faint voice, remember a woman with permed red curls and a straight back standing in front of a classroom: "What you are to be, you are now becoming."

It was the kind of remark that stopped you in your tracks and made you take stock, even at age thirteen. It fell from the thin lips of Miss Ida Himmelfarb, the most feared of seventh-grade English teachers at Troup Junior High School in New Haven, a place where lessons in the Horatio Alger myth were given strict attention.

It was 1950, and in that postwar period of ponytail hairdos and pegged trousers everything seemed within reach. Miss Himmelfarb, and many of the bright women who taught at Troup, ironically named after a local suffragette, knew with a sense of familiar frustration that they could not go "too far"—they dared not invade the upper reaches of any profession, the heights where only men could tread. But they hoped, in some small way, to fire up the odd student into crossing over the invisible lines. I got the message early.

When I arrived in the newsroom at *Newsday*, it was still rare for a woman to invest heavily in a career. Parents and society had set a more practical goal for young women: husband hunting. Working night rewrite, weekends and holidays didn't leave much time for a varied social life. But determination has a way of filtering out all that is not relevant to the target. I was going to be a foreign correspondent—a good one—no matter what detours and disappointments lay in wait.

One of these setbacks emerged with the disappearance of some great New York newspapers. Resisting the inevitable march of automation, the printers' union went on the warpath, refusing to make concessions. A rash of strikes began and papers folded one by one: the *New York World-Telegram*, the *New York World-Telegram and Sun*, the *New York Herald Tribune*. The *New York Post* hung by a thread, and only the *News* and the impregnable *Times* were left.

The networks moved in fast to hire men who lost their jobs. TV news had fed itself for years by recruiting refugees from newspapers and wire services; indeed, they had formed the original nucleus of the business. A shrinking print market, and an expanding TV news business that excluded women, did not exactly add up to an encouraging picture for an eager young amateur trying to break into news—except for two factors, at that point unknown to me.

The Times Square dance hall series I wrote for *Newsday* had caught the eye of Dick Kutzleb, WNBC's local news director, who lived on Long Island. He wanted to see me—especially since he had just received a directive from NBC president Robert Kintner to "find me a girl reporter." It was "about time." WCBS News had just hired a woman for its local program, and in the TV news business keeping your edge usually means having everything the competition has and more. Kintner put out a nationwide call for "a girl." About fifty auditioned all over the country. I was one of them—and I got the job.

In late April 1965, I arrived on the fifth floor of "30 Rock"—the marble palace that housed RCA and its wholly owned subsidiary, NBC. I shivered with the knowledge that harmonies of the great Toscanini and his NBC Symphony Orchestra had been broadcast from this hallowed place, the house that General David Sarnoff built. In the first few days there I met people, learned where the elevators stopped and why. I had made the transition from print to electronic journalism, but the equipment—the technology—remained a mystery. We were gearing up for a new program, "the first one-hour news show in New York, 'The Sixth Hour News.' " It was to be hosted by Robert (then Robin) MacNeil, now a fixture on PBS, at that time a rising correspondent who had been in the Dallas motorcade when Lee Harvey Oswald cut down a President.

On May 10, 1965, the show made its debut with virtually no planning. The executive producer was Bill Boyle, a tempestuous man with the vocabulary and energy of a master sergeant who tore around the newsroom screaming. A veteran of the wire services in an era when newsmen minced no words, Boyle knew it fell to him to put one hour of news on the air that night. The critics were waiting, the brass edgy. It was left to his band of renegades from print to pull it off. So he did what producers always do in a crunch: sent his reporters out on the breaking stories of the day and put them on the air.

The desk told Sy Avnet, a cameraman who had covered strife and stress in most of the world's crannies, to take me under his wing. Congressman John Lindsay, rumored to be considering a run for mayor of New York, was speaking at a B'Nai B'Rith meeting at the Waldorf-Astoria. My assignment was to cover the speech and tackle him for questions. We had no idea that Lindsay was to announce his mayoral aspirations within days. As far as the office was concerned, this was a simple, straightforward opportunity for me to practice innocuous questions on a real politician, a rehearsal, a good beginner's story for my TV debut. To Lindsay that day it appeared we knew something, especially since NBC was the only news organization on the scene.

Tall, chisel-faced, moving with the confidence gained of a privileged life, the handsome congressman strode into the parlor leading to the ballroom. Smiling politely, I approached him as the camera crew hung back. After introducing myself and stating I was from NBC, I asked if he would answer a few questions on camera either at that moment, or perhaps after his speech. Still striding, barely looking at us, he snapped a rude no and entered the dining room.

I was crushed, convinced I would be fired. My first outing, and it was a disaster. I had no story. The notebook and pen I was carrying were useless. *You had to get them on camera.* I ran for a phone booth and called the desk. As soon as I spilled out my account of what had happened, I could hear the clicks of telephone extensions being picked up. The henchmen were counseling and the verdict was to declare war. "Tell Sy to go portable," ordered the assignment editor, Bob McCarthy, seething, "and chase the bastard to hell if you have to. Just keep asking questions."

"Going portable" meant nothing to me, so Sy explained. The twenty-seven-pound Auricon camera was fastened to a cast iron brace which Sy put on his shoulder, still attached to the sound man by a cable. As a moving phalanx of three, with me carrying the microphone, the plan was to ambush Lindsay and hunt him to ground. We did just that. And even though Sy had warned me not to go up or down any steps, we found ourselves on the congressman's heels, at his elbow up and down the red-carpeted staircases of the Waldorf. In his desperate effort to escape, Lindsay forsook the elevators, couldn't find the right staircase, and presented a picture of a confused, petulant, panic-stricken public official trying to duck. Finally, after several "no comments" through clenched teeth, he wheeled around hissing, "What is your name, young lady?"

I told him.

"Well, your station will hear about this," he threatened.

"Mr. Lindsay," I said, half-pleading, "this is my first day on the job and I'm doing what I'm supposed to be doing." The rest of the exchange dissolved into a diatribe from the mayor-to-be about my "rudeness."

Whether or not he realized what we had in the camera, and how it would make him look on the evening news, was unclear. These were the pioneer days of the dance between the establishment and TV news, and politicians were not yet attuned to the mortal damage they could do themselves when left to their own devices, especially if they are innately arrogant, a birthright of John Vliet Lindsay.

The story leading "The Sixth Hour News" that night showed an angry, almost belligerent Lindsay running from a persistent brunette who wasn't taking no for an answer. A critic on the *Herald Tribune* noted my performance the next morning: "A new reporter, Liz Trotta, was very much on the job with one of those chase interviews (of Rep. John V. Lindsay) that strike TV newsmen as enterprising and the average viewer as in aggressive bad taste."

More important, after the piece ran, the president of the news division, Bill McAndrew, bolted from his office to exclaim to his attendant cronies, "Well, at least she's not a lollipop."

I had just earned my first stripe.

2

"BUT I DON'T DO WEDDINGS"

*I*f there is such a thing as a re-
porter's paradise, it has to be New York—the city, as A. J. Liebling
wrote, that "shrugs its shoulders" even in the grip of its routine chaos.
No budget crisis, ax murder, water shortage, building collapse, political payoff scandal, drug bust, skyscraper fire, or vice ring interrupts
the steady beat of its merciless heart, buried deep in the island's
bedrock.

Three reporters, four camera crews, and one "silent" cameraman
constituted the staff available to cover the city when local news went
to an hour at WNBC. By contrast, that number is likely to be tripled
or even quadrupled to fill the same amount of airtime today. The
lightning march of technology—tape cameras, "live" coverage—

would distend rather than streamline the operation. TV news, barely out of its infancy, was on its way to bloat and bureaucracy.

But in the rough-and-ready early days of local news, the wise-cracking, fly-by-the-seat-of-your-pants methods of frontier journalism were still in place, side by side with the professional discipline of writing and reporting on a deadline. Even the loudest jokers and drinkers knew that speed and accuracy—finding the right lead as you faced the blank page—were their ultimate masters. No one, of course, ever actually talked about "good writing." It would have been just as gauche as a fighter pilot talking about courage. It just wasn't done. Instead, the pride of work came out in other forms, such as the popular newsroom game of seeing how long you could keep up a conversation by using only clichés.

"Hey, you know that storm off Cape Hatteras is 'packing a wallop'?"

"Yeah, and it'll be worse once it hits the 'dread Bermuda Triangle.' "

"You're right. 'Only time will tell.' "

That last cliché was generic—usually the last line of a reporter's on-camera piece when he has said all there is to say and hasn't a clue about what will happen next. One always had the impulse to add: "Only the Shadow knows."

Nicknames abounded, usually conferred by the redoubtable Boyle. He was quite scientific about who merited his sobriquets and traced the origin of this newsroom game to the day of a major airplane crash at Idlewild Airport. It seems a public address system had been installed in the newsroom, ostensibly to reduce the noise level but actually to update the executives who resided in the little adjacent offices. So when Boyle announced over the PA that a major disaster was in progress, heads began popping out of the tiny enclosures, and vice-presidents dashed toward the news desk. Boyle, a malevolent glimmer in his eyes, sensed he was about to be second-guessed and grabbed the microphone: "Attention, all news executives. Get back in your hutches. Repeat: Get back in your hutches."

From then on, the executive corps of NBC News was known to the cognoscenti as the Rabbit Network. There was White Rabbit, Crusader Rabbit, Killer Rabbit, and so on. Soon, Boyle's exercise expanded to even more original names: Reuven Frank, "the man who brought Huntley and Brinkley together," was White Fang; the inordinately handsome Bob Mulholland, who had risen from writer to network president, became the Dancing Master; Irwin Margolis, a rapacious bureau chief with the shifty conscience of a serial killer, evoked Jaws; Richard Wald, a president of NBC News, was variously the Velvet Shiv or the Smiling Hangman; Les Crystal, another president of NBC News, answered to the Marshmallow; Bill Corrigan, a fidgety old-womanish vice-president, earned the Empty Suit. And I was—for better or worse—the Black Orchid.

IN contrast to the national mood, New York's usual hurly-burly politics in 1965 were humorous, gritty, and even at times bizarre. After three terms in the job, Mayor Robert F. Wagner stepped aside, and the Democrats were running city comptroller Abe Beame. Lindsay stood for the Republicans and the Liberals, and his coterie of young thinkers pledged to stamp out the "power brokers" and revive "Fun City."

Still smarting from our initial encounter, Lindsay never missed a chance to needle me. One day, as my colleagues and I elbowed our way into the usual circle that forms around a politician ready to answer questions, Lindsay, noting my efforts, put his hand over the NBC microphone and announced to the all-male group: "Women should only be allowed in the bedroom and the kitchen." The locker room responded with laughter.

Just when it began to look like another raucous New York election, in walked the man who would transform the race into a cross between Monty Python and a course at Oxford. Handsome, patrician, wealthy, superliterate, savagely funny William F. Buckley became the Conservative party candidate. As Lindsay devoted himself to righteous comments on bossism in New York and Beame sounded the themes of big-city government, welfare, crime, housing, and jobs, Buckley, sprinkling his speeches with Latin aphorisms, made headlines with ingenious proposals. To ease traffic congestion he recommended construction of a twenty-foot-wide path—a bikeway—to run almost the length of Manhattan. When a reporter wryly asked if this plan might be called the Buckley Bikeway, the candidate parried with "Yes, my finest hour."

The press, even grouchy liberals among them, loved the Buckley technique—eyebrows arching each conservative idea, tongue flicking out like an adder's—as he moved in on a liberal target to deliver a mortal debating blow with malicious glee. A mischief-maker but not a serious candidate, they reasoned, so editorial writers held their fire.

Even New York's official liberal establishment treated him with kid gloves, on the whole, ignoring his political philosophy and delighting in his oratory and ability to entertain.

I asked his wife, Pat, one day in an interview what she thought of this foray into the sidewalks of New York, and she dutifully said she thought it fine.

"What's he like to live with?" I pushed on.

"Well," she replied, "he's just the most fascinating man I've ever met." Mrs. Buckley epitomized insouciance, exiting shabby press rooms with her mink coat dragging the floor.

I had admired Buckley ever since reading *God and Man at Yale* as a teenager in New Haven. He was Catholic and conservative, as I was, but my experience of that sleepy town in the fifties was quite different. He went to Yale (as did John Lindsay), an unreal bastion of white Ivy League upperclassness, while I grew up in the real city that surrounded it, a mélange of ethnic groups that gave the town its texture and its politics. Before the Civil War, Yankees predominated. Then came the Germans and the Irish, driven by the potato famine; and by the 1870s Italians were arriving in droves. Streaming in among them were my parents: Gaetano Trotta, a farmer's son, born in Amalfi among the lemon groves and grapevines, and Lillian Theresa Mazzacane, daughter of a surgeon, and perhaps even a baron, born in Benevento, an ancient region of the Samnites.

In the case of my father, heavy taxes, class inequality, a hunger to work—and just plain hunger—sparked the kind of desperate courage that it took to become an emigrant, to go against the grain, to revolt. It is said that in 1896 Amalfi had 10,000 residents. By 1900 the town had only 3,000—the rest of them had gone to New Haven. Today an estimated 25,000 Italian Americans in New Haven call themselves Amalfitani and trace their roots to this jewel of the Tyrrhenian Sea.

Politically, the Elm City, as it was known before Dutch elm disease and frenzied urban renewal made blight fashionable, teemed with ethnic intrigue. Initially, the Italians were drawn to the Irish-controlled Democratic party, as the Yankee-controlled GOP seemed a far cry from their own background. It didn't take long, however, for the cries of "wop" and "dago," as well as discrimination in the labor unions, to disenchant the sons of Italy. Capitalizing on this disaffection, the Ullmans, a Jewish couple who manufactured corsets, took control of the GOP and extended a hand to the new Italian Americans. Two alliances were formed by these events: a political bond between Italians and the GOP, and a social bond between Jews and

Italians in New Haven. It was most evident in the Trotta household, where favorable mention of a Democrat would cause an eruption at the dinner table. Names like Dewey and Nixon were the most acceptable, and Jews were automatically smart "because they study."

For my mother, it had been a different story. To this day, the remaining Mazzacanes like to trot out the family coat of arms, proof, they say, of my grandfather's baronial rank. Poverty had not spurred his departure from the old country. In fact, he had attended college intending to practice medicine as did his father in the town of Cerreto Sannita (Cominium Ceritum of ancient times). Family lore, unwavering in its detail over the years, has it that Giorgio Mazzacane did not emigrate from the land of the Caesars. He fled.

At a town dance one evening, Giorgio was observed by the chaperons, one of whom was his fencing instructor, in the company of a lady whose virtue was in question. The town prostitute, to be exact. Indeed, she was Grandpa's date. The fencing master demanded that this brash student divest himself of his companion "rapido," and what happened next might have worked its way into a Verdi opera. Giorgio refused. A classic mano a mano erupted. They fought a duel. And Grandpa won, dispatching his instructor forthwith. At nineteen years of age, my grandfather was on the run, booking passage on the next boat for America.

Giorgio settled in New York City and married Luisa Barbieri. He returned to Italy several times, once in 1897 as a volunteer for King Humbert to participate in Italy's disastrous invasion of Ethiopia. He was stationed for thirteen months with the Italian medical corps in Massawa, and on one expedition traveled over mountains and desert by mule to fight an epidemic of dysentery ravaging the ancient Abyssinian city of Harar.

After the Ethiopian adventure, my mother was born while Giorgio and Luisa were en route back to New York. Eventually, the family moved to New Haven, where earlier pioneers from Cerreto Sannita had settled. My grandfather bought a pharmacy and in his spare time taught Italian and history at the Sannio Club, one of several men's clubs set up in the 1890s by new Italian Americans hoping to preserve their heritage—and to chew the fat.

When I grew old enough to give names to what people did, I realized that Grandpa was a newspaperman and a broadcaster. He published a weekly in Italian, about Italian-American matters, known as Le Forche Caudine, a reference to the Caudine Forks, which was a narrow pass in the Apennines on the road from Capua to Benevento.

Here, in 321 B.C., the Samnites trapped the Roman army and forced it to pass under a yoke.

Every Sunday morning, my grandfather could be heard on the radio over station WELI in New Haven. "L'Ora Italiana" was a two-hour program of news from Italy and the Italian-American community, with a heavy sprinkling of opera recordings, principally Caruso. Grandpa wrote his own material and even chose the music. The show aired for nine years until his death in 1943. Perhaps it was this Italian tradition of flouting authority, of taking on governments, churches, classes, that created an atmosphere of boundless opportunity, despite the odds, in our household. I inherited my family's religion and its politics. And surely it was my grandfather's example that sparked my own ambitions to become a journalist. That was why so many times, even working the streets of a throbbing city, I looked back and saw Grandpa in his study, bent over his papers, writing in Latin—a persistent unmoving image, the first "freeze frame" of a life's film.

WHILE I hoped someday to persuade WNBC management that I wasn't a "girl reporter" but a reporter who happened to be a girl, I knew immediately that it wasn't going to be easy to convince the camera crews. They were for the most part chauvinistic blue-collar men, who for starters harbored a lower-middle-class resentment of the brass; and working with a woman on equal professional footing aroused Freudian fears still unplumbed. It was uphill all the way. Most were courteous, and in truth, I learned the front and back ends of a film camera from them—subtleties of lighting, intricacies of sound, and sometimes even the right question to ask. But unhappily, a noticeable percentage of the crews couldn't handle a woman on the job. It wasn't until years later, around the time I returned from my first war tour, that they arrived at a philosophy they could comfortably accept. "She's got balls."

Many of the cameramen I worked with had been shaped by the old Movietone News school, and though still working in black-and-white film, the good ones were creative, quick, and excited by events. The adjustment to shooting in color only further demonstrated their ability—an attention to detail and depth of feeling that seemed to dissipate in the harshness of videotape. In the early days of tape, it was easy to tell who shot the pictures, a cameraman from the old film school or a newcomer from a university "video project"; long shot, medium shot, close-up, pan up, pan down, over and over. Tape did offer an astonishing clarity of image, and on hard news stories it added an appropriate edge. But something vital and artistic from the old days disappeared in the conversion as the subtleties of film gave way to the easy definition of the tape picture. The clarity worked against the results in much the same way that colorized versions of old movies diminish the black and white original. In a deeper sense, the same thing was happening to TV news: complexity, depth, and shading were losing ground to the easy and quick fix.

The days unfolded long, hard, and wonderful, all of us members of a family, or better, a professional fraternity house under the watchful eye of an elite faculty. The age of touchiness had not yet arrived, so it was considered perfectly acceptable that Rex Goad, a vice-president in the news department, would counsel me even before I went to work that there was a standard "morality clause" in every contract and, what's more, NBC frowned on in-house romance. Little did I know at that point that wives had already been exchanged or stolen in two cases involving overseas correspondents and cameramen.

Invention resulted routinely from the pressure of getting an hour of news on the air five days a week. It was extraordinary how people who had spent their lives in print employed the technology—toys of the trade—and somehow made it work. This was the age of film, which had to be shot, developed, and edited before it was shown. The atmosphere vibrated with thoughts of "what could happen," and when a studio director called for a "roll"—a cue to start the film—chances were the machinery holding sound and picture would fail to obey. Pretaped packages were at a minimum, so the ever-present spectre of dead air haunted every anchorman.

One day a fire broke out—at least a "three-bagger," or three alarms—at Forty-ninth Street and Eighth Avenue, just a few blocks from the office. When Robin MacNeil opened the program the fire still raged, and every fifteen minutes new pictures would appear on the broadcast, unedited, owing to a relay set up from a cameraman on the scene to a courier to the developer—and into the projector. Raw footage of a breaking story: the news business in its most exciting form. Then, in the last half hour of the show, disaster struck: the building collapsed, disintegrating into a heap of dust, rubble, and smoke. And it was all on film.

"It's on the way," came the triumphant voice of a courier on his Harley-Davidson, speeding through crosstown traffic with this exclusive prize.

With minutes to spare, the processed film was loaded into the "chain," or projector, and MacNeil heralded the arrival of this dramatic development. Before the viewer's eyes an amazing series of pictures popped up: first a dust-filled plateau, rising into a pile of rubber, then mortar, wood, and steel springing into the air until a complete structure materialized. The film was *backwards!* Crazed, hell-bent to get pictures on the air, the techs had loaded the film in reverse, celluloid perforations hopelessly entangled on the wrong tracks. There appeared to be "something wrong," MacNeil said shakily and then mumbled good night. The control room shook with laughter, not to mention living rooms throughout the five boroughs.

While news expertise scored high for any TV reporter, keeping a story to ninety seconds or two minutes always tested mettle. It took me a while to learn that basically TV news reporters were paid a lot of money to gather a mountain of details and then whittle them down to plausible generalizations. But God help you if the conclusions were off. To do the job right, I wound up probing as much and more than a counterpart in print. Still, the picture proved the point, and unless that concept took hold in your mind and gut, no story would get off the ground.

"It's just a question of Dick and Jane," Drew Phillips, one of the show's producers, used to say. "See Dick, see Jane—just like in the storybook—is how the script should read."

Drew, who came from the *World-Telegram*, had the pro's ease of simplifying matters, but he was, in essence, quite right.

In my second week on the job, the desk dispatched me to a settlement house on the Lower East Side to do a report on a poor people's program. I sat for two hours asking questions and taking notes. Finally, a long-suffering cameraman tapped me on the shoulder and suggested that we ought to "start shooting." In one terrible flash the first lesson of working in TV news started to dawn: the camera has to be on, and all the pencils, papers and wonderful notes in the world are not going to get a story on the air unless it's "in the camera."

I covered an average of four to six stories a day, the scut work of the business—tenement fires, oil tank explosions, bank robberies, mob murders—and the important events: civil rights protests and meetings, race riots, elections, city council fights, budgets. Many nights I stood in the rain for hours at a stretch, shivering, as firemen or the police searched for bodies. Many days I wilted in the August heat on the JFK tarmac awaiting the arrival of various worthies. After my first fire, I couldn't look at a hamburger for weeks, so strongly did the stench of burnt flesh linger in my mind. As with all reporters everywhere, surviving the weather ranked second only to locating the nearest telephone and bathroom. Dinner dates, weekend outings, vacation plans evaporated on command when the news flag went up.

Equipment failures and traffic jams were ulcer material. A battery running down in the middle of an interview, a "hair in the gate," a camera jam—a million paths to disaster. It seemed you always had the slowest cameraman on a breaking story, when the blood flows to your head and your guy hasn't even found a parking place. When we agreed "It's a wrap," the cameraman reached into a black cotton changing bag fitted tight up to his elbows to keep out the light. Inside the contraption he removed the film from the magazine and placed it in an aluminum can. George, a cameraman notorious for his turtle speed, seemed to lose himself in the bag forever, oblivious to deadlines. There were days stories broke around me while he was slowly pulling the Auricon out of the trunk, methodically inspecting it, slowly getting into gear. The man's very name aroused "Arghs" from anyone assigned to him. Inexplicably, during one of the worst Harlem riots, while surrounded by menacing blacks, he raised his camera overhead, stood his ground, and captured the best demo pictures of the year. From then on, even when he compulsively took his dozen light readings (usually in the middle of a strong statement), we made allowances for George. Still, he drove me to chain-smoking and pacing like some windup Bette Davis.

Local news was a good place to join the fallible human chain that attempted to ferret out and broadcast news every day. For national coverage, and especially foreign, the supply line got longer and so the margin for disaster increased. Here, on the smaller scale of New York, the trick was to get a fast fix on the story, shoot the pictures, interview the key people, capture the essence of what was happening, and underscore the points you wanted to make with specific shots. A good cameraman could read your mind and the story at the same time. Otherwise, it was a case of street corner diplomacy, negotiating for shots, working around the male ego. It could be as simple as a news conference, or as complicated as the problems of a welfare family. This was spot news, with little time to ponder, so it helped to be a quick study and know at least a little bit about a lot of things.

Invariably, just before the camera rolled, interviewees wanted to know what questions they were going to be asked. I always replied that I didn't have a clue until the talking started. It was important to listen and work from answers. But even when I knew precisely what to go after, I didn't tip my hand. As a newspaper reporter, no one ever asked me, and besides, giving away the questions always implied censorship. Anyone egotistical, confident, or desperate enough to sit in front of a camera should be ready to take the blows as well as the compliments of his immediate family and friends.

Stand-uppers—the reporter talking into a camera, usually in the middle or at the end of a piece—remained the last thing to do before wrapping it up at the scene. The reporter had to have a pretty firm idea of the story's structure—the little movie that is a TV story—and basically summarize the piece in this short segment. After scratching the "on-camera" out on paper, you memorized and delivered it. Ad-libbing, always dangerous, was at a premium.

Later at the office you wrote the story, if you hadn't already started it in the crew car or taxi returning to the studio. Ahead lay a gamut of producers to run for approval; they assigned story length and kept track of the process in-house. If time permitted, you looked at the film with an editor, that is if it had come out of the soup (developing fluid), and continued writing, all the while checking wires and news-papers for the latest developments. If you were "on top of a deadline," you wrote the story blind, recalling from memory the shots taken at the scene, but never seeing them. The worst criticism threatening a reporter, even if he wrote like Hemingway or sounded like Huntley, was that he didn't "know film." It was the insiders who knew how to splice if they had to, or that the sound on film was always twenty-eight frames, a little more than a second, ahead of the picture, or—without checking a watch—that a 400-foot magazine of film had reached its end. It was called having "a clock in your head," the highest compli-ment these film magicians could pay a reporter.

The executive producer of the program determined finally if the piece made air, a decision that might be made and changed, and remade and rechanged, right up until the anchor introduced the story. If the piece had low priority alongside more important events, then it became a "tell story"; the anchor read a short narration over some of the film shot and the reporter who had been at the scene was never seen or heard.

Not all my stories got on the air; it depended on what else hap-pened that day, an occupational hazard in TV news. The 1964–65 World's Fair, plugging its dubious message of "Peace Through Under-standing," appeared on my assignment sheet with tired regularity: a sick mountain gorilla or dancing Watusi warriors at the African pa-vilion, a fight over whether the Italians would agree to ship the Pietà for the Vatican exhibit, constant racial demonstrations against the fair's hiring policies. Indeed, while still at *Newsday*, I had acted as a tester for the Congress of Racial Equality (CORE) and applied for a job. The fair people offered me a hostess job, but when CORE sent over a black candidate she was rejected. It was a pretty good story.

After much ballyhoo, the sprawl in Flushing Meadow had more to do with corporate—Pepsi-Cola, General Motors, Kodak—then national culture. Nevertheless, when the smoke cleared the fair was a fiscal flop, winding up in very bright red, and having served at best as a substitute amusement park for the decaying Coney Island.

Robert Moses, the pugnacious urban wizard from my hometown who ran the fair, functioned as the scourge of the New York press corps: great copy, but dangerous for interviewers. He liked nothing better than to challenge reporters or even correct their grammar, and he had no qualms about blaming the fair's troubles on the press: "We have been listening too much to the raving hyenas, scavengers, jackals, parrots and vultures who should be kept behind moats in the Bronx Zoo," he said. "It's too bad that the rest of America does not realize how few and unrepresentative these discordant voices are. The shallows murmur, but the deeps are dumb." Moses did what Spiro Agnew hadn't yet dreamed of doing—savaging the press before the public. It was another milestone for TV news. Once viewed by public figures as a novelty or a nuisance, it had become an enemy, a threat.

On really big stories, network affairs, I functioned as a spear carrier, especially that frigid October day in 1965 when the first pope ever to visit the New World paraded down Fifth Avenue. The fifteen-hour visit was one of television's early media extravaganzas, viewed by more than 100 million people in the United States and millions more around the world via the Early Bird satellite, another technological innovation that would change the face of TV news—and the faces that were seen on it. Bitter cold, a Mediterranean blue sky, the day seemed wrapped in clarity and drama for the benefit of people watching in twenty-two nations. Paul VI's motorcade traveled through the city up to Harlem and then ended at home plate in front of St. Patrick's Cathedral, where I was stationed. The pope, his heavy red cape swirling in a stiff wind, blessed the crowd and went on to address the United Nations. "No more war, war never again," the pontiff told the world's delegates. "Peace, it is peace, which must guide the destinies of peoples and of all mankind."

Even as he spoke, America and North Vietnam were squaring off for the longest war in our history.

*   *   *

THE presence of Chet Huntley pervaded the NBC news department; and if he loomed large on the TV screen, face to face he was indeed overpowering. At that time, David Brinkley was based in Washington, and Chet, in New York, sat at the old rolltop desk his father had used as a railroad telegrapher in Bozeman, Montana—beside it, a brass spittoon and an 1870 Winchester rifle. So intimidated was I by the very sight of this gentle giant, so afraid of making a gaffe, that I instinctively darted into corners or a side corridor when he came in range. Despite all the polish and confidence necessary for on-air work, it didn't cure me of a lifelong habit of dissolving into bad grammar and general tongue-tiedness with my superiors.

Huntley and Brinkley had entered the American lexicon like bread and butter; both joked openly about the many fans who approached them in public asking which was which, or who was who. They were the first of the big names in TV news, and although they made nowhere near a million dollars, both men received the deference accorded to stars. Except—and it was a big except—they were solid, serious professionals, totally devoid of any instinct to entertain instead of inform.

A local reporter, no matter how proficient or well known, operated light years away from the world of the network correspondent. Network people were perceived, and usually with good reason, as the best broadcasters, writers, and producers. It amounted to an important class distinction—even more pronounced at CBS—that was to become blurred as the caliber of network personnel changed and the standards for admission to that upper stratum began to erode. There were, of course, exceptions to this class division, rare ones, such as the brilliant Edwin Newman, who worked as a commentator for the local station in New York as well as reporting and anchoring on the network.

Educational and cultural differences often came into play. The strength of the local reporting staffs derived in large part from management's tendency to hire newsmen from New York, people who had gone to city schools, knew the terrain, and had experience covering a very tough town. On the network side, correspondents represented a cross-section of the country, often graduates of Ivy League schools, and if they didn't know how to order wine or find a three-star restaurant in Des Moines, they learned fast.

In the early 1960s, when the industry began to explode, a bunch of roistering old newspaper guys found themselves smack at the center of an unprecedented communications revolution. A new way of transmitting news was taking the nation by storm, and this unlikely band of journalistic rock-throwers was suddenly seated in the eye of a corporate hurricane. As former newsmen, executives in TV news departments had no lessons of history to steer by, no body of tradition to draw on, no course at the Harvard Business School or the Columbia Graduate School of Journalism to teach them how to manage people and pictures. While General Motors and the rest of corporate America had long before invented boardroom culture, the men leading television news were just getting their baptism into a new order—one that was by definition at odds with the tenets of pure journalism: independence versus team playing, truth-telling versus playing it safe, full disclosure versus holding your cards close, courage versus timidity. To the rank and file, these once free spirits appeared so riddled with insecurities that fear became a department unto itself.

"I see the vice-president in charge of fear is at it again," said Sander Vanocur one day, the man credited with finally characterizing the new ethic of the men who were taking over TV news, graduates of raucous newspaper city rooms who now sat awkwardly in carpeted silence. They were making it up as they went along. Inevitably, the stewards of TV news were on their way to becoming what other corporate leaders had become: managers. But that is getting ahead of the story.

Many in the business regarded NBC as a "correspondent's network," just as CBS came to be known—more for worse than better—as the "producer's network." Bill McAndrew prized his correspondents so much that he threw a special Christmas party for them every year, gave advice on career problems, and knew their families. As a Knight of Malta, he genuinely practiced Christian charity in an unlikely environment for such a skill; his correspondents could do no wrong. The word in the newsroom: "Bill McAndrew is so proud of his correspondents you'd have to pee on his desk to get fired."

Local news was not beneath McAndrew. He followed every story with interest and liked nothing better than getting involved in the actual coverage. Sleeves rolled up, tie loosened, he would lean over the assignment editor's desk with a light in his eyes: "Hear you got a two-bagger going in Flatbush." McAndrew reported to Robert E. Kintner, regarded by many, at least at NBC, as the "father of television news." Kintner was a natural titan, a former hotshot White House correspondent for the old *New York Herald Tribune* and coauthor with

Joseph W. Alsop of a well-known syndicated column called "Capitol Parade."

Kintner was a confidant of the powerful and above all a lover of news. Stories about him glutted the daily diet of in-house gossip. How he was seen turning off the lights after hours in the various small offices, admonishing a secretary not to waste electricity. How he was spotted in the dimness of a studio, on a catwalk above the floor, listening to the eleven o'clock news. He sent memos like confetti, missing nothing, insisting on the use of English instead of jargon. "Give me some more of those signs," he would command the director during a broadcast. The "signs" were "supers" (now called fonts) superimposed over the picture on the screen to identify the person or the place. Kintner embodied a commitment to straight, no-nonsense journalism, dignified reportage without gimmicks. During his time the phrase "CBS plus thirty" became a rallying cry at the network. In other words, no NBC News broadcast of a breaking story or major event went off the air until thirty minutes after CBS had said good night.

From my first week at work, Kintner began sending me memos, tips on story treatment, critiques, praise, and even a gentle hint to "do something" with my hair. The problem of "Liz's hair" reached hilarious proportions until, under orders, I was fitted for a hairpiece. After two wearings, I rebelled and threw it in a hatbox where it lay for the rest of my career.

Then the "lighten up" chant began: "We don't want you to dye your hair—just lighten it a little." These suggestions, happily, didn't come from the news staff but from an assortment of managers and network flacks who wanted in on the act of creation—the Bride of Frankenstein lives again. Desperate, I made an appointment at the swanky Kenneth's, where Jackie Kennedy was getting her bouffant done. Seated in an expensive chintz chair, I said bravely, "Straighten it." The soigné sleek look lasted only a few months. Then I reverted to Italian curly.

Opportunities for embarrassment abounded. The very first time I appeared on the air, live, in the studio, new hairdo in place, wearing a crisp green linen dress, I took a cue from the anchorman and waded into my copy, a story about the latest skirmish between Adam Clayton Powell, Jr., and white members of Congress. Ten seconds into the piece my bra strap broke. Struggling to keep my eye on the script and the camera, I speculated wildly that the sound of fragmenting elastic had filtered through the microphone, that my chest had dropped for all the world to see, and that I was now the laughingstock of TV news. I hunched my shoulders to appear concave by nature, trying to act as though if, indeed, the worst had happened, this feminine inconvenience was of no matter. The pretaped story came up, I continued the voice-over, "tagged out" on camera, and then bolted from the set after the camera switch.

Leaving the studio, I ran into one of the associate producers who complimented me on the piece. I waved his compliment aside and hysterically related what had happened to my upper body. Had anyone noticed?

"Notice?" he said with a sneer, addressing the space between my neck and shoulders. "Who would notice?" Thank God for small favors.

Getting into the building tested your patience on some days, especially when one of the hourly tours snaked its way through the corridors—gawking at the cavernous studios, peering through the glass in front of the newsroom, hoping to catch sight of "someone famous." Bob McCarthy, a former *Daily News* crime reporter, who functioned as the city editor for local TV news, usually went into his "Front Page" personality when the relentless stares of the ladies from Tacoma began to irk him. Grabbing the microphone, he would shout to radio cars carrying reporters and crews: "KEK 322 this is 520. Attention all hands—a shootout in progress at Broadway and Forty-second Street." Or to the newsroom at large: "Tell that guy to get the lead out or he's fired—we're on deadline!"

"Tell the mayor to kiss my ass," he bawled into the mike one day. "We're not interested in what he has to say." When it really got purple, McCarthy was usually pulled aside—and talked to. Years later, when he gave up drinking, the craziness seemed to go out of him, but he was still a newsman to his half-bitten fingernails.

Drinking was still an integral part of the journalistic life in the 1960s. Generations of newspapermen had passed on the rite of booze as part of the mystique and legend that went with pride in the craft. In the mid- to late 1950s, as the networks discovered that a prestigious news department meant more viewers for the entertainment side, too, they decided to reach for the best. That so many drinkers should arrive at one time in TV news was no accident.

The networks needed men who could write for the ear, short declarative sentences that radio and television audiences could easily grasp, what someone once called "lean, muscular prose." Logically, they turned to the press associations, AP, INS, UPI, places that demanded this skill. Eventually, the reach extended to newspapers, and so the networks caught the end of an era, a time of hard-boiled, two-fisted, liquor-swilling rogues who could do the job.

Tales were handed down of newsroom heroism, great prose written while under the influence, on a deadline, proof that a "real man" could take his spirits and keep them under control. The Hemingway code of macho gave justification to every martini lifted after hours of working under the gun in a very public profession—grace under pressure at any cost. But for many, that grace lasted only as long as it took to get through the latest deadline and down the elevator to Hurley's bar.

The storied Hurley's stood stubbornly on the corner of Forty-ninth Street and Sixth Avenue, hard by the RCA Building in the heart of Rockefeller Center—not only a hangout but a symbol of the rebellious spirit associated with being in the news business. Old Man Hurley, a dour Irishman with a craggy look, simply refused to budge when RCA became his neighbor, and so it built around him. A dingy, smoky pocket of ribaldry and bygone days, smack in the shiny granite belly of a corporate giant. Old Man Hurley was succinct about the outcome: "I've seen sonofabitchin' Rockefellers come and sonofabitchin' Rockefellers go and no sonofabitchin' Rockefeller's gonna tear down my bar."

You never knew who would be standing next to your lifting elbow at Hurley's. Jason Robards, Jonathan Winters, jazz musicians from the local clubs and the "Tonight" show, starlets, football players, the lot. If a stranger appeared in the doorway, Old Man Hurley would quickly take his measure, and if he didn't like what he saw, the surly Celt would stare down over his glasses, tuck his chin in and bellow, "Out, out," in a brogue that would have stirred the spirit of Parnell himself.

If you were on his OK list, there was no limit to how high you could run a tab. In fact, one tab at Hurley's was in the service of news. During the racial troubles in Selma, there was a flare-up one Friday night that looked as though it could get out of control. Bill Boyle, then the night news manager, wanted to send a correspondent fast and realized there was no money to support the assignment. The finance department boys had gone home, so he went to the drawer where money was kept from the NBC tours, all nickels and dimes, a total of twenty dollars. With the competition breathing down his neck, and management demanding that he cover the story, Boyle did what any hot-blooded newsman in his place probably wouldn't have thought of: he went to Old Man Hurley. Cash was dredged up from the Irishman's stash in the basement under the bar and Boyle signed an IOU for $500 in $50 bills, declaring the money to be for the use of NBC News. On Monday, the front office went crazy and called him on the carpet, which in those days was a rubber tile floor. "Never again," intoned the money men, determined to shore up this unprecedented loophole in their neat little world of numbers. As a result, a petty cash fund was established—in perpetuity—so that henceforth NBC would never be indebted to an Irish bar.

That wasn't the only encroachment on NBC's news operation by Hurley's. One of the desk men, a perpetually red-faced southern gentleman, Buck Prince, spent the better part of his day at the venerable well, an unofficial greeter to the regulars. Buck spent so much time on the frayed red leather stool that he decided to move his operation. So, a telephone extension was installed from the NBC newsroom to Hurley's bar. It functioned faultlessly until the front office found out and pulled the line. Buck eventually retired and opened a liquor store.

Uproarious stories abounded about how these athletes of alcohol made merry while in their cups. What one didn't hear was the plain truth that alcoholism was rampant and taking a heavy toll in marriages and careers. Few would admit before the end of the decade that liquor was indeed quicker—and deadlier. A producer of "The Sixth Hour News," who was struggling to stay dry, fell off the wagon in the helter-skelter pace of the program. One day, shaking in his clothes, he simply walked off the floor and said, "I can't do this anymore." He spent three months drying out in Payne Whitney.

The alcohol problem didn't confine itself to the troops. Even some in the executive suite had a problem, whispered the crowd at the Coke machine. At first I paid scant attention to the gossip and worried only about Kintner's voluminous memos. It was intimidating to receive notes from the network president I had never laid eyes on—nor would I until years later. Meanwhile, I took Boyle into my confidence, asking him what he thought about Kintner's attentions. "Terrific," he said. "But don't tell anyone or they'll think you're sleeping with him."

The presence of the great Kintner, a bulldozer of a man who squinted through lenses as thick as Depression glass, capped this rough-and-tumble operation: hard-boiled news guys with the requisite hearts of gold toiling for a man who came out of the same tradition: honest-to-God writing and reporting on a deadline. Unfortunately, from that same tradition derived the tragic flaw that would bring Kintner down in the prime of his career: he, too, was a drunk. Not just a quiet or sporadic one, but a rip-roaring boozer who spoke his mind even more under the influence. Unfortunately, he did this one time too many at an affiliates convention—and the man in charge, Robert Sarnoff, chairman of RCA, son of the founder, decided "no more." Kintner was out in twenty-four hours.

Dear Miss Trotta,

February 9, 1966

In watching the WNBC-TV local news shows, and the promotion on your behalf, I thought it appropriate now, since I have resigned as President of NBC, to congratulate you on your outstanding development as a broadcast reporter over the last months. You have continuously improved and I appraise you as one of the better news broadcasters—male or female. Congratulations and good luck for the future. As you probably know, I am very pro "female reporters" when they are good.

Sincerely,
Robert E. Kintner

When I received that letter, I could only admire the man whose bellowed command, "Get me a girl reporter," had opened the door for me at NBC. Years later—an old man now—he asked to see me and, true to his style, picked me up in a limousine. After dinner, he suggested we go downtown to visit Toots Shor, once the most famous nightclub owner in New York. Shor, in financial trouble, had given up his old landmark on West Fifty-second Street and moved to a cheaper trade around Madison Square Garden. Kintner said, "Let's go see him. He's down now—and that's the time to be a friend."

As we glided down Fifth Avenue, passing 30 Rock, the red neon RCA sign on top of the building glared in the summer night. Kintner, looking out the window toward his old kingdom, was silent for a moment. Then quietly, he said: "One thing is very important. You have to separate the job from yourself. When I went out that door for the last time, it didn't kill me because I had known all along where the perks and the power came from. Not from me—but from the job."

I was still living in the Greenwich Village apartment, paying ninety dollars a month (non-rent-controlled), the night the NBC switchboard called and said Chet Huntley wanted to talk to me. I froze. His wife, Tippy, who had been a "weather girl" at the Washington NBC station, was also on the line. The reason for the call was to ask for my help—(my help?)—on a possible local story. A young friend of theirs had been awarded an internship with the White House Scholars program, and perhaps it might be something I could do for "The Sixth Hour News." Here was the world's number one anchorman *asking* if I was interested. If it didn't inconvenience me, said Huntley, perhaps Tippy could come down right now and deliver some background material. Would I mind? And if I didn't think very much of the idea, then no bother.

No bother? Were they kidding? My shock was complete, as was my immediate cooperation.

Tippy arrived as I tried wildly to spruce up my shabby retreat, plumping the studio couch pillows, throwing open the garden door for an al fresco effect. She politely appeared not to notice, charmingly stated her case, and left me with some written background on her friend. Within days I did the story, and from that time on a relationship began with Chet that consisted of idolatry on my part and, I do believe, admiration on his. Television people like to talk about their "rabbis"—an old police department expression to describe the person who would watch over you, a kind of Jewish guardian angel. Mine was a Protestant from the Old West.

Chet was a big man in nature as well as stature. Often, strolling across Fifth Avenue on the way to lunch, he was stopped by fans every few feet, but not once did he ever exhibit the kind of amiable condescension that was becoming so typical of network celebrities. He wore the mantle lightly and with the basic decency of a man who had not lost sight of his mortality.

Those were still the days of union solidarity, so when the American Federation of Television and Radio Artists (AFTRA) went on strike, not just on-camera personnel but writers, directors, camera crews, couriers, everyone walked. It was a general strike with a celebrity picket line. Each bitter cold morning the news staff walked the length of Forty-ninth Street in Rockefeller Center, passed through the legendary Hurley's, downed a quick shot of brandy, exited a back door and still managed to march without missing a beat. Meanwhile, management manned the store and, to our chagrin, did surprisingly well. Everyone went out except Chet Huntley. No Western individualist was walking any picket line because a union he didn't believe in told him to. A furor went up, and one night as he left the building, unknown assailants tried to mug him. Unruffled, he stayed on the air and for years tried to convince newspeople they needed a separate union of their own, exclusive of actors, dancers, and jugglers. It never got off the ground, for as news became more like entertainment, there was hardly any need.

My days were getting longer. In addition to reporting for the evening broadcast, I anchored two five-minute programs, inserts into the "Today" show at 7:25 and then 8:25 A.M. when local stations across the country broke away from the network for their cut-ins. Everybody said it would be great "exposure." The first time around this sounded like some kind of electronic fan dance. But as people began to comment, I realized how potent showing your stuff can be. Indeed, the more you showed 'em, the more likely they would remember your name.

To launch this daily chore meant rising at 3 A.M. and arriving at the office about 4 A.M. Cabbies, drunks, and ladies of the evening calling it a night made up my company in those magic hours. Once at the office, I cut and read the wires, screened film from the previous night, and wrote the script. At first it was overwhelming, and on the odd morning when the clock was overtaking me, a seasoned veteran of the *Herald Tribune,* Bob White, would fly to my rescue, making it look as though his help didn't count at all. It did. Bob was a roly-poly man who hugged the typewriter like a cello player. Peering over his eyeglasses, wisps of gray hair framing a cherubic expression, he had the knack of pretending deadlines didn't matter and so let's just take it slow and easy. His prose was clean and hard, a pro's, and his manner was unfailingly gracious and kind.

Unlike Bob, newspeople, by necessity and natural temperament, are often fast-moving and fast-talking. In television especially, the instant deadlines and merciless limits of airtime can do mortal damage to your concentration. Attention spans run about as long as that of a hummingbird. Flitting is substituted for thinking.

Alec Gifford was one of these quicksilver people, but with a hard intelligence to back it up. I never knew anyone who spoke so rapidly with a southern accent, a fast-forward drawl. Alec had recently arrived from WDSU in New Orleans. With his manic metabolism, he anchored the 9 A.M. ten-minute broadcast, assisted by the unflappable Bob White. We were the dawn patrol.

The dangerous waters of TV news, which included an array of ways to make a fool of yourself on the air, had long ago been charted by Alec. "Remember," he said to me one morning as I munched on a scrambled egg sandwich, "in this business, always fold your own parachute." I pondered that. And to further make his point, as I was on my way down to makeup at 6:30 he shoved a fistful of miscellaneous AP and UPI copy into my hand. "Stick this in your bag," he said. "One day you might need it."

I figured Alec might be a trifle too insecure. Especially since the copy boy assigned to the morning shift knew the drill. After I had finished writing, his job was to "break the script," that is, to separate the six-page book of carbons and paper so that all parties to the broadcast would have a copy. While this was being done, I went to makeup.

From the newsroom on the fifth floor, it was only a short elevator ride to the cavernous third-floor studio. Usually, copy boys ran down the fire stairs, taking them three at at time, arriving breathless with my copy of the script. Others went to the director, the tech staff, and the file. With copy for a five-minute show, minus a commercial, it wasn't as though I faced a run-through of *War and Peace*.

Then dawned that fateful morning in Studio 3B: hair in place, makeup on, back straight, adrenaline rising—and still no copy boy. A moment of reckoning approached, that abyss down which careers disappear, the darkest phobia of anyone who has ever been on the air. Egg-on-the-face time.

As Hugh Downs told the nation that "Today" would be back after news from your local station, I reached for my bag, pulled out the unread wire copy I had stuffed into it, barely smoothed the creases, and after a tight "Good morning" began reading.

There was no teleprompter in those days, so eye contact was paramount, but straining to read the faint AP carbon copy that morning, I barely looked up. If I had tried intentionally to pull the most trivial, the most boring stories in the world, it could not have been worse. A zoning fight in some obscure corner of Long Island, a bar brawl in lower Manhattan, a lost dog—on and on it went. I kept talking, pretending there was someone out there actually waiting for word of these important events. When it was over, the crew applauded. I slunk back to the newsroom waiting for the telephone to ring. The "Today" show was watched by every executive at NBC.

Not until late that day as I walked by the foreign editor's office did I have any inkling of reaction. Mac Johnson, no stranger to bottled spirits, beckoned me in and said in a stage whisper: "Were you drunk?" When I explained what had happened, the fistful of wire copy in the bag, he beamed. "Great recovery," he said paternally. "Good thinking." I blessed the name of Alec Gifford and never forgot my parachute.

The "Today" show writers and producers who prepared the network news segments anchored every half hour by Frank Blair worked
alongside the local newspeople. In addition, a special Vietnam broadcast, a daily diary of the war, was launched, and correspondents such
as Dean Brelis and Garrick Utley, fresh from the front, rotated on the
program. They were doing what I wanted to be doing, and the drama
of Indochina became a siren call. Banging out the details of the
Brooklyn Democratic leader's latest complaint, I would look up and
savor second-hand the romance and excitement of a war in progress.
It took no expertise to see it as the biggest story of my generation.
Silently, my resolve began to form.

The conflict in Vietnam was widening like a bloodstain, offering
up a series of horrifying images to a nation for the first time watching
itself at war: praying monks drenched with gasoline setting themselves
afire, soldiers in agony crying for a medic, thunderous bombers and
screaming fighters streaking over a deep green landscape, children
fleeing napalm. At home, ragtag hippies intensified their protest
marches, burning flags and draft cards, intoning, "Hey, hey, LBJ! How
many kids did you kill today?" All of it made the morning and evening
news, day after day after day.

By the end of 1965, 200,000 American troops were on duty in
Vietnam, a number that would double in a year. What were they
doing there? The message came through garbled for both reporters and
the public. There was nothing clear-cut here, no obvious transgression
of a line as in Korea, no liberation of Paris, no territory held, no cities
captured. And no victories to celebrate—just a feeling of not getting
anywhere. The opposing camps had squared off: hawks who saw a
reason for the war and a reason to win it, doves who saw neither, both
sides sleepwalking in a nightmare. The press, although still "on the
team," lamented the death of civilians and understandably admired
the courage of the other side, but many sensed that we didn't have the
bearing of a victorious army. Watching it all, I just didn't know what
to think, but I was determined to find out. The problem was that
Vietnam was not a local beat. It was network.

Color portraits of the NBC News network correspondents lined
the fifth-floor corridor of 30 Rock. This exalted group offered a high
point for the RCA tours: Huntley, Brinkley, Harsch, Newman, Mc-
Gee, Frederick, Chancellor, Dickerson. Most of the pictures on Murderers' Row—so dubbed by the producers—were of people who had
come to the network after print careers. Rare was the local station TV
reporter promoted to the ranks of that royal company. One had to be

noticed for exceptional work for even a remote chance of "making network."

It was discouraging, but again an opportunity came up. My good fortune was New York City's misfortune as the biggest transit strike in its history appeared on the wintry horizon in late 1965. Dick Kutzleb, as director of local news, had plotted out a game plan for covering such a disaster, although he and Gabe Pressman thought it most unlikely to happen. But Mike Quill, head of the Transit Workers Union and one of the city's more colorful and profane labor leaders, sounded the trumpets and vowed to teach the new whippersnapper mayor a lesson in practical politics.

Dismissing Quill's threats as blarney, the brass decided on places where "live" cameras would be set up to report the outcome of the confrontation. Equipment was still bulky and primitive, and a "live" van had to be pointed at the transmitters atop the Empire State Building in order to send its signal. Gabe positioned himself at City Hall, where he expected a deal to be announced at the eleventh hour—almost a foregone conclusion—and I was penciled in at the Americana Hotel on Seventh Avenue and Fifty-second Street where the bargaining teams had holed up. For some time now, most of my work on stories had amounted to interviewing the principals, seeing that I had enough "cover" pictures to illustrate what was happening, and dropping a stand-upper into the piece. I had done virtually no live work from the field. That was about to change.

As good as his word, Quill stormed out of negotiations with Lindsay, calling him a "little shit" (not publicly), and took his men out on a strike that paralyzed New York. The story had dropped into my lap. Just before 6 A.M. on the morning of January 1, 1966, the director sitting in the studio at 30 Rock said, "It's all yours now, Liz. Just take a deep breath. And, oh yes, they want you to wear suits." I owned a total of one.

That seemed the least of the problems ahead—as thousands of cars gridlocked the city, crushing the economic lifelines, creating serious emergencies. New York stood on the brink. The network side got on the story, and in the days that followed I lost track of the number of times I heard, "We're coming to you in five, Liz." Baptism, Holy Communion, Confirmation—all in five. Negotiations resumed at the Americana, and one night, after doing hourly live reports all day on where and how the two sides stood, I looked squarely into the camera and confidently reported, "There will be clocks around the talks." A producer congratulated me on my first king-size blooper after we switched back to the studio.

Meanwhile, one of the three-man federal mediating team, Dr. Nathan Feinsinger, took pity on me as he watched the male veterans elbowing me in the tight clinches. At 4:30 one morning, calling me from his suite as I sat in the empty ballroom downstairs, he started to ramble on about the talks and the dark implications of an impasse. About five minutes of this and I realized he was willing to be interviewed, if I asked. So I did and he agreed. It would be a live broadcast—but only if I could please get the exact text of that part of Milton's "On His Blindness" where standing and waiting is discussed ("They also serve who only stand and wait.") Feinsinger had something to say and needed the precise text to underline his point. The alarm went up: the first break—and an exclusive one at that—on the transit story. The newsroom exploded in a furor, the brass issuing an all-points bulletin for a copy of *Bartlett's Familiar Quotations*.

Once we had it, the problem became how to sneak Feinsinger down from the upper floors of the hotel into the ballroom—where CBS and ABC also had hot cameras—and break into our network without alerting them. To complicate matters, Feinsinger used a wheelchair.

It was a masterpiece of coordination. Elevators were silently commandeered, studio-size cameras and six-inch-round cables stealthily dragged behind a thick curtain, out of the competition's sightline. We went on the air, breaking live into programming. Feinsinger was dynamite, Miltonian to the point of melodrama as he painted a dire picture of the negotiations. In retrospect, there was little doubt that he delivered a masterstroke to frighten both sides into real negotiating.

An agreement was finally reached on January 13, and NBC had news of a deal first, again exclusively. The redoubtable McAndrew had been in touch with his "sources" and scooped his own staff. Contacts in the New York power structure are part of the trappings and perks of network executive jobs, and while they are often used to further one's own private agenda, such as social climbing, McAndrew always had his eye on the story. During that week he worked the phones like any cub reporter. It was the only time in my twenty-year TV career that I competed with the boss.

The strike coverage brought me into focus on the network side, and co-workers began to say that perhaps it was time for a "girl" to be hired as a real-life reporter for general coverage. Pauline Frederick was nearing retirement, and Nancy Dickerson would fade as President Johnson began to withdraw from the scene, so it wouldn't be as though they had "too many women." But the brass had to be careful in that department; network radio had already banned the respected and highly professional Frederick from the air because "station directors don't like the sound of a woman's voice."

At this turning point in my career, with the prospect of perhaps vaulting another barrier, something else was happening. Celebrity. I had started doing interviews with celebrities for the local news and soon after became a celebrity myself. People on the street and in restaurants began to do double takes. Party invitations flooded in, especially after I had talked to the likes of Sophia Loren, the Beatles, the Rolling Stones, Mme. Chiang Kai-shek, Nelson Rockefeller, Senator Jacob Javits, and even Frank Sinatra. Of them all, Sinatra seemed the most daunting, before the fact. He was at the height of his favorite pastime, reporter-bashing, screaming epithets at gossip columnists. One night he arrived at a local nitery, surrounded by his New Jersey goons, some of whom played backfield for various football teams. I waded in, widened my eyes, and lowered my head. "Will you give a break to an Italian kid just starting out?" I inquired. It was shameless.

Meeting my gaze were the deepest blue eyes I had ever encountered. Even Paul Newman looked stone-washed next to this.

Obviously amused by this earthy question, Sinatra smiled and sat down. "Shoot."

Heady stuff.

Equally beguiling, and no less formidable, was the taut, tan figure of a wily newcomer to the United States Senate. After skillfully changing his legal residence from Massachusetts to New York, Robert Kennedy had grabbed center stage on the New York political scene. It was unnerving when he would look around a pack of reporters, walk up to me and say softly: "Well, so what are we going to do today?"

Heady stuff.

With it all came the entrée into insider information, the kind of behind-the-scenes gossip rarely made public in those days. Nelson Rockefeller, then governor of New York, always had an eye for the ladies, to put it politely, quick to comment on a new dress, a change in hairdo, a loss in weight. He possessed a devastating combination of raw sex appeal, patrician charm, and the aphrodisiac power that money bestows. So I listened keenly one day as Kutzleb moaned, "Rocky is acting stupid." He said he had warned Leslie Slote, Rockefeller's adroit press secretary, that the governor might at least *try* to lower his romantic profile. After all, the press could just look the other way for so long. Now, Kutzleb told me, Rocky was playing with someone on his staff—and it sorely tested the propriety of the news personnel. But, remarkably, propriety prevailed, and Rockefeller never had to reckon with what befell Senator Gary Hart of Colorado more than two decades later. Sadly—and almost inevitably—a lifetime of philandering became a major story only after Rockefeller was no longer around to deny it.

All heady stuff. Still, it was not enough, and, in truth, I was vaguely uncomfortable. Somewhere a puritan voice, no doubt an ethic that had penetrated my psyche growing up in colonial Connecticut, kept reminding me that reporters are supposed to *cover* stories, not *be recognized for covering them.* Worst of all, the days seemed to pass in a blur. I was running out of time. The war would be over if I didn't get there soon.

My campaign to get to Vietnam was waged like the war itself, first a guerrilla action and then an all-out offensive with major battles. The strategy actually grew out of a conversation with my old mentor, George Barrett, who had distinguished himself in World War II and the Korean War. "The first thing you do," he counseled, "is tell everyone that you want to go. Not the brass—because it will eventually get back to them and that's the point of the exercise—but everyone you come in contact with."

It worked. And it didn't work. Bill Corrigan, the network news vice-president in charge of coverage for Asia, asked me if the rumor about my wanting to go to Vietnam was true. Corrigan was constantly on the lookout for people to coerce, although the official policy stipulated volunteers only. Up to that point mainly network correspondents covered Vietnam. A hunch told me that they might be thin on volunteers. Corrigan seemed interested and said he would get back to me. A few days later, after contacting Ron Steinman, then bureau chief in Saigon, he said no dice. "Steinman says he'll be on the first plane back if we send a woman in there."

Now came the time for an all-out offensive. I nagged and bitched, left copies of Marguerite Higgins's Pulitzer Prize–winning stories out of Korea on executives' desks, became a general—to use a favorite TV news phrase—"pain in the ass."

Meanwhile, despite the general evenhandedness shown in my

assignments (except the war, of course), stinging reminders of the automatic double standard surfaced. Some were hilarious, such as the wedding dress caper. Lynda Bird Johnson's wedding to Captain Charles Robb of the Marines was shaping up as one of 1967's great political and social events—a relief after her prolonged exposure and curious relationship with actor and perennial escort George Hamilton. It would be the first marriage of a president's daughter in the White House in fifty-three years; and the groom was slated to go to Vietnam within four months. Naturally, the networks planned special coverage. The fan and women's magazines were all atwitter, too, especially about what the bride would wear. Catfights broke out about whether *Women's Wear Daily* had the right to print a sketch of the wedding dress, and the hype began in earnest. Walking in the hallway outside the newsroom one afternoon, I was stopped by a man I didn't know, except by reputation: Bob Shafer, a new network producer working on specials. "Liz, I'd like you to meet with me soon as possible. I'm going to have something for you in the wedding coverage."

Not a bad opportunity for a local reporter, I thought, and asked what he wanted me to do.

"The wedding dress," he said. "The dress is shaping up as a hell of a story and I'd like you to find out everything about it. That'll be your piece for the special."

I distinctly remember blinking, Then, recklessly, I blurted out, "But I don't do weddings."

His eyes narrowed. "I'm talking about a network special," he replied, leaning on the word *network.*

"Oh, I don't mean to be rude," I sailed on blithely, "but I don't work on women's stories."

He said nothing for a few seconds, mumbled something inaudibly, and walked away in a clear and present huff.

The next morning, Don Meany appeared in my cubicle. A quiet, scholarly-looking man who seemed to be perpetually blushing, Meany was a vice-president and very much in charge of the coverage of special events such as the wedding. He allowed as how he couldn't believe the conversation I had had with Shafer, as it had been reported to him. The guy's a network producer, he went on, and in case you forgot, you're just a local reporter and should be grateful for the chance.

"Don, don't you understand? I want to cover a war—not a wedding."

Meany turned redder than usual, shook his head and, like Shafer, mumbled and left.

The wedding special in all its storybook glamour went on the air without my assistance.

The months slid by, and on January 30, 1968, the newsroom crackled with the electricity of a big, breaking story. Dark-suited executives appeared amid what seemed to be every available body in the news division. The Tet offensive was under way; all eyes were glued to the monitors, waiting for the pictures shot in Vietnam and about to come through by satellite from Tokyo, where Jack Perkins would do the voice-over. Excitement turned to wonder and then a kind of shame. Images of an enemy firing within the U.S. embassy compound seemed otherworldly, a bad war movie about American losers. In retaliation, the Allies decimated the Vietcong network. In terms of enemy killed countrywide, it was clearly an American victory, a fact even Hanoi's commanders would admit years later. Still, this audacious gamble—to turn a war not going their way—would succeed in breaking American will. As for how the story hit back home, the facts never caught up with the pictures: all anyone would remember were Vietcong on the embassy lawn.

It was by now clear that the way to win the war—applying overwhelming force, an invasion of North Vietnam—had been abandoned in favor of protracted limited war in an effort to force Hanoi to the bargaining table. But as the casualties piled up, the weekly toll of blood spilled only whetted the American, not the North Vietnamese, appetite for resolution. When the war escalated, so too had the peace movement, its ranks falling into marches on the Pentagon, down Fifth Avenue, and anywhere they could count on the presence of a TV camera. After Tet, the administration's credibility, whatever its strategy, had about as much currency as the Bank of Saigon.

In the next few days, the sight of correspondents like NBC's Howard Tuckner, lying wounded as the battle raged around him, seemed to underscore the futility of the war and give the doves yet another springboard for their campaign to abandon South Vietnam. Hawk, dove, or do-do bird, it was not an argument that concerned me at that point. I had missed another seminal event in the conduct of this war and all because management didn't want to offend a bureau chief with a macho problem.

Antiwar demonstrations coincided with race riots in the early weeks of 1968. Locally, the waves of unrest hit the city hard. New

York, with its large black population, reeled in the turmoil of the civil rights movement: Harlem, Newark, the South Bronx, Brownsville— all battlegrounds of the struggle. Even the serenity of the Columbia University campus was smashed when antiwar demonstrators occupied and ransacked the president's office. And near the Quad, a Vietcong liberation flag hung over the headquarters of the Marxist-oriented Students for a Democratic Society (SDS). At that same moment an embattled Democratic president was fighting for survival. And as the war moved to the top of the political agenda, a man with an unsmiling face and priestly demeanor appeared on the scene, like Jesus Himself beckoning believers to follow Him: Eugene McCarthy, a Democratic senator from Minnesota, Messiah to the antiwar faithful.

The spirit of upheaval did not spare NBC News. After seven consecutive years, "The Huntley-Brinkley Report" no longer had a lock on first place. Suffering a freak accident in his own bathtub, Bill McAndrew died, a turn of fate that would gravely affect the course of the news department. He was replaced by the talmudic Reuven Frank, whose strength lay in documentaries, not administration, a portent of shaky times ahead. More important, I had a reporter's hunch he didn't think much of women in broadcasting.

Against all this turmoil surged my own. Finally, a chance came to move to the network side. I was assigned to Gene McCarthy's presidential campaign. In April 1968, I headed west to join the McCarthyites in Indianapolis as the Indiana primary drew near. There could be no better introduction to the war in Vietnam than from the man who epitomized the opposition. I had to start somewhere.

3

CARTHAGE
BURNING

Solitude is standing alone on a midwestern plain in the thin light of a day in May. Here, it was the sounds you didn't hear that stayed with you, like the roll of cumulus clouds across the biggest sky you had ever seen, and the surge of growth beneath the moist ground, already set in motion by the spring rains. It was difficult to believe this void of silence existed in the heart of a country on the verge of a nervous breakdown. Only the crackling of dried corn husks from another season reset the clock, dissolving the sense of timelessness.

I was stranded in central Nebraska, wandering through a cornfield at high noon, wondering what ace reporters do when they have missed the boat, or in this case, the bus, the campaign bus. For one mad moment I was seized by an urge to shout, "Free at last" and run wildly through this pocket of rural sanity. No, that would never do. The national desk had no doubt already heard that their girl reporter had done something very girlish. Somewhere between Broken Bow and Beaver Crossing, I had lingered too long on one of the many farms included in the day's schedule, and the followers of that year's political Pied Piper had left without me. It was that kind of campaign.

No coddling of the press in 1968, and certainly not by Gene McCarthy, who never looked behind, but simply assumed you were walking in his footsteps. No Secret Service agents to round up the troops, carry the bags, plot out the moves, make sure one and all were where they were supposed to be. Even though a president had been assassinated five years earlier, presidential candidates were still psychologically out-of-bounds in the minds of those in the security business. As a result, the McCarthy campaign consisted of his student-crusaders, members of the press, and close friends. You ate on the run—usually stale cake and bitter coffee at the latest truck stop—and looked after yourself in the tradition of rugged journalistic individualism. Add to this McCarthy's own studied indifference to the untutored Fourth Estate, and even filing your story, calling your desk, finding time to ship, were challenges in no way made easier by his aides. There was, of course, the usual bellyaching all reporters indulge in—almost a requirement in the world of TV news—but it never seriously occurred to anyone that it should be otherwise. Besides, it all had a certain rustic charm somehow rooted in the rough-and-tumble spirit of early America.

"The Huntley-Brinkley Report" had been broadcast in color for almost three years at this point, so to the public, the business of TV news seemed to be moving with the times. In fact, stories were still shot on film, a medium long on artistic effect but short on efficiency and flexibility in the bone-crushing hours of a breaking story. The unwieldy Auricon camera produced picture and sound on film that had to be developed. Although invented in the 1930s, it had become the workhorse of this brand-new medium. Clumsy and primitive, the Auricon did a job for which it was never designed, day in and day out. An average 400-foot magazine of film meant anywhere from thirty to forty-five minutes in the soup, if someone wasn't there ahead of you. Add to this the editing and splicing time, the writing and narration of a script that was recorded on a separate track, the actual feeding time (as you prayed the film splices wouldn't break), and most dicey of all, the logistics and travel time involved in where to go to feed the story, and you had the daily makings of a very big accident about to happen before the eyes of 8.7 million Americans.

On the road, as in the 1968 presidential campaign, a field producer kept track of our proximity to either an NBC news bureau or an affiliated NBC station, the only two sources from which a piece could be "fed" to New York. Because there was no daily satellite capability, TV news pieces were sent by catching a "loop"—literally, a loop, or series, of telephone company lines covering various sections of the country. A signal sent along these lines allowed you to feed a film spot, a story, to New York, but you had to be in the bureau or affiliate where there was access, and, of course, enough time—time, the final reckoning in TV news, the grim definer of who could take the heat.

If you had a story—if the candidate actually "said something"— after shooting the pictures, the next critical step was getting the story to the feed-point. Airline schedules were as important as getting the facts right, and riding single-engine charter airplanes in rough weather with mail-order pilots became part of the daily routine. Once you got to an airport in the town or city with a feed-point, say station XYZ in Seattle, you often raced by motorcycle—desperately clutching the driver's black leather jacket—to the bureau or station, threw the stuff into the developer, reminded New York of your status, and checked on the line bookings. Then, as one veteran producer used to say, you "sat around and scratched your ass" waiting for the developer to work its magic. The correspondent might use the time to write a script, or if he had finished the script and recorded a narration on the scene, he might have stayed behind to keep up with the candidate. The field producer at the feed-point worked with a film editor to edit the story, again praying with each click of the splicer and eventually, the cut story was fed by the mysterious loop into the electronic arms of a two-inch-tape machine at 30 Rockefeller Plaza. Within minutes, sometimes seconds, New York rewound the tape, counted it down into the show, and made it part of "The Huntley-Brinkley Report."

Russian roulette all the way is how many veterans remember their dismal batting average: you made it a little more than 50 percent of the time. That is to say that in a given week, two or three stories out of ten failed to make it through the electronic gamut. The videotape camera would soon replace the film camera and cut editing and transmission time in half; satellites would dot the sky, eliminating the loop, and getting a story on the air would be routine instead of apocalyptic. TV news was about to come out of the open-cockpit, biplane generation into the screaming sleekness of the computer jet age. But with it would come a kind of slick prepackaged journalism that seemed less immediate, less real—a difference comparable to the transition, in the early days of television, from "live" broadcasts to those that were prerecorded on film.

Meanwhile, it was the ever-present threat of the "feeding" frenzy that kept a correspondent's adrenaline up, and on this particular day in Nebraska, looking for and finally finding a telephone had done me in. As I was filling in the national editor on the morning's events, the bus had taken off and left me stranded in heartland America. Once I began to imagine the scathing comments already being voiced across the newsroom back in New York, I took a hard look at the situation, headed for a dirt road winding through the valley ahead, and stuck my thumb in the air. Soon, an amazed farmer, driving a pickup truck he might have borrowed from the *Tobacco Road* prop man, slowed down, and I was on my way back to Campaign '68 in Lincoln, Nebraska.

That night, at the Cornhusker Hotel, I called the desk in New York to give them an update on the candidate's whereabouts.

"You're where?" roared the voice at the other end.

"At the Cornhusker," I said smartly.

"Well, have you been shucked yet?" he howled.

As I stood there forcing a laugh and telling him to eat his heart out, I gazed down from my tenth-floor room and saw fire engines racing toward the hotel. Sirens blazing, they parked in front of the entrance, and men in rubber boots and funny hats raced into the lobby, carrying a large hose.

"Hey, Ray," I interrupted. "I think the hotel is on fire."

"Is McCarthy in the building?" he asked quickly.

"No, he's out with his family," I replied, uneasy at the smoke billowing up from the sidewalk toward my floor.

"Well, forget it, and give me the rundown for tomorrow, will you."

Midway through my recitation of tomorrow's schedule, I heard hollering in the hallway. There was little doubt that hanging up on New York might be hazardous to my career, but better for my health. "Call you back," I snapped, and raced for the door.

First abandoned in a cornfield and now fleeing a hotel fire. By the time I got out on the street, it occurred to me that the degree of understanding between headquarters at 30 Rock and their correspondents roaming the world was tenuous at best.

*   •   •

WHEN I picked up the McCarthy campaign on April 19, it was only two weeks since the assassination of Martin Luther King, Jr. The country was dazed, newspeople frantic. And television news executives, in particular, were making decisions, about how and what to cover, that they would defend and debate for the rest of their lives. Walter Cronkite's on-air declaration in March 1968—that the United States should pull out of the war—jolted both the public and the media. Was it the pronouncement of a newsman who had hit upon the real story, or just a spectacular example of a country fragmenting? Whatever the reason, Cronkite's stunning pronouncement planted a seed of partiality in a business that vaunted objectivity, remaining above the fray. A very fine line had been nudged by one of America's most respected and authoritative journalists. Even President Johnson is said to have remarked that if he had lost Cronkite, he had lost the country. Weary and resigned, Johnson announced to the nation on April Fools' Eve that he was pulling out of the presidential race. His political retreat only fed the journalistic appetite for power, and that of television news in particular. It had brought down a president. Television was becoming the great leveler as the remoteness and inaccessibility of authority figures crumbled before the electronic age.

Theatrically and inexorably, news film documented the disintegration of the good old days. The early months of 1968 were a made-for-TV movie: Tet, an assassination, the fall of a president, race riots, antiwar demonstrations and violence, the waging of a disputed war, a presidential election up for grabs. Nelson Rockefeller, thinking he could stop the reemergent Richard Nixon, made his third bid for the GOP nomination. On the Democratic side, McCarthy, Kennedy, and Vice-President Hubert Humphrey were the leading contenders. For newspeople as well as politicians, careers and fortunes—big ones—were made or were broken on the back of these events.

Competition was stiff that year, not only among the candidates but also among the correspondents who covered them. Sam Donaldson of ABC News vaulted aboard McCarthy's DC-9 the day I made my way down the aisle of the aircraft to begin my first tour of national political reporting. Fresh-faced and unfailingly polite, Donaldson had not yet made a specialty of yelling questions at people ten feet away from him. He was a rather good reporter with a sense of humor, not the court jester he would later become.

CBS News had David Shoumacher in place, short in stature and charm, long on the killer instinct his network fostered in its line reporting staff. Donaldson and I forged an informal alliance during those weeks to block the often underhanded tactics of Shoumacher, who seemed particularly irked that his competition from NBC was a "girl."

"Oh Senator, Senator, do you have a moment?" The NBC field producer was about to introduce me to the man who had forged a lightning rod for a generation of war protestors. "This is Liz Trotta, one of our new correspondents," he said, maneuvering me opposite the tall, gray-haired figure.

McCarthy gave me the once-over as I stood there with my hand outstretched smiling nervously. "Well, well," he said mockingly over his shoulder to Shoumacher, who was lurking nearby. "NBC's gotten so desperate, they've sent a girl." Every man within earshot, including my own producer, joined in a hearty laugh.

Everybody who had given me advice before I left for this first network assignment said I should put myself in the hands of the NBC field producer on the scene. Little did I know how close this advice was to what he had in mind. When he wasn't pushing me around, telling me how to write, what to say, whom to interview, and where to go, he was knocking on my hotel room door—ostensibly for story discussions. Parrying his amorous advances became part of my daily routine. At that point sexual harassment was not even a concept, let alone an actionable offense, so I swallowed hard and decided it was just another affront to be absorbed by any woman who wanted to succeed. Meanwhile, while I was congratulating myself for having fended him off, he lingered on the phone to New York, bad-mouthing me to whoever would listen. Not for some months did I realize the extent of the damage he had done. The "Trotta is trouble" myth began to build, and even the usually discerning Reuven Frank, now the president of NBC News, began asking close associates if "Liz had a sense of humor."

Worst of all, this same producer kept me away from the crew—calling all the shots, interposing himself between me and the people with whom I should have had the most rapport. In desperation, I appealed to the national editor, Van Kardisch, a hard-boiled newspaperman with the proverbial heart of gold, whose innate good news sense told him something was wrong. Within days, the word was sent upstairs and my panting and pawing companion was transferred to another part of the political landscape.

The relationship with the news desk in New York was close and critical, an umbilical cord between you and the organization. The organization had to know where you were and what you were getting, against the backdrop of what it knew and gleaned from the wire services and other sources. Kardisch was a product of old-fashioned newspapering days. Short in stature, with a head of deep auburn hair, he was the epitome of the newsman on top of a story. His voice was always strong and level as it gave authority to a thick streets-of-Brooklyn accent. One could imagine him as city editor of the storied *Brooklyn Eagle* and on the copy desk of the *New York Post*, which was, in fact, the life he had before TV news.

His passion was keeping all the troops in view, no matter how far afield they were scattered, their locations and latest moves logged on a clipboard that he carried by his side. And his advice to correspondents was simple in its routine, difficult in its execution. "I don't care how hard it is to find a phone, how tired you are, where you are, or how much you have to do. All of this is useless unless we know where you are, what you're doing—especially if you have a story—and how we can ship the film. So call in every time you hit a new spot, at least every hour." Then he would add, without changing the monotone of his desk voice, "And if you don't—I'll find you. I can find you anywhere. Just try me."

I tried him one day, inadvertently. The press was hurtling in a bus through rural Indiana, riding behind McCarthy, who was about to face his first primary against Bobby Kennedy. There were still enough small farms left in mid-America to make it interesting and friendly, and for two or three stops I simply forgot to call in. Besides, the standard campaign speech was still intact; I practically knew it by heart. Eventually we rolled into Kokomo, a town famous as the title of a hit song in the 1947 Betty Grable movie *Mother Wore Tights*. It had such great hick appeal that we were all yelling the refrain, "In Kokomo, Indiana," just as the city limits sign came into view.

We pulled into an alley on the fringe of the downtown area, barely fitting into the space, and even before the door opened I could hear someone calling my name, a strange sensation as I knew no one in Kokomo. Darting around the bus was a small boy, exhorting me to "Call the desk." Kardisch had struck from New York, somehow finding and employing this local urchin and directing him to an alley in Kokomo. I dived into the first building I saw and called Kardisch. He was, of course, exultant, and would gloat over this feat for years to come. At that moment, however, he was chasing a story. "We've got a report that Paul Newman has had a heart attack and may be dying in a local hospital. It's unconfirmed, but you'd better move and check it out. And get back to me fast."

He was, of course, referring to the movie actor Paul Newman, a regular presence in McCarthy's entourage. I had met him once already in an Indianapolis hotel lobby and chatted for five or ten minutes about the campaign. Heart attack? The campaign kids derided the report, and eventually, after I had performed the usual routine of checking local hospitals and the police by telephone, Newman turned up. He was sitting on the dais at the next event, a McCarthy speech in downtown Kokomo, looking as healthy as he was handsome.

Newman was among the first of a new type of "politically aware" performer on the scene in that election year: Shirley MacLaine, Warren Beatty, Jane Fonda, Joan Baez, and others traveled with the candidates, entertained, made speeches, shook hands, and generally lent their glamour to the daily grind of campaigning. That glamour often translated into a cynical exploitation by both candidates and press. Stars guaranteed at least some coverage of otherwise lackluster campaigns. Meanwhile, the stars felt they were "relevant."

Most of the actual work the three nets were doing on McCarthy's campaign, apart from photographing the "color," consisted of listening to his set speech in hopes that one day he would depart, elaborate, or trip himself up into the waiting arms of a reporter who would file a story. McCarthy's message—stop the war, listen to the young—was gathering moss, and the question of whether he could beat Kennedy or Humphrey was, of course, new material. It was the pursuit of this information, or even a nuance in McCarthy's view of how his campaign was going, that gave me an opportunity to accomplish two things: establish some credibility as a "girl reporter" and get even for his humiliating welcome the day I arrived.

An opportunity came, luckily, while we were still in Indiana. One afternoon at Indiana University in Bloomington, we were listening to still another recitation of The Speech, struggling to sustain concentration, trying to avoid the ever-present danger that he might "say something" while we weren't paying attention. Suddenly, while all three network cameras were switched off, he began to depart from the prepared text. The remarks were vague, but nevertheless he was offering an assessment of Humphrey and his chances, something he had not done before in any detail.

Something new—and that meant news. The reporters and producers began waking up, and a wave of hurried whispers began:

"Whaddee say?" "Didja get that?" Nobody really had got it, not even the print and wire guys. Luckily my tape recorder at the foot of the podium had been running. I could file for the radio network, but what good would an audio tape do for a TV story? None.

After the speech the entourage broke and ran, unable to catch up with the candidate until we all boarded his plane. But McCarthy had secluded himself in the front compartment and sent word back saying that we had misunderstood his remarks, that he hadn't said what by now was being discussed as the headline of the day. We took off, still panicked at being caught with our guard down and in possession of only half a story. I sat in my seat, replaying the audio tape, wondering what to do next, when a gravelly voice from across the aisle rose above the takeoff roar. "You want to nail him?"

The voice belonged to Jack Bell, veteran supreme of the Associated Press, a man I so idolized that I had never gotten up enough nerve even to introduce myself. "Yes," I stammered. "But how?"

"Just play that thing back for him," he answered, grudgingly jabbing his finger at the tape recorder in my lap. "After we land, we'll stop him on the tarmac. If he doesn't own up to saying what he did, play back the tape for him."

It was perfect. And, of course the idea would come from a pro in the world of print. For a split second, I felt a twinge of conscience that I was no longer part of that world.

When we landed, McCarthy was halted by the crush on the tarmac. According to plan, I asked him about his Humphrey statement and actually quoted what he said. He denied it. I switched the recorder on under his nose, and with all cameras rolling, he flinched in embarrassment, stammered, equivocated, and said he had been misunderstood. It was great television. A politician caught in the act of dissembling. The story led the "Today" show news segments the next morning. More important, from that day on he looked at me in a different way, nothing obvious, except he knew that I could not be easily dismissed.

Meanwhile, whatever he may have thought of me, McCarthy was having his very own midlife crisis in public. Rumors continued to circulate that he was having an affair on the campaign trail with a well-known magazine writer, scandalizing his wife of many years. Still, the valiant Abigail flew in whenever he needed her to shore up his support with the respectable family vote. All this, and my own personal experience with him, added up to a man who thought himself above charges of infidelity, disloyalty, or chauvinism.

On still other counts, McCarthy seemed an unlikely candidate to lead any movement, let alone one that was challenging America on just about every institutional level. His intellectual vanity appealed to students, as did his touch of originality and the occasional flashes of Irish charm, although it always had a bite. Watching the Nixons on TV one night he said to me, "Pat is really animated these days. Her eyes are moving." But self-deprecation was not his style; remoteness and piety were, the kind of island-calm interior discipline which, frankly, I remembered from my years at Catholic school.

The day came when I counted seventeen ecclesiastical buzz-words in just one of his speeches, and they kept reappearing; phrases like "community of spirit" and the "ultimate good of sacrifice" that were fashionable in the days of the lay-apostolate revolution of the 1950s. It recalled a time when "Catholic intellectuals" decided to counter the widely held opinion that such a category of thinkers was a contradiction in terms. Philosophical journals of so-called Catholic thought became the outlet for these men, whom I suspected of being priests-with-privileges or simply those who couldn't give up wine or women, and so they formed this lay-apostolate army of scholarship.

My suspicion that McCarthy was among them became a certainty when John Cogley, foremost of these new Catholic writers, appeared one morning on the press plane, his Catholic mysticism a natural companion to this candidate's secular cynicism. The staff described Cogley as one of the new "advisers," a commodity that McCarthy used up frequently throughout the campaign. The last time I had seen Cogley, a dozen years earlier, he was speaking on academic freedom at Fordham University. Desperate under the yoke of a regiment of nuns, I had cut class at the ladylike College of New Rochelle to hear him. Afterwards, we had a long discussion about what could be done to break the stultification of the Catholic academic curriculum, and with his encouragement I went on to great feats of insubordination, such as buying a copy of Boccaccio's *Decameron*, which was high up on the Church of Rome's Top Ten—the Index, an official proclamation of what would wreck your mind. Forbidden books.

I had entered the College of New Rochelle after my father decreed that only a strict Catholic school would curb my natural rebellion—"a wild streak" he called it—that registered as insurrection in the placid 1950s. At CNR (aptly rechristened the College of No Romance), one wore high heels and stockings to dinner every evening and needed written permission to take from the school library any works of Voltaire, James Joyce, and a host of other subversives. In time, I found myself captaining a very small academic freedom movement, fueled by not just the strictures of the Ursuline order but the growing lay-apostolate movement within the church, the same Catholic intellectuals that Eugene McCarthy brought to mind during his campaign. Our merry band of malcontents espoused their ideas, made speeches when we could, and challenged interpretations in the classroom. "I'm sorry, Mother, but the Holy Ghost has nothing to do with either the swan or Leda" was one comment that aroused their suspicion early on.

Our rebellion took other forms not so lofty, like a raid on the locker room where the palm fronds were stored for High Mass on Palm Sunday. We hid them—and only an eleventh-hour stool pigeon (not one of my band) gave us away—enabling the mass to proceed as scheduled. Then there was the Toilet Paper Caper, where we gathered all the rolls in the dormitory and in the still of the night tiptoed down to the main staircase overlooking the great reception hall, where an intimidating statue of the Blessed Virgin watched over the scene. We wrapped this austere plaster icon in a swath of Scott's best—white, of course. These actions didn't have the dash or political force of burning draft cards or "taking a year off" to join the McCarthy campaign, but for those days it was the closest we could come to defiance.

Although demanding, the academic requirements at CNR were stifling (our favorite word), and one goal emerged: a Catholic marriage and more children for Mother Church. It seemed a terrible waste of time, putting in four years of brainwork and then holding out for the bridal registry at Tiffany's. Where were we going? Why, with few exceptions, were the young women winning the Dante Prize and the Latin Prize and membership in Phi Beta Kappa suddenly setting their graduation caps for a husband? It was a giant failure of the imagination, a buying-in to a system and an attitude that held up as models women like Jean Kerr and Clare Boothe Luce: very talented, but more important, Catholic, married, and rich. Safe. For most of my classmates, the brass ring was the wedding ring, and years later how could they not blow up with rage and despair, wondering where it all went? They could have been contenders.

What sealed my fate, however, as a wild Italian intent on living a blasphemous life, was the picture I hung on my dormitory room door: a six-foot color photo of Elvis—shirt unbuttoned, hair greased, lips pouting, legs parted in a sinful pose of lust. The floor monitor—an elderly Victorian named Mother Cordelia (nicknamed Fang) pounded on the door, demanding to know the identity of this pornographic representation. I told her it was my fiancé. From then on, it was downhill. After two years of friction, I was asked to leave, albeit with an A average. And yet, one image did last from that cheerless place: the sight of Mother Madeleine, a diminutive dynamo who, in a whoosh of black crepe, directed our attention to the writings and broadcasts of Eric Sevareid. Not a day went by when this tiny scholastic didn't begin class with an analysis of "what Mr. Sevareid said last night."

Rebellion still festered as I entered Boston University in my junior year and immediately set about finding a companion in discontent. Not an easy task when most of America's students, reflecting the postwar prosperity of the Eisenhower era, sleepwalked through college. But there was a way: *The Razor's Edge*, an unauthorized newspaper, made its appearance. My partner and coeditor, Rick Gelinas, wore the only beard on campus and had a single-minded devotion to shaking up the administration. We managed to wangle secret funding from the Newman Club, thanks to the shrewd patience of Father Norman J. O'Connor, a progressive priest always on the lookout for something to challenge Catholic dogma and complacent students. We printed the paper photo-offset and handed it out on street corners. The *Edge* was a mixture of trendy philosophical thought, Beat Generation essays, satires of university officials—especially the philosophy professors—the rah-rah student leaders, and very earnest fiction. I even contributed an unsigned short story about a lost love, certain it would find shelf space among the likes of Edith Wharton. The newspaper, alas, was short-lived, as the university threatened to throw all of us out—including the Newman Club—if one more issue hit the campus. We ceased publication and desisted from public comment. It was a bitter lesson in censorship, but my crusader blood was throbbing with satisfaction.

The force of O'Connor's personality attracted all sorts of characters to the small Newman Club office, which functioned as a kind of unofficial resistance to the 1950s sweetheart of Sigma Chi campus ethic. Joan Baez, then an awkward and bashful girl studying at the School of Fine Arts, visited regularly with her chum, the very Bronx-like daughter of a New York cabdriver. Even then, her long and gleaming black hair turned heads, the dark Indian looks and soulful eyes singling her out as someone different. On odd evenings she sang in the local coffeehouses, very bohemian in those days. We thrilled to the pure, clean sound of this remarkable voice, and when she sang, even in those noisy student hangouts, no one spoke. How could we have known that the yearnings she stirred—of innocence and longing, of righteous certainty—would one day urge a generation of middle-class kids to dress up in silly clothes and make love instead of war, to challenge the highest authorities in the land. Some of them were right here on the McCarthy campaign plane, and I was among them, an observer, keeping my opinions to myself but remembering the many battles I had fought in my own college days.

"I can't believe it," said Cogley, when I reminded him of our past association and my subsequent misdeeds. "But then I should have known you'd become a reporter." And he winked. There it was, I told myself, a campaign propelled by Irish whimsy and academic martyrs. The Golgotha Express.

McCarthy wore his mantle of intellectual angst very heavily. As "the U.S. Senate's only published poet" (I never heard the poetry community claim him as its only senator), he seemed dedicated to his remoteness, his appearance of being in touch with Someone way beyond the campaign. He spurned the usual candidate walks down the aisle of the plane that politicos used to ensure that at least one reporter would write about how they were just plain folks in their "off-guard" moments. Not for Clean Gene. Most of the time he sat in his front compartment staring into the eternal blue or hunched over a book which always looked leather-bound, like a missal. The first time I saw him in this mode, I noticed he was wearing a wool shawl draped in the manner of a stole over his shoulders, just like the ecclesiastical stoles worn by priests hearing confessions!

As for his "kids," many of whom had taken leave from college to be part of this crusade, they were suitably enigmatic. Many were getting their on-the-job training, poised to resurface in later campaigns as experienced apostles of the Left. Meantime, scheduling the candidate, staff coordination, advance work, and the like were hit-and-miss processes. Oddly enough, there was virtually no byplay between them and the candidate they held in humorless reverence. Perhaps the seriousness of their goal—changing the world—required more solemnity than I could appreciate.

Watching McCarthy in those weeks, I began to see a man who while vainly confident in his worth appeared to have a low opinion of the world, a man whose outlook seemed shaped by his distrust of those around him, who felt a chill at the heart of things. He was to prove this later conclusively, when he turned his back on the young crusaders who had followed him from New Hampshire out across the country to crown him king of a new age. As the police raised their clubs in Chicago in the summer of 1968 to do battle with antiwar forces in the streets, the political poet did a vanishing act. It was an abandonment—McCarthy watching from the safety of his hotel window—that the sixties generation would never forget, a sad end to their dream of a man who understood and carried their message.

Someone familiar with the classics might have been reminded of Scipio, the great Roman general, looking down from the heights of the citadel walls upon the fleeing citizens of Carthage as their city burned. "A glorious moment," he said, "but I have dread foreboding that some day the same doom will be pronounced upon my own country." It was as if McCarthy knew from the beginning that the crusade would never work, that, like the world, it would break in his hand.

Even as early as the spring of 1968, McCarthy was losing the thrill of the chase. The war's prosecutor was now a lame duck, peace talks were just getting under way, and a determined and combative Bobby Kennedy, seeing his opportunity, had jumped in to spoil McCarthy's party and set the stage for an inter-Irish class war. McCarthy could scarcely conceal his contempt for the middle Kennedy, a rich upstart siphoning off young votes from his dream.

It is perhaps too easy now, from this distance, to castigate that sad campaign. For me at the time, it was an exhilarating leap into national affairs, a side of the business I had only dreamed about. The reality was sometimes uncomfortable, but as my confidence increased, and local press coverage of the NBC "girl reporter" became a theme in the primary states, more of my stories made air and I began to hit my stride. The very fact that there was any fanfare at all about my presence on the campaign was puzzling. It took me a while to realize a basic axiom of television reporting: the index of your importance is the frequency with which you appear. I was hardly a household word, an unknown really, but the fact that I was different attracted the curious, and that meant press coverage.

With the sanction of the NBC press department, which beat the bushes to publicize its on-camera reporters, I submitted to interviews, chatting about how I cut my hair so it would be easier to take care of on the road and rattling on about decorating my new apartment in New York. I was ill at ease in my new role of being on the receiving end of questions and cynically aware of capitalizing on my persona as a "girl reporter" when I wanted to bury it forever. It was pure Hollywood starlet stuff; although reluctantly, I went with the flow.

Even more disconcerting was the amount of attention given to the entire road show of journalists on the campaign trail. Crowds formed to gawk at all the press and TV people, who, even as they landed in the Podunks of this country in 1968, were carving themselves a niche in the celebrity hall of fame. We were becoming the excitement and often the story. Talking to a farmer leaning on his hoe was the appropriate cliché (even if he was talking nonsense) to certify that you were getting the story when that image appeared on the evening news.

Those print reporters who were quietly writing in their notebooks for the next edition, alone, unsung, unseen, were merely carrying on a tradition. We, the television newspeople, were marching toward glory. In years to come, the process would become more important than the event, and political campaigns and conventions grabbed center stage as supernovas of the televised news follies. For the moment, however, both the writing press and the TV news reporters still acted in their usual role of spear carriers, although it would probably be the last political campaign in which this was possible. McCarthy, for all his aloofness, had succeeded in manipulating the boys on the bus to his advantage. And while the candidate continued to be overestimated by reporters: the issue that very nearly drove him to victory in New Hampshire, the war, seemed to take second place beside the man. In fact, it is amazing to realize now that McCarthy, such a towering figure of the time, was a roman candle with a nine-month life span. In January he was a virtual unknown. In April, post–New Hampshire, he was white-hot. By September, he was fading fast—and for good.

FOR election-night coverage of the important primaries that year, "The Huntley-Brinkley Report" was broadcast from virtual cities created within the capitals of the primary states. Acres and acres of trailers, trucks, sets, studios, storage houses, garages, the works. No expense was spared in those fat days of spend-what-you-need to cover the story. And, too, NBC News had already begun its slide from the number one spot, and there emerged a new urgency to hold off Walter Cronkite, already on his way to becoming the country's most trusted man. But it wasn't the kind of dog-eat-dog competition that would come later in the TV news ratings. Responsibility for the evening news program was still largely in the hands of the executive producer and not a major topic for discussion in the highest levels of the corporation.

Primaries and all big stories were a field day for TV brass, such as existed at that time. More romantic roughnecks in pinstripe suits than boardroom habitués, they proved their old skills when the alarm went off on a major story, such as the AFTRA strike a year earlier; but they also warmed to the perks of the medium. Primary election nights offered rich opportunities to bask in the glitter, get a free trip out of town, and even kick up a heel or two. Expense account food and wine rarely prompted an audit, and office romances denied the oxygen to bloom back at 30 Rock became hothouse orchids out on the road. One vice-president in particular, bald, slight, married, a virtual Mr. Peepers of the newsroom, was known for his amorous adventures in the field. How to explain this remarkable transformation? The answer in the news business, I was soon to learn, is that married guys take it where they can—and usually that is away from home. My defense was the tactful exercise of my dumb brunette act. One simply pretended *not* to get the message, so the dialogue never got around to yes or no. For me it was protective coloration. For the randy executives, it was probably confirmation of what they thought of me in the first place—a no-win situation if I ever saw one.

McCarthy lost in Indiana and Nebraska, but his Oregon victory perked up the campaign. Meanwhile the siren call of Vietnam continued to dominate the front pages and the first four minutes of the evening news programs. Three years had passed since the Ninth U.S. Marine Expeditionary Brigade—3,500 rifles strong—had landed at Da Nang, but the war was still the main event: the relief of Khe Sanh; the siege of Dong Ha; a raid into the A Shau Valley; mines blowing along Route 9; stepped-up infiltration across the DMZ—on and on it went. Primary campaigns, protests, and demonstrations were only a sideshow to the story I really wanted to cover. If peace broke out, I would never get a crack at it.

We were fast approaching June 4, the California primary, when the desk left word that Bill Corrigan wanted me on the line in a hurry. Corrigan, a moon-faced fussbudget who perennially popped pills for a nervous stomach, was the man who rode herd on Vietnam coverage and all the headaches and heartaches it entailed. At least two correspondents had been seriously wounded so far, and one, half out of his head, sent home. The minimum tour for the combat assignment was six months, with every opportunity to re-up if you were still in one piece. But the Tet offensive had scared off a lot of would-be volunteers, and correspondents' wives were not allowed to live in Saigon. It was a bachelor's game. Still, cannon fodder was getting scarce. My chances were improving.

If the newsroom had been a barnyard, Corrigan would be mother hen, clucking and scolding, scurrying from phones to telex to wire room. A product of World War II, he liked to pride himself on his own record in the Orient. In fact, on one of his routine tours of the Far East NBC offices, at least one American based in the Tokyo bureau suggested respectfully that in the presence of Japanese, perhaps references to his time as a B-29 tail gunner might not be in the interests of diplomacy.

When I got through to Corrigan in New York, he said, "Looks like you're going to be a war correspondent—that is if you still want to go to Vietnam."

"Yes, yes—of course, I do. When?"

"You'll be coming off the campaign as soon as Elie Abel gets there within the next few days—and then you'd better start wrapping up your life in New York. You'll get your marching orders when you get back, but think about heading East some time in early August."

It was clear that Ron Steinman, a New York tough guy who didn't want his Vietnam fiefdom infiltrated by a woman, had finally decided to rotate out. In fact, he had been shifted to Hong Kong as director of Far East news, largely because of an incident in the Saigon office. Steinman's Vietnamese secretary, later to become his wife, had been shot. A sound man was cleaning an AK-47, which he had brought in from the field as a souvenir. As he laid it on a table in the equipment room, a round discharged and after ricocheting off a doorjamb smashed through her head. Miraculously, she survived, but the treatment she needed made it imperative for Steinman to take her to Hong Kong.

Frank Donghi was slated to replace him. They were complete opposites. Steinman was a terrier, an intense street-fighter who covered the war like a city editor assigning his police reporters. He was also an adroit manipulator in network intrigue. Donghi was quiet, gentlemanly, a lover of art and music, a man who spoke French elegantly—and a disaster when it came to arming himself for the backbiting jousts. Frank had made it very clear to me, during the months he lobbied for the job, that once he became bureau chief he would clear the way for my assignment to the war. He was keeping his word.

Despite the prize that lay ahead, I felt a sting of disappointment about leaving the campaign. No matter how many times a reporter has to bounce in and out of a story, there is still a feeling of incompleteness when you can't follow one to the end. And in 1968, with sides so clearly drawn on explosive issues, I ached to be around for the conventions and a dramatic national election. And yet, no sooner had I left the flatlands of the Midwest than my thoughts turned to how one goes to war.

Back in New York, I was sleeping off the McCarthy campaign and jet lag from the Los Angeles flight when the telephone rang at about 4 A.M. It was from Jake Burn, an NBC network producer who had Far East credentials stretching from Vietnam back to World War II. He had been given the dubious job of initiating me into the mysteries of being a war correspondent, pointers on everything from what to think about when the flak flies to which Saigon tailor made the best bush jackets. I fell for him during the basic training course, trying not to imagine what the farewell scene would be like as I went off to war. Jake was not, however, calling me to discuss the war.

"Kennedy's been shot," he said brokenly.

I heard it halfway through that tunnel leading from deep sleep to consciousness. "I know—I know. That's happened already. . . . Dallas . . . . What?"

"No, no, it's Bobby. Some Arab shot him right after a speech."

There was no going back to sleep after the call, and I lay there in the early light thinking of another time, a cold, sunny day in Manhattan. It was St. Patrick's Day, and Bobby was marching smartly before cheering crowds up Fifth Avenue, flashing a smile that could melt a Republican. My crew and I were covering the parade, marching along, getting interviews and pictures for our piece. When we had enough and the dignitaries had peeled off, certain of their appearance on the evening news, we repaired to a favorite watering hole near 30 Rock, an Irish landmark called Charley O's.

As we leaned on the bar, watching some college kids order green beer, in walked Bobby—unannounced. He shook a few hands and then headed toward our group of four at the bar, ordered a draft, and joined us laughing and talking about the wildness of the parade. Suddenly, he seemed to lose the room and was staring off into a distant place.

"My brother Jack would have loved it here today," he said, almost as if there were no one around to hear him. He continued a kind of rambling reminiscence about President Kennedy. The mood of his delivery was ghostly and tantalizing. We were eavesdropping on history, mesmerized, but at the same time, there was the impulse to run, to escape the anguish of not knowing what to say, how to react. We stood like sentinels, listening, the memory of Dallas being drawn before our eyes. Eventually, Bobby returned to the warmth of the room and the Irish spirit of the day, making small talk, finishing the beer, wishing us the best. After he left, I looked at my three hard-bitten news colleagues; we were all silent.

And now that scene was played back in my memory in the early hours of a New York morning, while on the other side of the country, the man in that memory was fighting for his life. He would be dead before the next dawn. Another agony, another staggering event to cover, to absorb, to make sense of. Once again the country seemed to be losing its grip. So too did Eugene McCarthy as the life went out of his campaign. The way to Chicago was clear now. While the police and war protesters bashed each other outside the convention hall, Humphrey would win the Democratic nomination. Richard Nixon, hailed as the "new" Nixon, would seize the Republican banner.

It was 1968—the year of change, revolution, and flower power.

It was also the season of death.

4

SOME
ENCHANTED
EVENINGS

August 10, 1968

Dear Mom,

First of all—stop worrying. I'm here in Saigon and everything is going along fine. I'm living at the Continental Palace Hotel, which is right across the street from the office. I have a very large room with a terrace overlooking a park. Everyone here has been very nice to me, especially the bureau chief, Frank Donghi. The American soldiers are, of course, all over the place. They're terrific guys and very eager to protect me.

By the way, don't be alarmed about anything you hear about attacks on the city. It's well known here that no matter what the Communists try at this point, they'll never get into the city as they did in the early part of this year.

Besides, the American troops fire heavy artillery every night. You lie in bed trying to sleep and you can hear the pounding from far away. It's very strange.

Thinking of you.
Love,
Betty

"I don't think she's going to make it out there. The story's too big and too tough." Such was the opinion of Les Crystal, second in command on "The Huntley-Brinkley Report," who had dropped by Bill Corrigan's office to pass on the good news.

Bill, fidgeting more than usual, listened to these encouraging words from the seat of power and, months later, passed them on to me in his gossipy *entre nous* stage whisper, the kind of elbow-in-the-ribs stuff executives are so good at when they've been proven right about something. By then, of course, Crystal had become one of my biggest supporters. There was really no risk—to NBC News, at least. Indeed, it was the thing to do.

Sending me to war at all was a roll of the dice in that man's world, so there was no fanfare. But there scarcely ever was in the days when reporters left for assignments unburdened by the imperatives of show business. The "Dan Rather in Afghanistan" school of journalism had yet to be founded. It was still the predawn of an era in which the person covering is more famous than the story covered. In any case, there I was, the first lady-type TV reporter to take on a full-time tour in a war, about to fly silently into the Asian night.

My last day in the office, a flurry of one-liners rose from the male chorus. Most of them were good-natured. Some were not. "Well, Liz, let me put it this way," confided one well-meaning colleague. "If you give it all you've got, you may do as well as the worst guy we have out there."

On August 4, with the hot tarmac at JFK hinting at what waited at the other end, I prepared to board a Japan Airlines flight for Tokyo. An overnight there would set me up for a couple of days in Hong Kong and then on to Saigon by Air Vietnam. There to see me off was my mentor, the man who thought reporting the most honorable work one could do, George Barrett of *The New York Times*. He was so thoroughly a pure reporter that when his old friend A. M. Rosenthal became the major power at the *Times* and wanted George as part of his inner circle, George demurred. "I don't want to manage people," he would say. "I just want to be a newspaperman." His resistance eventually boxed him in, and after 40 years with the paper he ended his career, exhausted, as an assistant city editor on the night desk.

Part professor, part friend, wholly loyal and protecting, he was proud of me and my new assignment. I was still mindful of George's poignant warning about what it meant to be a reporter: to leave airports with no one to say good-bye and to arrive with no one to say hello. Neither had George forgotten. "This is an exception," he said. "We've got to get you launched as a foreign correspondent, so just this one time you'll get a guaranteed send-off."

This was followed by lots of good-natured kidding, how lucky it was for me that this wasn't a dangerous assignment, like covering a real war, World War II for example. George was downplaying it all and at the same time making a valiant effort to minimize how "this pipsqueak war" had affected his own life. His son, David, had already left for Vietnam, a medic with the Fourth Infantry Division in the Central Highlands.

As we headed for the gate, I noticed George seemed to avoid looking at me; and when he did, all the city room sophistication couldn't hide the softness of his gaze, the look you see in the eyes of those who have spent their lives reporting other people's stories, not elaborating their own, the look you get after years of working to do it right, not just the words but the tone and insight. His last words to me were, "Keep your head down."

As I boarded the plane, there came a sharp pain of loss, and even fear. The first of many.

The powerful jolt of the retracting wheels broke the last connection to a normal life. The aircraft's thrust against gravity, the upward surge through invisible resistance only heightened and embodied what I was setting out to do. There were no clear thoughts telling me this, no heroic paths to take on the world, only a knot of nerves and a rush of blood.

I looked forward to the flight and the lack of anything to do except eat and read. Now there was time to sit back after weeks of running around getting shots, picking the brains of those who had been to Vietnam, saying good-byes, buying cotton underwear, keeping appointments with the dentist and doctor, and even checking in with a psychiatrist. When Corrigan ordered me to see a shrink, I hit the ceiling. When I cooled down, he patiently explained that all correspondents bound for the war were now routinely sent to shrinks for a general consultation, lest instability manifest itself in less favorable circumstances. What had triggered the new rule was already the stuff of NBC legend. One of the reporting staff in Saigon had been jilted by his girlfriend, had beaten her up, tried to burn down the hotel, generally flipped out, and been taken back to the States in a straitjacket by military aircraft. Just another flame-out in the bureau. The policy of recruiting bachelors, so that anxious wives would not be roaming around a war area, clearly had its own drawbacks. Still, girlfriends took care of the morale, or sex, problem (they were usually one and the same), and it was safer than leaving all the sad young men to bar girls.

The psychiatrist evinced extreme suspicion of my desire to cover a war, concluding that it was nothing more than the naked expression of a frustrated libido. Funny how sex seemed to be on everybody's mind. Even Corrigan slipped it into his farewell address the day before I left. After the usual admonitions of "never let the risk outweigh the story" (a line that haunts all war correspondents, as it is meant to), and tips about keeping my powder dry, he looked at me pleadingly and said, "And whatever you do—please, please—don't get knocked up." For a nice Catholic girl from New Haven with the sexual IQ of Mary Poppins, his advice seemed less than romantic.

Gazing out the 707's window, I tried to focus on what I actually knew about Asia, apart from the briefings and a dozen or so books read in the last few months. The Japanese stewardesses mincing up and down the aisle in their kimonos aroused memories of World War II. Two uncles had served in the war, one in the Pacific, where a tree sniper got him on Okinawa, winning him a Purple Heart and a ticket home, but not before he had made the whole Mariana Islands run, sending grass skirts to me and my sister, and letters that looked like confetti because watchful censors had snipped away any reference even remotely suggesting his location or future movements. While Uncle Ray took on Hirohito's hordes, his brother, my Uncle Lalo, marched with the famous First Division under Bradley, hitting Omaha Beach on D day. He spent the last years of his life staring at some infinity beyond the walls of a nursing home, and answering questions by reciting the numbers on his old army dog tag. But my mind's eye still replayed a slow-motion memory of that day in 1945 when, after three years of fighting in most of the major campaigns in Europe, he was coming home.

Amid a crowd of relatives a little girl cannot shift her gaze from the heavy combat boots coming straight for her as the smiling man with the cloth sack over his back walks down the stairs of New Haven's railroad station and scoops her up in his brawny arms. She, of course, falls in love with her hero. Perhaps planted there was a psychic seed, a romantic notion about war, steering me all the time to still another place where the most ancient and deadly ritual of mankind was being reenacted.

Crossing the Pacific, chasing horizons farther away than the end of the world, I conjured up every possible Occidental cliché about the Orient and its ways—everything from the sayings of Confucius to songs from *South Pacific*, which I had first heard in the old Schubert Theater in New Haven. Clutching a small yellow press card from *The Troup Trumpet*, my junior high school newspaper, I turned up regularly at the Schubert on rehearsal days, requesting—and usually obtaining—interviews with show business greats. It was an early lesson in the power of the press card, the doors it unlocks, the prestige it confers.

I struck on Saturday afternoons, confidently walking through the theater's open front door, to the right of the marquee, or flashing my press pass to the old man who guarded the stage door, announcing that I had an appointment with one of the stars. He took pity on me, while I silently imagined that I had performed the magical feat of gaining entry. I was working press.

Making my way to the back row of the darkened theater, I would sink into the maroon velvet seat and enter the world of the rehearsal. Whenever someone declared a break, that meant time to nail the stars and line up the interviews. Nine out of ten times I scored, mainly because the brazenly appealing spectacle of a thirteen-year-old girl who called herself a reporter, with a straight face, was hard to resist.

When *South Pacific* came to New Haven in 1949, I sat through a Saturday afternoon rehearsal, watching Ezio Pinza create the elegant magic of "Some Enchanted Evening" before my eyes. Is that what I imagined Vietnam would be like: handsome French planters, perky nurses, lovesick GIs, beautiful native girls? There it was again: the romance of war.

My reverie continued on the flight from Hong Kong three days later, except, of course, for the anxiety of knowing that the hour had come. By the time we broke through a cocoon of clouds over the South China Sea and began to descend over the hard green line of the Vietnam coast, my eyes closed, entertaining more realistic visions of missiles, bullets—whatever projectiles the enemy had— cutting upward to our destruction. I would learn soon enough that commercial airliners did get shot at, and usually on takeoff or landing.

As we angled in over Tan Son Nhut Airport, cutting lower, I could see white dots, no, more like smudges, all over the place. Lower and closer, and then the definite shape of the white specks emerged— stars, hundreds of them, white stars plastered on everything. This was U.S. territory, all right—stars on jeeps, trucks, planes, helicopters, hangars, helipads, rooftops, you name it. The familiar signature of power was everywhere to be seen. By God, I thought, we really *are* in Vietnam. And what is all the delay about? There were winners down there, Americans with white stars on their jerseys. How could we not be winning?

Frank Donghi, laconic and smiling, emerged from the rush of Vietnamese faces at the air terminal, offering a pale cheek as he leaned his lanky, six-foot frame toward me for a hello peck. He wore the civilian uniform of Asia, a short-sleeved white shirt and khaki trousers. He looked a bit haggard, I thought, his mid-fiftyish face beginning to show the strain of working all day and most of the night. The thirteen-hour time difference was a killer for all bureau chiefs, requiring their supervision for the day's coverage and all it entailed, and demanding their availability to the New York office at night. Stateside deskmen have very little regard for what time it is on the other side of the world, and the same holds true for vice-presidents. No question is so small that the guy in charge can't be awakened. Besides, that's his job. Still, behind Frank's good manners, something was wrong.

"So you made it, finally?" he said amidst the clatter of duck sounds which I would soon take for granted as Vietnamese conversation.

"Thanks to you, chief."

"Welcome to Vietnam. It's a great story." With that, he began to clear a way through the bureaucratic maze, introduced me to the gold-toothed Mr. Long, one of the two NBC office drivers, and for the next few days generally began initiating me into this place everyone seemed willing to kill for. Meanwhile, from Hong Kong, the eyes of

Ron Steinman homed in on his old bureau, watching Donghi's every move. Within days of my arrival, he sent a note to Corrigan in New York.

August 11, 1968
Liz Trotta has arrived and Donghi is spending too much time wet nursing her. I've told Frank that he must treat her like a correspondent, not like a woman. I don't think he understood me.

The rites of passage would not be long in coming. They began not on night patrol in a maze of jungle, not in the bowels of a tank plowing through the red mud of the Mekong Delta, not in a helicopter twisting to get out of enemy range. They began unexpectedly in Room 64 of the Continental Palace Hotel on Lam Son Square in Saigon, my new home. The top floor was laughingly termed the "rocket belt," a macabre comment on the flimsy sheets of tin and plaster beneath the slate roof that "reinforced" it against a hit from the Vietcong. The city had been rocketed routinely earlier, but now with peace talks in the wind attacks had abated. Besides, only philistines would assault this lovely old relic of French colonial grandeur, this storied palace of swashbucklers—journalists, spies, adventurers, war profiteers, and ne'er-do-wells—who by some slant of the stars found themselves in Southeast Asia. Even the venerable Graham Greene had stayed here for a year to write *The Quiet American*. More than any other book, this evocative tale of a disillusioned British newspaperman and a criminally naive CIA agent in the final days of the French Empire had become the magic mirror for correspondents in Indochina.

My room, with its fifteen-foot ceiling and marble floor, opened out onto a balcony framed by a graceful spread of tamarind trees, and beyond them, just below the panes of the French doors, stood the white stucco opera house now housing the South Vietnamese National Assembly. Its orange tile roof seemed within reaching distance, completing this graceful tableau of the days when Saigon was indeed the "pearl of the Orient"—another time when East and West had tried to live side by side at this ancient crossroads.

After a few nights of tossing in the trampoline-size bed, I realized it was infested. Under Donghi's watchful eye, the management owned up to the presence of bedbugs and changed the mattress. By the second week, I could actually fall asleep amid the rumble of distant B-52 strikes and the nocturnal lullaby of outgoing artillery fire. The VC were probing the city's perimeter after a two-month lull.

Wars have sounds that never leave you, and recognizing those sounds can save your life—whether it is a company commander listening for the direction and range of the enemy's fire, or just knowing the difference between "incoming" and "outgoing." Making the distinction is crucial and not as easy as it may seem. "Incoming"—an exclamation of terror meaning "hit the deck fast"—was a rallying cry. I heard it first in the corridors of the old Continental.

On the night of August 22, I was awakened by a sound I had never heard before, a sickening thud from somewhere in the night. Then silence. It was shortly after 4 A.M., so I rolled over and went back to sleep. Perhaps a half hour passed, then a second thud, louder and closer. What happened next replays in great detail. I got out of bed, went to the glass balcony doors and searched the flare-lit sky and the empty square below for an answer. It came. A fiery curtain of red, a blast of blinding white light and an eardrum-splitting crash. I heard the shattering of glass and the shuddering of the earth. Slowly, I backed away through the shards blown out of the doors, dimly registering that the roof of the old opera house below my broken window was ablaze. Pandemonium broke out in the corridors. As though in a trance, I opened the old armoire by the bed, took out a bathrobe, put it on, and walked without haste to the door. Two thoughts ran through my mind: I was still asleep, and "What the hell are they shooting at me for? Don't they know I'm 'press'?"

In the corridor, a German correspondent who lived next door was heading for the staircase. In midflight he halted, cocking his head like a resistance fighter to the distinct sound of airplane engines. "Listen," he said in a stage whisper, his hand cupped to his ear. "Zee Americans are in za air. Efferyting will be alles right."

He darted down, leaving me to remember that Germans didn't say that in World War II movies. The floor boys were huddling in corners, wedging themselves in where the walls met on the landing, supposedly the safest shelter from a direct hit. Everyone was waiting for the next round of Russian-made 122-mm rockets. These self-propelled rockets packed a forty-two-pound warhead and with a range of up to seven miles could be fired from just a bamboo tripod on the outskirts of the city. I hurried to the ground floor in search of my fellow NBC correspondent, Ken Bernstein, banged on his door, and waited tensely for an answer. Nothing. To this day, he swears he slept through the whole attack, and I still laugh and tell him he picked a fine night to lose himself in the charms of some local lovely, with me and the rest of the free world in peril.

"Where's Treaster?" I heard a loud Brooklyn accent, turned and saw a short blonde in a diaphanous baby-doll nightgown. Barbara Gluck, the American matriarch-cum-social-arbiter of the Saigon press corps, was looking for her sweetheart and husband-to-be, Joe Treaster of *The New York Times*. I was now crouching on the landing, as more crashes echoed through the streets. In one of the great incongruous moments even of this mad place and time Barbara looked down at me and said, "Hey, aren't you Liz Trotta from the 8:25 news on NBC?"

Grotesque, funny, terrifying, just one night in a war zone. When the incoming stopped, a sense of giddiness set in, all of us silently congratulating ourselves on staying alive. We hadn't yet heard the news. A young Japanese correspondent asleep in a nearby building was killed—by the rocket that struck the opera house as I stood watching at my window.

The war had come to me—even before I went looking for it.

THE business of getting outfitted for the field and accredited by HQ MACV (Headquarters, Military Assistance Command Vietnam) took some days. Finally, I owned a green poncho, a set of USMC fatigues and another from the South Vietnamese airborne, the latter a more realistic fit. Jungle boots, malaria pills, knapsacks, web belt, insect repellent, water canteen, salt pills, the works. And last but most important, my DOD (Department of Defense) ID card, No. 099135, which conferred on me the assimilated rank of major and even included a note to the enemy.

NOTICE: THE BEARER OF THIS CARD IS A CIVILIAN NONCOMBATANT SERVING WITH THE ARMED FORCES OF THE UNITED STATES, WHOSE SIGNATURE, PHOTOGRAPH AND FINGERPRINTS APPEAR HEREON. IF THE BEARER OF THIS CARD SHALL FALL INTO THE HANDS OF THE ENEMIES OF THE UNITED STATES HE SHALL AT ONCE SHOW THIS CARD TO THE DE-TAINING AUTHORITIES TO ASSIST IN HIS IDENTIFICATION. IF THE BEARER IS DETAINED HE IS ENTITLED TO BE GIVEN THE SAME TREATMENT AND ACCORDED THE SAME PRIVILEGES AS AN INDIVIDUAL IN THE GRADE, RATE OR RANK OF THE MILITARY SERVICE OF THE UNITED STATES INDI-CATED BELOW, WITH ANY AND ALL RIGHTS TO WHICH SUCH PERSONNEL

ARE ENTITLED UNDER ALL APPLICABLE TREATIES, AGREEMENTS AND THE ESTABLISHED PRACTICE OF NATIONS.

Somehow the civility of the message didn't jibe with what one knew of the guys in black pajamas and the horror stories that came out of the prison camps. Still it provided great material for sarcastic banter on the Continental veranda, where the war's expatriate colony gathered every evening to trade stories, line up a whore for the night, or peer at the latest pornographic postcards sold out of a big valise by one of the dozens of street peddlers. Sitting on the "Continental Shelf" over a *citron pressé* seemed a relatively civilized ritual in this never-never land that at times seemed to exist for only the most basic human urges—greed, sleazy sex, and the art of killing. After a neat gin or two, one could pretend to see romance in the raw beauty of it all, the sheer exoticism. One could even rationalize the loneliness with a fragile hope that you had been drawn into the brave march of great events.

It was one of these evenings on the Shelf, not long after my arrival, that I was introduced to still another rite of orientation. He was Major George "Speedy" Gaspard and he could have been a double for Steve Canyon of comic strip fame. It was generally believed he was the model for the hero of Robin Moore's *The Green Berets*, a best-selling novel and even more popular movie starring no less than John Wayne. Speedy was a dashing mercenary, big, blond, and broad, with the neck and shoulders of a stevedore, the manners of a prince, and the body of a stud. His chest accommodated an array of medals that bordered on parody. Under his tilted green beret blinked a pair of innocent gray eyes said to have melted the hearts of ladies from Fort Bragg to Phou Bai.

Speedy had greatly distinguished himself in the Korean War and went to Vietnam in 1962, when as the Special Forces used to say, "It was a nice quiet little war." He had built a Special Forces camp at Dak Pek in the mountains of the Central Highlands near the Laotian border, smack in the middle of the Ho Chi Minh Trail, by which the enemy moved its supplies into the south. For a while he functioned as a civilian in the USAID program (U.S. Agency for International Development), but by 1968 he was back in his SF uniform working as a member of the highly clandestine SOG (Studies and Observation Group), which among its other activities ran secret patrols into North Vietnam.

He seemed the boy next door, except when you caught him at the right time—glancing sideways at the screech of car brakes, alert to the report of a motorcycle—and realized Major Gaspard had spent much of his life ready for action. The coiled spring was buried deep. As a "beret," he was of course regarded by the press as CIA, and so his unofficial job seemed to be befriending them. It was a game where everyone knew what parts were being played and by whom. A good spook knows how to listen and maybe even plant a story or two. So, on any given night Speedy would work the Shelf, especially when there were newcomers.

We were introduced, and within minutes it was apparent Speedy had rightfully earned his name. He invited me to dinner at the Hotel Caravelle's rooftop restaurant, a favorite perch from which one could watch the war's fireworks at night, streaks of incoming and outgoing, even the light of B-52 strikes, piercing the darkness beyond the edge of the city. Under a flare-lit, brooding tropical sky, he plied me with champagne and crayfish. A torrential rainstorm and crashing thunder provided a dramatic backdrop for the sensuous turn of his monologue, which soon became an all-American pitch for spending an amorous night together. The downpour boiled in steam off the pavement below, aptly matching his mood. Lightning lit up the driving rain as it flooded the square. We ran for my hotel, our clothes drenched and clinging. He was hot on my heels to the elevator, pulling me into an embrace as the storm increased its fury. A soldier, a girl, a rainstorm . . .

And a very angry Vietnamese night watchman.

"No—no—she is good girl," shrieked the scrawny figure at this trained killer of the secret war. He was shaking his finger under Speedy's nose and directing me into the elevator at the same time. Speedy stood there, for once helpless. The cage closed. Reaching the top floor, I rushed to the open veranda and looked below. A romantic figure from out of a storybook squared his shoulders, adjusted his green beret, and bent his head against the storm. He disappeared beyond the glistening trees—my defeated soldier in the rain.

THE city itself had been transformed since the Tet offensive. The rakish air of adventure among foreigners had given way to bald fear, and the protective glamour of the GI uniform seemed to fade into the dusty depression of a people who knew it was all just a matter of time. No more did European tourists come to board "La Semaine à Saigon" bus tour, which wound through the avenues under arches of shade trees. The grand ochre-colored public buildings and fine villas covered with orchids were a pale backdrop to the ever-present military hardware, and even the Romanesque Catholic cathedral was attracting fewer worshippers to High Mass on Sunday. Membership at the Cercle Sportif had thinned considerably as the French drifted home. In the nightclubs, slinky Korean and Filipino singers had a harder edge of desperation in their songs as they played to a shrunken audience. In the street stalls, cheesy velour panels of stalking tigers were outselling the watercolor portraits. Military souvenirs were set out for sale alongside the trident-shaped peace pendants— the very same ones worn by the antiwar crowd at home. Perhaps the happiest people in town were the owners of the massage parlors, where business mounted with the tension. Five dollars for an efficient and mechanical moment of "love."

Contrasts—relief from the grim presence of the war and its toll— were getting hard to find as the fascination of the old East seemed to recede into the ugliness of despair. There was a sense of things coming to an end, with no thought to what consequences the future would bring. Thousands of refugees swelled the city. Traffic jams of Hondas, trucks, pedicabs, jeeps, and Renault taxicabs on their last cylinder filled the air with fumes of gas and sounds of havoc. Roadblocks and car checks slowed the city's pace to a crawl. Piles of garbage and human waste merged with the putrid smells of durian, a local melon, and nuoc mam, a fermented fish sauce, to win out over the fragrance of jasmine and bougainvillea. Vietnamese girls in miniskirts outnumbered those in the graceful au dais. Beggars and lepers obscured the sight of schoolchildren holding hands. Sandbags and barbed wire formed silhouettes of warning against every golden sunset. And holding it all in its sticky grip, a relentless and stupefying humidity, an exhausted companion that never left your side. This was no Bali H'ai.

"Is that Liz—hey, Liz Trotta, what are you doing here?"

I turned around and looked down the path to the old stucco villa I had just left. The daily South Vietnamese military briefing was letting out and the man calling my name seemed a creature from another world. Craig J. Spence of ABC News, a great character of the Manhattan scene, headed toward me resplendent in a perfectly tailored bush jacket and matching khaki trousers. He was the only man I ever knew who wore a Cartier dress watch in combat. As he gestured me to a halt, he lit his corncob pipe—an accessory he had borrowed from his hero, General Douglas MacArthur.

Spence was the dandy at war, a reincarnation of the "traveling gentlemen"—adventurers of wealth and family—who visited battle-fields for a thrill during the nineteenth century. He was at the same time winning and despicable, a concentrator of emotions who drove people either to loving or hating him. Although he had no journalistic credentials to speak of, with his talent for promotion, for boring from within, he had gone far on naked nerve. He could get you to do things you would do for no other person, make you bend your imagination to his own, usually for his own advancement. He was the Great Persuader.

We had met months before at a press conference in Leonard Bernstein's apartment, the very same digs where earlier the Black Panthers had attended a party in their honor and unwittingly occasioned the term radical chic. Our reason for being there had a Vietnam angle, if only a rarefied one. The conductor's wife, Felicia Montealegre, was unveiling her latest contribution to social justice, "antiwar Christmas cards".

Spence was very much a member of the colorful and closely knit Saigon press corps. It was heartening to see a familiar face in this scary place. Besides, his natural elegance and flair for displaying imperialist authority's hauteur lent ease and refinement to the whole crazy scene: from his appearances at Cercle Sportif, where the Saigon elite (including General Westmoreland) played tennis and sipped cassis, to taking his risks with the troops. Like everyone else, he slugged it out in the mud with the grunts, although never losing his flair. He began one piece about how the VC eluded American patrols by submerging himself in swamp water and breathing through a tube. Rising from the depths on a closeup, he began by saying: "This is how the VC hide. And this is the kind of war it is—you can't see the enemy."

Spence and I renewed our acquaintance, in the field and on the limited Saigon social circuit. One night we were sitting in his room at the Caravelle just across the square from the Continental, listening to Mozart and watching fist-size cockroaches scale the shower curtain. Suddenly, gunfire. At first it seemed like just another round of shots in the air from the jittery "white mice," the white-shirted South Vietnamese national police who enforced the 10 P.M. curfew. After the second burst, Spence grabbed his tape recorder, bolted for the door, and began running wildly through the streets toward the racket.

I was right behind him. "Don't be crazy," I yelled as he pulled ahead. "You don't know where it's coming from—don't run into the line of fire."

He ignored me. Finally, I screamed, "For Chrissake, remember Ted Yates, you idiot!" Yates, an NBC producer, had been killed in Jerusalem during the 1967 Six-Day War when machine-gun fire raked the lobby of the Intercontinental Hotel and instead of diving for cover he tried to identify the source. Apparently, someone mistook the NBC camera for a weapon; it was not the first or last time a TV camera would attract fire in combat. But this evening's shoot-out in the streets of Saigon amounted to one drunken GI letting off steam and two MPs firing into the air: a drunk and disorderly arrest, a night in the brig. For years after, whenever I saw Spence, his fond greeting would be, "Remember Ted Yates."

Although he was unalterably prowar, Spence was eventually forced to leave Vietnam when the U.S. command pulled his accreditation. Some said it was for his constant harassment of the U.S. military spokesmen, the "boy majors" at the Five O'clock Follies, the daily briefing that was so named in tribute to its veracity. Others said for gold smuggling, a rumor Spence relished and only slightly discouraged. The consensus held he had been caught trading on the black market; everyone did, of course, except that in Spence's case the U.S. command may have seen it as an opportunity. He went on to Cambodia and then wound up in Tokyo where he lived for about a dozen years, returning stateside a wealthy man with important Japanese connections. We would meet again in Washington, D.C., years later, where Spence operated as a shadowy figure, both Scarlet Pimpernel and Dorian Gray. It was the romantic exploits of "our war" as he liked to call it—our youth's adventures—that bound us. Like so many Vietnam correspondents, he had been drawn naturally to the circle of fire and relived it long after the ashes had been scattered.

THE press corps itself was the stuff of legends, many manufactured by its own members, who created tales of derring-do and the devil-may-care stories all too often related as "how I escaped my last close call while laughing all the way." Personal mythmaking required the storytellers to live off the politicians, diplomats, soldiers—and one another—to cultivate one vast reciprocity, a paramilitary brotherhood of men. In the early days they were selling undoubted physical courage. Later, they were hawking an "immoral war." Above all, aggression in the face of danger, a driving male force, roared out of the locker room into the hallowed halls of media heroism.

Male dominance also figured into their personal arrangements. Not unlike the Saigon-based service officers, civilian construction workers, spies, diplomats, and other symbionts of war, many journalists, married or single, lived in villas with Vietnamese housekeepers tending to their domestic needs and mistresses to their sexual requirements. This arrangement was infinitely preferable to a thirty-dollar romp with one of the Tu Do Street bar girls, or a fifty-dollar drop-in on a local brothel. Indeed, one of the favorite cartoons passed around showed a war-weary newsman in a silk "aloha" shirt at home in his villa. Holding a drink and cigarette in one hand and balancing an Oriental playmate on his knee, he is hammering away at his typewriter: "As I write this, perhaps my last dispatch, the bullets are whizzing 'round my head."

It wasn't a bad deal. For fifty dollars a month, the man of the house got his meals cooked, his laundry washed and ironed, his house cleaned, and sometimes sex at no extra cost other than occasional gifts or trips for a mistress or her family. With rent, food, and utilities thrown in, a man could live like a potentate on somewhere between $700 and $800 a month (network or news chain money exchanged at the black market rate). Maintaining a mistress cost even less. And Sherman said war is hell.

Women were the surplus product of the Orient. Paradise for Western men, Captain's Paradise in some cases, as they deftly concealed their cozy wartime menage from the Mrs. back in Boise. Even so it sometimes went awry, as when an NBC correspondent completed his tour and his girlfriend's love letters, forwarded to the nation's capital, were read by his wife, no doubt worrying about what her man was going through in the war zone.

Once the newsman was transferred back to the States or Europe, the girl was passed on to a friend or simply dumped amid rash promises to return and reclaim her as a bride. The echoes of Madama Butterfly were heard too often. Some did marry their girlfriends and take them back to the States, more often than not to contribute to the divorce statistics. All in all, the basic lack of sexual sophistication that characterized so many American men new to the Orient drove them to some degree of silliness. For example, all of their contacts with local women—be they the farmer's daughter or a bar girl—were rationalized in the most wholesome all-American terms: murmured asides about how the lady in question was, despite what you may think, a descendant of mandarins. God forbid anyone should think Mr. Clean actually had anything to do with whores! I took great silent amusement in this lack of sangfroid and vowed one day to write a piece about American men and their below-the-belt encounters in the Orient, to be entitled, "But She Comes from a Very Fine Family."

Membership in this exclusive club of veteran correspondents was for life, standing in apposition to the visiting journalists, that horde of stateside reporters and editors who drifted in and out for the usual two-day tour—one "fly-over" of the war, one briefing, one aperitif on the Shelf. It gave small-town editors, local anchormen—and even famous network presences—a chance to tell their children they had "been in Vietnam." The permanent press contingent was of stouter material, 500 to 600 strong who covered this gigantic murder beat day in and day out.

For a time Vietnam television coverage had been secondary to that of print. And while in 1968 there were still those who would debate the relative importance of each, the argument was ultimately dwarfed by the blistering impact of the war's *pictures*. The balance shifted—and with it the expository importance of the print reporter gave way to the vivid impresario-like celebrity of the TV newsman. Why, one could *see* him dodging those bullets. Just look at him! The evening stars of America's living rooms had become the Greek chorus of this faraway drama.

The newspaper, magazine, and wire service men appeared in marked contrast to their TV brethren, who seemed a few shades lighter in weight and color. And the general run of TV type, especially in the war's waning years, paled beside the network correspondents who came from print and therefore had its dash and depth—Dean Brelis and Welles Hangen of NBC, Charles Collingwood of CBS, Peter Kalischer of CBS, for starters: two of them Rhodes scholars. Unlike the new electronic breed, they cared more about the story than their Q-ratings; this older generation of correspondents didn't have to worry about the star system.

NBC forced no one to go to war. You could refuse, and many did. In fact, by August 1968 when I arrived, the news department was out of experienced old-line correspondents who wanted to cover the war. Many of the men simply said no. Some went for "limited" tours—great for me and other Young Turks wanting to show their stuff, but a nagging problem for headquarters. By contrast, CBS, perennial boot camp that it was, made their correspondents offers they couldn't refuse.

In fact, Roger Mudd's refusal to cover the war influenced the network's choice of Rather over Mudd to replace Cronkite years later. Dodging the war haunted a CBS career. Nobody at NBC seemed to hold it against those who refused.

The Associated Press bureau occupied an office twelve feet down from NBC News on the fourth floor of the shabby old Eden Building, Saigon's Rockefeller Center. The elevator, an elderly mahogany French construction, bore the grime of brigades of journalists coming in from the field and soup stains left by children dripping their lunch. As it was often out of order—no doubt from lifting six large Americans instead of the three slight Vietnamese it had been built for—we made good use of the marble stairs from the *rez de chaussée* to the *quatrième étage*, breathing hard under heavy equipment.

This was the hub of Saigon: a sprawling complex of dim offices above cheap jewelry shops and souvenir stores in the lobby and food stalls with hot rice in baskets spread out under the arches outside. On its corner the Eden formed an angle of Lam Son Square, a crucial box for the foreign journalist, completed by the Continental and the Caravelle, which housed much of the press contingent, and the Rex Hotel, a high-class BOQ (bachelor officers' quarters) with nightclub and sun deck. At the center of the square, a grassy patch bore the gigantic black stone figure of a South Vietnamese infantryman with fixed bayonet charging his unseen enemy. The statue loomed, overscale and brutish, against the wide, graceful boulevards, its ferocity of pose made ridiculous by primitive craftsmanship. A metaphor for our allies?

AP was every journalist's backstop, furnishing a hefty file of stories, the backbone of daily war news read by Americans. It was the best news operation in town. As the premier wire service on the world's top story, AP had to get it all and get it right. Living up to the challenge was a roster of reporters and photographers who would have brought an approving tear to the eyes of any grizzled news veteran, a dirty dozen of rogues, roués, and hard-core professionals.

Peter Arnett, who won a Pulitzer prize in 1965 for his powerful coverage of the American entry into the war, was the unelected but undisputed dean of this Grand Guignol of journalism. A born reporter—tough, romantic, innately fair, with a spongelike mind, taking it all in with the laugh of a pirate and the courage of a saint. Short, square, broad-headed, with brown convex eyes, Arnett looked like a bull pawing the ground when he set out on an assignment—or when he saw a pretty girl. He traveled with an amazing AP photographer, Horst Faas, another raging bull, who wound up with two

Pulitzers. What a team: the doughty New Zealander and the indefatigable Hun, covering the war day by terrifying day for nine years, logging more combat hours than any Marine battalion in-country.

Also with AP was George McArthur—hard-drinking, uncontested womanizing champ of the Orient, who claimed to include Imelda Marcos among his conquests: a fading matinee idol who never said hello to me in six months, and I knew why. He simply couldn't handle the thought of a woman taking part in anything that he did out of bed. Why, I wondered, did men so often think that war was their exclusive property, as if that was something to be proud and possessive of?

Another AP photographer, Rick Merron, a driven supermacho bantam rooster, wore a Montagnard bracelet of elephant hair, the mark of those who had gone native. Long after the Americans left, he went back to find his sweetheart, stopping in Singapore on the way to sit staring into the night from my veranda and reminisce about the war. Merron never returned home with his girlfriend. He eventually drifted out of the business and disappeared. But destiny and the ties of Vietnam would intervene. Arnett, by now with AP in New York, had heard of Rick's disappearance and even tried to find him. One day, on a routine story about bodies that surface in New York waterways after the spring thaw, he found his old war brother, perhaps a suicide, on a slab at the Brookyn morgue. The body had been fished out of the Hudson River and lay unclaimed for four months. Arnett identified the nameless corpse from a 101st Airborne insignia tattooed on the left wrist. Perhaps the turbulent waters of Manhattan had finally offered Merron what he couldn't find in the fields of fire. Like so many, he had gone to war "seeking dark brides," driven by the same impulses that eventually led him to the overpowering river.

Henri Huet, still another AP photographer, born in Vietnam to a Vietnamese mother and a French father, served in the French army, and had vivid memories of Dien Bien Phu. Often, on days out of the field, he would bring sandwiches over to my desk for lunch and delight me with tales of his many dangerous exploits. Then, in 1971, Huet and Larry Burrows of *Life* were in a South Vietnamese chopper hit by enemy ground fire over Laos. It crashed into the jungle and their bodies were never found.

Hugh Mulligan was the AP bureau's Falstaff, a leprechaun with the complexion of a blood orange, Bugs Bunny teeth and a mop of gray hair. He had gone to war as a GI in World War II, and although seasoned in wire service, this was his first time out as a war correspondent. His most memorable contribution was coining the term "Bufe," a proper noun he employed in several wire stories to describe the large ceramic elephants made in Vietnam and functioning as coffee tables in living rooms across America. Shipping Bufes home was as much a cliché as sending pink grapefruit from Florida. Little did Hometown, USA, know how the Bufe got its name. Mulligan simply used the acronym for what he thought it was: a "Big, Ugly, Fuckin' Elephant."

Behind the black humor, by 1968 an air of defeatism pervaded the Saigon press corps. Tet seemed to have smashed any hope of winning, especially since the press itself, feeling betrayed by the occasionally sound but wrongly based optimism of the American command, deemed it a stunning setback for the Allies. Evidence to the contrary, such as the shattering of the VC infrastructure in the south, paled next to the riveting pictures of the VC running around the U.S. embassy compound. Even without the popular uprising in the south that Hanoi had counted on, the countrywide attacks by the Communists had fulfilled Clausewitz's goal of war: "to compel our opposition to fulfill our will." The message for America was to get out fast.

"You'll be going with Vo Huynh tomorrow," said Donghi.

It would be my first time out in the field, and the incomparable Buddha standing before me was to be my cameraman. Vo Huynh had been Vietnam lore for years, once described as "the kind of man who rode with Caesar and Alexander," proud, fearless, tiger-smart and loyal. Correspondents schemed and fought to work with him. I knew I was getting the royal treatment this first time out, but it took, and we wound up working together for most of the months I was in-country. We understood and watched out for each other as only those who have shared desperate moments and a tin of C rations can. Not once did he treat me falsely; he was neither condescending nor subservient. It was odd. When I left New York, the conventional wisdom said I would be mistreated by the American military and the Vietnamese because I was a woman. As it turned out, the best treatment came from these two patriarchal groups and the worst from my "liberal" news confreres, who for the most part felt threatened by a woman competing with them.

Huynh was the continuity of NBC News in Vietnam. He had grown up in the north. The Vietminh had killed his grandfather, a landowner, and that single act turned him against the Communists for the rest of his life. The French, who regarded him as a possible Vietminh sympathizer, had arrested and imprisoned him for a month. Like so many Vietnamese, he was caught between colonialism and Ho Chi Minh's new order. In 1955, he went south, picked up a camera, and wound up working for NBC in 1961. He was the brain and guts of the Saigon staff, and every bureau chief throughout the war sought his counsel and his nerve.

Howard Tuckner was one of Huynh's protégés. They were an unlikely and, for Howard, a lucky combination: the hard, quiet courage of a Vietnamese and the self-conscious bravado of a New York sharpie. Huynh saw Howard's gnawing insecurities, but he also recognized his tenacity in pursuit of a story. Howard had become a celebrity among NBC's war reporters. With the eyes of the world on the war, and the eyes of NBC management in New York on the Saigon bureau, working there was life in a fishbowl, but the tragic path Howard was already committed to eluded even the people looking on at the time—all except one. Ron Steinman's memos to New York, routine assessments of his correspondents, were notable in Howard's case for their sense of foreboding. "I will have to wait and see how he turns out," Steinman wrote, "but with each succeeding story of his I become less optimistic for the future."

Howard was a writer for "The Sixth Hour News" when I arrived at WNBC in the spring of 1965. He had made the switch to television early in his career, moving over after nine years with the *Times*, where he covered and wrote sports. Once a week, he went out part-time with a crew to do stories and then appear on the air; every staff writer who did this aimed for a permanent reporting slot, but few made it. Howard was bitten hard by the on-camera virus and determined to break out of the writer's bank. He volunteered to go to the war and left within a few months. How I had envied him.

At thirty-three, he was trim, muscular, just under six feet, with bedroom eyes and a slick head of Rudolph Valentino hair he combed constantly with a little greasy comb that must have been a hangover from high school days in the Bronx. He walked—glided—silently, with his head pitched slightly forward, giving the impression he was sneaking up behind you. With women, his confidence soared; fully aware of his appeal, he instinctively knew how to handle them. Speaking about his track record with the many Vietnamese women he squired, he once told me: "You know, the sad part is you can fuck 'em, but you can't touch 'em"—a pioneering observation of its time.

Howard's ambition was epic, a Sammy Glick who really didn't even try to mask it. Vietnam was his big break. He was in the thick of it, the buildup, the big U.S. operations, the insatiable appetite for combat footage. Hooking up with Huynh, he couldn't miss. Had he been less lucky, his ambition would have put him in a body bag early in his tour. Instead, he was making his name, and when Tet came along he got the biggest break of all: he was wounded. Not fatally, a flesh wound from shrapnel he caught during a firefight in Cholon, but America watched the heroic war correspondent deliver his on-camera closer lying in the street, bleeding, while a medic knelt patching up his injuries. It was dynamite.

The piece should have taken him over the top, except for one detail—Howard had done the on-camera closer in three takes. As Huynh told the story, Howard couldn't decide whether or not to let the first take go since it contained a profane word. He had concluded by saying that anyone who claims he isn't afraid in the war "is a damn liar." Huynh told him to leave it, New York would buy it. Howard insisted on doing it twice more without the "swear word." When all three takes were screened in New York, even the film editors guffawed at what was supposed to be the unrehearsed reporting of a wounded man. Reuven Frank asked to see the outtakes and then, said witnesses, hit the ceiling. What had appeared on the air as spontaneous and courageous reporting was, in fact, a calculated attempt to play to the cheap seats.

Despite his long experience in covering the war, Howard was already in trouble with management even before the Tet attack. Steinman had become even more disenchanted. "He was constantly coming in with stories about Russian MIGs and tanks before they were actually in the country, troop movements in Cambodia," Steinman later told me. "He blew stuff out of proportion, full of hyperbole. He just wasn't reliable. Once we had an argument about a revelation from his latest 'source.' He'd been to an army base in Tay Ninh province and heard that MIG fighters were seen flying overhead. So I asked him, 'Who told you?'

" 'I can't tell you,' he says.

"I said, 'What do you mean you can't tell me? I'm the bureau chief.'

"Then he tells me he heard it from a PFC at the gate. Can you imagine, he wanted to say, on the air, that MIGs were over Tay Ninh because he heard it from some private?

"I told him he couldn't use it. 'You can't verify it, Howard. Have you checked with MACV?'

" 'No, no, of course I haven't,' he says. 'If I do that, then they'll know my story.'

"I gave up. You know, he was one of the first guys to use hair spray in my bureau."

Still wearing his bandages, Howard went back to New York after Tet ("without authorization," said Steinman), hoping to capitalize on his wound. Although Howard's vanity was a given, I noticed something new in his demeanor on his first day back in the newsroom, an awareness that people were looking at him, even when they weren't. He seemed to have incorporated a sense of the camera into the reflexes of his daily life, presenting a profile to the world for its admiration.

He told me Reuven Frank wanted him to go to the Moscow bureau, but he turned it down. What he really wanted was to "anchor," in those days a brash admission. A mortal blow came in the wake of Bobby Kennedy's death. Howard was assigned to cover the funeral train as it wound its way from New York to Washington, D.C., passing through New Jersey, where he was to do his report. In it, he referred to the train bearing the senator's body as "twenty-one cars laden with grief and sorrow." The newsroom scuttlebutt had it that Frank had bolted from his office, looking for someone to whom he could express his outrage. That kind of prose was too purple, even for a former New Jersey newspaperman. Soon after, Howard was out.

I went to see him at the Warwick Hotel, where he was living just before I left for the war. He was sitting in a chair as though part of it, immobile, speaking softly, still not comprehending what had happened to him. He kept repeating he couldn't believe that Reuven Frank had fired him. Years later, Frank presented a different version of the episode. He said Howard told him he wanted to anchor, and he had replied that he wasn't going to guarantee that or anything else. "He also told me he had an offer from ABC News," Frank added, "so I told him to take it."

When we talked about Vietnam, Howard brightened, reporter to reporter, filling me in on all the pros and cons about working there. As we said goodbye, he went numb again, retreating into his wounds, the ones he got at 30 Rock. I thought of him sitting in that chair a few years later when I covered a story about paraplegics recuperating from their war injuries. They couldn't talk about present or future, only about what life was like before the bullet hit.

THE NBC office was functionally gloomy and curiously devoid of any of the jokey artifacts typical of overseas news offices. No personal effects, bulletin board postcards, smart-ass notes. Just a bizarre memo from Reuven Frank, dictating that "rice paddy" was redundant, so say "rice fields" instead. And, don't forget, we never say "Communists." The word is "enemy" or "North Vietnamese" or "Vietcong." Was this an editorial or a political statement?

Frank Donghi sat in the main room of the office facing the entrance, and on each side were adjoining rooms, one for reporters, the other for crews and technicians. There were about twenty people on the staff, which included five or six American correspondents and about the same number of cameramen and sound men, all Vietnamese with one or two exceptions. The air-conditioning was loud but superb, that is if the electricity didn't cut out, which happened several times a week. Inside the main doors, hanging over the entrance, was a curious scroll bearing Chinese characters. Nervous laughter and sheepish glances were exchanged whenever I inquired of its origin, but never an outright answer. Years later I learned the scroll was a souvenir from a brothel in Thailand. It had been drawn by a woman using a paintbrush manipulated by her vagina. (Is there no end to the mysteries of the Orient?) No one seemed to remember how it came to NBC News Saigon, but it was definitely an American donation.

The world of electronic journalism was anything but instantaneous in those days. Vietnam, in fact, was really the last big story in which TV newsmen still relied on paper. In the bureau, we were connected to New York—to "the world" as the GIs liked to call anything outside of the country—by a telex machine on which we could "talk" to the newsroom back at 30 Rockefeller Plaza. Two telephone calls from New York were a standard daily booking for radio reports, but there was no picking up the receiver and dialing direct anywhere. We simply could not call out, and only with great difficulty was New York able to call us. The sense of isolation, of living inside a hand grenade, was complete. If anyone wanted to find out what was going on in the outside world, he would run down the hall to AP and read the wire files.

Xuan Thuy, the chief Vietnamese negotiator, and former ambassador W. Averell Harriman were still slugging it out at the Paris peace talks, the United States charging Hanoi with using the lull in the fighting to prepare for another offensive, Hanoi charging the United States with a "vicious calculation" in using the bombing limitation actually to intensify the raids. While news such as this directly affected us, it seemed remote and dim. Our reality was the war, night and day, and there was no sign of an end.

New York, of course, was always looking for action, for the "bang bang" as it came to be vulgarly known. With this philosophy came a built-in distortion of the story that was of great concern to those who were serious about getting it right. Ken Bernstein was one of these people, a former newspaperman; a veteran of the Moscow bureau and other foreign capitals, he was getting "short," near his departure date, when I started my tour. As a parting thought to New York, he wrote a letter to Corrigan that I didn't see until many years later.

Dear Bill,

The complaint "no action" is still received from time to time. This is depressing because some of the most significant stories in Viet Nam are hardly conducive to "action." If it is true, as TV's deprecators charge, that only blood and guts make a story in Viet Nam, then the war is certainly being badly covered. I think of two of my stories that didn't make the grade. . . . One was about "miracle rice". . . . Huntley Brinkley rejected on grounds, as I recall, that there was "no action." About all we could muster were peasants sowing and threshing rice, but I think solving the rice deficit in Viet Nam is a significant subject.

I think you should know, too, how things are for our safety nowadays. Old-timers say it is much more risky than before Tet. . . . I sometimes think the people in New York continue to imagine us taking walks in the sun with not much to worry about except a few scattered VC with stolen carbines. On the contrary, the enemy is now in mass and has weapons at least as good as ours. And the US casualty figures show it. A fellow needs motivation to go out into that situation. With so much to fear, fear of New York's displeasure is not effective motivation.

> *Sincerely,*
> *Ken*

Corrigan never replied.

Getting stories out of the country was by today's standards as primitive as sending messages on a tom-tom. There were two daily Pan Am flights on which we could ship, one in late morning headed for Tokyo, where a piece could be satellited. Because of the high cost, satelliting was as rare as ice cubes in the Delta. The second flight left in the afternoon and stopped in Hawaii and San Francisco. There were other assorted ways out, such as a U.S. Air Force flight to the Yakoda base in Japan, but they required someone to handcarry the package of film, audio tapes, and scripts, as well as military permission, which was usually automatic. Once a story was shot and scripted, the odyssey began: from the field to Saigon (usually by chopper), from Saigon to the States by fixed-wing aircraft, from the airport to the NBC office, to the developer, the viewing room, the editing room, the film chain, and then, miraculously, on the air. On average, anywhere from thirty-six to forty-eight hours elapsed from the time the story happened to the moment it went before the American public. Someone once said that if we had had daily satellites then as we do now, the war would have been over much sooner. Perhaps that is true. We might have won it, too. And many more newsmen might have died trying to keep up with the demand.

IN preparation for my first time in the field, following the usual procedure before moving out, Huynh and I took a look at the office map to get an idea of the terrain. Huynh squinted hard, put on his brilliant grin and assured me we would find "a good firefight." He said the name of our destination was Trang Bang. Surely he was kidding. What a silly name for such a dangerous place.

In the correspondents' room, Andy Guthrie, another reporter, was writing a letter to the wife he had left behind in Hong Kong.

"It's a good-bye letter—oh, I'm not kidding," he added, noting my disbelief. "I'm going into the field tomorrow. And I always write a good-bye letter—even when it's not intended to be one. Hey—this is Vietnam." He popped a malaria pill and went back to his task.

How strange. I wondered how many men before him had sat in this room setting down last words.

I went back to the Continental, stretched out on the bed beneath the blur of the ceiling fan, and ordered tea, which arrived on an antique sterling silver tray with a pure linen napkin. Next door I could hear Bob Flick, also newly arrived for NBC, giving laundry instructions to the room boy. Flick—a refugee from marital trouble—lasted just a few weeks. After an ugly experience under fire at Da Nang, he headed home for California. "You can get killed in this place!" he proclaimed.

Little did he know that even worse terror lay ahead of him eleven years later. He went to the jungles of Guyana as a field producer on the NBC team assigned to do a story on Reverend Jim Jones and his Peoples' Temple. Flick barely escaped with his life when five people—

including a congressman and two of his NBC colleagues—were gunned down.

My copies of *Stars and Stripes*, the armed forces newspaper, which arrived each morning with breakfast, had piled up for deeper inspection. In just three weeks, the Soviets invaded Czechoslovakia, bloody rioting broke out at the Democratic convention in Chicago, the North Koreans demanded an apology for the release of the USS *Pueblo* crew and the New York City school system was imploding from racial strife. How quickly things became irrelevant. Like my next-door neighbor and a few others I had already met, this was not a place to come if you wanted to forget your personal grief. On the contrary, Vietnam had a way of squeezing you against your inner torment until you fought it to a finish or went under. Among the reporters I knew who were covering the war, survival was clearly beginning to look like an art. Facing my first day in the field, I was terrified, but with six months to go, there was no point—at least not yet—in letting the fear of war become worse than the war itself.

Tomorrow, Trang Bang. Perhaps Andy Guthrie was right. Time to write letters. First to Jake Burn, who knew this place and would understand. He cared deeply about this war and these people, often reminding me that "the trouble with the Domino Theory is that the only people who really know it's true are the dominoes." In the wake of our separation he had become the feel and wonder of this place, not to mention the heartache. I was trying to see it all through his eyes, with his professional cynicism, humor, and compassion—to unlock what he called the mysteries of the black and gold. I wanted to love or hate it in the same way. At the very least to understand. Missing him was daily bread. We had had an affair back in New York, and if he had asked me not to go—to stay for him—I would never have come to Vietnam. No career seemed worth leaving him. Yet in the end, I did go—as he knew I must.

I finished the letter just as the sun went down in a shameless display of orange. Just one more letter before I would try to get some sleep.

Aug. 29, 1968

Dear Mom,

Tomorrow I'm leaving for a place called Trang Bang, which is just north of Saigon. . . . This war is going to be over soon. Already the fighting is beginning to die down. Thank God. These poor soldiers are going through hell. . . . Please don't be nervous. Life could be a lot worse, as it is for the people here.

> Be home soon.
> Love,
> Betty

5

RAW
FOOTAGE

"You can't make it longer, asshole! You'll never get it on the air."

Fred Flamenhaft, supervising film editor for "The Huntley-Brinkley Report," was haranguing his boss in the shabby dimness of a ninth-floor editing room at 30 Rock. Freddie was in character. No matter what he said, it was always in the softest of voices, just the opposite of the articulations of his boss—and best friend—Shad Northshield. That brooding, irrepressible, and hard-spoken man may not have grown up in the mean streets of Brooklyn as Freddie had, but Chicago in the thirties had left mark enough. Two tough guys who had fought to get where they were, exerting a crucial influence on how tens of millions of Americans saw their war—indeed, their world. As executive producer from June 1965 to January 1969, Northshield had final say on what war stories would appear on the NBC evening news; and as chief of film editing, Freddie supervised the weaving of sound and picture.

They rarely argued and had never disagreed fundamentally over a piece. Then, about eighteen months after America sent troops to Southeast Asia, while watching miles of film, they were about to make a reciprocal discovery. Shad hated the war. Freddie was committed to it. "Can you beat that?" said Shad almost a quarter of a century later. "He was a hawk and I was a dove. It took us months to find out—and only because we were arguing about the length of a piece—that, politically, we were unalterably opposed. I was sobbing because the troops weren't coming home. He was sobbing because they weren't winning."

Shad arrived in TV news as a hard-trained reporter and writer from Chicago, where he and John Chancellor had been young reporters on the *Daily Times*—in fact, where, so the tale ran years later, the police picked up the august NBC anchorman-to-be as a drunk on a fire escape and supposedly looking at a lady undressing. Shad, who remembered the incident as a boyish prank, appeared at the police station the next day and then in Chicago's municipal court to speak up for his colleague.

He had been born in the suburb of Oak Park on July 21, 1922. "On the same day as Hemingway," he said. "And even on the same day of the same month. On top of it, both our fathers committed suicide." Shad quit his last job in Chicago at the *Sun-Times* in 1953 and had come east. Once he was in TV news, documentaries became his specialty, but in fact there was virtually nothing in the business he hadn't mastered—except management. He was too mercurial and scathingly intolerant of screwups. "Every month I'd get dressed up in a blue suit and tie and wait to be called up as they made vice-presidents, but it never happened."

Shad's career paralleled TV news's noisy coming of age in the sixties. "All of a sudden it exploded," he remembered. "NBC News became enormous. In one year we went from four news producers to twenty-eight. In another, I remember turning out at least forty documentaries and sixty instant specials." Shad also ran the coverage of five national election nights. But it was the war that drove "The Huntley-Brinkley Report" in the years he was executive producer, and his views were hardly exotic in the antiwar climate of New York. He thought it "useless, a waste of American manhood, a failure—and Tet proved me right."

Shad's opposition did not come out of conventional antimilitarism. Indeed, as a second lieutenant during World War II, he had led his mortar platoon across the Low Countries—173 days in the line at a stretch, wounded three times—helped storm the Siegfried Line, then all the way to join hands with the Red Army at the Elbe, across a wilderness that had called itself the Third Reich. He had paid his dues.

"I was in love with combat soldiers then—and now," he says. For that reason—and in spite of it—Shad's private judgment of the war was consciously stamped into the program. In at least one staff meeting he made it clear that he was going to push the point on the broadcast: the war should be emphasized, especially for its stupidity.

Flamenhaft was a perfect foil to his hard-charging chief. Theirs was a Mutt and Jeff act: counterpoints. Shad's grammatically flawless English, Freddie's unconscious and thus flawless mimicry of a Broadway hotshot out of *Guys and Dolls*. Where Shad was tall, rangy, and darkly attractive, Freddie was short, pudgy, and reassuringly cuddly, a Jewish elf with a mad scientist's high forehead and wild curly hair. His favorite comment on the passing scene was a muttered "bullshit." He had drifted into TV news by way of many jobs, including developing pictures—of nightclubbers on flashy East Fifty-second street, the old "Strip." He got a job at NBC News because the editing department needed someone to carry the film cans. Freddie had an abiding faith in his country and the opportunity it gave him—a son of poor immigrants—to become something. He was slow to rage, except in defense of anyone he thought mistreated—such as the people of South Vietnam.

A third unheard voice on "The Huntley-Brinkley Report" belonged to Gil Millstein, the chief writer. He knew little about covering a story for TV or what to do with film, and he really didn't pretend to. He was a warden of words only, the man who wrote a grammar and style book, referred to as "The Millstein." About a thousand words a day went by him for approval before they went out on the air. Gil was a graduate of *The New York Times*, which gave him a special cachet in the shop. In addition to functioning as a kind of walking Fowler's *English Usage*, he read all the wires, making sure no story moved that we didn't know about, flagging down Shad if something began to develop.

Gil's main task and special talent was to write for the anchors, working their cadences and idiosyncrasies into the copy. But it was his work with correspondents that made him famous among those of us in the field. No reporter dared record a script for air unless he had clearance from New York, and it was Gil who ordered the corrections. Other editors and producers would pick up their extensions to be in on the process, but he called the shots. In some very assorted corners of the world, I prayed the phones would be out so I could ship the recorded script and film without the obligatory vetting call. Gil could be withering, especially, God forbid, if he caught you in the thrall of a cliché. He was high priest of the purity of the language.

"Oh, so, 'Only time will tell' will it? How about *you* telling it for a change instead of writing crap like this." Or, " 'Under cover of darkness' was it? Hey, guys, did you hear that one? Now there's an original line. I bet you were awake all night thinking that one up. For Chrissake, stop leaning on the clichés and learn to write!" So, of course, you learned in a damn hurry.

In places like Vietnam, where there was no ready telephone access to New York, Gil couldn't reach the correspondents, so if you were not in the field—where you were entirely on your own—then the script was recorded in the office after the bureau chief edited it. In both cases lurked the spectre of an irate Millstein pouncing on an unnoticed error *as it aired.* "I remember a few times a story would come out of Vietnam and I suggested a change," said Gil many years later. "I got laughed at. You know, they said how in God's name are we going to get in touch with so-and-so. And, of course, I had to pass it up." He still sounded regretful.

Gil's politics were not just left, but Old Left, very old. The last time he voted in a presidential election was in 1940, when he cast his ballot ("a protest vote") for Earl Browder, candidate of the Communist party. As for the war, Gil predictably loathed it. He still does. "But most of the correspondents who went to Nam became better than themselves for having been there," he told me years later. "I'm not being patriotic or unpatriotic about it—but they finally found out what it was all about. And now the stuff is made into movies."

Shad, Freddie, and Gil were the key men on the broadcast, but overlooking them and the whole news division was Reuven Frank, the talmudic, white-haired news savant from Canada, an early legend as one of the multiple but not numerous fathers of TV news. He was another import from print, having worked as night city editor on the *Newark Evening News.* He took a bachelor's degree at City College of New York, then a seedbed for bright young men who would make a mark in New York. He won his master's in two stages at the Columbia School of Journalism, taking time out for the war in France where he clerked at an army hospital ("I got a battle star because I could hear the Bulge"). In 1950 he joined NBC as a TV news writer.

At NBC, Frank became especially known for his work as executive producer at the national conventions. NBC's PR credited him with "such innovations" as a booth for the anchormen and a special group of newsmen—floor reporters—to cover the state delegations. His personality hardly matched his reputation. A reclusive, shambling man, he seemed to retreat within the shiny folds of polyester jackets, his symbolic connection to the then poor but assertedly honest world of the newspaperman.

Normally, in those days there was little input from the anchors, unlike today when the news stars often make major policy decisions from the choice of stories to that of personnel. In the tumultuous 1960s the men behind the camera were calling the shots and shaping the history of a different kind of broadcast news. Men like Shad, Freddie, Gil, Reuven—hard-nosed frontiersmen in this Wild West— might not have been household words but nevertheless wound up imprinting their personal philosophies on generations of Americans. They were not unlike Callisthenes, Alexander the Great's historian, who proclaimed himself more important than the great warrior. After all, he reasoned, the boss may be conquering Asia, but I'm the one getting the message out.

The message from most of the correspondents in the field and the producers, writers, and executives back home was that Vietnam was shaping up as a costly mistake. So there I was, about to risk my life to report a war many hated and few expected to win. Still, it was where I wanted to be.

THE lights on the helicopter's control panel were the only reference point in the night, haunting the cockpit with a deep red glow. The pilot, in silhouette, moved slowly like a robot, his head and hands made grotesque by a huge flight helmet and thick gloves. Voices exchanged somewhere in the moonless dark spoke of the jargon of flight, barely audible under the whine of a warming engine.

I checked my watch: 5:15 A.M. Chill dampness would soon yield to a rising sun. The Huey shuddered and swayed as it lifted just a few feet above Hotel 12 at Tan Son Nhut Airport, a routine departure point for journalists leaving Saigon for the field. It hovered, rotated, lingered higher, and then leaned into a sharp-angled turn as it mounted toward a star-strewn sky. Ahead lay Trang Bang.

Soon the sun was stage-lighting the dozen hues of green below. I peered over the door gunner's shoulder and followed our whisking shadow across rice paddies, bamboo forests, and the thatched roofs of shantytowns. The still surfaces of unending chains of lakes and lagoons lulled me into serenity until I realized these were bomb craters flooded by the monsoon. Within an hour we landed just east of the village. Luckily, on my maiden outing, the landing zone wasn't hot. We touched down without being fired on.

"We go find the company commander," said Huynh, off-loading himself and his gear within seconds. Green and groping, not having the foggiest practical notion of how wars are fought, I was relieved to take my cues from him. In the weeks ahead he would patiently transform me into a war correspondent.

Huynh was lugging the then-standard equipment of the TV combat cameraman. The Auricon camera, about twenty-seven pounds, a power pack, five to six pounds, plus personal gear, including food and a water canteen. About forty pounds. Our Dutch sound man, Hugh Van Ess, carried the film, an amplifier, tape recorder, microphones, cables, and his own gear, weighing in at about fifty pounds. Then factor in the suffocating heat, the merciless sun, the muck and torture of the terrain—and the fear, the fear, the fear. That was how TV crews operated, under normal circumstances, in this war. The trick was holding it all together and getting the pictures when the action started.

We were to hook up with a unit from the elite 101st Airborne Division, the Screaming Eagles, whose exploits went back to the Normandy invasion. Unfortunately, there were no daring jump operations for airborne units in Vietnam, not in the triple-canopy jungle that had regularly swallowed up whole battalions of French paratroopers in colonial days. This work was earthbound—walking, running, crawling, shooting—the grim, unspectacular murderous toil of infantry. "Grunt" work. Most of the 101's activity was farther north in the war, but elements of the third brigade were working this area through clusters of villages along Route 1, about halfway between Saigon and the Cambodian border. With memories of Tet so deeply ingrained, American military commanders were taking any probe by the Communists very seriously.

Alpha Company had been in a firefight the night before. The men spotted and cordoned off an understrength battalion of about 300 Vietcong believed to be the Cu Chi Regiment, named for the nearby headquarters town of the U.S. Twenty-fifth Infantry Division. For three years, men of the Twenty-fifth had been taking on this old-line VC unit. Now the Eagles were added to the mix. The VC tried to make a run for it during the night; helicopter gunships and fighter-bombers were brought in to support the ground action. The initial estimates said ninety-three enemy had been killed. American losses, eight killed and twenty-six wounded. At least that's what the official report said. It didn't mention that the unit was operating at half strength.

In the light of early morning, what we saw on the faces of the men of Alpha Company were raw fear and grinding fatigue—the "thousand-yard stare" of the soldier still standing amid his fallen comrades, fixing his gaze on some distant point beyond the reach or understanding of those who have not "seen the elephant." They were trapped in a little universe of death, grief, and misery. Yet despite their ghostlike presence, my own appearance—"a round-eyed chick from the world"—seemed to ease a few of them back into basic all-American kidding and ogling.

The company commander was a first lieutenant right out of West Point, handsome crew-cut looks, lean and smiling through the grime and weariness that gripped him. He gave us a quick briefing, referring to a well-creased plastic-covered map to lay out our objective: a walk through the bush in pursuit of the elusive enemy. We started off into the brush and saw those killed the night before lying chalk white along our route, staring vacantly through half-open eyes. In a silenced machine gun emplacement, a North Vietnam gunner slumped over his Chinese weapon, which had struck down so many GIs just a few hours earlier.

The jungle was an extremity of death and beauty. I began to reach for an exotic yellow blossom rising from the grass. "Don't do that!" barked a trooper. "Don't pick up anything—ever—not even a flower. It's probably booby-trapped."

We walked single file, silently, every snapped twig a thunderclap. My very breathing seemed loud enough to alert the so invisible, so real and determined enemy. It was strange, a jungle without sounds, no birdsong. Were there eyes watching us, settling us into their sights like hunters in a blind? A hand pulled me back into line. It was Huynh. "Don't walk with the radioman," he said. "The VC always try to kill him first to knock out communication." But by that time, the radio guy and I had become rather chummy, and it was difficult to shake him.

We continued for about a mile or two. I was beginning to realize how out of shape I was, how leadlike the Army jungle boots were getting with each step. Fourteen years of ballet training at Mme. Annette's School of Dance in New Haven were all that stood between me and physical collapse. Max Nash of AP was behind me, making shots all the way, waiting for the electric moment of "contact." We all had one goal, soldiers and journalists, a good firefight with the hated Cong. They wanted to win the war. We wanted to be introduced by Chet and David.

I watched Huynh's every move, every expression. Before my eyes, he turned into a jungle creature, electric and cunning. The ancient spirit of the hunt had taken over. The ancient spirit of the nest was more my speed. I felt the muscles in my legs shaking. Huynh made no comment, but he knew that behind the Girl Scout cheeriness I was terrified.

"If you 'make' the first shot, you're okay," he whispered. "The first shot is the one that they aim at you and you don't see them. But after first shot, you know where it's coming from. If it's AK-47, then it's sniper. If it's machine gun, then it's not small unit. One machine gun, a platoon. More than one, could be company-size unit. You have to listen."

He knew the game. It was NBC's guerrilla against Uncle Ho. All the stories I heard in New York and Hong Kong about this man drifted back, how on at least two occasions he had rescued American units, one of which had lost its way in the jungle and another when its commander was killed and panic set in.

Suddenly, as we approached a clearing, loud voices, first in Vietnamese, from the company interpreter, then in English. "NVA. Out in the open!"

The instant yet slow-motion chaos of deadly collision had begun. We hit the dirt, all except Huynh, of course, who seemed bulletproof in every firefight, standing to get his pictures. We could see men running toward a treeline across the clearing as the company commander called in the 81-mm mortars. The grunts opened up with M16s and machine guns. If there was incoming—and later they said there was—I didn't hear it, not in that devil's smithy. Besides, I was face down, saying a Hail Mary into the mud.

No one was hurt. Only a skirmish, but the postbattle excitement of being alive was electric. We walked on, eventually stopping to break out our C rations for lunch. I wrote a stand-upper—an end to the piece delivered to camera—saying that the Americans knew that the elite VC formation and North Vietnamese army elements were trying to make their way back to Saigon for another Tet attack. It was the kind of timeproof conclusion that would hold up even if all hell broke loose in the remaining hours, unless, of course, there was a major development, like being overrun, or worse. The rest of the script would be written in Saigon; in effect, backwards, like so many stories for TV. If we decided to stay on with the unit, if it looked as though things might really get interesting, I would have to write the entire script in the field. The crew would record my track, and the whole package, in a bright red shipping bag, would be flung aboard whatever bird was flying to Saigon. Our bureau drivers were trained to off-load stories from choppers coming in from the field and then ship them out of country as fast as possible.

We interviewed the company commander and several of the men, our protectors and friends, for friends are made fast in combat, sometimes in the split second needed to register the sound of an incoming mortar. Many of the men talked about their fear, how Charlie would hit them when they least expected it. I got the usual questions in return. Why do you do this? Do they pay you extra? What's a nice girl like you doing in a place like this? Apart from their curiosity about how and why we were covering the war, there was the added distraction of seeing an American woman, a jarring sight for soldiers whose main contact with the opposite sex usually involved a quick ten-dollar screw with a Mamasan who cleaned the barracks, encounters with the massage parlor maidens or bar girls from Tu Do Street in Saigon, or the GI's traditional last resort, a visit to a whorehouse. In any case, I felt extremely self-conscious, instinctively trying to act like their kid sister or Miss No-Nonsense News Lady.

Once we had our sound, Huynh and I hung back while he put a new magazine on the camera. There was a commotion behind some bushes to our right. A burly warrant officer was having it out with a young trooper. The private looked desperate, as though he was on the verge of coming apart. The WO slapped him twice across the face and shook him to an accompanying denunciation the more chilling for being muttered. Combat was tearing even this crack unit apart.

Midafternoon, the usual 3:30 to 4 P.M. monsoon time, water began pummeling us. The enemy had already faded into the forest. We huddled under our ponchos, waiting for the rain to abate and then for clearance to land a chopper that would take us back to Saigon. Huynh and Hugh hurriedly pulled out plastic bags to cover the equipment, especially the camera. If the humidity or mud hadn't triggered a malfunction, then the rain would. Camera breakdowns in the field were the worst nightmare of all, and given the weather and terrain, it was a miracle that any film whatsoever got on the air at all. Most of the credit had to go to the Vietnamese crews and a German technician, Detlev Arndt, who kept rewiring and gluing the well-worn parts. Here was a war being fought with the most sophisticated machines of the age, yet recorded with equipment built for anything *but* war. It was like taking a horse and buggy to get to the launch pad at Canaveral.

"When can I tell my parents it will be on?" asked the young commanding officer, a question posed to TV journalists all over Vietnam. I explained that the story would run too soon for him to alert his parents, but maybe they could request a film copy of the cut story from NBC after it aired. He shook our hands, a big, boyish grin on his face. I knew he wasn't eager to say good-bye. After all, we were "the world," somehow connecting him and his men to the people and the country he was defending.

A smoke grenade spewed a mist of gold against the gray aftermath of the storm, marking the landing zone. The helicopter descended, and as it hovered before ascent, we exchanged the traditional "thumbs up" sign of the military world, signifying that everything was and would be all right. I can still see that young lieutenant holding on to his helmet in the dust of the downdraft, watching out for us right to the end.

Back in Saigon at the bureau, I finished the script and recorded it, ready to ship with the film the next morning. As with all stories out of Vietnam in those days, there was no way to develop the film in-country; correspondents couldn't see what they had. Notes, or a shot list, your cameraman's skill and memory, and your own eyes were the only guides to continuity. Basically, you were flying blind. Many of the stories you might never see. In the case of Trang Bang, I wrote it straight and dully competent. At least that was my verdict when I saw the piece for the first time, twenty years later.

Exhausted and dehydrated, I repaired to the Shelf, where Jack Russell, our radio correspondent, and Bob Flick were into their third round, eyes fixed in fascination on the wall facing them. Two geckos were copulating. "That's Vietnam," said Jack. "Even the lizards do it out in the open."

"Disgusting," I snorted. "Can't they at least go behind a palm tree? Is everything horny in this country?"

They assured me this was the case.

Looking around, I thought how surreal it all was: the clink of cocktail tumblers, breezy humor, potted palms, and all after a day on the battlefield.

The Trang Bang story aired within the next forty-eight hours. Once they had telexed the play report to let me know that the piece had run at two minutes and twenty-five seconds, I put Alpha Company in the memory bank and went on to other stories. But a week later, one of the AP guys poked his head in the door and said there was something I might want to see. Max Nash was filing a story on a military line from Cu Chi. A company of the 101st had been hit, one of nine surrounding the village of Trang Dau, about nine miles from the American base at Cu Chi. Max had talked to the survivors and was piecing it together over the telephone.

U.S. intelligence had learned that a meeting of Vietcong leaders and political cadres would take place in the village on that night. Although the airborne troopers were alert to possible trouble, peering into the darkness, they could see nothing. Then, suddenly, at two in the morning hundreds of Vietcong and North Vietnamese troops stormed out of the darkness and hit them hard. Using women and children as shields, they came in waves, charging into the company shoulder-to-shoulder, quickly smashing the American defense line, firing wildly with AK-47 assault rifles, pushing the frantic civilians in front of them. Brigade headquarters back at Cu Chi heard the strident voice of a radio operator: "They're coming! They're coming!" Then it went silent.

One trooper who had been hit in the head, arms, and legs, lay in a pool of his own blood as the second assault wave broke over him. He felt himself being roughly turned over and then left for dead. Through a film of blood he saw the Vietcong shooting other wounded troopers nearby. Then they gathered some of their dead, lashed the bodies to bamboo poles and carried them away quickly and silently, fading into the darkness.

"We'll get the bastards," said a survivor.

The battle lasted only fifteen minutes. When it was over, thirty-one had been killed, twenty-seven wounded: the men of Alpha Company.

The following day more details emerged. Among the dead, the company commander, that West Pointer with the big grin, identifiable only by his fingerprints. So this is how it works, I thought. Same unit, same place, same enemy—but just six days too early. In the midst of my disbelief was the realization of how absolutely random this dying process seemed to be. And so, back home, instead of sitting down in their rec room to watch a real TV home movie of their soldier son, two dazed parents were making altogether different arrangements.

IF the war was one of guerrilla tactics, so too was coverage of it. This was no cohesive campaign with a single front. No major cities were taken, no territory invaded, no massing of armies in pitched battles that would turn the tide. This was not one story but a collection of small half stories, fragments shifting in a kaleidoscope. The front was everywhere. Like an episode of "Laugh-In," the hit TV comedy show of the time, you simply opened one of the many small doors on the set to get a quick peek at the latest snippet of lunacy. A B-52 strike in the Highlands, a terrorist attack in Saigon, an F-4 raid in the southern panhandle, a naval bombardment in the Tonkin Gulf, a deadly walk through the booby traps of the Pineapple, slices of winning and losing and dying in a hundred different ways.

As the military fought a battle for hearts and minds, so too did the artillery of the press, and of television especially. Guerrilla war and guerrilla journalism had found each other. The haphazard freedom of the way reporters covered the war perfectly complemented their appetite for risk. The button-down, establishment-type heroes of the press corps—senior staff correspondents from newspapers and magazines—were pitted against the anti-heroes influenced by the counterculture of the sixties, younger newsmen like AP's Rick Merron or, more often, the free-lancers who sought adventure and drugs: the midnight cowboys of the war, crashing motorcycles through the jungle, strung out on the local grass. Usually, they worked as photographers, accentuating their hippie Nikon chic with headbands, cartridge belts, western boots, and tight jeans, inventing themselves as they went along. Much attention was paid to these romantic hucksters during and after the war; the so-called underground press of hip journals canonized them for their life-style, since there was little journalistic achievement to salute.

The most colorful acolyte in this cult was Sean Flynn, slender, handsome, smoldering, and bearing an eerie resemblance to his famous father, Errol. A swashbuckler-in-training, Sean took it to the limit in 1970 when he and another free-lancer, Dana Stone, both high on grass, rode their rented motorcycles along Cambodia's Route 1 and disappeared.

Sometimes the war's psychedelic appeal added religion to the possibilities for self-indulgence. A familiar figure on the Saigon spiritual circuit was John Steinbeck, Jr., son of the writer and regarded officially as "a newsman." He worked as a part-time technician for CBS until his accreditation was pulled for joining a peace crusade led by the Palm Tree Prophet, a Buddhist monk who liked to meditate atop trees—always to a great deal of press coverage. Steinbeck made the news again when he went to jail in Thailand for possessing a kilo of marijuana.

It was, at best, a wild and crazy war—as opposed to those sober, reasonable wars which one can find anywhere. And if the high command did not understand what was going on much of the time, newspeople were only slightly better off. Each day you carved yourself out a slice of the war pie, nibbling on a battle here, tasting a reconnaissance there, trying to make some sense of it all. Ambiguity was everywhere, as the mistakes of American politicians and commanders aroused, if only by contrast, a certain admiration for the single-minded, cold-blooded dedication of the other side. The Vietcong were world-class low-tech jungle fighters, sweating their noncombat hours in miles of fetid underground tunnels, surviving on a daily fistful of rice and promises from Ho Chi Minh.

Ambiguity descended over both sides of the Pacific as the sense of great achievement that had prevailed in America since the end of World War II came undone in 1968. The heroes of that war, drowning out of their depth, were being made the villains of this one, discredited by academic sanctimony, adolescent self-righteousness, and not least the weariness and frustration of a country to which they had been unable to keep their promises. It was street theater—at war and at home. While Communist guerrillas were slicing up Alpha Company, urban guerrillas were stepping up their outrages. In both cases, they got media attention that would eventually influence the war's course.

If anyone epitomized a generation caught in the raw iconoclasm of the sixties it was Frank Donghi. Here he was, fifty-three years old, running from the womb of Dobbs Ferry, New York, to get in on the action. From the day he met me at the airport, when I first suspected something was eating him, Frank seemed increasingly distracted, reacting slowly to New York's demands. His bid for the Saigon assignment had not been just an aging newsman's lust for one more good story. He needed the money—bureau chiefs made fortunes by trading their network dollars on the black market—and his family was coming apart. In fact, Frank had fallen in love with a California girl not long before he left the States. A son had run away from home. His wife was in a daze. His daughter, Diane, was a freshman at Barnard College on her way to becoming a disillusioned flower child. I had met her several times in New York, trying to help find a place for her to live during the first year at school. She had seemed a shy, intelligent girl with no still, deep waters of anarchy discernible. Then in Saigon, I saw a photograph in one of the news magazines of a familiar-looking girl with long ash-blond hair seated in front of a picture of Karl Marx: Diane, in full revolutionary pose, photographed in an SDS hangout near the Columbia campus.

Some months later, it became apparent that she had joined up with the Weathermen, a violent spin-off from the flower power revolt, and soon she was on the run from the FBI, eventually to be arrested and indicted by a Federal grand jury for plotting a campaign of bombing and terrorism. The government later dropped the charges, saying that a trial would reveal its methods of obtaining evidence. I never saw or heard from Diane again.

If the scene back home was phantasmagoric, Vietnam was Looney Tunes. Fear, black humor, and general madness ceased to intrude; they now hovered permanently through the fog and filthy air. Things were normal only if bizarre, predictable only if unexpected. One of our cameramen, a German, Peter Bellendorf, was a great source of daily hilarity. He kept a cobra and a python in his apartment, and they functioned as a security detail for the cash and cameras he kept around. He acquired the cobra in Ceylon, concealing it in his laundry bag: and when the bag began to move under the eyes of Vietnamese customs, Mr. Long, the bureau's driver and fixer, came to the rescue with a bribe. Despite this reptilian guard, Peter's rooms were burgled, and he was so livid he rigged a claymore mine in his bedroom. He was mildly disconcerted when someone in the office pointed out that in the event of another break-in, his goods would go up with the intruders. As for the snakes, they became a bother, especially when Peter was on the road and it was up to members of the bureau to feed them live chickens. The solution emerged when it was decided to pit the cobra against the python on Peter's bed. For posterity's sake, lights and a camera were set up. The python followed its natural bent and swallowed the cobra whole. This was one piece of action footage that never made the evening news.

At the end of my first tour in early 1969, Peter and I left Saigon on the same Air France flight—me for the States, he for Germany—both of us vainly swearing never to return. By nature he was a loner, especially when it came to taking pictures. Going into the field with correspondents irked him, so he often went out alone, light and quick with a silent camera. He was reported missing on April 8, 1970, in Cambodia's Svayrieng Province. Some said that he was captured by the Vietcong. Whatever happened, he is still numbered among the fifty or more newsmen in Southeast Asia listed as "missing, presumed dead."

Cables and telexes from home offices to overseas bureaus are the stuff of many legends, and have a particular flavor in war zones. With no handy telephone or fax machine, the telex was the two-way voice directing war coverage—without benefit of nuance, the raised eyebrow, the qualifying tone. You got what you read, so it was important to remember the same in sending. An angry or stupid message could seriously hurt your career.

One of the most renowned home office communiqués was a message attributed to ABC News in New York expressing frustration that in firefights the camera angle always seemed to be from behind the friendly forces. How about a reverse shot? Somebody suggested telexing to ask if they would like that reverse shot over the shoulder of a North Vietnamese machine gunner.

There was no underestimating how little the desk guys at 30 Rock knew about the war. It sometimes seemed they thought we were on a movie lot, not in a war zone, covering a Cecil B. De Mille spectacular, where with a wave of his hand he could marshal huge armies or part the Red Sea—all for the benefit of our cameras. Office-brand producers simply assumed the war to be at the service of the networks, but a telexed answer to even the most absurd request had to tactfully instruct in the art of war while sedulously avoiding sarcasm—even a scintilla of smartassness that could register on the high command. One could never be too wary of the invisible man we all kept in mind: the Vice-President In Charge of Fear.

"New York," of course, loomed omnipresent. Images of vest-wearing vice-presidents dancing around the telex machine seemed to be everyone's darkest vision. Incur their displeasure and you got a "rocket"—a nasty message personally addressed to you, but for the whole world to see: PRO SMITH EX JONES: CBS AHEAD PLEIKU AMBUSH STY. YR H-B SPOT LAST NIGHT HAD NO REPEAT NO INTVWS WITH CASUALTIES. PLS EXPLAIN SOONEST.

New York was never so close as when a visiting executive came to town. Apart from the obvious terror of being asked to extend their tours, bureau chiefs and correspondents were expected to make these Westchester straight-arrows feel they were walking in the paths of the inscrutable East. Famous restaurants, which in Saigon meant those blown up at least once by a satchel charge of C-4 "plastique"; introductions to local luminaries, that is, U.S. embassy or top military officials and other bureau chiefs (meeting Vietnamese never rated); a stop at Minh the Tailor, immortalized by the press for his knockoffs of Abercrombie & Fitch safari or "TV" suits; and on the shady side, a lucrative visit to the Indian money changer in the Eden Building to double your assets.

Sexual excursions of a suitably executive and therefore furtive nature, normally took place on the way in or out of the country. Many an itinerary included an unlisted stopover at Peitou on Taiwan. This "resort" in a suburb of Taipei drew journalists, GIs, politicians, diplomats, and even a spy or two to its bucolic brothels, which according to one travel guide, catered to the "hot springs trade." But I had it on good authority that these clandestine visits served no medicinal purpose.

NEW York looked best when it stuck to the headlines: ordering reaction stories to the peace talks minuet and demands for a bombing halt from the enemy and the war protesters—all tied into an electrifying election campaign. The Vietnamese and the peace movement had toppled Johnson, and Hubert Humphrey, with half-hearted lame-duck backing from his commander in chief, could only pray for an unconditional cessation of the bombing if he was to stop Richard Nixon.

While both sides in the talks explored each other's weaknesses along the most devious of channels, the Communists kept up their pressure on the battlefield. News of an action shaping up around Tay Ninh near the Cambodian border, which lay on a major invasion route to the capital, caught the attention of the Saigon bureaus.

Donghi looked up from the wires.

"You'd better get your stuff together fast. It's Tay Ninh. They've got the city surrounded."

Huynh and I were ready within the hour. Just before we ran for Tan Son Nhut, Frank beckoned me closer, his face drawn and serious. "This is going to be it, you know. You're walking right into a fire-fight." He was genuinely worried.

I had other worries, lots of them. It would be a competitive story and the war lead for the day, if not for weeks. The pressure of getting the story and getting it *out* was already building, for the moment displacing fear. It was what drove all correspondents. The concentration kept you sane, the demands of doing the job, worrying about getting it right. Will the chopper come? Will the camera hold up? Will New York like it? And in my case, *If I fail, they'll say it's because I'm a woman.* I had so far received, I knew, only grudging acceptance from Ron Steinman, but I didn't know he was reporting on me back to New York. In fact, none of the correspondents realized the extent of the backstage information being exchanged.

In a letter to Corrigan, while he was filling in for Donghi in Saigon, Steinman wrote:

She is a problem in many ways, but she has been pretty well accepted by all our people. . . . However, if I had my way I still wouldn't want a woman out here. . . . With all that I think she is going to get better in the next months and could get a lot better if she had firm editorial and production type direction.

Three days later, he wrote to Reuven Frank:

Trotta has lots of drive and presents a number of minor problems, but she is working very hard and at least from me takes good direction. . . . One of the secrets of Liz is that she doesn't want to be treated like a woman and in particular like a woman correspondent. I treat her like any other correspondent and I think she is responding. . . . She is very much aware of the Donghi problem and worried about it because he is of very little help to her when she has to put a piece together. She would progress well if we had a man who could teach her and bring out the best in her. Her natural drive is the only real thing in her favor now and the fact that she looks good.

Of course I wasn't privy to those letters at the time. Still, it became apparent there were two hurdles for me to clear: could I do the job, and could a woman do the job? Tay Ninh would be the test.

The city was under siege as we bore down in full assault with a squad of Hueys carrying South Vietnamese troops, door gunners at the ready, escorting gunships slamming down their rockets and 30-mm machine gun rounds. We leveled in for the kind of hot landing that would be richly reenacted years later in *Apocalypse Now*, to a background of Wagner's "Ride of the Valkyries." But in the harsh original, full-screen stereo would have drowned in the din of guns and engines and the rush of your own blood. Into the grass, ducking the rotors, running at a crouch, making for the tree line. Head down, waiting for the liftoff and dreading the silence to follow. No more umbilical cord.

Soldiers and newsmen, alone on the ground left to the noiseless forces of the jungle.

Would we get out that night? In a few days? At all? And what was it I was supposed to look for? Oh yes, the trip wires connected to the booby traps that rip your legs off. But where were they? My next step. . . . Hell, how can you see the wire when it's so fine? *Stay away from fallen trees and twigs arranged too neatly!* Walk through the muck of the rice paddy, not on the bordering dikes, or one of Charlie's punji stakes will rip a hole through your sole. Did I take a malaria pill? What's the use, people were still coming down with the odd strain even when they took their pills. Are they in the trees, watching? They must know we're here. Christ, we made so much noise on the way in. If I get hit, how long will it take for the dustoff chopper to get me out? Stay low. Stay cool. On and on, a litany of cautions, my mantra for going to war.

The waning light had faded to dusk, so there was little we could do about a story. At least we were in place. We slept in hooches at the USAID compound and set out at dawn for Tay Hoa on the city's outskirts. A North Vietnamese battalion had moved in. Miltonian hell was breaking loose. Most of the 3,000 villagers had fled during the night. A few terrified stragglers ran as American air strikes "softened up" the area with 750-pound bombs and napalm, bringing at least a lull in the heavy enemy machine-gunning. South Vietnamese regional forces made a tentative move, only to recoil before heavy fire. More air strikes. The planes were working very close in, close enough for anyone on the ground to be hit by "friendly fire" if the coordinates were off by a single degree.

"You either get it—or you don't."

It was Huynh, camera propped on one shoulder, talking to me over the other shoulder. I froze in place. The idea was for me to make up my mind right there whether or not I was going to be a combat correspondent. To this day I don't know if he meant get the picture or get killed, but in either case it holds: you simply have to move out and take your chances, when all common sense is telling you to run and hide or catch the first stateside freedom bird. I moved.

There was plenty of shellfire coming in on the central market-place. The paralyzed regional forces crumbled back to the edge of the village. We huddled in a crater. Huynh rose, trying to entice me to do a standup to camera under fire. "Good picture. Lots of action." I hugged my legs closer to my chest. The provincial adviser, a Connecticut Yankee major who looked like Henry Fonda, was slouching next to me. When the mortars started crashing closer, we began a lively discussion about congestion on the Merritt Parkway. Eventually, with Huynh's prodding, I climbed out of the hole and did a crouching standupper (even though he wanted me to stand), a popular compromise in covering a war for television. Even as I spoke into the camera, I thought of the mud on my face, the greasy traces of old lipstick, and the sweat pouring down my face into the open collar of my filthy shirt. Corrigan would undoubtedly send me a memo about my hair.

By midday, the nerve center of the battle shifted to a schoolhouse on the other side of the village. To reach it we had to cross an open field, commanded by high ground in enemy hands. "We go now," said Huynh. "We can make it. But don't run."

I wanted so much to run I would have qualified for the Olympic track team. Only that inscrutable certainty told me to do exactly what he said. We made it, of course. Huynh's reassurance never failed.

Diving for cover alongside the schoolhouse, I wound up nose-to-nose with Horst Faas of AP. Now I knew I was in the right place. But he did look worried.

"Dammit, I thought I had the best picture of the war!"

"Of what?"

"Of you and Vo Huynh getting hit. You know that NVA had you in clear sight walking across that field. I had you in focus and was ready. Dammit."

"Very funny, Horst." Except I really don't think he was trying to be funny.

Overhead, the Cobras were laying down a deafening, stunning, pulse-beating carpet of fire, making conversation impossible and reminding us how close we were to the target area. The *Paris Match* photographer and some other French journalists were among us, pouting as usual. Their disdain for Americans was palpable. The Dien Bien Phu syndrome: we couldn't do it, so neither can you—even if you can.

The fighting raged on. With Huynh filming all the way, and no camera jams to slow us down, I talked to anyone I could get to, anyone not too busy trying to stay alive. During a rare lull, the crew and I huddled against some sandbags to record a sound track of the script I had been scratching out between incoming rounds. The humidity matted the pages of my notebook, and the ink ran from the scribbled names and notes, but somehow, the routine discipline of the job prevailed in this mayhem. In the end, it's the discipline that saves you.

In late afternoon we broke off and fell back to the village. Now we needed a way out. CBS and ABC crews were lurking around with the same thought. It would soon be dark, little chance for a night chopper. Huynh and I found a general. I put on my sultriest voice and asked about transportation. Within minutes, he called in his own ship to take us back to Saigon. Later, someone asked me if that wasn't using feminine wiles to get a story. You bet it was. A small victory measured against the number of times my male colleagues bedded secretaries or took majors drinking to get a beat. It wasn't a point I felt guilty about, especially in Tay Ninh. We were ahead—great combat footage and a bird to take it home. Huynh's face was set in the well-pleased half smile of Buddha.

"What do you think?" I asked.

He nodded once, his black moustache twisting above a proud grin.

"We got a good story." Understatement was his specialty.

At 4 o'clock in the afternoon Vietnam turns violet. The chopper corkscrewed south into the mauve fog that separated day and night. I turned my face to the wind rushing through the open door and tasted the salt of the perspiration trickling over my lips. My face and back still burned from the scorch of the sun. We were hungry, tired, and alone with the long, lonely thoughts of what we had seen. Below, the darkness was now complete, except for the occasional glow of a lantern on a river sampan, or the flashing lights of another aircraft.

A chill filled the cockpit. Heat, hunger, thirst, fatigue, and now cold. Almost as a reflex I thought of Mac Johnson, the foreign editor for NBC News. During World War II, he had been a UP correspondent in the Pacific, flying twenty-three combat missions. As a reporter for the *Herald Tribune*, he sat atop a gun turret of the USS *Missouri* to cover the surrender of Japan. Mac's gravelly voice and prize-fighter face only added to his gruff image. I, of course, was terrified of him, particularly on the day he called me into his office to brief me for Vietnam. "This foreign correspondent stuff isn't always what it's cracked up to be," he began. "Do you know what you're getting into?" I indicated yes, but he knew I didn't have a clue.

"There's glamour, sure, but that's a lot of bullshit," he said. "Most of the time you're going to be wondering what you're doing so far away from home. When you're cold and there's no way to get warm. When you're hot and there's no air-conditioning. When you're hungry and there's no time to eat or the restaurants are all closed. When you're thirsty and you're out in the middle of the jungle or the desert and your canteen's empty. When you're bone tired and there's another deadline to make. And when you're frightened out of your mind and there's no place to hide. This is what it's really all about. And I don't know why any sane person would want a job like that."

Mac knew the answer to that one as well as I did. The hard-boiled act would never let him say it.

A couple of hours later a motley trio straggled into the empty bureau. We had already handed the shipping bag containing the film, script, and recorded narration to an NBC courier at the airport, who loaded it onto an air force flight to Japan. Huynh stored his gear, while I checked my mailbox, hoping it would offer some relief from a better place. Instead, I found a phone message from David Barrett, George's son, a medic in the Highlands. He had called on a military line from Pleiku, a New York friend leaving a perfectly normal message in an absolutely abnormal environment. George had been in Europe, touring his beloved France, and had sent David a poppy from one of the old battlefields. "It seemed fitting to pick one and send it to you," he wrote, "a reminder of other wars, and I guess man will never learn." From Flanders fields to Pleiku, the torch was passed.

I left the Eden Building and numbly picked my way through the night roaches toward the Continental, wincing at the familiar foul odor rising from the streets, that unmistakable stench of the Third World, where people and garbage live side by side. The "white mice"—Vietnam's national police—gave me the usual fishy stares. Exhausted, I flung off the heavy boots and collapsed on the lumpy bed. I fell asleep thinking about the story we had shipped, the film I had never seen, although the images had been burned into my brain.

Tay Ninh made "The Huntley-Brinkley Report" the next night, although given the thirteen-hour time difference, it was actually the same night, September 12, 1968. In this case, the time lag enabled New York to know and report the battle's outcome.

CHET HUNTLEY: *"The enemy offensive at Tay Ninh, a key provincial capital on the main road to Saigon, has been smashed and the Viet Cong and the North Vietnamese are in full retreat toward the Cambodian border. . . . At the height of the Tay Ninh battle, the enemy occupied villages to the south, east and west of the city. Here is a report on the fighting from NBC News Correspondent Liz Trotta."*

Huynh's pictures and my words followed, including twenty-five seconds of a bedraggled woman crouching before the camera. Then Chet tagged out live with what happened after we left Tay Ninh. While our film was on its way to Tokyo, the regional forces had caved in; but for air strikes and the Vietnamese rangers, Tay Ninh would have fallen.

Frank was already in the office when I turned up early next morning, eager to see the play report. Along with it was a message: GREAT REACTION HERE PROFESSIONALLY AND IN PRESS VERY GOOD. PROUD OF YOU. HUNTLEY

Ken Bernstein and I went to lunch down the street at Rumuntcho's, a French bistro frequented by South Vietnamese brass and foreigners. Apart from being one of the half-dozen good restaurants in town, it served Bloody Marys, a skill imparted to the owner by a couple of American correspondents—one of the few undeniable returns on the war effort. As we picked the ants out of the French baguette, I told him my war story. He was dutifully unimpressed. "The lead on H-B! This means, of course, you're going to extend your tour to a year. Or perhaps it just means I have to pay for lunch?"

Bernstein's humor, as usual, bucked me up. Truth was, I felt vaguely depressed, although I had every reason to bask in my triumph. Hadn't I just proven that I could not only do the job but do it better than anyone expected? Perhaps it was the letdown after "contact" that all the grunts talked about, or the loneliness and long thoughts of what lay ahead, or knowing I could explain and write about a lot of things except the wordless terror. Perhaps it was the war itself: so many young men ready to go the limit for a country that would not honor them. The night before I had dreamed my first war nightmare—no plot, no cast of characters. Just an endless expanse of blanched bodies stretching into infinity under a low gray sky.

6

ARMY
WITHOUT
BANNERS

The screen door opened with a long and piercing shriek, and somewhere in the twilight zone of wakefulness I heard a giant's footsteps crossing the old wooden floor.

"REVEILLE. REVEILLE. Four A.M. Rise 'n' shine. On the double."

A United States Marine was standing over my sweat-soaked body half wrapped in its gray sheet, the butt of his M16 prodding my feet as he executed his first order of the day. I understood the deep loathing of a recruit for his drill sergeant. I also felt it was this marine's cheap thrill for the week. Waking up in the Da Nang press barracks was a combination of sour mouth, heat prostration, and humiliation at the hands of our fighting forces. The most efficient alarm clock I had ever had. Check-in time for flights north was early. This was marine ter-

129

ritory. No candy-ass need apply for work in these parts. The press hooches reeked lean and mean.

Da Nang hangs on the coast about 300 miles north of Saigon. Even then it was a colorless city, redeemed by its perch on an exquisite bay reaching out into the South China Sea. The Hai Van and Tiensha peninsulas on either side extend from the coast like crab claws ready to close. On the cloudy, cooler days, sitting on a jetty behind the press center, I would imagine this was Shelter Island, nestled between the north and south forks of Long Island. To the left rise turquoise mountains stretching toward Hue. To the right, Monkey Mountain slopes down to the white sands of China Beach. Behind, the old tracks of the Trans Vietnam Railroad still clanking north to Hue.

The press compound itself lay at the end of a dirt road that ran beside a French colonial museum sheltering artifacts of the Cham period. Surrounding this travel agent's dream, the tortuous landscape of I Corps: the dense mountains along the DMZ from which the North Vietnamese laid down rocket and mortar barrages. Fighting here meant never straying far from a bunker. These were well-equipped troops operating on a short supply line. South of Da Nang, an area honeycombed with mines would in six years account for almost 50 percent of marine casualties. Khe Sanh, Con Thien, the Rockpile, Hill 881, Dong Ha, An Loc—they were all up here, places once screaming blood from the TV screen, now quiet again under their old scars.

Many lunatic conversations rang through the communications shack in the USMC press center—a row of telephones manned by military operators. The trick was to say you were "press priority" and to keep shouting "WORKING, WORKING, CAN YOU HEAR ME?" during the pauses, or the line was lost in the tangled communications web of the war. It was a queer relationship—Marine Corps hard-liners trying to run a civilian camp for a press they viewed as leftist and antiwar. Arguments and standoffs about where to go and how to get there were routine.

Because the terrain was so dicey and the marines so short on helicopters (being short on anything evokes a perverse Spartan pride in marines), correspondents constantly complained about transportation and information. It was one thing to hitch a ride to the base camp where a unit overnighted, but it could take two or three chopper rides to get you to the action from there. Working I Corps was an exercise in using your wits and hoping for luck. There are no kudos

from the home office when you have to "hurry up and wait"—
sometimes for days—to get near the story you want. In war and journalism, they give medals for results. One day, I bitched so loudly to go
out on an operation that one of the officers threatened to shoot me if
I didn't ease off.

"Go ahead," I said. "Shoot!"

He retreated.

The incident made the rounds, although it was not my first skirmish with the Corps. One public affairs officer, the memorable Major
Joel Martin, decided early on I was not manageable. Martin's practiced belligerence—evidenced in altercations with other correspondents and fellow marines—eventually earned him the title of "punch-
out artist." At least one newsman is said to have filed charges against
him for physical abuse, but later dropped them. Officially, his orders
were to escort and inform the press. You wouldn't have known it.

One day, out with the 101st Airborne around Hue, the battalion
commander took me into his confidence: his troopers were looking for
three marines lured away from their units by prostitutes working for
the Vietcong. We followed a series of grisly directions left by the VC
in search of the men: signs, for example, in which the men's dog tag
numbers were crudely carved. Eventually, the bodies were found, and
I returned to Da Nang. There was no way to file a story without
suggesting the identity of the men, and the sad, squalid circumstances
of their deaths could only add shame to the grief of their families. I
wasn't filing this one.

At the bar that night, I mentioned the story to Major Martin, who
automatically assumed NBC was going with it. He moved in for the
kill. "You run that story and it's your ass. If your network wants a fight,
we're happy to give them one. NBC will be out of this country in
twenty-four hours."

"Just try," I said. It was now a point of pride as well as good
journalism. Besides, watching him squirm made my day. The story, of
course, never appeared because I never sent it. Still, I made certain
that the good major knew my editorial judgment had nothing to do
with his bad manners.

At best, the press center brass viewed newsmen as enemies of the
Republic. How could it be otherwise when fellow marines were spilling their blood for a cause the press deemed counterfeit? Throw in the
woman factor—a female combat reporter who gave lip back with the
best of 'em—and there lay the makings of a different kind of war. On

the popularity charts, I was right up there with Hanoi Hannah, the radio propagandist in the north who was Charlie's answer to Tokyo Rose.

It was only when I got back to the States that I heard anything to the contrary. One day I was stopped by Chet Huntley, just returned from addressing a USMC convention on the West Coast. "The PAOs were telling me they really had it in for you over there," he said. "But they admitted it wasn't until some time went by that they realized you never stiffed them on a story. Never told it wrong, or gave them a bum rap. You know, they were really surprised."

In the autumn of 1968 I spent a lot of time trudging the mountains and valleys of I Corps with the marines. Again the old question: "Hey, why are you here? You're a civilian and you don't have to be," alternating with the even more familiar, "What's a nice girl like you doing in a place like this?" I would look at the ground and make my standard journalism speech, or on the nice girl matter, I would sometimes parry with, "Never mind that. What's a nice guy like you doing in a place like this?"

Not a day went by in the field without someone asking me if we got extra pay for being there. The fact was, NBC correspondents drew $100 a month combat pay. By the end of 1968, my salary amounted to $25,521. I knew I was getting paid less than my male colleagues, but I wanted the story so bad, wanted to be a correspondent so much, that I never complained about money.

Our preoccupation with marines at that point coincided with the on-again, off-again oscillation of the peace talks. We wanted to be in place to see what the North Vietnamese troops just north of the line would do in the event of a bombing halt, although one couldn't imagine the shelling getting any worse.

I was definitely learning the ropes: diving into bunkers in "Leatherneck Square" when the incoming started; choppering onto the red clay of "Firebase Sandy," 2,100 feet above the jungle floor, where on a clear day you could actually see the NVA moving south; hovering low over the mountains as our Medevac plucked from the jungle a soldier who had broken his back on recon; "returning" to Khe Sanh because going over old ground was all you could do in a war where we didn't hold territory and advance. What a shock of recognition to read some years later in an official Marine Corps history that "battles would be fought and refought against the almost invisible enemy on the same ground."

Apart from the obvious lessons of knowing what to be afraid of, how to lessen the risks of getting hurt and increase the chances of getting a story, there were larger truths to discover. All my John Wayne images evaporated the first time I saw a short skinny kid with fifty pounds on his back trying to make it up the steep side of a jagged peak along the DMZ. Hanging around the marines in this neighborhood dispelled other illusions, too. In Vietnam I learned the difference between men and women. Combat provided a rare view of that male primeval instinct to take territory and defend it against an outside threat. It was a stark contrast to the civilized world where men posture and women primp. Meeting a guy or gal at a cocktail party on Monday, making the date on Wednesday, going out the door all dressed up on Saturday, minding your manners. In war, the masks come off. When the shooting started, man's instinct was to hunt and defend—quite a dazzling sight. Mine was to retreat, and no course in basic training would have changed that.

I will never forget the blond, blue-eyed young man I interviewed after the NVA had overrun his position. In the hand-to-hand-fighting that followed he had whipped out a survival knife and slaughtered his attacker. "What were you thinking of as you cut his throat?" I asked.

"Well, ma'am," he said politely. "It was either him or me."

Although most men do not like to admit it, war is seductive—not just trumpets calling them to heroic deeds and glory but literally and sexually seductive. Flushed with excitement, raging toward resolution and domination, men in battle often feel an erotic rush. One late afternoon, flying "home" after a dicey day in the field, I struck a clinical pose and asked a young lieutenant about this. Nodding vigorously, he yelled over the engine noise: "Let me tell you, when a real good firefight gets going, it's like screwing six women at the same time."

As one of a very few American women among more than a half-million American soldiers, I gave up all hope of camouflaging sexual differences. But there were the inevitable wacky reminders of conventional modesty abandoned. For example, that day after a crushing downpour, when I stealthily stripped down to my all-cotton briefs to change clothes in the door gunner's seat of a chopper 1500 feet over the Delta. By instinct and then by hard-learned habit, I worked out how to minimize the sex issue. It was crucial to know when to become invisible, as on that day at a base camp up north when a marine general and I unexpectedly ran smack into 300 of his men—out in the open taking showers. I pretended not to notice; it would only have made it an episode.

The worst moments came when men, as is their wont, couldn't resist showing off, especially those who had mastered some of the war's more glamorous skills, such as flying helicopters. Often, we flew in formation into or out of an operation, perhaps a dozen ships. The pilots never seemed to be able to resist playing tag, getting as close as they could to the next chopper, waving or reaching out. Getting on top, in front, or ahead, any which way to show what they could do with these birds. They were all twelve years old again, walking the picket fence for their girls. And me with my heart pounding and my mouth gone dry, trying to smile and praying so hard they would knock it off.

As to what to do when nature called, I developed the refined technique of "thinking dry," keeping toilet trips into the bush at a minimum, even though the guys who stood guard—to make sure Charlie wasn't around—usually didn't mind. Life in the boonies had a way of equalizing. Still, there was always a silent message in the hush that descended when a woman showed up. Particularly in the field. Voices dropped to a murmur, faces turned toward you in awe. Primordial respect, born out of the agony of war: it went with entry into the world of men.

As reporters, all of us in some way had to harden our hearts to much of the nonmilitary agony as well, the Amerasian infants abandoned in the villages, the Vietnamese children maimed and scarred. I stopped looking at them early in the game—the scrawny arms and dirty knees, the rags for clothes, the unblinking almond eyes asking questions I couldn't answer. Combat wasn't as lethal as thinking about these children could be. Writing about them, taking their picture, making their case journalistically was one thing. To get personally involved would have meant the first trip down a road no reporter should travel— total myopia.

By the time I arrived in Saigon, a heavy sense of ennui had set in among the resident press corps, an attitude of futility, even exasperation, as to whether the war was winnable or worth the try. No one had to spell it out, but I had a sharp impression that getting in the paper or on the air often meant producing stories that buttressed gloomy assumptions about the war: all Americans involved were moral mutants, all South Vietnamese were corrupt, the Hanoi troops fought nobly for a just cause. In any war there are images and information enough to bolster any view. But early on I was shocked to learn that if you did twenty interviews in the field with GIs, chances were those who knocked the war would survive the editor's scissors. I complained to Corrigan when he was in Saigon one day—I had just come in with a series of interviews on Nixon's peace plan—and he put his fingers to his lips and told me to calm down. One NBC correspondent spent the better part of a week, waiting with his cameraman in the shadows of the Eden Building to get pictures of a street-corner black market exchange, even though he, like the rest of us, made our trades with the same man.

The war still had its champions in the press, but time took its toll; and reporters who had soured on the story made it clear over drinks, in the field, at the briefings, and, perhaps unconsciously, in their copy. They seemed so certain about it all, and perhaps owing to my inexperience or ignorance, I felt certain about very little. One night at a private dinner party Charlie Mohr of the *Times*, a solid critic of the administration's policy, lunged over the roasted chicken, grabbed another correspondent by his shirt front, and threatened to rearrange his face. The man had dared voice support for the war.

Young newsmen caught on early to the prevailing wisdom. Perhaps that was why so many of the celebrated pictures from this war depicted the miseries of the innocent. (Although separating the innocent from the VC could be a tricky business.) Whereas in World War II the focus of great photography had been on the troops, the GI slogging his way to victory, in Vietnam it often seemed to be the press's commentary on a war it didn't like.

Although reporters would bristle at the notion, the infantryman's inescapable world of grit, terror, and fatigue was not a way of life for most combat newsmen in southeast Asia. This was more true for print guys than television crews. We had to get the pictures and *be there*. And even when there, the pictures had to be interesting enough to tell a story and put it on the air. Words were never enough. But reporters were not "traveling with the army" in Vietnam, and no action was so far away that you couldn't get back home when you felt you had your story. The helicopter and its daily access to a warm bath and a restaurant meal in Saigon presented a powerful lure to come in from the field. Perhaps it was inevitable that this sense of imminent release affected everyone's commitment to the war itself, even the GI's. He couldn't leave when he chose, but he did have two guaranteed R and Rs in a set one-year tour. His relationship to the war was often as impersonal as the correspondent's to the troops. Both were counting down the days.

Money and class may have played their part, too. By the mid-1960s the poorly paid, ink-stained wretches of earlier decades had been replaced by a middle class of well-paid newsmen, not to mention overpaid TV types. What empathy could they truly feel, what language could they speak, to a GI who more often than not was their "inferior" in class and background? It shouldn't make a difference—but it did. A press corps, for the most part conditioned by liberal education and newfound affluence, felt estranged from the lower-middle-class men who were fighting this war. It was easier to talk to officers and less boring in so many cases, especially if the twenty-second sound bites (they were longer then) had to count for something. The press viewed the grunts much the same way leftist antiwar forces back home viewed the war's supporters—so many blue-collar types out of the wrong schools or none at all. Small wonder then, that a kind of repugnance crept into their stories: for this place, for these people, for the war itself.

"It won't bite you. Just sit in it for awhile and get the hang of it. It's a great ride."

I was crammed into the pilot's seat of an F-4 Phantom jet, the driver's stick arranging my legs in a position only comfortable if you are a man or a cello player.

"Oh, sure." My response, dripping with doubt, was lost in the thunder of another Phantom leaving the runway on its way to North Vietnam. I was going nowhere. Even the commander of the 366th Tactical Fighter Wing tried to persuade me. "Just a two-day training course to get used to G-pull. A real cinch. I'll fly you myself."

Frankly, I didn't care if Charles Lindbergh took me up. This lady was not leaving the ground at 200 miles an hour on top of a live bomb. Weighing the risk against the story didn't enter into this equation. The plane was a two-seater, pilot and backseater, which meant I would be going along for a 700-MPH joy ride with no cameraman and therefore no pictures. If a cameraman sat backup instead, the speed, altitude, and attitudes of the fighter, plus the limits of the cameras we used, could only result in either blurred images or none at all. The fact was, there was no story a TV camera could really do about the air war in North Vietnam. Although several of my male counterparts sought these joy rides, it was more bravado than journalistic enterprise. The print guys could at least give vent and space to colorful narratives about how it felt to challenge gravity. As for getting down to the nitty-gritty—an actual combat mission—there was simply no room for any extra bodies, a fact that also applied to rescue helicopters, the Jolly Green Giants, which were used to pick up downed pilots.

On the flight line this day, sitting prissily above the wings, even with the engine off, I somehow felt that this malevolent-looking piece of metal would go its own way. The thought must have worked itself into the furrows of a frown because the man making the sales pitch started laughing. "Hey, you'd get a real kick out of it once you're airborne."

Here it was, a fighter pilot right out of central casting. He was the squadron commander, and his name was Don D'Amico: a light colonel, heavy on the smart-aleck side. It seemed to go along with an occupation dreamed by many and held by few. You couldn't help wonder if flight schools held secret courses in cockiness, guts, and dash. Rakishness 101. D'Amico personified it, but his dark-eyed good looks and easy manner made you think it was all a put-on.

I met him at the Da Nang air base after Donghi, in Saigon, approved my idea to do a story on an ace—a pilot who had shot down at least five enemy aircraft. "We don't have an ace," I was told by one of the PAOs, "but we can introduce you to the hottest pilot we have." I agreed, especially after I learned D'Amico had flown 143 missions in the Korean War.

There were no aces up to this point in the war because of the bombing restrictions. To engage enemy aircraft meant penetrating their territory, so air-to-air fights were rare. In March 1968, President Johnson had suspended bombing north of the twentieth parallel, about 250 miles north of the DMZ, in the same key speech in which he announced he would not seek another term in office. By early April, the bombing limit had dropped to the nineteenth parallel. By July, pilots were forbidden to pursue enemy aircraft north of that line.

When it went into effect in March 1965, Pentagon poets had named the bombing program Rolling Thunder, one of those enemy-be-warned labels. The operation was carried out with frequent adjustments and lulls, so much so that Operation Window Shade would have more accurately described the frequency with which the northern boundary was changed. There were restricted zones in which aircraft could retaliate only if attacked, prohibited zones where they required specific authorization for any action, and buffer zones where American aircraft could enter air space but not bomb. Hanoi, the seat of the enemy's government, was on the no-no list because of concern about civilian casualties. The port city of Haiphong, a major supply point, was declared off limits for fear of hitting neutral or Soviet ships. And near the Chinese border any number of off-limits areas turned pilots into tightrope walkers for fear of violating Chinese air space. Many areas in North Vietnam were deemed "not hostile," a point of some confusion to men with orders to fight where the enemy lives. It was supposed to be a "policy of persuasion," a slow-squeeze master plan. In effect, the air war strategy added up to a crazy quilt of evasions and avoidances, a no-win plan destined to test the enemy's will but not to break it.

At home, antiwar protestors kept up the pressure, and on the battlefield, the North Vietnamese played the movement like a Bach fugue. Point counterpoint. For every peace march, another political or military offensive. Still, the administration thought pandering to the North Vietnamese—introducing a bombing lull or restriction—would establish good faith for a negotiated settlement. We were, in effect, begging for peace. It was a major policy shift for the administration, and for Johnson in particular an abandonment of his dedication to the war's legitimacy. This was a way out. The trouble was, the North Vietnamese weren't taking it.

Caught in the middle of this self-defeating policy were the fighter pilots. As warriors they marched to a different drummer, and D'Amico was true to type. He grew up in Rochester, New York, the son of Sicilian immigrants, which eliminated the need for translations or footnotes when we talked. He joined the army in 1947 after being thrown out of college for having beer and a girl in his room. As a young hotshot pilot stationed in Niagara Falls, he heard that the local newspaper's society editor wanted to do a story on his squadron, so he assigned one of his married pilots to take her up for a ride. "I was a young bachelor. I didn't want to be fooling around with some old biddy," he told me.

Then he saw "this good-looking woman," Dora. They dated for two years and broke up because "I just didn't have time to get married. I was flying." Dora became engaged to another man. Then one night, as drunk as any fighter pilot can get, Don turned up at her house, suggested she return the other fellow's ring, and proposed. They were married in 1956.

While there was no way to depict for TV what fighter pilots really did in this war, I started hanging around with Don and some of his friends whenever I could. The antiwar movement pinned the "murderer" label on pilots early in the war, and so sitting in a trailer in the late hours of a Da Nang night, hearing them talk about their patriotism and, at the same time, their moral reservations about the conduct of the war opened a new door. Bombing the same bridge, the same road, week after week. "Not only that," said Don at one point. "Half the time they know our destination while we're warming up on the runway. See that grass? How many VC do you think are in there monitoring our radios and relaying the targets to Hanoi before we're even off the ground? A lot, I can tell you." Professional pride is a staple of the fighter pilot business, and the air war in Vietnam did little for it.

As danger, fear, and dying are taboo discussion topics with fighter pilots, I stayed away from the heavy stuff. Don had had his share of riding crippled airplanes back to home base, stories told with the appropriate hand and arm twists and a mocking laugh. Still, like many fighter jocks, he harbored superstitions, certain rabbit's-foot quirks about playing the odds in the fighter game. D'Amico didn't like flying missions on Sundays. As squadron commander, he made sure Sunday was his day off. "I've flown three Sundays here, and they were all rescue missions," he told me. "Guys who were shot down. So I've decided to do my paperwork on a Sunday. Get up early, go to mass on the base, do my paperwork, and then go over to China Beach for a swim."

We wound up doing a piece on fighter pilots and their thoughts on the war. D'Amico predictably voiced his support, despite the bitter truth that he and his men were hunting the enemy at a severe disadvantage. He was a type all right, a generation of men who defended their country with conviction. D'Amico, and many like him, confirmed my opinion, not just about the "morality" of the war, but about the heroism of so many who fought it. I had a feeling that I hadn't heard the last of the colonel.

WHILE jockeying over the air war and the peace talks dragged on, we continued to slog through mud up north with the marines. On patrol near the DMZ, we could hear a deep rumble echoing throughout the valleys, a slam that made the ground quiver. No ordinary incoming. The battleship New Jersey, in service for the first time since the Korean War, spoke through her sixteen-inch guns. Another piece of hardware had been added to the American arsenal, debuting on station September 30. The old battleship lurked just a few thousand yards off the coast, tempting the Communist offshore batteries, hurling 2,700-pound shells into supply dumps and artillery positions, searching for the ineluctable enemy filing south. Firing with utter futility deep into a jungle that even by day under canopies of fog and brush protected its heart of darkness.

A change of pace came early one morning, when Nghia, one of the NBC cameramen, ran to my hooch. He had picked up some good intelligence. "Big firefight, big, very big. Thuong Duc, Thuong Duc."

Nghia, barely reaching my shoulder in height, was jumping around like water on a griddle. While I threw stuff into my field pack, he told me the Special Forces camp at Thuong Duc was under siege. It lay in the narrow valley of the Song Vu Gia near the Laotian border, about thirty miles southwest of Da Nang. At least three North Vietnamese regiments on the high ground encircled the camp. Enemy troops had already raised the NVA flag over five villages just one mile away. Villagers streamed into the district headquarters protected by the SF. Montagnard tribesmen, trained by the Green Berets, were taking heavy losses. The only way in and out was by chopper, and the NVA was shooting many of them down—including at least three Medevacs clearly marked with red crosses.

Nghia and I raced over to SF headquarters a few miles away, and even as we spilled out of the car, two choppers were coming in for a landing. They set down near a warrant officer who was gesturing at the pilots, waiting for them as he piled up boxes of bread. The rotors never stopped as dead and badly wounded Montagnards were unloaded. They could have come from only one place, and that's where we were headed.

We screamed through the noise, asking the pilot to take us on. He shrugged and gave us a thumbs up. The W.O., now loading the bread, shook his head. Two SF officers appeared, one of them a colonel. My heart lurched. Red tape, PAO traps, oh God no. But I should have known better. These guys weren't called the Jesuits of the armed forces for nothing. What was that SF motto I heard around the country: "You have never lived until you've almost died. And life has a flavor the protected will never know." The officers looked at each other, and then at us, with what I distinctly caught as a flicker of recognition. "You're clear for Thuong Duc—at your own risk. Good luck."

Once we were airborne, Nghia, Yashiro, a Japanese sound man, and I beamed at our good luck. Another chopper victory, another ride on the machine that could make your day or "mess up your afternoon," save you or kill you. Who could even imagine a picture of this country without a mechanical grasshopper in the frame. They went together, like a bird and its nest. Air mobility, we sure had it. From the air—wind in your hair, engine power in your gut—everything seemed possible.

Not until we had the camp in sight did I begin to realize that the risk-versus-story odds looked bad. Thoughts of Langvei came up, another SF camp on the Laotian border, except that the enemy held it now. The NVA overran it one February night—with tanks.

The pilot dropped us like a stone into a hot LZ. A mad scramble came out, and then we ran, hunched over. The warrant officer was pulling off the bread. Mortars and rockets slammed in around us, so close it seemed we would never reach the small rise about 100 yards away where the bunkers were dug. The movements of a nightmare, slow motion, running through glue, reaching for home. My head jerked up—and through the shimmering heat and flying dirt I got my first look at a Green Beret in the thick of it. Standing at the top of the hill, then stumbling toward us. A tall young man—about twenty-one perhaps—limping badly on a bloody and bandaged leg. Around his forehead, another bandage stained red. Dirty, exhausted, he staggered forward, trying to gather up the bread and get us up the hill at the same time. His eyes were dead, but he was animal alert.

The moment we reached the entrance to the main bunker, the chopper we had just landed in took off, reached 100 feet, was hit by enemy ground fire, and spiraled down. Rough hands pushed us into the bunker so there was no time to look back. Later we heard no one aboard survived.

Below ground, the SF team looked like regulars on Dante's tour of the hot spots. They accepted us as part of the team, with no big deal about having a "lady" around. "We figure if you've gotten this far, ma'am, you know what it's all about." That's what *he* thought.

It was noon, plenty of time left to film, except that looking for daylight meant tempting the patience of NVA spotters. Every time anyone popped his head up, the shelling resumed. In the bunker, we needed additional light to get a decent image, which meant a hand-held "frezzy" light, guaranteed to distract these kids already under pressure, and certain to produce a lousy image. Meanwhile in this small, dark space, the large-scale drama played itself out. Another chopper was shot down, along with two fighters. Finally, the radio-man, the most harried guy on the team, advised that no more aircraft try to land. The wounded, many of them children, suffered most.

There was no way to get them out under fire. The Montagnards kept taking heavy losses, staggering back to camp late in the day with their SF commander, looking like legions of the damned. We weren't getting out this day.

"They're gonna try to take us," said the young man in bandages.

Several interrogated prisoners confirmed this. They had orders to overrun Thuong Duc and hold it. Big surprise. All eight SF camps on the Laotian border existed for this very reason, to lure the enemy into the south, where they could be fought. Pursuing them into the sanctuaries of Laos and Cambodia was not allowed under another of these strange rules of engagement. We were all bait.

For the rest of the afternoon, air strikes around the perimeter set our teeth on edge. With all the priority radio traffic, it was impossible to get a message through to Saigon about our situation, so in the lousy light and cramped quarters we kept updating our film record of a camp under siege the best we could. It was going to be one of those stories in which the best and most terrifying parts would simply never be seen on television.

At 6 P.M. I had dinner by adding hot water to a frozen tuna casserole in a plastic bag, LURP rations, standard issue for long range reconnaissance patrols. At 6:30 P.M. an SF sergeant announced "all Americans" assemble for a meeting at 1900 hours. I was amused; it wasn't as though we had far to go. At 7 P.M. we sat in a semicircle as a young sergeant, bare-chested and limping from a leg wound, stood over us and began the "E and E" briefing: exfiltration (escape) and evacuation. In other words, how to get the hell out of here when the bad guys overrun the perimeter. He told us how to cut the barbed wire around the camp, at the spot where there were no mines laid, the E and E route (which way to run through the jungle), the passwords, the rendezvous point, alternate and primary pickup zones. As he spoke, I noticed another member of the team sitting next to me. He was fiddling with a bunch of wires and a block of C-4. I inquired. He was a demolition man and he was wiring the bunkers. Once we had the signal to run for it, they would blow the whole place. After that, it would be summer camp for everyone.

Nghia, Yashiro, and I looked at one another in united disbelief. They were, of course, smiling, the usual Asian reaction to impending disaster. I envisioned myself hurtling through the jungle, losing my glasses and my way, getting captured. They said that NVA officers might not kill you. Not so lucky if you're captured by the rank and file. Another great story, I thought, with no film to ship.

"Numbah ten situation," said Nghia, no longer smiling.

Cornered. No options. No control. Just take orders and don't run out of hope. Funny how danger makes your throat close and your insides shake. So much easier to be a woman when you're afraid, with no locker room rules to live up to, with total freedom to show your fear without shame. And yet, instead of panic I felt only crushing loneliness. A noiseless void. The sadness of the universe wrapping me in a veil. My mind raced to my father. He was my only hope for getting out of here, for pulling through. I remembered him standing on the bank of the frozen pond in Edgewood Avenue Park where he took me ice skating on Saturday afternoons—worried about the thickness of the ice, ready to rescue me if it proved too thin. Growing up in New Haven, when there was no Vietnam.

Thomas Trotta, the displaced Italian peasant, paterfamilias, heir to centuries of male domination, but never saying anything about the many who thought women should know their place. "A surgeon, a criminal lawyer—that is what you will be." It never seemed to occur to him I couldn't do what a man does, and so it didn't occur to me either. But when it became apparent I was on the way to a life of journalism, he balked. Given his liberalism about my career ideas, I was mystified. So one day I asked him why.

"Because it will break your heart," he said.

These were words I would understand many years later—always wondering how this soft-spoken man from Amalfi could possibly know about such things. If he was afraid of anything, even death, he never showed it. Call it girlhood faith, but I knew he was looking down from somewhere on this terrifying place, still steering me away from the thin ice.

The night was spent in fitful sleep on the bunker floor, Nghia, Yashiro, and I side by side. When the shelling stopped before dawn, we surfaced and sat outside. Fresh air, laced with the scent of phosphorous, but still fresh air. Fourth of July in the night sky. An AC-47 "Spooky" was working the perimeter. This fixed-wing airplane, another gizmo in the American bag of tricks, fired miniguns at a rate of 6,000 rounds per minute into the darkness below, every seventh round a tracer, etching an orange gash across a sky full of stars.

Then, suddenly, the enemy's rockets and mortars lifted from their resting place and rained on the camp. We dived back into the bunker and waited until first light filtered through and silence returned. All I heard was a ringing in my ears. Then the far-off muffled slice of a chopper.

Deliverance!

Filthy, worn out, exulting at the chance to get out, we made a break for it. Maybe the NVA spotters were eating their morning gruel. The chopper rocked and rolled as it hovered about shoulder-level to us. The pilot beckoned wildly. The shelling started. And diving off the chopper, on his way into this little part of hell, one of my colleagues from the AP. It wasn't every day you could get a beat on a wire service. Still, I felt sorry for him. He was about to serve his sentence at Thuong Duc. We twisted up and out horizontally, clutching the gear and the story in the red onion sack, watching the black spurts of flak, pushing and straining psychically to move this beloved hunk of metal into the safety of the clouds. "What the hell am I doing here?" The answer: Just trying to make a living.

Another flight home, leaning into the wind, heart still pumping and yet a voice telling me I needed a break. Even my St. Christopher medal was rusting. In a few days, I would be in Hong Kong on R and R, the precious ten-day rest accorded correspondents every two months. The very thought of it relegated Thuong Duc in my mind to what it looked like from 20,000 feet, a gray speck in a black valley shrouded in smoke.

Slowly, I began to reenter the little world of my own body. That's how it went once the guns were silent, turning inward and discovering you are besieged by your own biology. Time for a relief from the smell of a body that began to sicken you. A splash from a flacon of "Je Reviens" really didn't lighten the scent but helped the morale. Time for relief from those "lightweight" jungle boots so heavy on the march, especially through the paddies, rubbing against the heel blisters, swelling the feet; from the fear of scorpions stinging, leeches squiggling and sucking, driving you wild; from creepy surprises of the jungle, like that low-hanging hive of red ants I bumped into one morning on patrol in the Delta when it took four GIs to get them out of my hair and trousers; from the cracking thirst for cold water; the contracting pains of an empty stomach; the mildew and wetness in which even a scratch festered for days; the invisible parasites revealing themselves in red dots on your face; the chafe and burn of any two pieces of skin rubbing together; the thought of wetting your fatigues in fear; the nausea of motion sickness in choppers, fixed-wings, jeeps, armored personnel carriers, and trucks; the screech and thunder of noise; the choking on dust, the tasting of dirt. Time for relief from the slow breaking of your heart.

The Thuong Duc story aired the next night. It got two minutes on

"Huntley-Brinkley." Looking at the piece months later, I was shocked at how little resemblance it bore to what we had experienced—pretty aerial shots taken as we descended over the camp in no way conveyed the terrible odds of getting shot down; deadly incoming showed up only as pinpricks of light in the dark. The hundreds of ways to get hurt or killed remained invisible on the small screen in so many of the pieces broadcast from the war. Only the pictures of dead and wounded conveyed the horror, and by now it was nightly fare for an audience numbed by war. I wondered how many viewers had gone to the kitchen for a beer during the harrowing story of Thuong Duc.

Hong Kong revived me. My Amalfi of the East. I sat for hours, trancelike before the spectacular view, in the café atop Victoria Peak or on the veranda of the old Repulse Bay Hotel. The maitre d', a northern Italian, steered me to the lasagna with raisins, and although it didn't taste like home it was a dozen stars up from *bok choy* with *nuoc mam*. One night I went to the movies with Doug Robinson of *The New York Times*. We split our sides watching John Wayne jump out of helicopters in *The Green Berets*. The film was shown in an SF camp back in the Nam and the A-team nearly tore the place apart in rage and laughter. There was no getting away from the war, even in the seductive beauty of Hong Kong.

Going back hurt. And yet I would be lying if I said that I didn't need another fix. Jake had been right. I was on the Vietnam needle, and as I lay on the linen sheets in Honkers, all the phone calls from the brass in New York only boosted my ego and gave me more courage, more ambition, too.

There were no surprises when I returned to Saigon. The gloom, the air conditioner's drone, the sound of scuffling sandals, and the smell of old rice hit me all at once as I pushed open the black doors to the NBC bureau. Donghi, looking even paler than when I last saw him, made his usual gentle gestures. It had become apparent he was in deep trouble with headquarters, especially since they had an on-scene report of how the bureau was doing from Steinman, who had been in town. He spelled it all out in a letter to Reuven Frank in New York. He began by saying that Donghi was a very nice man, liked by everyone, but that he had withdrawn to the point where he couldn't read copy or help produce a piece. In short, he couldn't run the bureau. "He has built a wall between himself and all but a few people here," Steinman wrote, pointing out that Donghi had spent several hours looking for dried mushrooms to make a dish he was experimenting with and that he had esoteric taste in music and wines. It was a devastating report, even reading it now: the portrait of a man going to pieces slowly, a man turning within to shut out the horrors of the war.

"He doesn't know the names of all the Asians (they all look alike, right) and that hurts them because they recognize his blind spot. . . . In many ways he is a delightful man, but he is a hopeless snob." And then, the coup de grace: "He must be fired. It's a case where the head has to be chopped off to save the body."

With this assessment, it would be only a matter of time until management moved in for the kill. Even without being privy to what New York knew, I felt guilty about my own frustration with Frank. I wouldn't have got the assignment without him, and yet I had to face the fact that morale was low. Now the sense of doom in the bureau matched that of the war. More mirror images. It was time to get out of town. Frank gave me my next assignment. "You did so well with the Marines last time around," he said. "We're sending you up to Con Thien on the DMZ."

Mentally, I was already up north, where the Communists were shelling blazes out of the border outposts, their defiant response to the bombing halt, which had gone into effect on October 31. The basis of the understanding with North Vietnam was that they would cease all infiltration and shelling. They had foxed us again.

"You've heard. You've heard, haven't you?" It was Andy Guthrie, bearing down on me with all his combat gear, including a helmet. He loved wearing the costume of the realm.

He seemed flustered, not an uncommon state for Andy, but even more frantic. "D'Amico. Colonel Don D'Amico. He's been shot down."

I just stared at him.

"It was all in the *Stars and Stripes* while you were on R and R. He's okay though. They got him out of the sea. A real hairy rescue. He's all broken up, in the hospital at Da Nang."

Pictures of speed and fire and water zipped through my mind, unedited, without sound, not for broadcast. "What day was it, Andy?" I asked.

"What day? Let's see. Oh yeah. It was October 20th. A Sunday."

7

THROUGH THE SIFTER

Da Nang rattled in the storm. Tents flattened against the driving winds. Screen doors slammed. Ponchos flailed as officers grabbed for their caps in the sudden gusts. The hot rain shivered in mud puddles on the empty runways, promising a still meaner generation of mosquitoes. Mildew thrived as the downpour hammered a melancholy tune on the long rows of tin roofs. A typhoon was churning off the coast north and east of the flight line where fighter jets squatted motionless, mocked by the tropical force. The pilots had "gone to the mattresses." Out of sight, hunkered down. Grounded.

I was battering my way over to the Da Nang Officers' Club, thinking about ironies and coincidences. Bad enough for D'Amico to have gone down on a Sunday, but getting zapped ten days before the bombing halt just wasn't my idea of good timing. The officers' club was dreary: this war and this heat ground everybody down. No light-hearted banter and tales of valor as in those 1940s movies about "intrepid birdmen." No group singing at the bar, no limping wing commanders in sheepskin bomber jackets. No romance or bittersweet joy in fighting for the cause. Plenty of dancing and drinking and fly-boy nonsense, and at the same time a counting of the days.

I sat watching the fighter jocks lean on the bar. I had called D'Amico at the hospital. Visit, hell. He'd meet me at the club. There were stories about what had happened, but no pictures—not even a snapshot. All those Battle of Britain documentaries, all those grainy newsreels of flak hurtling toward Allied bombers over the Ruhr. This air war was invisible.

Fighter and bomber pilots were the unseen players in Vietnam. Television couldn't show what they did, and the policy makers and war managers found no way to make it possible. Besides, the television networks themselves, out of corporate inertia or ideology, weren't pushing for adequate equipment. So the war protestors could call the pilots murderers and make it stick, unseen men dropping napalm and high explosives on "innocent civilians." There was simply no way to offset it. Air time went to the grunts, 18-year-old kids sloshing through the mud to get their heads blown off, while the heroism of the air war went unrecorded.

D'Amico made a show of it, walking slowly into the club in his flight suit, gamely concealing his broken neck and back. He sat through dinner on a hard chair, skidding as fast as possible over the facts of that Sunday mission. He had been hit over Dong Hoi going in low to take out some antiaircraft guns. Except for a few cracks about the worthy enemy, he made it sound like a routine day at the office. But there was something different: a new look in his eyes, a hint of vulnerability. Part of the daredevil spirit seemed chipped away.

"What happened out there? Or would you rather not talk about it?"

"It was wild." He smiled crookedly. "The weather was pretty much like it is today." He leaned forward in his seat, looking toward the window, already reaching for the sky.

It had been raining for days. Word was out that a bombing halt was imminent, so the jocks were antsier than usual, waiting for the weather to clear. Every day the "frag" would come in—the fragmentation order which

*contained a list of the targets assigned to each squadron—but no one left the
ground.*

*It was Saturday night. D'Amico was playing poker in his trailer. The
roof leaked, so there were pots and pans on the floor to catch the drops. You
could hear the blink-blink over the muffled bidding. The trailer sat at an
angle, and water missing a pot flowed toward the bedroom. At about ten
o'clock the noise got fainter; D'Amico looked out. He saw a moon and
reached for the phone. The rain had stopped, and the overcast was breaking.
The frag was "up." Missions were posted. It was a go.*

*By 5 A.M. Sunday morning D'Amico was listening to the intelligence
officer's briefing at operations. He picked up his maps, photography, and
weather and briefed his backseater, Lieutenant Sam Wilburn, and his wingman in the second fighter. The call signs for the two F-4 Phantoms: Dover
Lead and Dover Two. D'Amico, as squadron commander, had assigned
himself the mission even though it was Sunday.*

*At 5:30 A.M. the faint light made silhouettes of the two Phantoms sitting
on the ramp. Facing east, D'Amico watched the sun lifting between the
horizon and the overcast. It was the first mission of the day, routine armed
reconnaissance, no specific targets, a shopping tour. He was carrying eight
750-pound bombs under his wings and on the center line an underslung
20-mm gun with 1,800 rounds of ammo. The gun meant strafing, a maneuver requiring low altitudes, except that pilots were restricted to no lower
than 4,500 feet. The unwritten message was, break the rule when absolutely
necessary—at your own risk.*

*At 6 A.M. the base was stone quiet. Then the deep rumbling and high
whine of the start-up shattered the stillness. Routine. Dover Lead taxied out
to the end of the runway, paused to call up its full power, and in six seconds
roared 7,000 feet across the concrete, trailing flame as it climbed. Dover
Two followed, and both planes vanished into the overcast at 4,000 feet,
emerging into a gray world at 6,000. A typhoon was sitting sixty miles off
the northern coast. It was quiet, so quiet. D'Amico studied his maps as he
soared through his familiar world of silence.*

*The Phantoms reached the letdown point over Hon Co, "Tiger Is-
land," just above the DMZ off the northern coast. There it lay, the Bermuda Triangle of the air war, a patch of enemy ground with enough
antiaircraft guns to bring down a squadron. Both planes dropped through the
overcast in close formation and separated in the clear, D'Amico low at
1,500 feet, his wingman high at 4,000. Beneath them they could see the
main supply route—Route 1A—going north to south. Dover Lead swung
over Dong Hoi and started jinking above the highway, trying to pick out*

"hostile" targets—trucks, supply depots, whatever. The people on the ground could see the two fighters, but there was no response.

"In the southeast corner of Dong Hoi, across a river, was a gun emplacement—three 23-mm quads, a total of twelve guns. I had that in the back of my mind because that town had shot down more friggin' pilots, including an old friend of mine.

"We couldn't see anything—I mean zip—so we headed north to Quang Khe. There was no activity up there, so both planes made a hard left turn and headed south. There's an inlet and a little bridge between Dong Hoi and Quang Khe—it's called Nordine's Pass—every fighter pilot knows it because it was named after one who took a bad hit there—so I told my wingman to hit the pass and then I did something I normally didn't do—I separated. Usually, I insisted in my briefings that planes stay together, but on that day there was no activity. Besides it wasn't that far away, and we knew exactly what our positions were in case of an emergency. So my wingman dropped off at Nordine's Pass, and I headed back south to Dong Hoi looking for that fucking gun.

"About six minutes later, twenty-eight miles south, I looked over my left shoulder and saw the river cutting through town. I knew it was where they off-loaded military supplies from boats and put them on bicycles headed south. I rolled in from the east at 4,500 feet and dropped eight bombs over the main supply depot. Then I pulled up—I must have been a mile away—and saw the guns."

D'Amico's voice, matter-of-fact when he began, now took on the color of his tale—tense, watchful, once more riding the F-4.

"Some guys say never go nose to nose with a gun—but it's more surgical and takes greater skill to go in with a gun than to bomb. You come in, dump two or three hundred rounds in there, then pull up, come back, and drop two or three hundred rounds more. Now you can imagine what that guy must think when he looks up and sees a big, ugly, noisy goddamn F-4 coming down and hears that gun going off. You know he has two choices: he can run like hell and hide in a hole or stay with his gun. This guy stayed. You got to admire his guts. He's got balls."

Dover Lead may have had a psychological advantage, but its firepower—one 20-mm gun loosing 6,000 rounds a minute—didn't match the artillery's:

twelve 23-mm guns getting off 4,500 rounds per minute. Unless he silenced it immediately, 54,000 shells were waiting for Dover Lead for each minute over the battery. They knew he was around; twenty minutes earlier the whole town had seen the Phantoms looking them over, and now they were waiting. D'Amico was about to break a rule he had insisted his squadron follow: never make more than one pass, unless absolutely necessary. It was, of course, a rule he broke when the situation demanded it, once going in eleven times over the same munitions depot.

Lighter now with the bombs gone, D'Amico flew straight. Then he began his roll over the target, his right hand gripping the steering stick, left on the throttle, adjusting the power setting to 450 knots (518 MPH) for the dive angle. Angle and air speed had to be right or the rounds would hit long or short. You have to be in range. Dover Lead was rolling on its back at a 150-degree angle, maneuvering into position to fire. D'Amico was riding a gun and aiming it at the same time, nose down, fifteen tons of steel shrieking toward the target faster than a stone can fall. The pipper, a dot, on the gunsight told him he was tracking the target. NOW. D'Amico squeezed the trigger on the front of his stick with his index finger.

"I rolled in at about 4,000 feet, dived to 1,500 and then just opened up, dumping two or three hundred rounds on this one position. Yeah, the legal limit for strafing was 4,500 feet, but the overcast is 4,500 feet and I'm fragged with a gun, so what am I going to do? What do they expect? The rules would say you shouldn't have been strafing, why didn't you bring the gun home, and I guess some pilots do that. . . ."

It was 6:50 A.M. The firing lasted only five seconds. D'Amico could see the dirt kicking up and the smoke rising as his shells sprayed the guns. He bottomed out between 400 and 450 feet over the target. Then he pulled up and out at a sixty-degree angle, four and a half Gs. His flying suit inflated, keeping the blood in his lungs, draining it from his face. His vision grew dim for a few seconds as he "grayed out."

"I rolled in, I rolled out like that. It was beautiful. I pulled up, and as I pulled up, I mean the whole sky lights up and I could see all this flak around me because it was so dark from the overcast. I'm cranking that thing around and I'm looking behind me and I call Wilburn, my backseater, and I say, 'Did you see where it's coming from?' And he says, 'Rog.' And I said, 'Let's get 'em.' "

D'Amico's voice hung in the air. He paused and sucked in his breath, as though still readying for the attack.

"At about that time, my wingman calls. He's coming back from Nordine's Pass and was watching me.

" 'Dover Lead. Are you in afterburner?'

" 'Negative.'

" 'You're on fire then.'

"I had been looking behind me, so when he said I'm on fire, I looked up front at my instruments. There are four warning lights in the cockpit that indicate engine fire, two red and two amber. All four of them were burned. That was it. That tells you, Sorry, guy, you'd better get out and walk.

"I rolled that sucker out and went into afterburner to get away from the target area. I hit the red jettison button, what pilots call the panic button, and cleaned the airplane. I dropped my gun, my rack, my tanks, everything. Climbing out, I picked up about 300 knots and tried to get to 10,000 feet.

"Almost as soon as I heard I was on fire, I heard another voice on the radio. It was 'Crown'—a big EC-121 aircraft miles away. It's a kind of airborne intelligence center that monitors and coordinates all planes in the area. He knew I was in trouble.

" 'Dover Lead, your pigeons to home plate are 135 and 125.' "

Crown was telling D'Amico what his heading was and how far he was from the runway at Da Nang. Crown kept talking to him, asking "How ya doin'?" keeping him company as he rode the burning fighter. Dover Lead's wingman, who would normally take over at this point in such an emergency, had gone silent. D'Amico called: "Dover Two, let's go Guard," which meant that the two fighters would switch immediately to the emergency frequency. No answer. At most, twenty seconds had passed since the Phantom took the hit. Instinctively, D'Amico headed for the water.

"The first thing I thought was, Shit, I'm hit. I knew I wasn't going to make it and I couldn't believe it. I couldn't believe they got me. I didn't even feel it as I pulled up. And I never thought about getting hit, much less about getting killed. So I sat there thinking, Well, I'll be a sonofabitch.

"The plane was moving, but it was rattling a lot. I was flying straight and level, trying to get the hell out of there—east—over the coast, around Tiger Island, and down the coast to Da Nang. I knew I had to eject, and I wanted to be as far away from shore as possible. That typhoon was still out there, and I knew the direction of the wind would carry me toward the coast while I was floating.

"Dover Two was on the radio again. He says, 'Boy, your right engine's really torching.' So I shut down my right engine, and the warning light went out.

"You're lookin' pretty good," my wingman tells me.

"And now I think, Jesus, maybe I can make it back. Crown is telling me they're alerting rescue, that a chopper's coming out to get me. Then my wingman calls again: 'Your left engine's starting to look bad.'

"So then I figure maybe the fire is out on the right engine, so I come back on the left engine and start up the right engine. And I mean just like the book. I hit the air start button, come around the horn, come into idle, tailpipe temperature starts going up, RPM starts going up, just like a regular start—and then the airplane goes BOOM! It blows up.

"I heard two voices. First, my wingman says: 'Oh, oh!' Then Wilburn in back says: 'I'm leaving.' "

The ejection rocket blew Wilburn's canopy and seat. D'Amico remained in the aircraft for a split second, the plane breaking up around him. He felt the crippled Phantom pitch and then roll nose down to starboard. Dover Lead was going down, its pilot twisted in the cockpit. He reached for the ejection handle between his legs, but the violent movement threw him to the left. Straining, he pulled the lever, firing the ejection rocket. He punched out at 9,000 feet, still twisting as the flying wreck fell away. Barely nine minutes had passed since the North Vietnamese gunner found his mark.

"I remember feeling a sharp pain in my neck and my lower back. Then I passed out."

Abruptly D'Amico sat up straight, still feeling the pain, returning to the present. "You know the rest," he said. "And here I am ready to go home in a few days."

I could see it was killing him, a mission uncompleted, a warrior without a war. "Hey," I said. "You've flown over a hundred missions. There's a limit."

"How can you put a limit on what you can do for your country?" he asked.

No answer. Perhaps because few people asked such questions in those years. A few days later, D'Amico was shipped out to endure eight months of hell in military hospitals. They said his flying days were over.

What had really happened on that mission? Television hadn't

recorded it. There was no one to see it. For Americans back home in their living rooms, had it really happened? If a tree falls in the forest and there is no one to hear the crash, is there a sound?

There were no pictures of the fall of Dover Lead—or of the hundreds of other planes flown by men who believed in the war and whose thoughts and exploits in defense of that idea were never heard nor seen. The air war sent no message, while war on the ground sent a cry of pain, exhaustion, and futility. Let's pack up and go home.

By the end of 1968, all those who thought there was a chance of winning couldn't be heard above the storm of the peace movement. Even if they got through, was anyone listening? Silence told its own story.

It seemed as though America itself, like a downed pilot, had been stunned deaf to the ritual radio message of a search plane, the eerie, mournful pleas into the wilderness begging for a reply if the missing man was still alive and free. Once every minute, for forty-eight or even seventy-two hours, a signal to the lost man, intoning the same words.

"Dover Lead, Come up Beeper, Come up Guard."

"Dover Lead, Come up Beeper, Come up Guard."

Dover, Charlie, Sparrow—whatever their battle call—that haunting plea sounded in every cockpit of every airborne plane, reminding pilots that a brother was down. Too often it was a call to the dead, answered only by the mute rebuke of the jungles and hills.

Vo Huynh and I were spending the night in a whorehouse. Where else do you go when all the hotel rooms in town are taken? My life seemed to be alternating between days of terror under fire and nights of wishing upon the stars. The quaint wooden bungalow stood flanked by coconut palms on the broad white beach at Nha Trang, with the South China Sea lapping just yards below—a picture postcard, except you wouldn't send it home to Mom.

Nha Trang drew the R and R crowd, guys from the field, journalists looking for a day off. We had just left an action at Ban Me Thuot and needed distraction, and in Vietnam you took it where you found it. This evening I was on a bawdyhouse porch, talking to a bunch of GIs between their carefully timed ecstasies.

At first the men seemed embarrassed by my presence, but on hearing I was a reporter from a set of initials that reminded them of home, they might just as well have been talking to their cousin Nellie. About

2 A.M., there were enough people on hand for a seminar. Even in war, women wind up listening much of the time, and as usual the talk turned to in-country gossip, lore, and legends. It always surprised me that even for those directly involved—whether journalists or military—despite the miles of footage leaving the country every week, much of the truth of this war was left to divination, obscured by a fog of gossip and rumor. No surprise to find it settling in over a Nha Trang veranda.

Did the VC really booby-trap a "crapper"? And had a luckless trooper used it? How about that attack from the "hoop snake," sometimes called "the step-and-a-half," you know, the one that rolled itself into a hoop, chased you, bit you, and left you dead one and a half steps later.

Persistent scuttlebutt revolved around phantom regiments, enemy units that never seemed to be where MACV thought they were, and mysterious non-Vietnamese military men seen commanding enemy forces in action. One day it was a black marine sergeant who had gone AWOL, on another, a White Russian officer, on still another, a German mercenary. Other such people, especially ex-SS and Wehrmacht, had been here with the Legion not so long ago.

Some tales revolved around the idea of shared territory. There were Special Forces men who swore they recognized VC officers on R and R drinking at the bars in Bien Hoa. One assured me he could "tell from their hands." Another accommodation with the enemy was said to have been worked out at Nui Ba Den, the mist-covered Black Virgin Mountain. No one argued that American forces held the peak and base while the VC occupied the middle, but no one could prove they both used the same water hole. Similarly, American and VC troops had their own sections on China Beach, or so it was said, each side observing an invisible line. Let the diplomats talk fruitlessly in Paris. The fighting men had long worked things out in the field.

In fact, the peace talks in Paris remained stalled as grown men argued over the shape of the negotiating table. Meanwhile, more than 28,000 Americans had been killed as the Christmas season approached. Back home in "the world," Richard Nixon was elected president. He would assume direction of this unhappy war while his vice-president, Spiro T. Agnew, prepared to do battle with their common enemy, TV news.

.   .   .

BACK in the furnace of Saigon, the bureau was in turmoil. Corrigan had come out from New York to fire Donghi. The front office just didn't trust him on the story anymore. They'd heard enough about his bridge playing and reputation for fine cooking, effete pursuits on a blood 'n' guts beat. Donghi had let his guard down, going laconically through the motions of running the bureau, distracted by his personal problems and counting the months to retirement. Theodore and Flick, both of whom left the country in a big hurry, blamed their departure on Donghi's management when debriefed by New York. Steinman, who deplored Donghi's elitist approach to life, delivered one of the fatal rounds. "I went to Saigon to see him one day. When I arrived at the bureau he wasn't there. He was out shopping for pâté and brie."

Everyone tiptoed around Frank after the deed was done, afraid to look him in the eye. He said he was relieved; he couldn't take the second-guessing anymore, but he knew it was just one more fragment in a string of personal and professional defeats. Fittingly, it all fell apart for him in the desperate setting of Vietnam, a civilization's metaphor for failure. "Anyway," said Frank, "I'm taking the long way home, around the world, and I'll be in Angkor Wat for Christmas."

I felt rotten and exasperated. This man's life was a wreck. Why wasn't he going home on the next plane to rebuild? Perhaps if I had been older, less interested in my own career, I might have caught on to how he was breaking apart. Easy to say now, not then. Who could have known the war would entwine and alter everyone who went to it? It got us all: all nations, all sides, all callings.

Meanwhile, at 30 Rock, they were having new ideas about story coverage. TV's "role" in the war was becoming almost as big an issue as the conflict itself—at least in the executive warrens and among certain politicians and television pundits. Network defenders insisted that everyone was "blaming the medium for the message." Its detractors attacked the seriousness and depth of what they saw on their screens. Television news, wrote Michael Arlen in *The New Yorker*, was "just another aspect of the world's greatest continuous floating variety show."

Ouch. The word went out to start reporting the Big Picture. Relating an encounter with the enemy wasn't enough; the reporter must now tell how it fit into the entire context of the war. Easier said than done since everyone on both sides of the Pacific was trying to figure out a context for the decade, let alone a single firefight. "Take-outs" were fine, but on a day-to-day basis, out chasing the troops, the Big Picture didn't seem as important as dodging bullets or sidestepping land mines that took off your legs and ripped open your belly—and still shipping the film back on time. Besides, nobody I knew had a clue as to what the Big Picture was. The little pieces, the disjointed fire-fights, *were* the context of the war: a tiny, determined nation ready to struggle to the death against a dazed giant growing weary of battle.

Steinman—who once splendidly told me to "do a story on mud" when I reported we were rained out on an operation—didn't buy this new approach. The war was his police blotter. "New York got holier-than-thou and started taking away the freedom of running a bureau, of moving on a story," he said looking back years later. "Why, in two years time we must have turned out, easily, about 1,500 stories. Then they decided every piece had to have 'depth,' and so it began to take a week to ten days to finish one, to do what passed for reporting. It was a waste of time to do 'special projects,' and I told them so. Vietnam was a combat story."

It was difficult to take the so-called high road in this argument as so many effective stories materialized precisely because they were only a slice of horror rather than a cosmic analysis. Take Fire Support Base "Julie," which was quietly enclosed one night by North Vietnamese regulars, who hurled themselves into a wall of firepower laid down by the defending Americans. Many of the attackers died in the wire, a testimony to their iron resolution. We arrived early the next morning and I saw the G-2, the intelligence officer, going from body to body among this township of the dead, searching pockets and rucksacks. Tailor's dummies. Eyes staring, arms akimbo, heads twisted, some in one piece, many draped over the concertina wire. I followed him, looking at the pictures of girlfriends, wives, and children, listening to the interpreter translate the letters home, going through the pitiful belongings left behind in a blast of light. It was a slice of war all right, no Big Picture here, just a reminder of the two things that sobered me about the enemy: his inhumanity alive, his humanity dead.

In line with the new edict, I went south to check out the Big Picture in the Mekong Delta. It was the dry season, not a small detail if you plan to operate among the channels of a monster river that begins more than 2,000 miles north in the freezing high wilderness of Tibet. Getting there was half the fun, so I hitched a ride on a joint army-navy operation—along with Yunichi Yasuda, a twenty-four-year-old Japanese cameraman, and Vi Giac, a forty-seven-year-old Hanoi-born sound man. The navy's Mobile Riverine Force, a Civil War concept using small "monitor" gunboats, hooked up with the second brigade of the Ninth, ostensibly to simplify the logistical nightmare of chasing Vietcong in that amphibious world. We choppered out of Tan Son Nhut toward Long Binh, about twenty minutes away, to take on extra fuel for the ride south, skimming treetops to stay below the outgoing artillery. By dark, we were circling over the USS *Benewah*, flagship of the task force, which would link up with the ground forces down the coast the next morning. I spent the night in the captain's cabin. "You know," he said, "I've been in the navy for some years now, but I must say this is the first time in my career that a woman has spent the night aboard my ship."

A less favorable welcome came from one of the junior officers.

"What if we get into trouble?" he said. "Have you been to jungle survival school? What right have you to be on this ship?"

Another officer invoked the old seaman's superstition of how it is bad luck to have a woman aboard.

At 6 A.M. a helicopter lifted us off the *Benewah* toward the coast. I had been out with the monitors in the canals before, but this time we were going with the army, in pursuit of the 516th Vietcong Battalion. Operation Tiger Claw, they were calling it, another remarkable example of the Pentagon's penchant for linking advanced technology with arrested development.

"Well, you must be the NBC team," said the battalion commander. "We heard a woman was coming. We'll give you a good ride *over* the operation."

"Sorry, Colonel, but we have to go *with* the operation."

"You mean on the ground—with the troops?"

"Well, sir, we didn't come here to waste time." He could see my patience thinning.

"Okay, if that's what you want. But it may be rougher than you think."

There seemed no point in telling him it was rougher than anybody thought, anytime, anyplace.

This was river and canal country. Networks of them cutting through the dense foliage, creating a floor of mud for the troops. Every twenty feet or so water rose chest-deep. Each man waded through, and then by a hand-to-hand helping process, he was lifted to the opposite bank by the man in front of him. We were in Kien Hoa Province, two miles north of the village of Mo Kai. It would have been a routine combat operation but for one young soldier who seemed to embody even this war's daring and strange romance. When I first saw him he was holding an M16 in one hand and a prisoner in the other. Blond, wiry, a bantam at five feet, five and a half inches, 130 pounds, a twenty-four-year-old wood sprite in khaki. Soldiering doesn't get any better than this. Sergeant Pearle Chauncey "Skip" Ettinger, Jr., was a Green Beret on the second of what were to be five tours in Vietnam. He was a believer long after the press and America turned away from the war.

As a "pathfinder"—a scout assigned to pick the jungle trails because of his exceptional ability to detect and survive the enemy—Skip had leverage. Not to mention a decided renegade charm, what the British military call "OLQ," officerlike qualities, a broad gauge of indefinable traits that separated good leaders from average ones. The test was simply, Who would follow this man? He was perfect for Vietnam—small, light, and fast, a VC-style guerrilla trying to make a difference in conventional war.

Even over the yelling and clanking of "moving out," his voice seemed hushed in tight control, modulated fittingly to the volumes of his shadow war. Immediately, he took charge of our long trek through the jungle. First, the prisoner—walking "point" at the head of the column—then Skip. I followed with the crew. The canals never ended. I could see the leeches in the water. We struggled across the muddy banks, Skip urging me to pull myself up by the butt of his M16. Yasuda arched his back to keep the camera dry, stopping only once to shake his head and mutter, "crazy American woman." We moved quietly, for hours it seemed. Then, a shot—snipers! The line hit the dirt. Our side was blasting back as Skip pushed me down a bank. "Don't move."

Yasuda was on his feet, filming the crouching column. Silence. The sniper had vanished.

It wasn't until we got up to walk again that a deadening fatigue hit. Combat is a high; and like most highs, exhausting. Five hours into this walk in the sun, we ran out of water. Stopping to rest, I rolled up my trousers for a leech check and there it was, a black bloodsucker on my calf, merrily feasting on what little protein I had left. War is good business for leeches. I wanted to leap out of my skin. Let somebody else wear this sweaty, aching, bruised, scratched coverall, complete with its own lunching leech. I wanted my mommy. Skip steadied me, pulled out a Ronson, and burned it away.

Down the trail about an hour later we stopped at a sign nailed to a tree: Tu Dia—"that area," loosely translated. Usually the VC left such signs to warn their own of booby traps ahead. "Off the trail," snapped Skip.

We cut right through the clinging, sodden canopy of branches. "Does this mean we don't have to worry about traps?" I asked.

"Not really. Sometimes the signs are put there to lead us off the trail right into booby trap zones. You never know for sure."

That was it, the psychological terror the enemy counted on. Moreover, when somebody did trigger a grenade trap, the ensuing confusion slowed down the column, giving the enemy time to escape while the Americans waited for Medevacs to evacuate the wounded. Uncertainty has its own exhaustions—that's what the Cong were playing on with virtuous authority.

Finally, we reached a village. There was little question it belonged to the Vietcong because the men were gone. The troops moved through, searching the grass huts. Then the word came down the line that a fleet of choppers would land in a nearby rice field to pick up the troops, but as we approached the field, someone yelled that three people were running into a nearby tree line. The company commander, a square-jawed six-footer in his mid-twenties, gave the order to shoot. Mortar shells flew. Fifty-caliber machine gun bullets tore into the tree line and the village huts that lay in the line of fire. And amid the deafening noise, the sound of an infant crying.

Standing near me was a South Vietnamese soldier, interpreter for the unit. "You damn Americans," he screamed. "Why do you shoot? How do you know who they were?"

When he cooled off, I went over. "Does this happen often?" I asked.

"Often? All the time," he said. "And when I complain, they tell me, 'That's war.' "

I asked the company commander the same question. "Maybe they weren't VC," he said. "But if they were, they would ambush us later, or shoot down our choppers. You can't always ask questions first."

Later, talking with the battalion commander, it was clear that the most controversial point in the war—civilian casualties—had arisen again. And realizing my quandary, he said: "Look, I won't tell you how to tell your story. But when to shoot or not to shoot is the grayest area in the war—and it will always be."

He had struck the heart of it—how do you tell the enemy from a "friendly?" Despite the pasting the VC took during Tet, there was no way to disperse the suspicion they were everywhere, that, as the barracks wisdom went, "The only definition of a Vietcong is a dead Vietnamese."

Skip was talking to the C and C (command and control) ship on his PRC 77 radio, guiding the choppers in and calling for fire cover.

"Tiger flight leader, this is Leopard 12. The PZ is ready at this time. Over."

"Leopard 12, this is Tiger leader. Roger. Pop smoke. Over."

"Tiger flight leader, this is Leopard 12. Smoke out. Identify. Over."

"Roger, Leopard, we have red smoke. Over."

"Tiger flight, clear to land. Get us home. Over."

"Roger Leopard, coming in. Out."

As the choppers swooped to take us out, Skip said, "Please come back again. You've no idea how good it is for our morale."

Good-bye time, addresses and phone numbers exchanged, another soldier became brother and buddy in just a few hours. It always haunted me that I would never see any of them again when lift-off time came. But this time I was wrong. Skip Ettinger was in my life to stay, a metaphor for a generation.

The piece led "Huntley-Brinkley," running two minutes and forty-five seconds. Just another mission, another tiny piece of the huge jigsaw puzzle that was Vietnam. If it somehow fitted into the Big Picture, I couldn't see how.

KAITAK Airport in Hong Kong crawled with businessmen, tourists, and the influx of people connected with events in Southeast Asia. A tour of editors, mostly middle-aged, from small-town newspapers took up many of the seats on the flight in. They had spent the usual few days getting a grand tour of the war and come away with enough anecdotes to last them through several editions and a lifetime of cocktail parties. Brainwashed or not, they were eager, polite, and full of the cub spirit. Waiting by the baggage turntable, I noticed a patrician-looking man in a well-worn trench coat standing confidently with his foot on the rail edge, an elbow on his knee, sucking on a cigar. It was the venerated Washington journalist, Joseph W. Alsop. He had spent several days in Saigon piecing together the Big Picture— as a guest of Ambassador Ellsworth Bunker at the American embassy. His sojourn underscored the need print reporters in general seemed to have to "talk to someone at the embassy," for a quote from the ambassador or one of the faceless "Western diplomats." That need escaped most television types whose lust was for pictures. I had never been inside the embassy.

Just a few days earlier Peter Arnett had been a guest at one of

Ambassador Bunker's little dinners in honor of Alsop. The learned journalist was seated next to Bunker at the formal dining table, both directly across from Peter. After the entrée arrived, they got down to the nitty-gritty, which in Saigon meant war talk. Alsop, a staunch supporter of administration policy, looked up from his filet de boeuf and said to Peter, "So you're the guy who fabricates all those quotes from Khe Sanh."

Peter, unamused and "a little hair trigger in those days," leapt to his feet and started around to the other side of the table. "I cannot accept that," he snarled, as the other men rose.

Arnett charged and Alsop jumped behind the ambassador, who stopped the attack. It was probably the only time in the history of the Vietnam War that a diplomatic effort brought immediate success. "Bunker is a brave man," Arnett said later.

Horst Faas also had an Alsop story. One day he had staggered onto a chopper after a couple of hellish hours in a firefight, and there was the imperturbable columnist in unwrinkled fatigues—reading a book on Chinese ceramics.

At Kaitak, as I watched him retrieve his bag, one of the traveling newspaper editors turned to me. "That's Joe Alsop, you know, the famous Washington commentator."

"Yes," I told him, "I know."

"It's funny," he said, "I really feel bad. I always thought of Alsop as one of my heroes, you know, one of the guys we look up to in this business. Well, when we got on the plane in Saigon, I went over to him to shake his hand and told him how honored I was to do this, and, you know, what a fine job he does and all that. Well, I'll be damned if he didn't cut me dead. Just kept his cigar in his mouth and barely said hello. Makes you feel kind of let down."

Out of a misguided sense of embarrassment for the national press, I suggested that the great Alsop was having an off day. Yet in my heart I knew it had happened just the way he said.

Alsop, Luce, Sulzberger, they were all pensive elder statesmen of a press elite traditionally "on the team," newsmen who co-opted authority from the powerful men they covered long before the TV journalists of the sixties caught on to the game and dealt into it for themselves. The difference was that most of the next generation wasn't buying the party line. What a change from the days when the butler answered the front door and announced: "Four reporters, Milord, and a gentleman from *The Times.*"

*   *   *

R AND R was coming up again, right smack in time for Christmas in Hong Kong. World War I had St. Petersburg; World War II, Vienna and Casablanca. The Vietnam War had Hong Kong. It hosted glittering parties, welcomed illicit lovers, transshipped illegal drugs, filtered intelligence, and relayed television pictures—the romance, the intrigue, and the transience of a wartime crossroads.

At night, the lights on Victoria Peak—1,800 feet above the sea—merged with the heavens. Driving up the tortuous road to the summit, it was easy to mistake a shooting star for a string of tiny lanterns strung in the garden of somebody's terraced villa. Such was the enchantment on the night of the big Christmas party in Welles and Pat Hangen's home. The British Empire once kept this majestic white house for its tax collector, in the days of black tea and tiffin, opium wars and officers wearing swords and white gloves.

The blaze in the huge fireplace warmed a crowd caught in the excitement of a glamorous time, a new empire, the generation of the American. Foreign correspondents, world-weary at any age, tracked handsome CIA agents, who talked softly and vaguely. Always seated to hold court, the experts and scholars disgorged tidbits from their latest "fact-finding" binge. Working the fringes, rich local businessmen stalked the teak floor, looking for yet another angle on war profiteering. Foreign diplomats found safety in small groups, where they exuded confidence in direct proportion to their country's status. And making it all shimmer like the colored glass balls of Christmas, beautiful Chinese women drifted by in satin cheongsams, on the lookout for a Western devil, preferably with money. All the currents of an electric time grounded in that single room.

Pat Hangen radiated charm and an intelligence rarely found in the wives' colony of the overseas press corps. Welles, never good at small talk, yet unfailingly polite, made the rounds, even more handsome in his Ivy League suit than in the usual bush clothes. "And this is Liz Trotta," he said in introducing me to one of the more distinguished China-watchers. "She's already had her first firefight."

It was just like him, making me, a newcomer, feel I was part of this exclusive circle. It was the last time I saw Welles before he vanished in the jungles of Cambodia.

Four days before Christmas, the alarm went up. Although the State Department wasn't yet making it official, the crew of the USS

Pueblo might be released by the North Koreans at any moment. R and R and hanging mistletoe went up in woodsmoke as I shipped out for Seoul on the first available flight.

The capture of the *Pueblo*, its captain, Commander Lloyd Bucher, and a crew of eighty-three burned just one more whorl of shame into the American consciousness. North Korea, a third-rate Communist power, had attacked and seized the spy vessel, claiming that it had come within the twelve-mile territorial limit.

The *Pueblo* was hardly a ship of the line, but it did contain electronic equipment of particular interest to the Russians. How it had been taken so easily was never fully explained. It never fired a shot; the tarpaulin on two .50-caliber machine guns was not even lifted. The suspicion grew that Commander Bucher had surrendered a highly secret electronic monitoring vessel too readily, and worst of all, that he had ignored the sacred navy tradition "Don't give up the ship." To make matters worse, the crew lacked the time to destroy all top-secret material, so much fell into enemy hands. Then, after exacting a confession from Commander Bucher and holding the crew for eleven months, the North Koreans negotiated a release agreement in which the United States admitted to and apologized for espionage (although it was repudiated before the ink dried).

The deal was that the three networks could have their own correspondents and one pool camera (NBC won the toss) at Panmunjom, the site chosen for the release of the crew. We stood on a rise overlooking the Bridge of No Return, connecting and dividing the two Koreas. Bitter cold seeped into every bone as a light snow fell. A tape of Bucher's confession boomed through a loudspeaker on the other side. Finally, the captain appeared, walking evenly across the 250 feet to freedom. A pause. Then the coffin of a sailor killed in the attack, followed by a solemn single file of men, some limping, some smiling, most grave and tentative.

Shortly after the crew moved from the joint security area of Panmunjom to the United Nations Command's advance camp about four miles away, the navy presented Bucher at a news conference. He said he had confessed to violating North Korean waters for purposes of spying because of the beatings and abuse suffered by the crew, and threats of more.

At another news conference the following day, Rear Admiral Edwin M. Rosenthal, who would escort the *Pueblo* crew back to the United States, said there would be "a routine court of inquiry" but blithely pronounced Bucher "a hero among heroes" and likened the *Pueblo* saga to *Apollo 8*. It seemed ludicrous, especially since for the first time in many turbulent days, Americans, savoring their first close-up of the moon and a wondrous look at the earth, felt a surge of old-fashioned pride. They had done something right.

That was not exactly what everyone was thinking about the ill-fated spy ship. Once again the military had shot itself in the boot, and the cumulative shame of our efforts in this part of the world continued to gnaw away at the old Yankee confidence. This was the year of getting beaten up by the little guys.

By the end of 1968, U.S. troop strength in Vietnam stood at about 550,000; U.S. fatalities had passed 30,000; and at the Paris peace talks they were still arguing over the shape of the table. The new bureau chief, Jack Reynolds, had settled into Donghi's chair, ushering in still another NBC era in Saigon. Reynolds, a pipe-smoking bachelor who bore a biblical resemblance to Charlton Heston, didn't come from hard news but from producing public affairs programs for the local station, WNBC. His idea of a good war story for the holidays was a nice homey tale about troops in the field eating a full-dress turkey dinner with champagne. Our loathing was mutual, so my relief as I neared the end of my tour was even sweeter. New York begged me to extend, but the law of averages seemed less and less in my favor.

As a final assignment, I was scheduled to do a Tet first anniversary series. Jake was flying in from New York to produce it. We had exchanged letters since I left, mostly about the war and how it was playing back home. The old romance seemed to have evolved into a teacher-protégé exchange, and the moment I saw him through the dust at Tan Son Nhut, I knew that we, too, had been put through the great sifter of the 1960s. Everything had changed. And while for the first few days we imitated the ritual of picking up where we left off, it was apparent that one more romance had gone the way of fleeting encounters in this Age of Aquarius.

I was learning another basic lesson about women in the TV news business, the ones who work in the field without benefit of a regular routine and access to a normal social life. How many times had I been envied for "meeting such interesting men," when more often than not there wasn't any time to get beyond hello. Canceling a dinner date as you dash out on the first available to East Nowhere is not the stuff of lasting relationships. Most of the time men see you at your worst: harried by deadlines, sweating in haste, hair wild in flight, makeup long erased, clothes disheveled, snapping orders, cussing in rage, and no time for the flirty demure stuff. It is a rare man who wants such a creature to bear his children and stroke his brow.

Living such a life, spending so much time chasing stories, it was difficult to form attachments outside the business and so I had turned inside, to Jake, to a relationship bound by the weariness of long hours, the tension of office politics, and the emotional shorthand of a pro-fessional romance. Even then I had worried about appearing "loose," about accusations that I used feminine wiles to get a story, instead of whatever talent I had. Now I resolved that it was safer to stick to the story, adopt the morals of "Caesar's wife," go it alone. An expensive trade-off, but certain choices had to be made, prices paid, all along the way.

Putting on our reporters' faces, Jake and I went looking for a three-piece Tet anniversary status report, up and down the length of the country, covering the one thing that lasted, the war. And as the days melted down toward departure, I filled my mind with thoughts of chocolate malts, silk stockings and real bookstores, anything to shorten the final jittery hours of wondering if something might go wrong. A piece of plastique on the Shelf, a rocket on a city street, a terrorist on a motorcycle. By the time I turned to close the door of Room 64 for the last time, I had seen enough of war. Only on the way to the airport with Jake did I begin to feel a sense of finality, even of nostalgia as I watched the blur of bicycles and conical hats through the window of Mr. Long's old Mercury.

It must have been the overhead blowers squirting cold air in my face that sent me on a train of backward glances, like all recollection more powerful in comfort as well as tranquillity. Wheels up again. That had become the punctuation of my life, the cue for starting and ending chapters and stories. The green curve of the land and the whitecaps floating coastward evoked a parade of phantoms. Visions of the past drifted in and out of focus like a homemade movie, forward and backward: the afternoon when our chopper took a hit coming out of a firebase, hearing it whine and lurch in a baby blue sky; the dirty, sweat-stained faces of the grunts; the Sunday when Don D'Amico's luck ran out; Skip Ettinger pulling me up out of the muck with the butt of his M16; Huynh asleep at the foot of my bunk when he sensed trouble ahead; the morning fog rising from the elephant grass; the Foreign Legion patches behind the old Majestic bar; the mauve shade of the jungle; the smell of papaya and French coffee in the Continental garden; the body in the rubber sack next to me on a chopper, and thinking over and over that I knew before his mother did.

I had been to Vietnam all right. I just wasn't prepared for remembering.

8

THE FORGETTING OF MARY JO

Central Park had disappeared. From 59th to 110th streets a cathedral of ice rose out of the island's center. So pristine, so imposing was its frozen splendor that only princes and their ladies should have trodden those crystal paths that clear, cold February day. Instead, Donghi and I threaded the corridors of ice, heading for hot dogs and chocolate. I had only been back a couple of weeks—from the stifling streets of Saigon to the frigid clarity of a city silenced by winter.

"Are you going to try to find another job in broadcasting?" I asked Frank, knowing full well the prospects at his age.

"I don't know. I haven't really decided yet, and I'm sick of the Corrigans of this world. I want to see what Mary Kay says, too. You know, I'm in love with her. In a few days, I'm going to see her in California."

Frank was a man who could profess his love that easily, who seemed unembarrassed at putting his life into somebody else's hands. His natural recklessness played nicely into the spirit of the sixties. Having cut off the past, he was walking into a future that wasn't there.

Quite a pair we two, home from the war with heartaches. We walked for hours swapping sadnesses, all the while feeling safe and suspended in that motionless ice palace. During dinner at the Praha, an old Czech restaurant on the East Side, Frank began to ramble. I thought it was the red wine, until he turned the palest I had ever seen him and said he might kill himself. Not maudlin, or threatening, but matter-of-fact, almost apologetic. "Oh well, if it doesn't work out— like everything else, maybe I'll just pack it in. You know . . ." His voice faded. I started to protest.

"Really, Liz, it just doesn't make sense anymore."

Never before had I heard anyone make such a threat, but I knew all the psych books said that when someone does it's a good sign he will probably do it. "Will you make a deal with me?" I said.

"Now don't give me any inspirational stuff."

"No—no. Just call me when you get this way again, if you get so depressed. Any hour, just call me. Promise?"

He smiled paternally and agreed.

Room 520, home plate for 30 Rock for local, national, and foreign news, was unchanged after six months, except that everyone in it looked alike. Now I could appreciate why the "gooks" called us "big noses." Ah yes, how travel does flatten one's prejudices. I told no war stories, although the demand was there, and relished the compliments on my work and new figure, now minus twenty-three pounds. Although technically I was still part of the local WNBC staff, "they" (the dreaded and collective vice-president-in-charge-of-fear) made it clear that I was "going network," those days the closest to a peerage in news. In the meantime, I stayed hungry and humble on the New York beat, fitting back into the crony circle at City Hall. The best compliment came from Governor Rockefeller, who noticed the weight loss and made sure I knew he approved.

Each morning it was routine to check three clipboards at the desk in the center of the newsroom. The man behind the desk in effect coordinated all the news flow of the day. Years later, a blizzard of memos and menus would come from in-house computers, but then four 8-by-11 plastic boards told the story of what had been happening at NBC News in the last twenty-four hours. The messages on the Number One Board, enclosed within a red border, were priority.

One morning, the manager on duty, Walter Millis, gave me an odd look as I sauntered over to his desk for the morning read-in. "Anything earthshaking?" I asked.

He said nothing.

My eyes went immediately to a red bordered message on top of the Number One Board. It was a *New York Times* item.

GUERNEVILLE, *Calif., March 14 (AP)—Frank F. Donghi, former National Broadcasting Company news bureau chief in Saigon, was found dead late yesterday in his room at a resort lodge here.*

Coroner Andrew Johanson said an empty bottle of sleeping tablets was found near the body.

Mr. Donghi, who was 54 years old, had been staying at the lodge since Feb. 28. NBC said in San Francisco that he resigned his Saigon post about three months ago.

Twenty years later, I asked Reuven Frank about Donghi. As president of the news division at that time, he would have approved the firing.

"I don't remember anything about his work out there. He was an old-line middle-level executive who came over to us from CBS—kind of a sad sack."

BY now I was peeling off from the local beat to work on stories for the network. A series I reported and wrote on hunger in America during early 1969 won an Emmy, which didn't hurt my "she's a ball-buster, but she knows how to get a story" reputation. Eventually I eased into the on-call, at-the-ready, cancel-all-other-engagements (better still don't make any) life of the national correspondent covering "general" news. A utility infielder for "The Huntley-Brinkley Report." Anything from the food program in South Carolina to the development of the Boeing 747 in Seattle. Often, of course, correspondents had their assignments the night before, but usually it was worked out on a spec basis. For example, at 7:45 P.M., after we went off the air, one of the senior producers might order you to Dallas the next day—an oil rig controversy was shaping up. Not for tomorrow night, maybe not ever, but take a look. Nothing was "locked in" because news departments had the money to bounce their correspondents all over the country

without casting assignments in stone. Once the corporate side tightened purse strings in the late seventies and early eighties, then everything had to be nailed down. Reporting by appointment—once the
province of Washington bureaus—became the standard procedure.

Doing the story was one thing. Airing it was still a technological
crap game. Often a story died for lack of satellite access. Processing
and transferring film still kept us in the dark ages. For every ten stories
covered, perhaps three would never be seen because the satellite wasn't
booked or in the right place at the right time. Only big, manageable,
and expected events could be covered "live." The idea of an anchor
talking to correspondents halfway round the world at the wink of a
computer remained science fiction, not journalism, and the average
newsman wasn't looking that far ahead anyway. "Today's news today,"
as one of the "520" producers used to say.

"People were very serious about what they were doing, but they
didn't take themselves seriously." Only a line producer who knew the
pitfalls firsthand could talk like that; and Al Robbins, with whom I
traveled a lot in those days, surely did. You just had to roll with the
cues, because banging your head on the control room door wouldn't
change a thing. Most of the men there operated with an ease they had
gained from working in newspaper and wire services. Even the
typewriter-throwing temper tantrums were a holdover from city room
days.

There was, above all, a great deal of fun in what we did, perhaps
because the risks were so big. The New York stories required a lot of
derring-do, mainly because they came in dangerously late on the theory that anything happening in the NBC News headquarters area
could be put together quickly. When a very late story hit the building
and there was time enough to develop and transfer the film, but not
to cut it with a recorded narration, then the fun began for the correspondent. I would sit next to Huntley in the studio, off-camera, listening as he introduced the story into the live broadcast; then,
watching a nearby monitor, I would read a script I had written over
the passing pictures. Sometimes I had "times" written on the script—
the number of seconds for each paragraph as measured by a
stopwatch—but I had never seen the pictures until that moment. It
was like driving through a blizzard, hoping not to skid. The intense
pressure of knowing you couldn't flub a word or miss a beat—because
this was your only shot—made its lasting impression. Nor did it hurt
my morale to get an "atta girl" from Chet.

Wallace Westfeldt replaced Shad Northshield as executive producer of "Huntley-Brinkley" in early 1969. The word was out that Northshield couldn't get along with Brinkley, whereas Westfeldt, successively a correspondent, writer, and producer in New York and Washington, was a Brinkley confidant. It was a sea change, Shad's hard-edged, mocking style giving way to the soft New Orleans tones of a gentleman who made "goddammit" sound like a response from a church choir. Wally had inherited the war, "Shad's issue," his own being the civil rights movement, which he had covered for eight years for the Nashville *Tennessean*. Wally's friendly, down-home nature and change of pace transformed the atmosphere, like Johnson taking over from Kennedy. His crew cut, a hangover from Marine Corps days, and Brooks Brothers blazers gave him the look of a prep school English teacher at first impression, replaced—once you had factored in the pug nose, the deep whiskey laugh, and the tall, beefy frame—by that of a Newport yachtsman courteously but single-mindedly determined to win.

Humor was Wally's strong suit, minus the Northshield bite. Sometimes he would deliberately throw me a late-breaking story to write for a quick voice-over and then pace up and down behind my typewriter chanting: "Trotta, it's five minutes to six. Get the lead out. What do you think this is, a weekly?"

During one broadcast, there was a break in the film chain, and a series of pieces went down the tubes with nothing ready to replace them. Richard Hunt, a correspondent standing nearby, rushed up the back stairs to the ninth-floor editing room, grabbed a long feature on Japanese flower arranging off the shelf, and rushed it to the projection room. Huntley ad-libbed, and America's evening news roared on uninterrupted. Meanwhile, Wally had disappeared. After Chet and David said good night to each other, a producer found him under his desk, hugging his legs and muttering, "People are no damn good. I'm not coming out anymore."

Wally's approach to the war seemed fashionably liberal, although many years later he argued it was not the country's involvement in the war he opposed but the way we fought it. "I think Chet and I felt the same way. If we were going to do this kind of thing, this war, then we should have gone in with all flags flying. But if we're not, then we shouldn't. As for Chet, although skeptical at times, he never harbored cynicism, he didn't operate on those terms. In many ways he was kind of naive."

Chet and David never declared themselves for or against the war on the air as Cronkite had over at CBS, but Westfeldt told me,

"Remember, Brinkley was a very close friend of Lyndon Johnson and used to play poker with him, although I do think they separated at one time over the war."

Despite Wally's late disclaimer, a flagrantly personal statement on the war did make its way into the lineup of the show one night, built around a song made popular by Kenny Rogers, "Ruby, Don't Take Your Love to Town." It told the story in rock-country cadence of a veteran returned from the war sexually incapacitated, pleading with his gal not to look elsewhere. There was no script, no reporter, just a "self-contained" piece produced by a crew and a producer in the Los Angeles bureau. The pictures centered on the kind of cheaply furnished room you find in SRO hotels, highlighting Ruby's and the vet's simple possessions, clothing, pictures on a dresser. Wally had got the idea listening to his car radio on the drive from New York to Washington and "decided to experiment." Brinkley, ardently against the war, approved.

The airing of this statement in pictures was followed by a leaden silence in the newsroom, its intensity matched by an avalanche of viewer protest. "I'm not sure I would have done it again," Wally said later.

Every night, within seconds of the "Huntley-Brinkley" sign-off, the phones in the newsroom erupted in concert. "For you, Liz, on two," one of the writers yelled one Friday as he was putting on his coat. "He won't give his name. Says it's a surprise."

"Oh great, probably the Boston Strangler."

"Hello?"

The voice on the line was faint, but familiar, an echo of something bittersweet.

"It's your favorite fighter pilot."

"D'Amico," I shouted. "Where the hell are you?"

He was calling from Walter Reed Army Medical Center in Washington, D.C., exactly where he had been headed the last time I saw him in the Da Nang officers' club. Everything that had seemed so far, so finished, came roaring over me, the first of many flashbacks to that corner of the world I was trying to forget.

D'Amico had just "caught my act" and had to call. He was going nuts after three months in the hospital.

"Do you want to go back?" I asked, knowing the answer.

"Of course I do, but these bastards say I'm never going to fly again. Just watch. Are *you* going back?"

"Are you kidding?"

"No, but I thought maybe you wanted to."

"Well, sometimes I do," I admitted—only then realizing that it was true.

ON-AIR personnel—"talent" as they are derisively if legally named—are the candles in the window for TV news. Promoting correspondents through the network press departments, while not the extravaganza it is today, has always been a ritual of the business. In the late sixties and early seventies the pitch was still low-key, with an emphasis on foreign affairs and sobriety. The Flo Ziegfeld ethic had yet to infiltrate the executive suite, although Hollywood flesh peddling and campaigns about who was more trustworthy loomed over the horizon. At NBC, correspondent "tours" were part of the promotion machinery, usually twice-a-year whirlwind sweeps concentrated on a particular section of the country and such audiences as foreign affairs councils, civic organizations, and most important, local TV viewers. The idea was to mingle with the townsfolk, appear on the local stations, shake hands with the mayor's wife—grass roots contact with NBC's ultimate consumers. Most important, it massaged the affiliates and gave the news directors an opportunity to drop your name at their next Jaycee meeting. The gig usually took the form of individual speeches by a half dozen of us correspondents, and then Q and As, which often erupted into debate among ourselves. One night Douglas Kiker, who covered Washington politics with the easy confidence of a snake-oil salesman, got so bored with an audience that he dared me to stage a fight just to wake them up. Our mock battle over admission of Red China to the UN (he for, me against) was a smash.

The tour that spring—"The First 100 Days of Richard Nixon"—swept Pauline Frederick, Irving R. Levine, Frank Bourgholtzer, Carl Stern, John Chancellor, and myself through eight western cities. Nervous about all these veterans and being the new kid on the block, I asked Pauline's advice. "The point is to stick to what you know," she said. "The men—Chancellor, for example—will refer to their great experience and say things such as, 'Well, I mentioned that to the president the other night and he told me, etc. etc.' What you should say is, 'Well, I don't talk to presidents yet, but there's a GI in the Mekong Delta who told me, etc., etc.' Get the idea?"

Did I ever. And so one night in San Diego before an audience including many officers from the huge naval base nearby I put Pauline's tactic to the test. After delivering my opening remarks, among them a reference to the "heroes" I had seen in a war which was wrong not in itself but in the U.S. government's half-hearted commitment to it, Chancellor leapt to his feet. He pressed his points against the war, referring to me over his shoulder as "Mme. Nhu over there." Then, "Heroes? There are no heroes in this war." But Chancellor had miscalculated. When I rose to defend myself, the audience burst into applause.

As we stood in the wings during intermission, one furious anchorman turned on me. "You're just lucky I didn't tear you apart out there," snorted Chancellor.

We were forever cool to each other after that. I don't believe he ever forgot what he said. I know I didn't.

So many questions wherever we went, wherever any reporter went in those days, zeroed in on "how the news was slanted." People hammered away, looking for confirmation of their darkest suspicions—that someone was managing the news for some ulterior cause, whether against the war, for integration, or for some vaguely-defined "radicalism." Across the millions of square miles west of the Alleghenies, many suspected that every correspondent covering the war had been brainwashed. I took pains to point out that no one had herded me into a dark little room before I left for the Far East and programmed me to report that the war was wrong. And this was true. What was also true, of course, was that New York edited and selected the stories. More important, a majority of newspeople held liberal views that included bitter hostility to the war.

The newspapers in each town we visited usually ran two or three pieces on the NBC road show. Pauline and I drew a lot of interviews from the "women in a man's world" angle, at that time a legitimate field of inquiry. Who knew that it would become a cottage industry? The women's movement was still in its early, ladylike stage, but an awareness of that next frontier was beginning to surface. After all, hadn't a big TV network hired this "girl" who incidentally was also "not a bad looker," as one reporter wrote.

The *Los Angeles Times* showed us more respect, asking our opinions of Nixon. Then came the obligatory feminist observations. Pauline said: "Most women listeners would prefer to hear the voice symbol of the husband and lover, rather than the sister or mother." A sharp observation, especially since the NBC brass had kicked her off the radio hourlies because the affiliates held that listeners gave no credibility to a woman's voice.

I told the *Los Angeles Times* that "if there is a woman in this field who can make it, she's got to be twice as good as the next guy. She's got to be. She's open to criticism. But if she criticizes, she's labeled a prima donna or a bitch. If a man loses his temper, he is described as someone fighting for a cause, doing the manly thing."

Near the end of the tour I could feel my patience giving way. I began to long for the grit and chaos of Vietnam. Even the network stories dulled in comparison, the normality of daily living, not to mention the nonsense on the party circuit. It only underlined the fact that I needed another dose of the war. Besides, I was still in practice. Wasn't I automatically looking for tripwires, even in the most manicured lawn, waiting for something to happen even in the stir of the leaves? Back in New York, in a casual conversation with Corrigan, I mentioned it was getting a little tiresome responding to all the questions about what it was like to be a woman in the war.

He leaned back in his leather chair with a self-satisfied smile. "Well, you've got to admit it was a great gimmick!"

Late one night, the phone rang in my apartment on East End Avenue. There was no mistaking the soft, conspiratorial voice, even though I had never heard it on a telephone. Memories of green and khaki filtered in, made incongruous by the red velvet draperies of my bedroom window. It was Skip Ettinger. After Nixon's May 14 speech, in which he offered a new peace proposal, Skip had sent a letter of support to the White House, so certain was he that the president was out for a big win. He was home on leave, hurt and confused by the reception he was getting. The previous Sunday he had gone with his mother to the Baptist church in his little hometown of Pittsfield, Maine (population 5,600). The minister virtually denounced him from the pulpit. "He talked about how wrong the war was," Skip said, "and how anybody fighting it was a war criminal. And when the service was over, he cut me dead. I couldn't believe it. I thought I was fighting for my country." The antiwar movement had reached even into the quiet streets of this country town where people built their own flagpoles.

He never mentioned it on the telephone and for long after that, but Skip was awarded the Soldier's Medal "for exceptionally valorous actions" performed less than two months after we first met in the Delta. Three soldiers had miscalculated a river current and were in danger of drowning when Skip jumped in and rescued them. By the time the war ended for him in 1972, after four tours with two extensions, he had won twenty-three air medals as a helicopter door gunner, each one representing 25 combat assault hours, for a total of 575 hair-raising hours over hot LZs.

"I'm going back in nine days," Skip said. "Are you coming?"

I laughed and felt a stab of envy.

"See ya round," he said, signing off. "Meanwhile, keep your ass down."

THE New York Democratic mayoral primary on June 17 promised to be another Broadway show. The colorful cast included tough guy–novelist and reformed wife-stabber Norman Mailer and oafishly macho columnist Jimmy Breslin, who announced themselves as candidates for mayor and city council president respectively. Mailer, spearheading a "New Journalism," was an undisputed literary icon of the decade, chronicling the country's spasms—Vietnam, politics, and space—in a remarkable series of books.

"This is a dangerous thing for a writer to do," he declared, his renowned ego warming to the hustings. A phalanx of literary lights whose main outlet was *New York* magazine flocked to his side, including a leftover speech writer from the McCarthy campaign. Eventually, the literati faded away, leaving the McCarthyites and former Kennedy volunteers to express themselves in still one more crusade.

Breslin, who felt the body politic needed to be governed with "imagination," played Ralph Kramden to Mailer's Ed Norton, getting the laughs when he pointed out in true New York tradition that the front-runner in the nine-candidate race would undoubtedly be indicted, or instructing Norman not to shake hands with anyone who doesn't "look Jewish" because they're the only ones who voted. Their campaign slogan was No More Bullshit, which even in those emancipated times was reported with the expletive deleted. But their main message, their assault on the imagination, took the insiders by surprise: New York should become the nation's fifty-first state. Secession.

A media event was born, sired by experts.

That these two short, stout, dough-faced men got any votes at all was a tribute to their writerly skill (they had ready access to the newspapers and magazines and used it), their ability as end men in a minstrel show, and, most of all, the hunger of TV news for politics as jazz. They were regulars on the daily news budget, and I fell right in step, covering their peculiar performances at "campaign stops," interviewing them straightfaced, pretending this clown act was a legitimate political story. What we really wanted was a few laughs, some comic relief to use as a closer. They shrewdly complied; TV was calling the tune, and they played along. The road show didn't translate into votes—John Lindsay was reelected—but Mailer and Breslin were the hands-down winners on the evening news.

THERE is nothing worse than a midsummer day in Washington, D.C., hot, empty, dead. On the weekend of July 18, 1969, I was there to attend the wedding of Geoffrey Pond, one of WNBC's anchormen and reporters. On the 19th, shortly after noon, a cryptic wire story about an accident on Cape Cod began to attract attention in the NBC Washington bureau. New York was on the line. Something about Ted Kennedy. And a word no one in the newsroom could pronounce kept surfacing: Chappaquiddick.

"A car? You're kidding? A girl? Off a what? Holy shit!"

"Trotta. Go. Grab the shuttle to New York and call the desk from La Guardia."

It was typical of how assignments were given out. The nearest body at a given moment. Nobody consulted a list of favorite sons or a ratings sheet for popularity among viewers. A story broke, and the next guy up went. There were, of course, exceptions on specific beats, like the space program, which had a NASA correspondent, but for general coverage, the star system still only applied to show business.

By the time I was on the New York–Boston shuttle, more details had filtered in from our stringers on the Cape. After the Edgartown regatta at Martha's Vineyard, there had been a party in a rented house on the neighboring island of Chappaquiddick. Kennedy and a few of his cronies attended, along with some girls who had worked on his brother Bobby's presidential campaign. Kennedy had left the party with one of them, Mary Jo Kopechne, and somehow the car he was driving had gone off a bridge. Kennedy escaped; she was drowned. And although the accident had happened on Friday night, Kennedy did not report it until the next morning. It didn't add up; but so many stories don't in the first few hours. My overriding feelings were still at one with most of the press. It didn't seem fair, or even possible, that the "Kennedy curse" was still at work. I had met and covered Jack Kennedy as a Columbia student, carrying a fake press pass when he was campaigning for the presidency in 1960. Bobby had been a staple on my daily rounds during the two years I covered New York City politics—and now brother number three, whom I had never met, a senator and almost certainly a presidential candidate in 1972.

As for the obvious connotations of a "secretary" and a "party"— sex and drinking—it was still the era of keeping the lid on private lives of public figures, and in the case of the Kennedy family news was a sacred trust if it didn't fit the Camelot image. Indeed, the same approach extended to the space program and to the astronauts in particular (despite their peccadilloes at Cape Canaveral), three of whom were about to make that giant leap for mankind that very weekend. The Kennedy magic prevailed: rich, worldly, good-looking, Ivy League, and liberal. But this very magic—its irresistible power to co-opt reporters—would in the end be the legend's undoing. Reporters from most of the nation's major news organizations invaded Martha's Vineyard, and many more were on the way from Europe. The medieval morality play of handsome prince and tavern wench had begun. Journalism as allegory swept across the island—and onto the front pages.

While the networks sent their line correspondents, New York and Washington newspapers and magazines sent political point men and assorted pundits, some of whom would normally have access to the Kennedys, such as Hugh Sidey of *Time*, who blankly told me he "couldn't understand the silence from the family. Why, I was playing tennis with Ethel down at MacLean only last weekend." It was that kind of story.

Ted Kennedy's political aspirations overshadowed the story's criminal aspects, his chances for the presidency deemed more critical than whether Mary Jo Kopechne had died because Kennedy was drunk and speeding. The only newsmen on the scene who seemed to be approaching the story for what it actually was came from the Chicago newspapers, tough crime reporters who hung out at the bridge examining the skid marks. True, every reporter was interested in the details of the accident, but only Kennedy's presidential future made them significant; the moral vacuum exposed by the incident was of secondary interest, at least at first.

Reporters were met by a blank wall in a coverup executed by various waves of Kennedy linebackers, Irish Mafiosi, New Frontier phrasemakers, dozens of lawyers, and a state politically and legally wired by men in some way beholden to the family. The first person Kennedy was said to have told about the accident—apart from his friends Paul Markham and Joseph Gargan, who were part of the conspiracy of silence that night—was his administrative assistant David Burke. Burke, along with others in the Praetorian Guard, played a major role in constructing the story to feed the press and went on to become an aide to Governor Hugh Carey of New York, an executive at ABC News, and then president of CBS News, shepherding his staff in the service of truth for two years.

Dick Drayne, the senator's press secretary, left the safety of Washington for Edgartown and its encampment of four to five hundred reporters. A master of the velvet con, Drayne donned his khakis and shetland sweaters, affected a melancholy walk, not unlike those much-photographed lone beach strolls taken by Jack and Bobby, and then allowed sotto voce as how the senator was sailing on the family yacht. A portrait of a brooding man in shock and mourning emerged with spurious ease from such as Drayne, but not the hard, cold fact that Ted Kennedy was pulling out the stops to save his skin.

Much of the prepping and snooping for our coverage was done by a formidable old-guard film cameraman, Nemo Gaskill, a lumberjack of a man who in World War II days wrote a basic, classic primer for newsreel cameramen. Nemo lived on the Cape, and it showed in his ruddy sailor's complexion and flat *a*'s. Towering over his colleagues, he would part the crowds with his bulk and folksy confidence. "Network News, step aside, please." He was so well liked, that almost everyone did make way.

Nemo's plug into the local rumor mill was paying off, so the day Kennedy got back to Hyannis after attending Mary Jo Kopechne's funeral in Wilkes-Barre, Pennsylvania, we were ready for him to step off the family DC-3. Up until now, four days after the accident, Kennedy had made no statement of any kind to the besieging army of newsmen, whose sympathy and reverence to the Kennedy name was beginning to unravel. Nine hours after the accident, he had made his ambiguous statement to the Edgartown police chief, Dominick Arena, sneaked out the back door of the police station, and gone into seclusion at the family compound. All we had was the police report, contemptuously incomplete, as we would later learn. Thereafter the silence was deafening.

Apollo 11's spectacular landing on the moon had offered glorious if brief distraction, but by Wednesday, most of us covering the story were straining at the bit. News desks were clamoring for details, color, anything. Here was our first crack at the senator outside the towers of Camelot, and when Kennedy and his pregnant wife, Joan, deplaned at Hyannis shortly after 2 P.M., a wave of newspeople surged forward, the

TV cameras vying for frontline positions. Cables crossed and tangled, still photographers swore under their breath, reporters hung on to their mikes and note pads as Kennedy, his head swiveling in a neck brace worn since the accident, headed for a waiting car. This was not "the appropriate time" to talk, he said, and with that continued cutting his way through the mob, which started to melt away. I was walking to his left at a clip, not quite believing that a man who had gone off a bridge with a girl and just attended her funeral could have nothing to say. Didn't anybody around here wonder about Mary Jo Kopechne? The senator, his brain trust and connivers at the compound, the state Democratic party, and now even members of the press—all energetically committed to not mentioning the deceased.

I hit him with a stream of questions about Mary Jo, all of which he ignored. Then, "Do you think this will adversely affect your political career?" Scarlet bled into his face, the raw, beefy look that would increase with his age and girth. Who would dare challenge the prince? He wheeled on me, stopped short, looked directly down with deep-set bear eyes and hissed through clenched teeth: "I've just come from the funeral of a very lovely young lady, and this is not the appropriate time for such questions. I am not going to have any other comment to make."

Nemo was rolling throughout the whole exchange. Such loss of control before a hot mike and camera seems unthinkable today, as politicians have been schooled in the art of cool lest they commit ritual suicide on the evening news.

Our Boston affiliate, WBZ, ran Kennedy's reply unedited, but NBC in New York cut around it, uneasy about showing the sainted senator under attack by one of their own. But the story did prompt comment from the front office on another count. The only clothes I had with me on the Cape were a pair of blue jeans and a T-shirt. The crush of getting positioned on the story took precedence over shopping. Nevertheless, trousers, pantsuits, and especially blue jeans were verboten in the dignified days of NBC News. The airport sequence, much of it shot full-length, prompted no praise for sticking to the reluctant senator but a lecture from Corrigan on my wayward wardrobe. "Never—never—again do I want to see you in pants oncamera."

The next public development was Kennedy's appearance at the Edgartown District Court the following Friday to plead guilty to leaving the scene of an accident. He received a two-month suspended sentence and a year's probation. Reporters were stiffed again, but they only had to wait a few hours until that evening, when Kennedy bought fifteen minutes on the three networks to amplify his version of the accident.

By this time, Edgartown was overrun by reporters. The story had taken on the proportions of a major scandal. It had all the necessary ingredients: power, wealth, sex, death, handsome people and even a big white house—everything except a credible story line.

Even the logistics of the tale seemed designed to frustrate reporting it. The Kennedy compound was in Hyannis Port on Cape Cod; Edgartown, on Martha's Vineyard, was about twenty minutes away by plane, an hour by boat. A ferry made the channel crossing, from the Edgartown dock to Chappaquiddick, in about four minutes. The compound had to be staked out most of the day to spot Kennedy and his associates, while the legal and investigative action, such as it was, took place at Edgartown. Trips to "Chappy" meant feature stories, such as reenactments of how it might have looked through the front window of a car going over the bridge, scary even in daylight. Because nothing was predictable, especially the weather, and the ferry schedules were set, we had to ensure our own mobility with a flotilla of boats and a squadron of small charter planes. At one point, I had under my "command" six airplanes, four cars, a schooner, and a catamaran. We lived in both Hyannis Port and Edgartown, but all the pictures shot each day, plus the correspondent, had to be flown to WBZ in Boston, an hour away by charter, so that we could edit and send the piece down to New York for broadcast on the network. After the program each night, I boarded a Piper back to the Cape for the next day's story. If the fog rolled in, suddenly and silently as it often did, you took your chances on a white-knuckle express. One night we actually raced the lightning from Boston to the Vineyard, landing just as it streaked across the airport.

The hounds were loose after Kennedy's speech. Apart from his preposterous account of the accident, and what he left out, the cynical attempt to wrap himself in his dead brother Jack's shroud by quoting from his book was galling to a press that was beginning to suspect it had been "had." Borrowing quotes from Jack was a habit Kennedy did not give up, even after the accident, as I would learn later in another part of the world. His account of the accident, tersely offering no details, had admitted only that his delay in reporting the accident was "indefensible." In Kennedy's version, he wasn't drunk, wasn't sexually involved with Mary Jo, wasn't speeding, and was "in shock" after the plunge, which is why he didn't report the accident until nine hours later. Only a few new details emerged when he said that along with Gargan and Markham he had dived into the "murky current," trying in vain to rescue Kopechne. Most intriguing of all was Kennedy's claim that he swam ("nearly drowning once again in the effort") across the channel from the island dock to Edgartown.

If there had been a residual sense of respect, a fading ray of light emanating from the broken keep, it was dissipated by the triumph of insincerity and bathos in Kennedy's TV attempt to put it all to rest. It was one of the colossal failures of television manipulation. If television could make a presidential candidate, it could also break him. What might have cleared the senator for all time—a believable account of the accident—dissolved before the merciless eye of the camera. Kennedy had failed to convince the only court that could acquit him: the nation.

Back at Hyannis Port, Kennedy was either "secluded in his house on Squaw Island" or "sailing and going on picnics within the compound." The police reporters spent their days badgering officials and their nights drawing diagrams of the bridge. The Brits swam the channel between Edgartown and Chappy while their colleagues clocked them. The Washington clique of political writers sucked their thumbs over their typewriters, and the sick jokes began to surface, as they usually do with an idle press. If there was any trace of civility left, it was only that accorded to Rose Kennedy, the ever-staunch matriarch of the clan. Reporters showed up at St. Francis Xavier Church in Hyannis every Sunday when she arrived to attend mass, but no one had the nerve to question her. In fact, they backed away as though some invisible shield surrounded her person.

By late August, the battle was on for control of the inquest. Kennedy's people won a delay by insisting on the right to cross-examine witnesses, which they did not win, and, most important, the right to exclude the public and press. They wanted a secret hearing because of "a gathering crescendo of publicity." Meanwhile, something rather astounding was happening, not on the Cape but back at 30 Rock. It was no secret that Kennedy's front men, such as Drayne and Burke, were calling in IOUs from their friends in the press. In fact, Drayne systematically sidled up to reporters from the major news organizations, pitching them to go easy, just as if these were the good ol' pre–Mary Jo days. The night he got around to me I was less than cordial, especially since I was a New York–based reporter and we had no track record or friendship to draw on. The message was to get on the team, try for some softballs, let up on the bitchy stuff. In response,

I continued to play hardball, as had been my style since I arrived. And by the way, what about Mary Jo Kopechne? She still seemed to be the one person no one wanted to mention.

One day in the NBC newsroom, shortly after the court had decided on the inquest rules and we were waiting for a date to be set, a vice-president started asking about how I was being treated up at the Cape. A peculiarly subjective question, I thought, since I knew that management was satisfied with what I was sending.

"Well," he said, looking over his rimless glasses, "you know they made it very clear they don't want you around."

"You mean on the story? Someone from Kennedy's office complained?"

He hesitated, folded his arms, and said softly, "They did."

"And?"

"They wanted us to take you off the story."

He started to say something else and stopped.

"Go ahead. What else?"

"They wanted you out of NBC News."

I was silent, not sure I had heard it right.

"Don't worry about it. You're going back to cover the inquest. Just forget all about what I told you—for good."

I spent the autumn of that year covering Chappaquiddick maneuvers on two fronts: a campaign to exhume Mary Jo's body, and a preinquest drive by Kennedy's lawyers to limit the damage. By winter, two critical decisions had been made: the Massachusetts Supreme Judicial Court ruled that the inquest would be conducted in secret; and a Pennsylvania judge decided that Mary Jo's body should remain undisturbed. But judicial rulings could not erase her memory.

THE drumbeat of the sixties sounded loud and harsh that summer and fall. People knew something was over, finished, a chapter closed, but what next? *Apollo 11* had let in some light, but we couldn't colonize the moon. And the druggy self-indulgence of the counterfeit hip world that climaxed in Woodstock that August only underlined the sense of having nowhere to go. In Vietnam, 25,000 men left for the States, first of the troop withdrawals promised by Nixon, and Hanoi's armies lay low, waiting.

Two sets of alumni emerged from the decade, those who pressed their Woodstock tickets in the pages of Hermann Hesse and those who told their children about hunting Cong in Nam. Meanwhile, events roared on. If the psychopath of the year in 1968 had been Sirhan Sirhan, surely Charles Manson and his troop of crazies took honors for 1969 after a two-day spree in August, when they slaughtered pregnant actress Sharon Tate and six others.

If the Kennedy accident was Arthurian, the Manson murders took on the coloration of the Aquarian age: revolutionary slogans written in the blood of the victims, a killer who called himself Jesus Christ, a harem of love children who lived in the desert, homicidal hipness. But the same substances that kept the crowds tame at Woodstock drove Manson and his band to murder. It just depended on what kind and how much. And the smug argument of the decade—that a little marijuana never hurt anybody—dissolved into silence and depravity as smoking, snorting, and injecting began to kill more people than any M16 ever had.

Not everybody in the nation was drugged out. Not the New York Mets. The worst team in the major leagues, having lost an average of 105 games over seven seasons, the "amazin' Mets" were on their way from ninth place at the end of 1968 to becoming a national treasure that summer of 1969. The day they won the World Series I was in an editing room at 30 Rock, overlooking the roof of Radio City Music Hall. On warm days, the editors often amused themselves by looking out the windows at the Rockettes rehearsing their numbers or simply sunbathing in bikinis. On this glorious autumn afternoon, they were out there again, but this time throwing confetti and streamers, just as everybody else was from every skyscraper in Manhattan. A blitz of colored paper and ticker tape rained onto the city's canyons in honor of the boys who had made it up from the cellar. And from the editing rooms of NBC News, hundreds of feet of film sailed into the wind toward the skating rink, whirling above the gilded head of the great Prometheus who pondered it all. American optimism renewed itself, and violinist Isaac Stern told the *Times*: "If the Mets can win the series, anything can happen—even peace."

The casualty reports droned on from the battlefields. The peace talks were awash in bickering. The only good news came from the other side of the front: Ho Chi Minh died. By mid-October, I had agreed to go back for just one month more, "so some of our people can get leave." I couldn't resist. Just one more time. I missed covering the story, and besides, Jake was in Hong Kong now, having replaced Steinman as director of Far East news. It had been a long time since I'd heard from him. Never say die, in love or war: a mistake. We had returned to New York together, in a driving snowstorm, at the end of my first tour of Vietnam. For me, a heroine's reception, especially with the announcement that I had won an Overseas Press Club Award. It was ashes. Jake and I were finished. He had found someone else. There was a last attempt to resurrect the past, but the words rang hollow. Still, of all the memories, the shades and ghosts of lost loves, it is Jake's image that retains the sharpest outline and is most intensely part of the landscape of that time and place.

By November 3, I was back in the Saigon bureau. Lew Allison was in charge, one of our Los Angeles producers and a former newspaperman. Not only was he game—he had left a wife and three children behind—but he was deft, a first-class writer and editor. Lew invented amiability; he was a man who got along with everyone. Jack Klein, his number two, was trying to find a refrigerator on the day I burst back into the office. Another refugee from print, Jack had been working on the "Today" show in New York and wanted to try his wings. He looked incongruous in that musty place, especially since he had long ago earned the title of the best-dressed man at NBC News.

The story was the U.S. pullout, the "Vietnamization" of the war. The Ninth Division in the Delta would be the first to leave; by the end of the year the overall troop level stood at about 470,000. Much of what we did was in response to developments in Washington, talking to soldiers in the field about Nixon's plan to end the war, going home. Physically, the place hadn't changed at all, except perhaps that it looked sadder than my dreams remembered. About 9,000 men had been killed since I left in January.

The night of November 3, Nixon delivered a major speech on national television, saying that unilateral withdrawal would be a disaster for the country because it would encourage the enemy to continue their aggression and frustrate the peace talks. He asked for support from "you, the great silent majority of my fellow Americans." Nixon's message was not complicated: foreign aggression should be stopped; precipitate withdrawal of troops would only lead to more aggression. "Let us understand: North Vietnam cannot defeat or humiliate the United States. Only Americans can do that."

The public response to the speech was indisputably favorable. The polls, according to Brinkley the following night, showed "a division of somewhere around sixty–forty." A Gallup Poll indicated 77 percent approved of the speech. Even members of Congress from both sides of the aisle went along with the policy, except the hard-core critics like Senator William Fulbright, who stated the obvious, that Johnson's war had become Nixon's war.

During his administration, and especially later in his writings, Nixon often commented on the quality of war coverage, asserting that the media had come to dominate the conduct of the war. He conceded that television had showed the suffering of war as never before but added that "it conveyed little or no sense of the underlying purpose of the fighting" and "fostered the impression that we were fighting in military and moral quicksand."

There it was again, like an old telex from the New York desk. We hadn't really caught the war—"the underlying purpose," the Big Picture—in our cameras. But how could we, when even the high command, although intellectually committed to opposing communism, was fighting a war based on a compromised, confused policy. Every dead American on the evening news seemed a casualty of some amorphous American mistake rather than of the ferocious ideology of a brutal enemy. It wasn't the antiwar marchers that convinced so many that the war was wrong, but the American practicality that said, "If it doesn't work, throw it out." By the end of 1969, we were dedicated to that course.

Nixon had another battle on his hands—his perennial war with the media—and he chose Vice-President Agnew as the warrior to lead a counterattack. On November 13, in the Huntley-Brinkley newsroom in New York, Westfeldt got the word that Agnew would deliver a speech before the Mid-West Regional Republican Committee in Des Moines that afternoon. It was a blistering salvo aimed at TV news, and it targeted the "tiny and closed fraternity of privileged men elected by no one" who produced and broadcast the network evening news programs. He specifically cited the "instant analysis and querulous criticism" by TV commentators after Nixon's November 3 address, saying their minds had been made up in advance. Then Agnew took very personal aim at the men who ran the news broadcasts, who lived, he said, within the intellectual provincialism of Washington, D.C., and New York City, read the same newspapers, had the same opinions, and talked to one another constantly.

Vice-presidents-in-charge-of-fear headed for the windows. They had gotten away with a lot and they knew it. Whether they liked Nixon-Agnew or not—and they didn't—this was the White House talking, and they sat in their leather swivel chairs only by virtue of a license from the government. What's more, the "silent majority" did indeed exist and had shown its support of Nixon's new Vietnam policy not only after his speech, but more vividly in the wake of Agnew's attack. While he laid on the East Coast collusion theory to the edge of absurdity, still he had struck a chord: America was sick of TV news bias. The term "credibility gap," so often applied by the media to the official line, was now hurled back at them by an irate public. Calls to the networks rallied behind the administration. NBC News president Reuven Frank made the obligatory comments about the medium being blamed for the message, and Westfeldt, one of the invisible manipulators Agnew had indicated, swore he had never even met the CBS and ABC executive producers who were supposed to be managing the news along with him. Wally also took pains to point out that he read *Le Monde*.

A national debate ensued. Undeniably, TV news had many faults, but Agnew's description of its elite as "nattering nabobs of negativism" seemed to bury the medium's real faults in petulant jargon. Perhaps the most savvy comment came from a political science type who pointed out that junior producers in their twenties with little or no news background made some of the most critical decisions in the editing rooms, selecting which pictures to use and for how long. They called themselves filmmakers. And they would soon reshape the character of television news.

If the Nixon White House sought to intimidate the nets, it worked. Although professing business as usual, the news departments walked warily. No edicts went out, no public floggings, but "getting both sides" of the story was taken out of mothballs, and there was at least lip service to maintaining some emotional distance from the war. "Let the pictures tell the story"—always the clarion call when pictures are hot—came up for review, at least temporarily. Some suspected that perhaps pictures—without clear reporting and writing—weren't always enough.

The networks were so upset they even tried PR. Not long after Agnew's speech, I bumped into Huntley by the fifth-floor elevators. He told me he was disturbed by what he had just heard at an NBC affiliates convention. If there was any "pulse of the people," this was the place to read it. Huntley had been sent to calm the restless natives; it hadn't worked. "Our stations are furious at us," he said. "They agree with Agnew and are after us. I tried to placate them, of course, but they're mad as hell."

It was a friendless time for TV news in many ways. Both sides of the standoff, the Nixon White House and the antiwar movement, despite the wide coverage their messages received, remained convinced we were part of a conspiracy against them; and while the networks licked their wounds and issued pieties about their first amendment rights and the threat of government manipulation, North Vietnam was still skillfully playing the opposition in America to its deadly advantage. In fact, on the very same day as the Agnew speech, Xuan Thuy, Hanoi's chief negotiator in Paris, hailed the protestors and made it clear how much North Vietnam valued their support.

"So you're back." Everyone on the Shelf had greeted me on the day of my return as if they'd been expecting me. And for a while I was relieved to be there, relishing the sense of freedom—from screaming demonstrators, executive memos, nylon stockings, rumbling cities, ticking clocks, a plate for one with food enough for three. It was the wildness I had missed, living close to the edge and the patient desperation of a city fighting for its life. Nothing was tamed here—not the roads, not the houses, not even the weather. No, it hadn't been the dream I sometimes thought it was back in the States, that I had never been to a place called Vietnam, that it was all a hoax or fantasy. It was real. My Oriental Brigadoon.

The "Vietnamization" of the war added a new terror to combat assignments. Some old hands used to covering U.S. troops saw going out with Viets as an opportunity to qualify for "graves and registration," the official body bag collectors. I went out on a few, dropped in on some more Special Forces border camps, and concentrated on political stories from Saigon in the wake of Nixon's moves.

Most of the old gang was still around, even Craig J. Spence, who had managed to get back into the country despite his mysterious ouster by the military almost a year earlier. In the interim he had been "touring around," rolling his eyes for effect and tapping at his corncob pipe. One night the scratchy sound of Christmas carols played on an old hi-fi was wafting over the Shelf when a breathless messenger from the office came into focus under the veranda light. "Very important. Very important. You come, quick."

Spence and I finished our drinks and bolted for the office. When I picked up my desk phone, I recognized the voice immediately. Skip Ettinger was back. "I knew you couldn't resist," he laughed. He had picked up my whereabouts on the tom-tom circuit.

"Where are you? Down south?"

"Uh-uh. Guess."

"Hanoi?"

"Not this trip. I'm right around the corner from you. At the Caravelle."

Craig and I were over there in less than three minutes, picking our way through a floorful of sleeping room boys and a noisy assortment of French and German diplomatic types throwing a good-bye party.

We knocked on the door. Skip hollered for us to come in. He was about a bottle and a half into his cups, lying on the bed and staring up at the ceiling fan, a boy who had been spooking "upriver" too many times, now sprawled here, drunk and at least three days AWOL. He had come up to Saigon from My Tho to scrounge some parachutes for the Special Forces, and had been overwhelmed by the temptation to stay around the big city for a while. Now it was a question of getting out of town before the MPs spotted him, so Craig and I brought food and provided cover until he got his act together and slipped into the darkness, back to the war he just couldn't leave.

For the next two months Huynh and I prowled around looking for stories, sometimes waist-deep in the Big Muddy again, feeling an almost palpable despair creeping into the atmosphere. "They never learned to think like guerrillas," he said one afternoon as we slogged through another operation with a U.S. patrol. "Simple things, like, you know, the VC has to have water because they're far from their supply base so you must follow the water to find them."

That day remains stark among my recollections of the time, an unprinted negative, a reverse image, a moment turned inside out, with the sun bearing down on us and the airless suspicion that it was all falling apart. My foot touched something hard in the tall yellow grass and I paused. Lying in the weeds, rusty, crushed—an old Coca-Cola can. When had it been dropped? A week ago? A month, a year? We had been here before—and now we were moving around in circles. I picked it up and held it in my hand like a dead bird. It didn't matter anymore. The war was over.

9

KNIGHTS
AND
KNAVES

The bridge loomed black against the winter sky in late afternoon. The water looked deadly, its current rushing hard. A stiff wind riffled a growth of beach reeds that zigzagged beneath the thick timbers supporting its raised spine. Was it the accident that made this sight so foreboding? Without the memory, one could have mistaken Dyke Bridge for the lost fragment of a carnival roller-coaster.

"Mary Jo-oh? Mary Jo-oh?" My colleague Jack Perkins, hand cupped over his mouth, stage-whispered the name as we rowed under the bridge. It was the embodied voice of a press corps gone mad with cynicism and ennui. A secret proceeding, no sources to interview, the Kennedy veil in place.

Now, in early January, six months after Senator Kennedy drove his black Oldsmobile off the bridge, the veteran reporters of Chappaquiddick, hardened by stonewalling, returned to Edgartown for the inquest. Augmenting this band of originals and their innumerable reinforcements, an army of technicians turned Main Street into an appropriate set for what would be the next, and perhaps the last, act of this melodrama. The networks virtually owned Edgartown for the coverage of the inquest. One unit manager (the man in charge of the money) found out he was two bathrooms short, so he simply rented all the houses on an adjoining street.

Perkins, an aging love child of the sixties, was assigned to do the offbeat, special kind of pieces that would show off his singular wit and writing style. Jack's radical chic was the despair of network brass. It got so bad that Chet Huntley actually wrote a memo requesting that he discontinue wearing headbands and blue jeans on the air. But Jack's fertile imagination, supplemented by my natural instinct for trouble, helped fill the long hours with one madcap prank after another. By this time, reporters were gleefully mailing color postcards of the bridge, already much diminished since the accident by souvenir hunters pulling off splinters. And the night before the inquest opened, Cornelius "Connie" Hurley of AP in Boston began enrolling his brethren in the Chappaquiddick Press Club. A dollar got you a press card with room for your name and checkoffs as a "swimmer" or "nonswimmer."

On the first day of the inquest, Senator Kennedy turned up in front of the courthouse, now a vortex of cameras and microphones. History must have a record of the decade's biggest midlife crisis of all. He was, of course, the principal witness. The five "boiler room girls" who had been guests at the party arrived, tittering, decked out in boots and miniskirts. During Robert Kennedy's 1968 campaign, they got their gritty nickname as loyal workers who collected information on delegates to the Democratic National Convention. Newsmen lunged toward the steps when the senator reappeared, having answered questions for two hours and then telling reporters outside that his statements to Judge James A. Boyle were substantially the same as those in his television address of July 25, 1969, a week after the accident. It was the last time he would be legally required to talk about the death of Mary Jo Kopechne. His spokesmen immediately issued statements asserting that he was "confident and looking ahead." I ended my piece that night by saying, "The courtroom is closed to the world and the complete story of Chappaquiddick has yet to be told."

During the second day the boiler room girls walked in and out of the courthouse without comment to anyone. The boiler room was used to taking instructions from Kennedys, and indeed from men in general. They were the almost invisible inhabitants of a world where men still did the important talking, and the "girls" were completely loyal and even gave every impression that they regarded their labors as a sacred service. Working for a Kennedy meant they had "arrived" in the nation's capital. It was easy to shut them up, keep them in tow, and make sure their testimony didn't contradict the pat version of events. No one bucked a Kennedy.

We started and ended our piece at the bridge that night, recapping the accident at the top and ending with a picture of the new timbers added to the side of the bridge, replacing those which Kennedy's car had scarred as it plunged. We also reported that someone had carved into the bridge's center a heart, enclosing the names "Ted and Mary."

Headquarters for the newspeople had been set up in a church basement down the street from the courtroom: long tables of reporters screaming into telephones. Theo Wilson of the New York *Daily News*, last of the great trial reporters, sat behind me, filling me in when technology pulled me away from the scene. Theo was a typing machine: one night in particular, she turned out in succession an inquest story and a lengthy obit of Dr. Sam Sheppard, whose trial for murder she had, of course, covered in the great tabloid's heyday. Speed, accuracy, smarts—she had it all, and for years was a model of what I wanted to be.

Shortly before 6 P.M. one evening, in the midst of the panic before deadline, District Attorney Edmund Dinis shuffled in unannounced. It was a free-for-all, and when I returned to my seat, the one copy of my script was gone, swiped vengefully by a competing network or a lady from *Life* magazine who operated as a Kennedy defender in and out of print. With less than ten minutes to spare, and under the soothing words of Drew Phillips, our on-scene producer, I wrote like a demon and reached the live camera on Main Street just in time.

Reporters dusted off all the Currier and Ives clichés for the third day of the inquest. New England quaintness was being stretched to the absurd as great white snowflakes softened Main Street and blew up the many august noses. That day local witnesses were called to the stand, the most important of them Christopher "Huck" Look, the county deputy sheriff who said he had seen a car like Kennedy's approaching Dyke Bridge on the night of the accident. John Farrar, who ran a marine supplies shop, was the diver who brought up Mary Jo's body. He said then and repeatedly over the years that an air pocket had probably formed in the car; to his mind, this meant that Kopechne must have been alive for some time after the crash—three minutes, he told me in an interview, expanded in later statements to "easily an hour" and by the late 1980s to "perhaps an hour and a half or two hours." At the inquest, the judge cut him off just as he was about to offer this unsettling possibility.

Eventually, four days of testimony led to nothing. Judge Boyle's own cynicism was quite clear in the official transcript released four months later. But in the meantime, we were desperate for copy. How many features can you do on a bridge, how many thumb-suckers on Kennedy's "presidential future." Our frustration made itself felt in stunning silliness on the last day, when the state police announced that because it was all over and everyone had left, we could inspect the courtroom. Phillips and I darted upstairs. I spotted a full wastebasket and began searching its contents until a pair of high black boots came into view at eye level. I looked up from all fours into the barely concealed contempt of a state trooper. "You're wasting your time, Liz," he said. "We've already searched it."

Undaunted, I ambled into the library next door where the witnesses had waited their turn and, out of the trooper's view, hastily slipped a clump of torn notebook paper from a glass ashtray into my sheepskin parka. "Quick," I whispered to Phillips, "let's get out of here. I think I've got something!"

We raced down the back stairs, pulling up out of breath in the thin, cold air under a giant willow tree. Glancing furtively around, I stealthily pulled out the pilfered papers. Phillips panted in anticipation. I held them tightly in my frozen mittens and began to read: "One black and five regulars."

Phillips collapsed in a belly laugh, I uttered several four- and five-letter words, and we both went out for what the message requested.

The following April a grand jury—another secret proceeding— was convened for two days to reopen the case, but as usual the Kennedy network stymied any revelations. Only four witnesses were called. "The case is closed," said District Attorney Dinis, relief overwhelming his usual air of befuddlement. In closing our piece that night I said: "It appears that every criminal, legal inquiry into the death of Mary Jo Kopechne has been exhausted. And that, in fact, the case *is* closed so far as Dukes County is concerned. But in many minds there are still unanswered questions. Perhaps the transcript of the January inquest will clear them up. And perhaps it won't."

And it didn't.

Instead, the greatest miscalculation in modern politics continued to fester. Chappaquiddick haunted the public's memory: the specter of a young girl left to drown in the dark. The hopes, the plans for the last of the Kennedy brothers to unite a divided party were derailed as surely as the car that had hurtled off the Dyke Bridge. One by one, the knights rode out of Camelot, disappearing into the Arthurian mist.

Eventually, new information did emerge, not from Kennedy but from author Leo Damore, who interviewed Joe Gargan, Kennedy's cousin and fellow host at the party. Damore maintains that when Gargan went back to the bridge with Kennedy shortly after the accident to try to save Mary Jo, Kennedy suggested strongly that Gargan report the accident and say that Mary Jo had been alone in the car. Anything rather than implicate Cousin Teddy. The senator had nothing to say about the new revelations.

He was returned to the Senate by a loyal Massachusetts electorate in the fall of 1970. Joseph Kopechne, still grieving twenty years later for his only child, said it hadn't been all in vain. "Mary Jo's death kept the senator from becoming president."

Appetite comes with eating: the media had brought down a fine buck but not the leader of the herd. They were at the ready for a Watergate. No more getting massaged by the organization. The age of "boys will be boys," of keeping the gloves on when writing about the private lives of public figures, was over. Politicians were fair game. And the TV camera became the hunter's best weapon.

It was the cusp of the seventies, a time of marches and parades, seizing buildings, breaking into military installations, general mayhem. If the cavalier treatment of Mary Jo Kopechne's death hadn't influenced a spirit of rebellion among women, a sense that the world was flying out of control spurred them to take a close look at their lives. Only three women were numbered among heads of government: Sirimavo Bandaranaike of Sri Lanka (then Ceylon), who became prime minister upon her husband's assassination in 1959, lost power in 1965, and returned for another seven years in 1970; Golda Meir of Israel, who succeeded Levi Eshkol and served as prime minister from 1969 to 1974; and Indira Gandhi, perhaps the strongest and most truly independent of the three, who was patronizingly placed at the head of the Indian government in 1966 by a clique of self-satisfied gerontocrats as Nehru's unthreatening daughter. She lasted eleven tough years, returning in 1980 for four more until her assassination. Regarding this hard-boiled trio, feminists might have been well served to note that politics was, indeed, a very brutal business.

By this time, the sisters had burned enough bras for Westfeldt to order a series of stories on women's rights, or lack thereof. I did the first piece, starting with a stream of fathers pacing outside a maternity ward who told me they were waiting for "a son" to be born. The stories, of course, were assigned to the tiny group of women on the staff, Aline Saarinen, Cassie Mackin, Norma Quarles, and myself. I had little to complain about. Hadn't this network sent me to a war and just about any other assignment usually reserved for men?

Betty Friedan, who had got the whole thing going with her insightful book *The Feminine Mystique*, dropped by one day for a radio interview; and right in the middle, as I pressed her about "what women really wanted," she shot back: "Why aren't you Huntley or Brinkley?" My mouth opened, but no answer came out. The answer was, of course, that I wasn't good enough—not yet anyway. But the essence of the question—what would happen if and when I was— opened up a topic I didn't wish to debate on the air. And that fact alone disturbed me. I couldn't imagine the day when I would ever anchor a network show, because my ambition ended at being a foreign correspondent. Besides, the great reporters of TV news had not made their name sitting in a studio, reading what other people were doing around the world.

It was no coincidence that women gained confidence during an unpopular war. The grunts and the high command reeked of male chauvinism, as did the very pictures of the war itself. Worse, men were failing at it; the collapse of male authority was colossal, and it unleashed a flood of dismay, disillusion, mockery, and at last of action-generating resentment from blacks, women, and eventually even homosexuals. If they had been lacking in nerve to march for their places in the sun, the ever-present example of ferment against the war gave them steel.

On April 30, President Nixon announced that U.S. forces were on their way into Cambodia. It was to be a major offensive, a joint operation of sixty days' duration with South Vietnamese troops. Nixon was risking the political heat to go after VC sanctuaries declared off limits throughout the war, even though the enemy used them as bases from which to strike and resupply. His timing for the invasion couldn't have been worse: right around spring break.

A storm of protest ripped through the country. Campuses exploded in fury, and waves of protest swept into schools that were newcomers to the protest game—schools like Kent State. It was there, on May 4, that the reality principle set in, incontrovertible proof that violence invites violence. In a fusillade of National Guard gunfire, four students were killed.

To the antiwar activists it was a collegiate My Lai, and now both sides faced each other in terror. The kids knew they had gone too far. The government knew it couldn't take a harder line in Vietnam without catastrophic results to the national fabric. Neither cause had been served, and Kent State cast an ugly shadow over the war. No one was sticking posies into gun barrels anymore.

As the Kent State campus shootings took place, I was wrapping up our coverage of the latest revolt in Haiti. After a few days with President-for-Life François "Papa Doc" Duvalier's raggedy Tontons Macoutes, who at one juncture threatened us with burp guns, I was longing for the sleek efficiency of the Vietcong.

Back in the States, more than once I had the feeling I hadn't left the war but had just been transferred to the western front. The receiving end of the war could be just as tough. One day we received a tip that the staff at the Kingsbridge Veterans Hospital in the Bronx were mistreating Vietnam vets. It could have sounded faintly phony in that dizzy time, except that the complainers were paraplegics and quadriplegics. On arrival, the administrator told me I could talk to anyone I chose, adding that he thought some of the men were just plain "crybabies."

I began to worry about how you make small talk with shattered young men who couldn't even hold a straw to drink from a water glass. I practiced in my head, and everything sounded as though it would come out, "Too bad, old chap. Sorry you were in the wrong place at the wrong time, eh?" Finally, I just walked in, introduced myself, and blurted out, "Where did you get hit?" After that it was easy. They only wanted to talk about what happened before the bullet hit or the mine exploded.

In the therapy room, a muscular young man whose legs dangled lifelessly between parallel bars was learning to "walk." Then, exhausted, pale, he slumped into a wheelchair for an interview. His name was Bobby Muller, and biting his lower lip, he told me the story: emergency bells rung but never answered, waiting an hour for a pitcher of water, men lying in their own excrement, rats, verbal abuse. "I never cried in Vietnam," he said. "But I cry here all the time." We shook hands and I wished him luck, trying to hide my shaky composure.

Huntley introduced the piece that night by noting that so far in the war 42,118 Americans had been killed and more than 278,000 wounded, many thousands of them now in VA hospitals like Kingsbridge. An immediate outcry went up and a congressional investigation followed, resulting in an overhaul of Kingsbridge, including the staff. But much of the damage had already been done to the paralyzed men. Some tried drugs, others suicide. Some, miraculously, survived the ordeal. The next time I saw Bobby Muller, he was president of Vietnam Veterans of America.

Wherever I went that year, people were shooting at one another. And if they didn't use guns, they fell back on their fists. The situation was such that correspondents who never left the country might have qualified for combat pay. Some of the most violent fallout from Cambodia took place in the Wall Street area when hundreds of hard-hatted construction workers, carrying the Stars and Stripes, came off the steel girders, charged antiwar marchers, and slugged it out.

The chaos even invaded my sleepy hometown, New Haven, first a May Day antiwar demonstration that ended in a melée, then the upcoming trial of Bobby Seale, national chairman of the Black Panther party. Seale was accused of helping to kidnap, torture, and murder a fellow party member regarded as an informer. Dozens of protest groups of varying stripes showed up to support the Panthers. The president of Yale, Kingman Brewster, Jr., said he was skeptical that Seale could get a fair trial in this country and opened the university grounds to feed and shelter the demonstrators.

Free Bobby Seale, Get Out of Cambodia, Legalize Dope—all the causes melted into a three-ring circus on the Town Green. Abbie Hoffman and his ragged Yippie band were begging to be interviewed, bragging about how much they loved black people, when we showed up to cover the furor. "There's the house of death," he kept shouting on the way to the courthouse. He was weaving and bobbing incoherently, and even as we filmed his ravings, the police were straining to keep their cool and contain the hecklers. At one point, pushing and shoving erupted, and both police and radicals turned on us, not an uncommon development in an age when even taking a picture of "the other side" was construed as agreeing with them. Cameramen, sympathetic with the Right, were angry enough about having to take risks shooting pictures of ranting students, but when the cops turned on them—brothers in blue—then it became a matter of coaxing them to continue shooting.

The first person who greeted me as I entered the old Greek Revival courthouse on the Town Green had been my father's best friend, a local oil company owner of conservative bent who had trouble reconciling his hatred of the leftist press with the presence of his old pal's daughter. Looking around in the marble vestibule of the court at the unkempt and prostrate demonstrators, he said: "This is the end of the United States of America. And, Liz, you're working for people who are part and parcel of the whole decline."

It took four months to pick a jury, six months for the trial, which ended with a panel too terrified to reach a verdict. The judge announced he was dropping all charges against Seale because the "massive publicity" had made it impossible to retry him. After running unsuccessfully for mayor of Oakland, California, in 1973, Seale left the Panthers to do community action work and hit the lecture circuit. He even wrote a cookbook. Abbie Hoffman went on to become a comedian and lecturer and died of a drug overdose in 1989.

Getting on-camera had become a national pastime. Essentially it was where the debate over all the issues took place. As the fact of being on television mesmerized the nation and created instant celebrities, the merits and minuses of all arguments were occluded by the "well-knownness" of the person uttering them. This marriage of TV news and issues drove all kinds of people to scheme their way into air time. The tried-and-true press release was overtaken by the spokesmen, friends of friends, and often just going out into the fresh air and "doing your thing." Some virtually walked in off the street, like the short, swarthy man in the cheap suit who was introduced to me as a member of the new government-to-be of Bangladesh. Bang-WHAT?!

VIZNEWS, a British syndication service in partnership with NBC, was interested in an interview with him, and although no such country existed, martial law had been declared in East Pakistan because a number of people wanted independence under that name. I figured it was one more crackpot from another trumped-up revolution, and asked him polite questions about this new nation. He gave me his card with an air of authority, more assumed than real, and said should I be in the neighborhood, specifically the city of Dacca, please drop in for tea. I smiled patiently and bid him good luck.

"Thanks a lot, Van," I snorted at Kardisch back in the newsroom. "What do you have for me tomorrow? An Albanian city councilman?"

Politicians and antiwar activists were not the only people who took note of how to use the cameras for promotion purposes. A most unlikely newcomer to the game emerged from the morbid depths. The Mob. Even the kids never took on the Mafia, although its international connections may well have rivaled that of the CIA, a more homespun target. Joseph A. Colombo, Sr., head of one of the nation's first crime families, decided to go public. In the newsroom, even those with Mediterranean blood, myself no exception, had trouble keeping a straight face when we learned of the Italian-American Civil Rights League. Colombo's immediate (related) and professional (mob) families formed the nucleus of this group, which charged the FBI with discriminating against them. Bureau agents, up to their holsters in dealing with sandal-wearing anarchists, now came to work every morning to find dead-eyed men in fedoras and stout women in beaded dresses brandishing placards and chanting, "Down with the FBI!" in front of their offices on East Sixty-ninth Street. The league held rallies attracting thousands, called press conferences, issued releases and got space in the newspapers and time on TV just like any other cause. But ethnic equality counted less for their zeal than a new push by the Justice Department against organized crime. Thirteen strike forces— two in New York—had been set up to go after the dons, and Colombo was high on the hit parade.

Sy Kravitz, on the national desk, had grown up "in the neighborhood" with one of Colombo's lieutenants. We decided that with his connections and my last name, perhaps we could come up with some different mob stories. For about six months, we had a front office go-ahead to pursue our project, without having to answer to the desk every hour. We ate vermicelli with garlic in Brooklyn restaurants no one ever heard of, splashed in swimming pools at the fenced-in homes of people with funny nicknames, stole out in the middle of the night to secret meetings with "friends of the family." Sending back gifts— gold cigarette lighters, free tickets to "Vegas"—became a ritual. At least one vice-president started fearing for his kneecaps. The upshot of the skullduggery appeared on "Huntley-Brinkley" under the title of "Mafia Women": a long interview with Colombo relatives and friends who charged the FBI with harassing not only their men but the women and children, too. "What man would go over to a baby carriage and pull the covers down?" asked Colombo's daughter-in-law. "There is no such thing as a Mafia," declared Colombo's sister. "Does anybody call him Teddy the Swimmer?" demanded a friend, so incensed at the use of gangster nicknames that she supplied one for the senator from Massachusetts. The piece ran for seven minutes and ten seconds, an inordinate hunk of time for one story, and broke new ground. The wiseguys loved it, too, much to the relief of everyone involved.

The real payoff came later in the year when the league decided to hold a "charity show" in the Felt Forum at Madison Square Garden. Lear jets full of entertainers answered the call, delivering fellow paisans such as Frank Sinatra, Vic Damone, Jerry Vale, and Connie Francis to "donate" their time and show their respect for the Godfather. Black comedian Godfrey Cambridge quipped, "I got a strange invitation to this thing. A rock came through my window."

Limousines surrounded the Garden, cameras flashed, pinky rings sparkled. Every pastel-colored lace-front tuxedo shirt in New York came out of mothballs that night, mixing with women in white mink stoles and drooping earrings, pols from the boroughs with silky voices, lawyers on the lookout for a connection. Powerhouse stuff, a night on the town with the guys who ran it.

It was for many a command performance. Including Kravitz and Trotta wearing basic black. A Cadillac was sent for us driven by a husky fellow with a twitch. Two seats on the aisle, fifth row, placed us at the epicenter of "family friends" with whom we exchanged knowing glances. Men with bushy eyebrows stood at all the exits cracking their knuckles, flexing their knees. Joe Colombo, looking like the real mayor of New York, arrived to applause shortly before curtain time. He nodded to us just before the lights went down. Ed McMahon, everybody's uncle from the "Tonight" show, walked into the spotlight to emcee.

"Good evening fellow Italians," he said. "Before the show begins," he went on, "a few awards will be distributed to friends of the league, people who have worked to end discrimination against Italian Americans—and of course," he added hastily, "other ethnic groups." McMahon then read off a couple of names, and the required people rose from the darkness and were escorted to the stage to receive their plaques.

"They wouldn't, would they?" I whispered to Sy. He shrugged his shoulders. "Who knows? What's the matter, you don't want an award from the Mafia?"

Through the mists of dread, McMahon's voice sounded a familiar name. Mine. The words "noble participation in the campaign" filtered in, and I wondered how they would look in The New York Times the next morning. I began thinking small and slowly slid down deep into the cushioned seat, hoping to dodge the searching spotlight and the man in the baby blue ruffled shirting heading down the aisle in my direction. It was Vinnie, a soldier of long service to the family in his job as persuader. He stopped at my row, stood over me wearing a forced smile, and said: "Get up, Liz."

I rose, glided to the stage, and wondered which vice-president at the morning news meeting would announce that my contract had been invalidated for consorting with known criminals.

Sy was next, and took it all with much less gravity. "Don't worry," he reassured me. "We can always get a job with the league."

Sure, robbing banks in Altoona.

A parade of limos brought us to the Copacabana, New York's storied guys 'n' dolls hangout. A few whispered words to proprietor Jules Podell cleared the place of regular patrons as Colombo family and friends took over. "She likes Chinese food," the burly man across the table from me said flatly to a fawning waiter, who had dared suggest something from the late menu. Within minutes it appeared.

The women, looking out through layers of aquamarine mascara, chain-smoked and smiled politely, leaving the talking to their men. "I don't understand why they call us gangsters," my friend across the table said. "It's so bad, my own seventy-five-year-old mother asked me the other day about somebody who got iced, she read about it in the newspaper, supposed to be a big Mafia hit. I said, 'Ma, come on. I may take a number or two now and then, but your son don't go aroun' killin' people.' Can you imagine that, my own mother?"

I nodded weakly in assent. Sy kicked me hard under the table.

Colombo ("just a hard-working businessman," said one of the mascara women) table-hopped, kissing Sy and me, looking forward to working with us more in the future. He had plans, big plans. Sure, I thought, and Sy and I will wind up getting fired or fitted for a cement kimono.

Still, Big Joe, always impeccably turned out, had a menacing charm, smart eyes, and an electric quality that held people. He prided himself on his patriotism and had no use for flower power. Noting the hair length of a young man at one of his rallies he said: "Long hair—we don't put down anyone with long hair, because if you go back to the time of Our Lord you know he had long hair. We regret your hair—except that it would be neater if your hair was short. And so maybe you should cut your hair shorter." Some thought it was an offer that couldn't be refused.

Seven months later, as my crew and I stood in Columbus Circle covering another league rally, Joe Colombo was gunned down by a rival faction, or perhaps a member of his own Mafia family. Some even thought it was an FBI setup. For seven years he lived as a vegetable until his death in 1978. In a replay of the Jack Ruby–Lee Harvey Oswald affair, his attacker was shot to death on the spot, and the gunman disappeared.

*   *   *

Two events occurred that year that had an influence on my career at NBC. One grew out of Governor Rockefeller's election to a fourth term as governor, defeating Arthur J. Goldberg, the former Supreme Court justice. It was, as usual, an expensive, first-class campaign, right up until election night festivities at the Roosevelt Hotel. He was still a fantasy figure for the press, a rich and enlightened liberal Republican who actually thought nothing of borrowing a dime from a reporter to make a phone call.

I was at the hotel awaiting Rocky's arrival for the victory speech, milling with other reporters in an overcrowded anteroom adjacent to the stage. Staff members and security people were trying to clear the room for his arrival and then a short walk to the stage, where live cameras were waiting to record his victory speech. The three network reporters naturally had to be at his side to stop him for questions when he finished.

As the signal came that Rocky had arrived, we positioned ourselves. Suddenly, a provocative lady with whom I had no acquaintance, but who had been hanging around the anteroom, shoved me just as the newspeople began to close in. Maintaining the pole position in these situations was of extreme importance, so I pushed back. She responded by raking my face with five outstretched fingernails the length of talons. The front of my dress was torn, and blood dripped onto my chest from the scratches. Still edging closer to the stage and out of camera range, I tidied my dress and blotted my face—but only after I delivered an uppercut with the steel hand mike I was holding. She collapsed in pain. Under the hot TV lights I followed Rocky to the stage, smiled through the speech, asked the requisite questions, and then we went off the air from that location.

Returning to the anteroom, I found the irate lady of some pulchritude minus two front teeth and threatening to take the whole network to court. As it turned out, she was a campaign groupie, and everyone agreed that she had no business being in a restricted area without official status. Several people came forward to offer themselves as witnesses to the fact that she had initiated the fracas. True, but irrelevant.

The lady knew a possibly lucrative setup when she saw one and sued the network. The case was disposed of in an out-of-court settlement that paid her dental bills. Amusing, yes. The story played into the sneers and delight of the men who liked nothing better than to see a cat fight. If the war hadn't established me as a "bitch," an Iron Lady, that election night fight sealed my reputation as a tempestuous female who could be trouble. I knew management wouldn't forget it, could never be too sure that I wouldn't embarrass the network. It was okay for men to get in trouble—and they did with regularity—but women were expected to know their place. The fact that I had done my job, covered the story—and in my view at considerable peril—meant nothing. This was an industry in which, for women especially, "making it" often depended on being a deft intriguer and a model of self-control.

I asked a senior producer what I should have done under the circumstances: not defend myself? "No," he said, "but why the hell did you have to hit her with the mike?"

"Why? Because it was the only thing handy."

The second pivotal event was Chet Huntley's retirement from NBC News. Huntley was like the Rock of Gibraltar. No one ever thought he wouldn't be there anymore, NBC's commanding voice of authority who seemed to be part of the marble edifice itself. Although a Montana Democrat, he was in many ways the Ronald Reagan of broadcasting. Negatives, be it a divorce, a willingness to cross picket lines, or a fondness for martinis, simply didn't stick. Chet was too big, too well liked—too good at the job. "The dynamic duo" were indisputably the first superstars of the business. In fact, a consumer-research company found in 1965 that Huntley and Brinkley were recognized by more adult Americans than Cary Grant, Jimmy Stewart, the Beatles, or John Wayne.

Chet and I had become friends from the night he called me at my Greenwich Village digs, and it always amazed me how lightly he wore his celebrity. People mobbed him as we went out for the occasional lunch. "Hey, Chet, how's it going?" a tourist would yell across the skating rink. Or, passing by a restaurant table, "Hey aren't you—Huntley, no Brinkley!" His grace absorbed it all, cherishing the adulation but never letting it change who he really was, a very nice guy from Montana.

Huntley's last day, July 31, 1970, marked a turning point for the worse at 30 Rock and a windfall for Walter Cronkite. Already the leader, CBS News became the beneficiary of a flood of viewers who switched over from NBC, thereby gaining a solid hold on first place, which it retained for years. Sandy Socolow, one of two senior producers on the Cronkite show at the time, said it was a shock: "All of us—effete easterners—had always assumed it was Brinkley who was drawing the audience, his wit and charm. He was a breath of fresh air, and we'd wait to see what smarty thing he was saying tonight. But lo and behold, when Chet left, the audience left—and they came to CBS."

More intangible was the shift in atmosphere at 30 Rock. The absence of Huntley's easy, commanding personality left uncertainty and a sense of something very important being over for NBC. On the last day, I was at a Connecticut ski resort, Powder Ridge, covering a rock festival that had turned into a drug-out. The day brought its usual routine of news—the war, demonstrations, and there was nothing out of the ordinary about the program, that is until a pause and a shuffle of papers, just before the "backtime"—that closing section of a program which has been previously timed and counts the reader into the sign-off. Once you reach it, there is no changing, no going back. Everyone in the main newsroom and the "Huntley-Brinkley" office froze on the spot as Chet paused and said: "This difficult—uh—moment is here." It was the moment he announced his retirement. At one point, biting his lip once, brushing his cheek, he spoke of his faith in the common sense of the American people, adding that they were in no danger of being led down the primrose path by a journalist. "Be patient and have courage," he said, "for there will be better and happier news one day—if we work at it."

There wasn't a dry eye in the newsroom.

Brinkley responded with a few words and concluded with, "I really don't want to say it, but the time has come and so for the last time, Good luck and good night, Chet."

"Good luck, David. And good night for NBC News."

For me, Huntley's retirement meant not just the passing of a generation but the departure of a friend and supporter, not to mention an important catalyst in my career. As replacements, John Chancellor and Frank McGee coanchored the new "NBC Nightly News" with Brinkley for a while, and it was during this transition that the news programs began gearing up for coverage of still another demonstration. The National Organization for Women had called for a one-day strike to mark the fiftieth anniversary of American women's right to vote.

One early August morning, I called in from the road only to learn from Van Kardisch that my name had appeared in the News, in a story on the women's rights parade set for the 27th. To mark this, the "Today" show men were turning over their on-camera jobs to the women—just for that morning, of course. Pauline, Nancy, Aline, and I were to serve as the hosts and anchors. Trotta, said the story, would read the news from the anchor desk normally held by Frank Blair, a holdover from radio announcer days and, even by the most liberal definition, not a newsman. I started to fume, and Van sympathetically advised me to wrap up my work as fast as I could and get to New York to straighten things out.

I couldn't believe that management had so entirely missed the point. If anything, I had been apathetic to the movement's noisy posturing and its excessively liberal demands. They smacked of special-interest crankiness masquerading as the people's will. And, too, they bespoke a career-girl orientation that seemed more bent on arguing who's on top sexually than on the less glamorous issues of pay equality. Now that was a subject that did interest me, given that I was making far less than my male counterparts for performing the same job. To hear that I was to be queen for a day seemed a truly considered insult.

Aline Saarinen intercepted me when I arrived back in the newsroom at 30 Rock. "Have you heard?" And then seeing my face, "You don't like it, do you? What are you going to do?"

"I'm going to tell them to stuff it, that's what I'm going to do. How dare they throw me a bone for one day—call it liberation and not the outrageous tokenism it is—and release it to the newspapers without even telling me?"

Aline agreed readily, wittily adding that on Lincoln's Birthday they might just as well ask all the blacks on the staff to do the news. I stormed toward the elevator with her at my heels, and within minutes stood in Stuart Schulberg's doorway. The "Today" show's executive producer was holding a staff meeting. He started at my look of wrath and waved me in without dismissing his minions.

We had never really met before, just passing hellos in the hallway. Schulberg had a decent enough standing in the business. He was an able producer and was at that moment guiding the career of Barbara Walters, who had begun as a writer on his show and worked her way into the cohost chair. "You look as though you have something on your mind." He was seated at his desk, short, pudgy, red-faced, a small, fuzzy beard lending him an intellectual air.

"You bet I do." In lean sentences I told him what I thought of his Aunt Jemima plans, adding that I wasn't going to play.

He seemed genuinely shocked. "But the whole point of this is to give the women like yourself a chance, to show our support for the movement."

It was stunning. He genuinely didn't get it. "Look," I went on, fighting for control, and still standing in front of the headmaster's desk. "On a day when Frank Blair is sick or on vacation, you can easily reach for the phone and ask me to substitute. That's the day I'll do the news on the 'Today' show. And if you or anyone in the front office insist on my participation in this charade, I'll go to the newspapers."

Now he got it. All the liberalism he had been so sure of, all the noblesse oblige, evaporated. "I had no idea anyone would feel this way," he said. "I—that wasn't what we intended."

The show went on the air. All the other women—Aline, too, despite her privately asserted indignation—did the broadcast. Overnight I had become Joan of Arc, without an army.

While Schulberg's "unraised consciousness" was a normal in-house prejudice, in some quarters bias took on a certain deep and conscious meanness, a kind of exclusionary politics that viewed women as a threat. It certainly seemed to be at the root of Chancellor's behavior when I was assigned an ill-fated series of stories called "Women in Prison." His effect on my career was about to be as dismal as it was on the ratings. By then, McGee had left to do the "Today" show, and the stolid Chancellor sat in the main anchor position, with Brinkley doing commentary from Washington. The subject itself was ahead of its time for a network in 1971, but Westfeldt gave the green light and dispatched Al Robbins and me to cut a swath through the country, particularly in the South, in search of stories that would depict women in the prison system. No hand-wringing commentaries on whether or not society had put them there unjustly, but on how it treated them once they hit the slammer. Male convicts worked at any number of occupations. Women sewed and cleaned and mostly sat, special pariahs because they were women gone wrong—and to our surprise, so often because of a no-good man. We delivered six pieces of strong stuff, and Chancellor would introduce the series.

That gave me pause. I had had a queasy feeling ever since he came on the program, "Mme. Nhu" still ringing in my brain. More important, Westfeldt had told me right out—albeit with a chuckle—that "John sure gives me trouble on these women's movement stories. He just doesn't like 'em." Nevertheless he introduced the series, announcing that this was the first of six parts and that "tomorrow night" Part Two would run. To this day, whenever Al Robbins and I see each other, instead of hello it's, "Hey, whatever happened to Part Two?" The series vanished, and no amount of questioning could get Westfeldt or any of the senior and junior producers to say why. Nor did anyone tell the audience. The subject was changed every time we brought it up. Only in the corridors, on the grapevine, where the truth usually hides, did we hear a reason. Chancellor had killed it.

Sixteen years later, it came as no surprise when it was revealed that Chancellor, as a member of the grand old Century Club, had signed a petition to keep women out because it would "break down the effortless, unconstrained companionship among men." Funnily enough, I still believe that men have a perfect right to their own clubs, but it was a tonic to watch Chancellor's liberal credentials up for grabs.

I had other grievances. How I would have loved the men to stop telling me to smile, a countenance that seemed to be required of women in the seventies, perhaps because a harsh age needed a soft touch. "You never told me to smile in Vietnam. Why tell me now?" What correlation was there between achievement and sweetness of disposition? No man I knew at that point had been asked to smile on camera. So why abandon a demeanor that had served the credibility of all broadcasters, an expressionless, no-nonsense delivery that conveyed a seriousness of purpose and the requisite objectivity?

As for the women I encountered, many of them were fatigued housewives suffering an identity crisis, and they usually viewed me with a thinly disguised mixture of suspicion and envy. And the network wives—I could have retired if I had billed those who felt certain I was after their husbands. I was a liberated Jezebel, a single woman who actually paid her own way. As for the libbers, when I suggested to one of the NOW executive committee members that I had gone pretty far without a movement, she dismissed me with: "Well, you're just a freak." Sisterhood, it seemed, had its limits.

By early 1971, Skip Ettinger was back in Vietnam, and I was preparing to cover an extraordinary event in Fort Benning, Georgia, the court-martial of Lieutenant William Laws Calley, Jr. I had lost track of Skip for a while, especially after he turned up in New York, confiding that he wanted out of the army because nobody gave a damn anyhow. He toyed with the idea of finding a job in civilian life, perhaps the sky marshals' training program, designed to combat terrorism on commercial flights. But he gave up. "I don't fit in anywhere," he told me one night. "I keep thinking of the war. I feel strange here, as though nobody wants me around."

So, he put in for another tour. Instead, the army told him he would be permanently assigned to Fort Bragg. As wiliness is no stranger to the guerrilla mind, he and a friend in the same predicament drove hell-for-leather up to Washington. They arrived long after dark and spent the night getting drunk in the Pentagon parking lot until the business day began, then talked their way into orders for a Pathfinder detachment in Hawaii, and upon arrival there requested orders for Vietnam. A few months later Skip was back in action, on his fourth tour of duty.

If Skip Ettinger represented a soldier who took duty, honor, and country to heart, Lieutenant Calley embodied the freak, the short, strutting man in a leader's job with no leadership ability. On March 16, 1968, he was commanding a platoon from Charlie Company, 1st Battalion, 20th Infantry, Americal Division, a unit which had been mauled by booby traps and suffered heavy casualties in the days preceding the assault on My Lai 4. Ultimately, when the dazed men entered the hamlet they faced a situation calling for a cool, intelligent mind. Instead it erupted into the slaughter of 347 unarmed civilians. The fact of the massacre—with its sickening pictures of the bloody corpses of women and children lying neatly in a ditch—did not emerge until the fall of 1969. It provoked a sense of rage many thought had been worn down by the turmoil of the sixties. No other horror of the war galvanized forces on both sides of the issue as My Lai.

"Americans—you just don't do that," Skip said. "I was shocked. I never saw anything like this in all my time in that war. It's a disgrace. Shit, that's criminal. Calley could have refused that damn order if it came from above. And even if it is a VC village, you don't kill old crippled people and the women and children, man. No way."

The trial ended three years and two weeks after Charlie Company's rampage. I was in the courtroom when Calley was convicted of the premeditated murder of twenty-two civilians, felt my knees go weak when the verdict was read. All I could hear was the floorboards creak and the rustle of a uniform as he stood at attention and snapped a salute. In the days leading up to the jury's deliberations, I had visited him at the base apartment, where he stayed with his girlfriend. "So how does it feel to be served a drink by a killer?" he asked me one afternoon, handing me a scotch and water.

Jerry Rosholt, the "Nightly News" producer who had been living at Fort Benning for almost five months to make sure we got on the air, saw him regularly. "I remember being in his apartment one time—I think it was when we were sweating out the jury—and he kept saying 'Whadda ya think will happen? Whadda ya think will happen?' Finally he said, 'It's gotta be guilty. I did it!' He was a scared young man."

Calley's conviction and subsequent sentence—life in prison at hard labor—provoked a national outcry in his favor. Many felt it was the war that had gone on trial and not the twenty-seven-year-old lieutenant. The six-man jury, veterans of combat, had struggled for seventy-nine hours under enormous pressure to reach a verdict, torn by their own commitment to military principle and the cry for blood coming from within and without the army. After sentencing, one of them, Major Harvey Brown, fought to keep his composure, lost, and began to sob when I asked him on camera what had gone on in the jury room as they wrestled with the case. "I just wish to God we could have found that this didn't happen," he said. "This is what I was hoping for the whole time, that somebody would come out and deny it—that it didn't exist. American soldiers don't do that. But they did."

Calley served little more than three years of the life sentence. After his release he went to work in a family-owned jewelry store in Columbus, Georgia. A dozen years after the sentencing, I was working for CBS News and telephoned him, asking if he would do an interview. The first thing he wanted to know was how much we would pay him. I thanked him for his time and said good-bye.

THE war itself was winding down, although an incursion into the Laotian panhandle made it appear otherwise. Because of congressional restrictions against the use of American ground troops in Cambodia or Laos, it was a South Vietnamese show, with the United States flying critical air support and manning defensive positions along the DMZ and Laotian border. There was no enemy offensive that year, not surprising; the ever-patient North Vietnamese knew all they had to do was wait as American troops filtered home.

In early June rumors began flying around New York that the *Times* was sitting on a top secret story, so secret that even a separate composing room with its own operatives had been installed to work on it. On June 13, the *Times* published its first installment of the Pentagon Papers, a classified study of America's involvement in Vietnam that had been prepared for Secretary of Defense McNamara. The government immediately went to court to enjoin the *Times* from publishing any further installments and lost.

Within the next few days, Daniel Ellsberg, a Pentagon war manager who got religion and turned informer, was named as the man who had passed the papers to the *Times*. Every available network reporter was trying to figure out who he was and where he was. It was a test case example of a story television would never catch up with, just as Watergate would be. These stories emerged from serious sources, long-held contacts, the trust of the powerful, and TV news simply couldn't spare the time or the attention span to do them.

Even as the furor continued over the Pentagon Papers, National Security Adviser Kissinger was preparing his first secret trip to Peking, part of the Nixon administration's astonishing démarche to China. And détente with the Russians was at hand as the initiatives for strategic arms limitation talks acted further to change the great power equations. Economic problems—recession, inflation, wage and price controls, cutting the dollar loose from gold—seemed overshadowed by the pyrotechnics on the foreign scene.

For a reporter, that was the action, but NBC News was in the middle of a budget crunch, as RCA's ailing computer division headed down the tubes. Robert W. Sarnoff, son of the founder, had tried to take on IBM and failed. Before it was all over and the corporation said uncle in the fall of 1971, writing off $250 million, assignment editors and show producers were covering the news with care. As a direct result, Reuven Frank closed the Moscow bureau. The joyride was over, and the largesse of mighty RCA—which we had taken for granted—simply disappeared.

"Who do I have to screw to get a decent assignment around here?" I protested one day to Mac Johnson, standing in his doorway like some forlorn demimondaine.

"Well," he said, instantly warming to the challenge. "You could start here."

Anchormen and spies talk about "coming in from the cold," leaving the rigors of the field for the arms of the home office. As far as I was concerned, I had come in from the warm and wanted to go back out. Just when it looked as though I would have to launch another nuisance campaign, war broke out between India and Pakistan, and I was on my way to Afghanistan. No more screaming demonstrators, no more office politics, no more crawling through Manhattan traffic to make an airplane to another city with green street signs and chain restaurants.

The Khyber Pass was more my speed and, since all commercial flights had been canceled, the only way to the war. Who would believe that as my Japanese crew and I dashed over the dusty caravan route, we would be stopped by Pakistani officers and invited to have lunch with the commandant of the Khyber Rifles. He didn't look like Tyrone Power, but it beat lunch at a midtown steak joint with Reuven Frank.

The original dispute, a civil war between West Pakistan and its weak sister, East Pakistan, centered on the latter's demanding more economic and political independence from the government in the west. India supported East Pakistan, then under martial law, as refugees streamed out, and eventually invaded the country to dislodge the West Pakistan occupation. Out of it emerged the nation of Bangladesh, and East Pakistan ceased to exist. Simultaneously, a second front opened on the West Pakistan–India border. Not until the United Nations coaxed the parties to a cease-fire did hostilities end in mid-December.

Geography and strategy required four countries to be covered, about 2 million square miles, roughly half the size of the United States. Not just familiar names, but Hyderabad, Chamb, Sialkot, Jessore, Khulna, Chittagong, Hilli, the Sind Desert. Hundreds of news types swarmed across the subcontinent in pursuit of this elusive but no less deadly war, up against closed airports, severely limited telephone communication, and sporadic telex service. Indian bombing brought a strictly enforced curfew and blackout: once the sun set we were groping in the dark. We shuttled film by hanging onto our hats and a set of worry beads, roaring along at sixty-five miles an hour in an old wreck over rutted, unlit roads.

The Khyber Pass was critical, sole exit for stories to reach Kabul and then connect for a flight to a satellite point. Khyber closed at 9 P.M. One night, arriving late from the battlefield and desperate to ship, we encountered a local newspaper editor who took pity on us and called a friend. The friend happened to be the governor of North West Frontier province, a man who controlled access to the pass. Within an hour, Khyber was opened for NBC News.

It was difficult getting to the front, covering a war in which at the height of the fireworks soldiers were likely to lay down their arms and face Mecca for afternoon prayers. As they met the Indian army, devout Muslim Pakistanis yelled incantations to Allah, and this would make us even more afraid. The terrain further north as it rises through Kashmir into the Pamir Knot—the Roof of the World—challenged our stamina and common sense: cold and thin as a knife's edge, clouds so close you could feel their breath, the horizon so far and vast one pair of eyes could hardly take it in.

One frigid afternoon, a Pakistani major was driving us in his jeep along a harrowing road in the snows of the towering peaks, taking the hairpin turns on two wheels as he inquired about the activities of "the American president, Mr. Nixon." I directed his attention to our immediate situation, which was a little precarious. He smiled and said our philosophies of life were different. "You see, we Muslims say 'Inshallah.' If God wills. So we say if God wants us to die now, we will. There is no point in fighting it."

Half an hour later, a landslide rumbled down the road ahead, blocking our way, forcing us to unload our gear and make our way on foot, or else stay on the road all night and freeze to death. Forming a human chain, our brave major leading us on with pokes of his swagger stick, we climbed the icy mountain in the dark, guided by starlight and stark terror. At one point, we faced a two-foot crack in the rock, over the rushing water of the Jhelum River hundreds of feet below. The major leapt to the other side. "You can make it, but do not look down. Here is my hand. Now jump, now!" he commanded.

Cliff Watts, a British cameraman from our London bureau, did exactly what the Brits always do, and not just in war movies. He got more cockney and funnier by the minute. "What in bloody hell do these bloody wogs think we are. He's gonna get us killed and we haven't even had his lousy tea yet."

One afternoon, along with Yasuda and Yashiro, my old Vietnam crew, I was out looking at a captured arms cache along with a bunch of other foreign correspondents when an Indian Mirage fighter started a low pass at us. It was the first time any of us—veterans of the Southeast Asia campaigns—had ever had the sensation of sitting under an airplane that has you in its sights with no good intention. We dived into a forest. The plane circled low and climbed. We giggled and compared notes, the "Y-boys" telling me how, as children, they had listened, terrified, to the sounds of American B-29s over Tokyo, and how their mothers said the GIs would eat them when the invasion came. How sad it all seemed, as we sat in the grass, laughing about old enmities and long-gone wars. Here we were in another one. And one day this, too, would be an amusing memory—if we lived to remember it.

Some people become threads in one's life, acquaintances and then friends who emerge, fade, and reappear over the years, like Skip and D'Amico and Spence. And now, Shuja Nawaz. Handsome, husky, dreamy-eyed and smart, this twenty-three-year-old Punjabi reporter for Pakistan television attached himself to us and soon became our combination fixer, guide, and political adviser. He was a rare one, writer of poetry, reader of T. S. Eliot, cricket ace, and like so many idealistic young men of that time and place, an admirer of Zulfikar Ali Bhutto. Shuja was interested in studying in the United States, so I suggested that he sit down and write an application for admission to my alma mater, the Columbia School of Journalism. He was admitted, graduated as the top foreign student, and went on to a successful career at the World Bank and the International Monetary Fund.

It was to Bhutto and the Pakistan People's Party that the people looked for deliverance, for modernization of what was still one of the world's most primitive countries. Bhutto, the former foreign minister who emerged as Pakistan's new leader, remained out of sight for some days after the cease-fire. Newsmen were craving to buttonhole him for an interview. One day in Rawalpindi, he addressed a rally in his typical fiery manner, and just as he was leaving the stage, I dashed up and thrust a note in his hand before his bodyguards could react. "Please, promise you'll read it," I begged.

"I will," he replied, startled by my intrusion but taking my message.

I returned to the hotel, and within an hour there was a call from the president's house, summoning me for an interview with the new head of state. My crew and I arrived in minutes at the residence, a palatial legacy of empire once occupied by the British governor. Bhutto's reputation as a bit of a rake crossed my mind when I learned our conversation would take place in his bedroom, but what could have happened with my automatic two-man escort in tow? We had encountered very little technical trouble during the war, so naturally during the interview the camera jammed. I prayed hard and kept the president engaged in small talk as the Y-boys broke new ground in Japanese technology. Our exclusive left the country via the reopened Karachi airport, but still, for the next twenty-four hours, we kept our fingers crossed, hoping it wouldn't suffer the fate of those many network stories before us which had vanished like magic ink in a tangle of international airplane schedules, customs desks, and X-ray machines of the Third World.

When we weren't tracking Bhutto, or his daughter, Benazir—on leave from her studies at Radcliffe College—we ventured into the streets. If I had grown tired of ranting students at home, this was a country where political self-expression bordered on anarchy. During the war, the protesters in frenzied marches railed against the archenemy India. Then they turned on the United States, charging the CIA had engineered the war, aided and abetted by American TV and press controlled (of course) "by the Jews." The noise level went even higher as a Seventh Fleet task force led by the carrier *Enterprise* nosed into the Bay of Bengal for possible evacuation of Americans. When

wild-eyed rioters asked where we were from, we gave a standard answer: the BBC.

After Pakistan's defeat, rioters turned their wrath against the government until Bhutto calmed them down. Muslim women, many of
them still in purdah—veiled and confined—stayed away, and any
Western woman in the midst of the melée was open to a quick feel by
the locals. A long bush jacket helped minimize the random attacks,
but sometimes I had to resort to more drastic tactics. When I returned
to New York, Westfeldt asked me how I had managed it, the cultural
clash and all that. "Simple," I said. "When they got too close, I simply
picked up the smallest one I could find and threw him." It worked
every time.

Dacca, once the capital of East Pakistan, had been devastated by
war. Rain flooded the mud streets. Near-famine reduced our daily diet
to scrambled eggs, mulligatawny soup, and sweet biscuits. The Russians moved in soon after the fall, and we followed thuggish-looking
"businessmen" making their rounds like vultures over carrion. One
morning, I thought about trying to write still another forelock-tugger
on the country's future. We had already interviewed the new nation's
prime minister, Sheikh Mujibur Rahman, so I asked a friend where I
could find the president. He was, I learned, quite naturally in his
palace.

As we motored up the long, flowered drive to the beautiful structure, I realized I had better rehearse the pronunciation of this worthy's
name. My driver was coaching me: Abu Sayeed Choudhoury—a
mouthful, even in Bengali. But in reciting it over and over, I felt an
annoying familiarity, an unidentifiable mental nudge, which still
nagged me as I was pulled from my reverie by a turbaned servant in
gold and white sent to conduct me to the president. Huge mahogany
doors opened into an exquisite room, hushed by crimson oriental
carpets, ivory statuettes, and an intricately carved teak chair that
could have been a throne. On it sat the short, swarthy man in the
cheap suit I had interviewed months before in New York—except this
time he was wearing white silk and velvet slippers.

"Ah, Miss Trotta," he said warmly, his ruby-ringed hand outstretched. "I am so glad you accepted my invitation to visit me in my
country."

There's an old saying in the news business about how it pays to be
nice to the copy boy because you never know when he's going to be
your publisher. After this encounter with Abu Sayeed Choudhoury, I
learned it applied to sources, too.

My chief reason for rushing to Bangladesh was spelled out in a telex from Westfeldt, telling me to find the hundreds, maybe thousands, of young girls—some as young as eleven years old—who had been kidnapped, raped, and held prisoner in barracks by the West Pakistan army during the occupation. Many were pregnant and thus had been abandoned by their families. It was needle-and-haystack time, but we found a group of them hiding in a large house on the outskirts of the city. After interviewing these violated children, comatose from their ordeal, we returned to the hotel to pack and ship. It was the first and only time I swallowed three hard whiskeys back-to-back before sitting down at my typewriter. I was more than a little drunk, but it was the only way I could hold myself together.

Another test, this one of objectivity, presented itself when New York sent a message in early February that Senator Kennedy was on his way to Bangladesh. Every story sooner or later goes into its visiting dignitary phase, and here it was. "By the way," a producer in New York wired me, "don't forget to tell us the expression on his face when he sees you on the tarmac." Funny.

By now the Kennedy camp's disapproval of me had become something of an office joke. Months after the inquest, Lawrence Spivak, host of NBC's celebrated "Meet the Press," asked Kennedy to appear on the program. I was to be on the panel. Years later Reuven Frank told me that Kennedy's staff made it quite clear to NBC that the senator would agree only if I was dropped from the broadcast. I stayed on the panel, but found it irksome and inexplicable when Spivak insisted before the program that I not raise "the Kopechne issue." With benefit of hindsight, I realized later that he had obviously made a deal, and the show went on with no mention of Mary Jo by me or anyone else.

Kennedy and his wife arrived in Dacca to a reception tumultuous even by the subcontinent's instant hysteria index. They were trailed by a clutch of aides, refugee-specialists unaccustomed to meeting the faces behind the statistics. At Dacca University, where he made a speech, the old wooden bleachers creaked under the weight of chanting students, intoxicated at the sight of a real live Kennedy. Chappaquiddick obviously made no dent here. He began by telling them both America and Bangladesh were born in revolution. "For generations to come," said Kennedy, his head tilted, chin jutting, every inch his older brother, plus about forty pounds, "the story of Bangladesh will be a lesson to the world. . . . For in a sense we are all Bengalis. We are all Americans."

Once more, I heard an echo. Could it be? 1961: West Berlin. "Ich bin ein Berliner," President Kennedy had said. I sidled up to a Kennedy staffer and inquired. "Well, yes," he said sheepishly. "We do pull some of the president's old speeches from time to time."

A visit to a Bihari refugee camp topped it. The Biharis were Urdu-speaking Indians who had fled into the east wing during the partition of British India in 1947. They sided with West Pakistan during the war and so wound up a hostage people when the shooting stopped. Until an agreement on prisoners could be reached, thousands of them were shunted into an old jute mill which served as a concentration camp. Many starved to death. Others were hunted by the Mukti Bahini, freedom fighters on the winning side.

Kennedy decided to visit this camp of wretched souls. While the PR value had seemed inestimable, pandemonium reigned when he entered the mill. A mad mob of the starving formed, sensing that food would be given out—and it was, as our cameras turned on. Indian Army guards closed in to protect the official party and began beating the half-starved Biharis with long poles. The visit became a rout. Joan Kennedy, blindingly blonde, dressed to the nines, looked as though she would break as she picked her way through mud and garbage in patent leather dress heels. The Biharis stared at us through crazed, unblinking eyes. The army ushered everyone to an exit, fast, as the mob grew angry and surged toward us. It was an egregious exploitation of a people's suffering, a photo op for a visiting pol. In sadness and without pride, I filed a story.

By March I was back at 30 Rock on the fire brigade. By July I was buying sandals and more cotton underwear for my new assignment— bureau chief in Singapore, an Oriental backwater. "You'll be responsible for the whole area, about eighteen countries," said the new president of NBC News, Dick Wald, through a thin smile. "Why, you're on your way to becoming an Asia expert. And Singapore is very modern." Sure, and it just happened to be a short plane ride from Vietnam.

Only days before I left, an antiwar parade thundered through midtown Manhattan, its vanguard shouting "Hell, no, we won't go," and holding aloft a red flag with a yellow star. The battle flag of the Vietcong. I stood on the corner of Fifth Avenue and Forty-ninth Street and wept.

10

OUTPOSTS OF EMPIRE

"Get down, get down! They'll see you!"

The president of the Republic of the Philippines was pulling on the back of my bush jacket. He was crouching in the tall grass behind me as his army displayed their prowess in "routine" military maneuvers. To my knowledge, Ferdinand Marcos had no training in method acting; he didn't need it, not with his showman's knack for throwing himself into the role of battlefield commander amid the hail of blanks cracking all around us.

Marcos and I had become comrades-in-arms through a bizarre turn of events, the way things often happened in these 7,000 islands floating off the Southeast Asian mainland. In the fall of 1972, he had declared martial law in the face of what he claimed to perceive as a serious threat from Communist sympathizers and guerrillas. My arrival had coincided with the first day of the new edict. Without even bothering to stop for accreditation from Malacanan Palace, we started filming the outward and visible signs of martial law, such as the exterior of Camp Crame, an army post where hundreds of political prisoners—including the editor of *The Manila Times*—were held. Filming military installations was verboten, as I knew, but the risk didn't pay off, and we too were arrested. A staff colonel and the camp commander said that I could go, but that they would hold my Indian crew. Racism has no bounds, not even in Asia. I refused in a few well-chosen Yankee imperialist words. "They go where I go," I said, invoking the battle cry of correspondents. In response, a general on the scene tried to seize Vishnu Mathur's camera. Vishnu, an Indian free-lancer for NBC and a close friend, was by temperament and tradition nonviolent, so I took over and shoved the general, who fell back. A scuffle ensued, whereupon the general retreated. Now it was war.

For seven hours men in uniform interrogated us, using a tape machine that had no tape. All demands to call the U.S. embassy were turned down. For the first time in my life, I knew what it was like to be totally without freedom or redress. Deciding that the best course was a stiff upper lip and a good show of American grit, I squared my jaw and remained insolent. My real terror, however, was that Steve Bell of ABC would surely beat me on a major story. But all flights had been grounded, so no one shipped until a day later. Finally, three diplomats from the American embassy showed up to negotiate our release, which they insisted include shaking hands with the camp commander. It was one of those things that men understand so well from the playing fields of Eton to the sandlots of the Bronx—being a "good sport," not an easy concept for a woman wronged. I refused.

Meanwhile, in New York, people were noticing our absence. The wires moved a story, and someone showed it to Corrigan. "She's under arrest," said the desk man.

"God, let's pray they keep her," he replied.

Once we were released and a formal protest was made to the Marcos government, I was summoned to the palace for a personal meeting with the president. He ordered the defense minister to apologize to me, and thereafter, whenever in town, I was a regular guest of the wildly indiscreet Malacanan social set, not a bad place to pick up news.

As with most countries in that part of the world, there are really just two classes in the Philippines, the very rich and the very poor. Marcos and his wife, Imelda, were certainly among the former. Still, when we did a live two-way with "Meet the Press" in Washington, D.C., and I asked him if it was true that he was one of the richest men in Asia, he pounded the desk and put on his mock-indignant face.

The arrest and apology made getting permission to film decidedly easier. New York wanted a takeout on how the Philippine army was doing against the Huk guerrillas, and for one segment it was necessary to film the army on maneuvers at a training camp, which is how the president and I wound up in the grass.

Early one morning, my crew and I arrived at the sentry gate at Camp Bonifacio to find an honor guard and saluting cannon at the ready, unusual adornments for a routine training day. It became apparent we were waiting for someone important as the officer corps scurried around wearing the same look the brass used to wear in Vietnam when the commander-in-chief was due. Sure enough, Marcos couldn't stay away, and after a twenty-one-gun salute, he motioned us to join his motorcade to the bivouac area. The man in charge of the day's operation wore an enormous grin revealing a neat set of gold teeth and a name badge bearing the improbable name of Colonel Archangel. He briefed us on the "friendly" and "enemy" dispositions. Helicopters swooped in firing, machine guns clattered, recon patrols rappeled up steep slopes, rifle companies crawled through the dense mangroves, and smoke grenades of all colors lent this landscape the pastel air of Disneyland.

The president, when he wasn't ordering me to keep my head down, peered through his binoculars, giving a running account of the action. At several points, he turned to the crew to make sure the camera was rolling because, he said, "You should get this. This is good." And such shots were, naturally, being augmented by close-ups of the president concentrated in supreme command. We had been directed by amateurs over the years, but never such a high-ranking one. From time to time I really wondered if he was serious, but all I could manage was, "How fascinating, Mr. President."

After an hour or so, we indicated we had enough film, and Marcos left us with the certainty he was "looking forward to seeing your story."

Colonel Archangel, perspiring and relieved, ran over. "Well, how did you do? Did you get what you wanted?"

I assured him we had and thanked him for allowing us to interrupt his operation.

"Oh, no problem," he said, his gold teeth gleaming through a smile. Then turning to the troops, he cupped his hand over his mouth and shouted, "Okay, boys, strike the set."

So we had been had. The "routine" exercise had been an MGM production starring the president of the Philippines and directed by an American-trained colonel who must have had a shelf full of 1940s movies. Dramatic as it was, we couldn't use one frame. I told the story to Henry Kamm of *The New York Times* when we got back to the Hilton that night, and after laughing himself sick, he filed an add to his daily piece. He had a story, and I had a lesson in manipulation.

It was one thing to make your name while covering a famous war; it was another to hang on to it in the international world of political sharks. World leaders like Marcos understood the emergence of American TV news and its importance in keeping those American aid dollars coming, so he courted reporters. No sooner had you checked into your hotel than gifts from the palace would arrive, baskets of fruit, champagne, a shell lamp, embroidered shirts, colored wicker baskets and table settings, an array of local crafts. Kamm witnessed the arrival of one shipment and threatened me with exposure, that is until they sent champagne to his room.

Repelling sharks came with the territory, as did the unending battle to obtain "permission" to shoot stories. In Asia, of course, one needed approval for high-level interviews, but it could take weeks or even months to cut through the bureaucracy. India, for example, is a country from which more than one sane, soft-spoken correspondent has emerged a raving lunatic. Layers of civil servants once drove a British journalist I knew, much admired for his cool, to leaping upon the five-foot counter in the Bombay post office, grabbing the steel bars, and shrieking like a chimpanzee for service.

This former realm of the Raj undid me on several occasions, especially the time I tried to arrange an interview with Indira Gandhi. A formal written request and several cups of tea with dozens of polite bureaucrats produced no answer to my request, so I decided upon a somewhat daring approach. Once a week, the public was allowed to tell their troubles to the prime minister. Hundreds of people from the vast countryside made their pilgrimage to New Delhi to be heard by Mrs. Gandhi, not unlike the kings of yore considering the petitions of the peasants. I presented myself at the residence on the open house day and declared I was an American tourist wishing to bring greetings to Mrs. Gandhi. Within half an hour, an elegant lackey ushered me into a room where the prime minister granted audience. The door

closed, and after amenities I confessed my scheme and humbly requested time for an interview on-camera. With those shrewd obsidian
eyes, Mrs. Gandhi answered some questions, called for an assistant to
make note of the request, and bade me good-bye. Within a week,
Corrigan was on the phone to me in Singapore, hysterical. The Indian
government had made a formal protest to the U.S. State Department
about an impertinent woman journalist posing as a tourist.

"Did you, in fact, do what they are charging?" he fumed.

"Of course," I replied.

I thought I heard the sound of air leaving a balloon and, more
calmly now, he went on to say he certainly didn't want to dampen my
ardor as a reporter, but that on the foreign scene matters were usually
handled with more finesse. Lesson number one in international diplomacy.

THE Singapore "bureau," of which I was now in charge, consisted of
a spare bedroom in my apartment with a stack of a dozen or so local
newspapers, including the *Borneo Bulletin*. A clipboard, my battered
portable Smith-Corona, and several NBC News decals struggled to
lend an official air but met with no more success than old pictures of
Queen Victoria in the remaining fusty nooks of empire. My staff
comprised me and my cameraman, Vishnu. All in all, it was a quiet
corner in a steaming Asian backwater, a place to hang my knapsack,
get my laundry done, and regroup for the next far-off assignment. At
eighty-five miles north of the equator, it was a good place to leave.

As with most professions, in television what looks effortless is
usually achieved by much trial and error. Working in the field on a
protracted basis was the best way to pick up the so-called tricks of the
trade. Asia, where most stories were shot outdoors—challenging the
weather, the curiosity of onlookers, and uninvited noise, not to mention occasional danger—proved the crucible for learning how to report
and put together a story. It was one thing to have the story in your
head, know the shipping schedules, make sure the crew knew what
you were trying to show; it was quite another to have the tools at
hand. Take paper, for instance. Monsoon rains and mud smudged the
ink and soaked the paper of a score of notebooks, so I learned how to
make use of paper bags, sugar or candy wrappers, edges of newspapers.
A hard surface to lean on could be the nearest friend's back, the hood
of a car, or the stump of a tree.

Finding a quiet place to record the voice-over part of a script slowed me down every time, especially in places like India or the Philippines, where the masses of poor people, meaning no harm, would crowd around in fascination. Often, we solved the noise problem by setting up a mike in an open carrying case lined with foam rubber, an improvised studio. Although the public may never have seen me with eyeglasses, I was both nearsighted and sensitive to light, and even wore tinted glasses indoors. The Asian sun played havoc with my eyes. I squinted my way through the days, trying to avoid doing the on-camera sections in late morning or early afternoon, when the sun was directly overhead, or in late afternoon when the light slanted and darkened half my face. The most favorable time was somewhere in between, or preferably in the shade. Rainy days with their soft, even light flattered my face, but of course I had to wait for the downpours to abate or wind up looking as if I was on flood duty.

I was at a loss to solve the problem of squinting into the camera, especially since New York was now mentioning it to me in messages. Then a friend gave me a tip on how to keep your eyes open while talking and looking into the camera under a glaring sun. You shut your lids while tilting your head up directly into the sun for about fifteen to twenty seconds. Then lower your head, open your eyes, and start talking immediately. The adjustment to the brightness—even with eyes closed—lasts long enough to get through twenty seconds on camera without squinting.

Hand-held mikes—"licking the lollipop" in the trade phrase—were always awkward, especially when interviewing, and cameramen especially hated them because they "ruin the picture." The alternative was a lavaliere mike which fastened around the neck with a cord, at that time a rather clumsy affair compared to the minute Japanese models now to be had. The object was to hide the mike, as though the whole business were some deep, dark secret. That involved rigging the cable up the front of my dress or blouse, under my bra, and around my neck to clip it inside a collar or lapel or even the bra itself. In the field, this seemed routine, but in a live studio at 30 Rock, shimmying like a belly dancer always got a wisecrack out of at least one smart-aleck.

Looking good was important, but most critical was the ability to sound—and be—smart, *on deadline.* Recording a stand-upper amid the chaos of a breaking story on deadline always tested your mettle. The number of tries—or "takes"—a correspondent records to achieve a perfect stand-upper could wind up in the book of records. The crews loved keeping score, and somehow it was always the big anchormen who could do anything in one take while we mortals needed a full magazine of film, or so they said. "What is this, a remake of *Gone With the Wind?*" an impatient voice would pipe up from behind the tripod.

My record was the twenty-one false starts it took to deliver cleanly two paragraphs on a Saigon street with kids mucking it up in the background, cars backfiring, sun blazing, horns honking, and whole families watching "Gunsmoke" on sidewalk TV sets. The ultimate disgrace was to have all external factors perfect and then forget your lines. If they were long pieces to camera—a minute or more, say, about 200 words—then you needed a shortcut if brute memory failed and an airplane was waiting. One sure-fire technique (said to have been invented by Ted Koppel, who practiced it with finesse) required practice, but once mastered worked as well as cue cards back at 30 Rock. The correspondent recorded the text and plugged a wire from the tape recorder into his ear. Once the camera was on, he turned on the recorder and recited what he heard. The recording was just a few seconds ahead of the reading, but a skillful user seemed able to retain pages of script. More important, the take appeared natural, and the viewer's eye was undistracted by notes or imploring looks from a reporter verging on memory blackout.

All kinds of tricks could save your life: folding a paper napkin in the form of a handkerchief to dress up a man's jacket; using the all-purpose gaffer's tape—which can sustain the San Andreas Fault—to patch rips, tears, and unraveled hems; standing on camera cases, tables, walls, roofs, balconies, even the edge of a cliff to get the right background; reaching for a club soda when the willies or indigestion threatened to do you in before the last take. Animal backgrounds were always risky. People were even more unpredictable: those timid, tight-lipped folk who have nothing to say and then talk your head off when the camera turns on; or the loquacious and loud ones who clam up completely. Talking people into an interview—an off-camera skill—sometimes demanded more resourcefulness than actually putting the questions. "What are you going to ask me?" was a standard phrase that a newspaper reporter rarely, if ever, heard. The screen-size world of the camera imparted enough show business to the proceedings so that even the uninitiated somehow felt they were performers rather than the object of a journalistic inquiry. Men especially, I discovered, took extraordinary pains to insure they would look good on camera. Even heads of state inquired about their "best side" or the color of their shirt. Every story, every interview posed a new problem. Every day contributed another offering to my bag of tricks. Individually, they were simply observations, tactics, shortcuts, victories, and screw-ups. As a whole, they became a portfolio for survival.

Singapore itself was not unlike a self-conscious first-generation child, ashamed of its parents but proud of its ancestry, hell-bent on hard work to "make it," terrified at heart that it wouldn't. To be "Singaporean" amounted to schizophrenia: a Chinese nation with Western goals, trying to find an identity for a population that coveted money and success and spoke English, all the while paying lip service to the "great Chinese culture." The culture, meanwhile, had been stamped out in an urban-renewal frenzy unprecedented since postwar Japan. Whoever heard of a Chinese nation that actually had a section they proudly called Chinatown?

Unlike the rest of Southeast Asia, things *worked* here, and for news organizations that was reason enough to have a presence. If cleanliness is next to godliness everywhere else, in the City of Lions it *was* godliness. The penalty for dropping a burnt match was about $250 U.S. Flies and other airborne objects common to Asia didn't seem to exist in this island city-state. I used to say they couldn't get a visa. Once a tropical rain forest, and then a model of "New World Order," Singapore seemed a combination of Port Said and Switzerland, a Chinese, Malay, and Indian mix of 2 million people who spoke with the manners of British colonials and thought like Indian Ocean pirates.

When I arrived in the spring of 1972, pockets of "old China" had still held out against the bulldozer. There were unpaved streets full of freshly slaughtered pythons and shark, carts of bok choy, nha choy, and fresh coconut, a meat market big as a warehouse with steaks from Australia, rickety wooden houses where the "black-and-white" amahs in their jade earrings lived like Carmelite nuns, trained as servants from birth, deigning to work only for those they approved. Luckily I was one of them.

Tourists stayed only a few days to shop, on their way to livelier places, such as Thailand. Free-spending American GIs on R and R from the war added juice to the city, prowling the alleys for shortwave radios and low-priced girls. Most nights on the town ended with a trip to the notorious Bugis Street, a section down by the waterfront where men who had undergone sex change operations (then a popular medical practice in Singapore) dressed as whores and plied their trade amid the hundreds of sailors putting into port that day. The government looked the other way, its Puritan conscience subdued by the mountain of revenue Bugis engendered.

Overseeing the emergence of this Spartan paradise, Prime Minister Lee Kuan Yew ruled like an Oriental warlord in a Savile Row suit. Part Confucian moralist, part English barrister, part Chinese roughneck, he raised the hard-work ethic to a religious precept, making money the highest value. The "miracle of Singapore" with its banking and investment partnerships and commercial skyscrapers, its industrial park, became a clarion call for the young entrepreneurs of the "New Asia."

Kuan Yew, who used to be known as "Harry" in his days as an academic wonder at Cambridge University, was one of a breed: the Western-educated young lords of colonial Asia. After they had learned about freedom in their universities, they set about evicting their old masters. Was it any different with the young Vietnamese (Ho Chi Minh one of them) and Chinese (Chou En-lai another) who went to Paris, steeped themselves in the French Revolution, and returned home with burning fervor to oust the foreign devils?

Lee's native language was English. Political expediency forced him to learn Mandarin and Malay. The "PM" ruled a one-party nation. He had begun as a left-winger, but by the time Singapore became independent in 1965, Lee and his People's Action Party had already thrown his old revolutionary buddies into Changi Prison. Lee lived simply, and although he praised the virtues of his own army, even importing Israeli military advisers to train them, his old rambling house was guarded by the dreaded Gurkhas.

Vestiges of foreign decadence—Western influences that could threaten his grip, such as long hair—were discouraged. Posters delineating exactly what "long hair" meant (below the collar) hung in all government buildings, and any man landing at Paya Lebar Airport who fit the description forfeited his passport and was given twenty-four hours to get a haircut or leave the country. The local press was strictly censored, and the foreign press aroused Lee's paranoia almost as much as the red devil Mao himself. "Keep Singapore Clean" could have been aimed at journalists. One kept a low profile and refrained from arousing the natives with free-thinking ideas, or your expulsion order would come by express mail.

In almost two years, I sent only one story from Singapore, as New York's interest was still focused on Vietnam, Thailand, Cambodia, Laos, and occasionally Japan, Korea, or India. It was one of the rare cases where proximity—being there—did not confer newsworthiness. Each week I would send a list of story ideas—the emergence of Australia, a profile on the sultan of Brunei, political infighting in Sabah and Sarawak, oil drilling in the Indian Ocean. "No, no interest," came the reply. If "Nightly News" didn't want the piece, no one was interested; the evening program was still the tail wagging the NBC dog.

In the early days of TV news, foreign correspondents also functioned as bureau chiefs. They retained control of the story instead of having to answer to a producer type, the all-too-usual well from which most heads of bureau were later drawn. Bureau autonomy also meant financial control as well, no small consideration for a man with children, who in addition to his salary drew an education allowance for each child and a food and housing allowance arrived at by the family's size. If you happened to be a single woman, food and housing for one were available—an inequality I pointed out to various vice-presidents from the finance department. They always said they agreed in principle. But after all, the rules were written for married men, not single women.

Expense accounts, in general, were a windfall to most concerned. And while I tried to hold my own with an occasional eight-course meal prepared by Ayeen, my faithful amah, there was no matching the *US News & World Report* correspondent, Jim Wallace. Three parties a week were the rule, and guests consumed caviar, oysters, and champagne as if they were rice crackers. Expense account legends abounded. One correspondent asked that his clothes " 'n' junk" be shipped from Hong Kong to Los Angeles, never mentioning that his "junk" meant a Chinese boat. (It worked.)

I fully expected a snide telex after submitting for reimbursement an entry entitled "Air Fare For Nuns." In leaving Bangladesh, I encountered at the Dacca airport a small group of young women wearing white gowns with blue trim. Arms folded under their wide sleeves, they were standing by the hot tar runway in 120-degree heat. There was no space for them on any commercial flight, and as they were Catholic nuns not regarded as special in the crush of Muslim refugees trying to get out, they had to wait for the Red Cross plane due to arrive in about seven hours.

My old Catholic training went into high gear, and I started searching for the Indian colonel in charge of the airport. He was a dashing Sandhurst grad with whom I had often drunk Indian whiskey during the war. I spotted him by the ticket counter snapping his swagger stick against his tall leather boots.

"Can you get those nuns on a flight to Calcutta?" I asked.

Within minutes they had tickets, all charged to NBC News.

"Hell," I figured, "there are enough Irish Catholics in Business Affairs to let this one get through."

After landing at the appropriately named Dum Dum Airport in Calcutta, we prepared to debark. Suddenly, a small, bony arm reached out from under a white gown and stopped me in the aisle. A frail wren of a woman, her face lined by hard work and weather, fixed me with extraordinary eyes. Holding my one hand tightly in both of hers, she said: "We thank you for your kindness. I will ask Our Lord to protect you."

Somehow, it was difficult to respond, so struck was I by what must have been a kind of holiness I had never before witnessed.

Later, waiting for the gear to be off-loaded, I ran into a British journalist who had been on the same flight. "Well," he said, "I see you met Mother Teresa."

My life in Singapore became a frantic series of calls in the night, ordering me out on the first available flight. There were times I had to call the switchboard in the morning and ask what hotel it was and, by the way, which country. Even Singapore's geography, dangling southerly off a mainland, gave me the feeling of having been set adrift, that my friends would never find me. But they did, of course.

Skip Ettinger dropped me a note. He was on Okinawa studying karate. When he got out of the army, he couldn't adjust. He took a government job as an adviser to the army, stationed in Boston, but spent most of his free time in Chinatown getting drunk and hanging out. "It seemed the only place I felt comfortable was around Orientals," he said later. "I knew I had to do something. All my Vietnam buddies were either bums, alcoholics or suicides. Finally, I sold my car and bought a one-way ticket back to the Far East. So when I got to Okinawa I got a job as an army hospital receptionist and started studying karate. I knew it would help me."

Craig Spence, living in Tokyo and latching on to the upward curve of the Japanese nation, stayed in touch. A sad message arrived one day. His ABC cameraman from the war, Terry Khoo, a Singaporean in fact, had been killed by heavy small-arms fire covering an action near Quang Tri. The last time I had seen Terry was at a Chinese banquet in Cholon when he had regaled us with tales of near escapes in the bush.

Jake—the former love of my life and now director of Far East news in Hong Kong—had checked in with a welcome message on my arrival in Singapore. Good luck and all that. He was married now, enough reason to steer clear of that crown colony.

.   .   .

THE war and peace news ground on, except that, with American troops filtering out of Vietnam, the emphasis was shifting to Cambodia and Laos and the effects of the U.S. bombing. From early autumn through the end of the year, reporters crowded into Phnom Penh, now a city choked by refugees from the countryside, and Vientiane, a departure point for Hanoi-bound airplanes. After a Communist offensive in March and a solid impasse at the Paris peace talks, Nixon— committed to the warpath—resumed bombing North Vietnam and ordered the mining of its major ports. Meanwhile, both Laos and Cambodia were engaged in a life-and-death struggle with Communist-led insurrectionists. Staff correspondents from the major press and television companies went in usually during crisis periods, often acting on tips from their resident stringers. Some of these free-lancers were serious about the news business; many just drifted around Southeast Asia in search of excitement and free grass. Their animosity toward American policy was a given.

The city of Phnom Penh, its wide boulevards shadowed by willow trees and cream-colored stucco buildings, recalled old Saigon before the apparatus of war had disfigured its face. Television reporters had their work cut out for them: refugees, the bombing, and of course "running the roads," seeing how far you could travel past checkpoints without getting ambushed. While New York still pleaded weighing the risk against the story, the pressure to beat the other nets was always there. With no U.S. troops to draw the lines, no choppers to spirit you out from an action, it was a different kind of dangerous assignment, throwing you totally on individual nerve and judgment. Was that road safe? Was this Cambodian army unit—full of thirteen-year-olds— going to get me in trouble today? Add to that the lack of any American medical aid, and the imagination called up horrors of languishing in some swampy field hospital, bleeding to death.

Staying alive was always a serious concern, but staying healthy was tricky. Illness is serious business in Southeast Asia, not the common cold or a migraine, but malaria, typhoid fever, amebic dysentery. "If you can't peel it, don't eat it" said the old Asian hands, a convention I flouted for the first time on this trip. One night, David Hume Kennerly and I went to an open-air restaurant in downtown Phnom Penh; starry night, balmy breezes. David, a first-rate free-lance photographer who went on to become the resident camera guy in the Ford White House, was telling me about his recent series of rabies shots. He confessed he had made the mistake of putting his hand in an ocelot's cage at the Saigon animal market. Naturally, it bit him. Even as I laughed at his recklessness, I was blissfully consuming a mixed salad. I awoke the next morning in my room at the Hotel Royal with a harrowing fever, chills, epic diarrhea, the works. A Cambodian doctor arrived at my bedside and in true colonial tradition prescribed quinine, which had no effect. I worsened. New York expected stories, Hong Kong wanted to know where they were. The electricity and the air-conditioning in the hotel went out. Lumbering cockroaches poked through gaping holes in my bathroom. The floor boy, bringing me bottled soda and soup, shook his head sadly and padded away. Bordering on delirium, I lay there thinking that if the fever or the Khmer Rouge didn't get me, surely the cockroaches would.

After three days, I went back to work. Propped up against the front wall of the U.S. embassy, I did a stand-upper and staggered to my room to finish three scripts. When it was over, the crew—now also ill—and I headed for the airport. Customs hassled us about our gear, threatening to block our departure. And if that wasn't enough, when we did make the flight, it pirouetted through a typhoon over the South China Sea. We were the last plane to land in Hong Kong before Kaitak Airport was closed. After all that, it was simple—a doctor, a hospital, a diagnosis: amebic dysentery.

But it wasn't long before Al Chambers, who had succeeded Jake in Hong Kong, had me on the run again. Back to Cambodia, where we clustered around the radio to hear the BBC announce Nixon's stunning election victory over Senator George McGovern. What would he do now with this ringing endorsement of his war policy? By the time I arrived in Vientiane a few weeks later, the question was moot. He was bombing North Vietnam to the peace table. The price, however, was high. During the twelve-day period between December 18 and 30, a period that became known as the "Christmas carpet bombing," the U.S. command acknowledged that fifteen B-52s and eleven fighter-bombers had been downed by the intense antiaircraft fire over the north. Ninety-three airmen wound up as MIAs, and the Viets said they had taken thirty-one prisoners.

The raids would, in fact, lead to uncommon cooperation from Hanoi, but in the meantime they set off a new furor of antiwar demonstrations. A damaged Hanoi hospital became a symbol of American brutality; the Communists announced American POWs had been injured in the raids. (Many said later they were singing "The Star-Spangled Banner" as the B-52s rumbled over.) Foreign embassies—

most of them, curiously, from Communist countries—claimed bomb damage; peace groups who regularly took their shows on the road headed for North Vietnam. By Christmas Day, Joan Baez was strumming a guitar for her fellow travelers in a Hanoi hotel room, while Bob Hope, entertaining U.S. troops in Saigon, cheered on the Nixon offensive.

In Laos, the Land of the Million Elephants and the White Parasol, the noose tightened. The Vientiane government had made it clear it couldn't strike a deal with the Communist Pathet Lao guerrillas until matters were settled with Hanoi at the peace talks. Fighting, of course, continued in the country, two-thirds of which by that time was controlled by the Communists.

Laos, a modern-day Graustark, a land that time forgot, had everyone's vote as the saddest case in Indochina. Gentle, smiling, childlike, the people of Laos were not cut out for war, if anyone is. Who could begrudge a country once led by a man whose father-in-law was named King Jayavarmaparameçvara, and held court at the great Angkor Wat? A tropical forest, landlocked, hushed by jungle and crossed by hidden trails, Laos was a T-bone steak for the hard-headed North Vietnamese engaged in the business of supplying a war they intended to win.

On Christmas Eve, I was sitting alone in my room at the Lan Xan Hotel, finishing off a Yuletide supper of scrambled eggs. Al Chambers had swooped in from Hong Kong on a Caravelle and scooped up everyone in the tripartite coverage area so they could be home with their families. "Somebody" had to mind the store. No children meant no Christmas. This wasn't the first time. Working weekends and holidays so the men could go home was part of the territory.

It was lousy duty, although the chance of a breaking story was real enough. You never knew who would turn up at the airport on the ICC (International Control Commission) flights in and out of Hanoi. And the lefty traffic being what it was—Baez, Telford Taylor, Jane Fonda, whoever—networks kept a lookout for someone who would agree to carry a camera into Hanoi for pictures. But as far as I was concerned, North Vietnamese propaganda captured on film by Americans was a new form of giving aid and comfort to the enemy. I wanted none of it.

By New Year's Eve, the bombing had ceased, and the North Vietnamese had agreed to return to the peace talks within a week. On January 22, I was in Omaha, Nebraska, on leave for another NBC correspondents' tour, and waiting in the wings of a local theater to take the stage for another debate. As we stood there, someone rushed up and announced that Lyndon Johnson had died. Had he lived one more day, he would have seen the official end of the bitter struggle that brought him down: the initialing of a peace agreement to end the war in Vietnam. The list was so long, I thought, the roster of those whose credentials had dissolved in the mud of this war. Johnson, McNamara, Rusk, Bunker, Lodge, Westmoreland—they were the first to take the heat, the shining reputations that failed the test of Vietnam. Entirely different names would be added after a closer look at those who seemed so destined for success—so moral—at the time: Ellsberg, McCarthy, McGovern, Hayden. In the halls of power, in the streets of protest, and on the fields of battle, one by one the victims multiplied as the agony of this old war lived on through the failure of those who had dared to change its course.

From five feet of snow in Omaha, I raced back to Laos. Peace was breaking out, the prisoners were coming home, and a North Vietnamese military delegation would be passing through en route to Saigon. The accords would be formally signed on the 27th, and on the following day—a cease-fire.

But with an end to the shooting war, another old hostility erupted into full-scale battle. Some referred to it as the Real Air War. No strafing, no bombing, no napalm. Worse—because the combatants were the Big Three of American TV news. The networks, always at fighting weight in the competition for being first, went all out in a full-scale race, grabbing the best and fastest charter planes to shuttle breaking stories to satellite points in Hong Kong and Tokyo. Regularly scheduled airliners were not very dependable, and only operated during daylight hours, so bureau chiefs and correspondents had to be as adept at reading airplane schedules, identifying engines, and computing miles per hour as they were at reporting and writing a story. Names and phone numbers of anyone who called himself a charter pilot were guarded like coded targets. It also helped to have a degree in accounting, with rates running from $6,000 to $9,000 for a one-way trip from Saigon to Hong Kong. 727s—carrying only a flight crew and a bag of news film—dotted the skies over the three countries involved in this peace production.

Even as Henry Kissinger was hammering out the Paris accords, the nets secretly agreed to a charter truce, an agreement to share airplanes which they violated routinely. The history of internetwork relations abounded with tales of shipping bags kicked out of flying helicopters, rumors of engine sabotage and scenes of educated gentlemen grabbing each other by the lapels in the men's rooms of airport terminals. "Pool reporting"—having a single camera or a single correspondent for all three networks—was only a last resort in the coverage of this war. The name of the game was hardball. If word came that an important official was on a flight, and one network wanted to interview him on board, it would think nothing about buying out the entire first-class section so that the other two couldn't muscle in. I distinctly recall putting a "hold" on four planes in one afternoon to prevent CBS and ABC from beating us to Hong Kong. Money was not only no object, it was *the* object.

I arrived at the Vientiane airport shortly before the North Vietnamese delegation touched down en route to Saigon. As I stepped off the Royal Air Lao flight, there, squinting into the sun and laughing, was Jake. This was now getting to be the poor man's Hemingway. Girl meets boy. Girl goes to war. Boy meets other girl, marries her. First girl goes back to war. Boy meets girl again. War ends. It would never play in Peoria. As though no time had passed, no tears been shed, we went to work on a long piece for a documentary on the truce.

The Hanoi delegation landed within the hour, little men in frayed uniforms, small, tough bodies suited more for jungle trails than the glare of TV lights. Smiling like gargoyles, they marched across the tarmac, the enemy close up. "Look at them," Jake said. "These are the little guys who defeated the United States of America." We stood there dumbly, feeling a shame and sorrow neither of us dared admit. Somehow, the age of optimism had gone bust. And a great power—putting troops into the jungle at dizzying speed, spending its young men, yet never using its full might—had been drained and disgraced.

What had happened to the glittering and endless promise America had offered to the world in the wake of World War II? A decade that began with hopes of going to the moon, eliminating racism, creating a Peace Corps—all visions of goodwill uttered by a princelike president quoting Thomas Jefferson—had dissolved into riots in the cities, drug taking, and alienation. Was the war a symbol of this disillusion or perhaps a convenient issue on which to hang the failed hopes of the nation? And now, inflated optimism and American will were down for the count.

There seemed a sad symmetry in it all. I had listened, sympathetically, to the old British guard in Singapore talk about World War II, how the guns at the naval base were facing out to sea as the Japanese hacked their way through the jungle, how the colonials were still sipping Pimm's Cup on the padang as General Yamashita's 25th Army demanded surrender. The sun had indeed set on the empire, its first rays descending on the Malay Peninsula. Now, not very far away, it was going to be our turn.

For the next few weeks, Jake and I wandered through Laos and Thailand and then headed for Clark Air Base, north of Manila in the Philippines. The American prisoners of war were at last coming home. The first planeload from Hanoi would touch down on February 12. Overnight, the base looked as though MacArthur had landed once again, as an invading army of technicians and equipment moved in for this dream TV event. The arrival would be carried live on all three networks at 3:15 A.M. New York time.

Along with the equipment came the stateside reporters to fill out the coverage, and with no small amount of chagrin I learned that Jack Perkins would anchor the story from Clark. If there was one story I had boned up on it was the POWs; I had been studying their backgrounds for years and could recite what they liked for breakfast, and more important, what was known about them since their captivity. This was my baby, I thought, and while no one would admit it outright, the fact was a woman simply couldn't be trusted to carry the weight of such a big story. It was difficult to hide my bitter disappointment, but I trooped along doing pieces and staying on top of the story.

In the meantime, hardened Far East types, like Arnett and Faas and Jim Sterba of the *Times,* vacillated between chasing nurses and inducting their newly arrived colleagues who had never been west of Los Angeles into some of the local rituals. Most popular were the excursions to certain emporiums in nearby Angeles City, where Filipino girls did interesting things with bananas and other foreign objects while engaged in nude dancing. I told them I thought they were disgusting.

Erratic laundry service and general wear and tear left me low in the clothes department as usual. One day, stuck for something to wear for an on-camera situationer about Operation Homecoming, Peter suggested I borrow a pair of his trousers. It seemed a logical move, especially since the ban on women wearing pants never really applied in this part of the world. They fit quite nicely, and I wore them for the piece. Twenty-four hours later, Peter was called to the telephone. His wife, Nina, was calling from New York. She had seen me on the news that night and recognized her husband's trousers. Peter was in deep trouble.

The command was keeping a tight rein on the POW release, importing 66 public relations officers and enlisted men to deal with the 170 newsmen. They may have lost the hot war because of the press, but they weren't going to lose this one—not when their own were coming back. And who knows, what if some of the POWs had been weaned over to the other side and rolled off the airplanes singing Uncle Ho songs. All statements by anyone connected with the operation—medical personnel, flight crews, and the rest—were to be made only in the presence of one of these censors. Everyone had been coached and warned their careers were on the line if they broke rank.

One hundred forty-three men arrived with the first release. I recorded a track over the air force film shot in Hanoi, pictures of the airport ceremony in which the Vietnamese officially handed the men over to the United States. An escort guided each man, although all walked stiffly but on their own, as they boarded the huge C-141 hospital planes. It was their first airplane ride in the months and years that had passed since they were shot out of their cockpits. When the wheels touched down at Clark Field, they sent up a cheer from their seats, gawking out the windows. Perkins picked up the live narration at this point. When the door of the plane opened, in those few breathless seconds before the first man appeared, a current of anticipation, even of dread, shot through the silent crowd of newsmen and American residents. What would they look like? Led by Captain Jeremiah Denton—a man who had been held prisoner for eight years and whose voice cracked with emotion as he declared, "God bless America"—the POWs saluted the crowd and bounded down the stairs. They looked like underfed, weary men who had seen a great many unspeakable things.

I looked around and saw the rules of objectivity explode. Every cameraman, every reporter, setting aside mikes, pads, cables, and cameras, began applauding wildly. We were so overcome, not just by the joy of the event, but by the melancholy gaze of these men who had endured so much in a war we knew so well. Never, in any war, had American prisoners been in captivity so long.

For the third release about a month later, I was assigned to do the live portions for the "Today" show. I flew to Hong Kong to meet the satellite and, taking a deep breath, watched the men get off the planes at Clark, identifying them on sight, talking over the live pictures that were rolling from the base to New York. At last I got a chance to contribute what I had spent years storing up.

After the broadcast, New York called and told me I would be NBC's man in Hanoi for the final release. It was, indeed, a vote of confidence from the front office. It was also an occasion for a correspondent new to NBC to show his wrath at not being chosen for the job. Phil Brady, a former marine in Vietnam, had sold himself to NBC, and especially Westfeldt, also an ex-marine, on the basis of his special knowledge of the country and the language. Brady was all bluff—loud, theatrically serious, and a charter member of the macho brigade. His face turned redder than usual when I got the assignment to go to North Vietnam. First he began yelling at Al Chambers and the room in general, then, his solid six feet at full power, he lunged for me across a desk. Only the interdiction of Chambers prevented an even uglier scene.

"You bitch!" screamed Brady.

"Go ahead—and I'll sue," I answered, not budging an inch.

It made great copy for the international rumor mill.

Gaining entry to Hanoi for the last release meant getting positioned in Laos for the flight. I was wondering who my CBS competition might be—with luck, a foe worthy of my steel. As I walked into the lobby of the Lan Xan Hotel, I got my answer. In the center of the cool marble floor, a knot of people milled around an elegant man in a bush suit, sporting a British mustache. Great White Hunter type, I thought, until my eyes adjusted to the shade. It was Walter Cronkite. I felt a strong urge to borrow a razor blade and get it over with right on the spot, a kinder death than competing with America's most trusted man.

Someone moved me over for the introductions: "Walter, Liz. Liz, Walter." Without missing a beat, I leveled my eyes and said, "It's about time your shop sent me some competition."

Cronkite, a great sport, looked confused for only an instant, obviously measuring me as a brash and eminently beatable Young Turk. "We'll see," he smiled, and the eye twinkle that millions of Americans recognized told me he wasn't kidding. The NBC team was on full alert.

The next day, we threw him into the hotel pool.

The day after that, Walter was just another newsman on a stakeout. Still, at a Laotian banquet in one of Vientiane's old restaurants, he did sit at the head of a long table, taking the barbs from about twenty journalists, who loved the excitement of having him there, feeling even more important because of the presence of America's most famous newsman. We sat on picnic benches under arcs of colored lanterns, washing down piles of steaming rice with pitchers of watery wine. Most of the talk centered on an all-male escapade of the previous night when "we took Walter down to the Purple Pussycat," a well-known establishment where exotic ladies entertained. One story had it that someone took a Polaroid of a nude woman sitting in Uncle Walter's lap and then asked him if he wanted it. If the photographer had larceny in his heart, it didn't do him any good. Walter was reported to have calmly replied: "Do what you want with that picture."

Finally we got the word to proceed to Hanoi, the first group of American journalists to go north, to inspect the enemy's camp, to see his face. During the flight, everyone looked pensive, the intense curiosity to see the ravages of war mingling with the heavy dread of finding out.

David Kennerly was pacing up and down the aisle with that look all photographers get when they are just a frame away from "a great shot." All of us pushed our noses to the windows, trying to separate the rivers from the bomb craters in the red earth below. I went up to the cockpit for a better view, and just as Hanoi came in sight and we started our descent, the pilot jerked the aging Viscount violently to the left, turning and falling steeply, on the verge of a rollover. This is it, I thought. I could see the headlines. They'll play it for irony. War over. Big batch of war correspondents shot down in flames over Hanoi. We learned later that the pilot had been trying to evade ground fire coming from local farmers who for years had been shooting at American aircraft and hadn't got the word yet that the war was over— at least that was the official version.

On the southwestern edge of the city stood Nha Tu Dzu, once a film studio, now the place that POWs called "the Zoo." Robotic guides in civilian clothes asked us to mass in the prison courtyard for a briefing. A Communist official droned on about the fine care of the prisoners, whom we could not yet see. They ate meat and fruit and beer with regularity, he said through a fixed grin. They also received first-rate medical care, he claimed, even when they hurt themselves playing volleyball. I couldn't take much more of that, so I decided to investigate a fence with a closed door cut in it just across the courtyard. I signaled one of the UPI guys to come with me. We slid away from the group and opened the door.

There they were—American pilots playing volleyball, obviously for our benefit. They froze. We stood looking at one another in disbelief. By this time, the officials realized we had broken ranks. Along with the Viets, members of the American military delegation already on the scene, terrified that their own press would antagonize the Hanoi officials, began to see us as a common enemy. They tried to hold shut the main doors of the camp, so—as any true reporter would—we stormed them. The next thing I knew, Cronkite and I and our respective crews had pushed our way into a cell where a half dozen prisoners lived. I'll never forget the stunned look on their faces when they saw Walter. He pretended not to notice, and we proceeded to question them, men who had been living with a memory of home, now startled by the dislocation of seeing an American icon in their midst.

Tomes have been written about Cronkite's on-camera authority and magic, but watching him work in the field could only gain the admiration of a reporter: gliding into position for the interviews, turning to a rolling camera without notes and, on the spot, whenever a new development arose, delivering a vivid and literate summation of the action. It took skill to do this—and all the confidence and experience of one who has worked as a reporter, not just an anchor. Cronkite had earned his reputation.

Before we left, the Viets insisted on showing us the "massive damage" inflicted on the city by American warplanes. In fact, apart from a few isolated cases—the famous hospital that they showed every visitor—the bombing was surgical, virtually stopping at the edge of a railroad, within a few hundred yards of houses. The main bridge over the Red River and other logical military targets had been taken out with precision. The "terror bombing of civilians" had never happened, and I made this point clear in a March 30 piece that ran on the evening news, adding that the Viets were already talking about war reparations from the United States. Even as we toured Hanoi, the prisoners now home were telling their stories of torture. I closed the piece saying: "Until yesterday, until the POWs broke their silence, many Americans were sympathetic about the suffering of the North Vietnamese people, but today, in the wake of what the prisoners have said, North Vietnam's search for sympathy could be longer and harder."

The actual release took place at the airport, where each prisoner was officially handed over to U.S. military officers waiting at a table set up in front of the terminal and within a few hundred yards of two C-141s. One by one, they crossed over until the last man had stepped forward. A shuffle and then a surge started toward the planes. As I jockeyed into position at the edge of the crush, I heard a familiar voice. "Hey, Liz. Liz!"

It couldn't be. It was.

Running toward me in his flight suit, smiling as though he might have been released that day himself, was Don D'Amico. We smashed into each other's arms, crying and talking at the same time. Out of the hospital, he had fought his way back onto flight status so he could come to Hanoi and fly prisoners out. I hadn't seen him in five years—since that rainy day in Da Nang after he had been shot down—sitting in the officers' club, watching him pretend he was in one piece.

"Could have been you," I said.

"You don't need to remind me," he replied, looking over at the grim-faced Vietnamese encircling the flight line.

Watching this scene, a nearby North Vietnamese soldier, pointing an AK-47, angrily motioned for us to get back behind the barriers. By this time I had had it. In a display of pure aggression, I wheeled on the little man and snarled. "Get away from me you son of a bitch or I'll knock your head off." It is not wise to address people this way when they are carrying weapons. D'Amico collapsed in laughter. The soldier retreated.

While the POWs came out of the north, in the south the last of the American troops—those not attached to the embassy or offshore carriers—were leaving the country. Almost overnight, as the American military command dissolved, so too did the staffs of the news organizations in the Far East. The war, which had galvanized the world's interest and the personnel needed to satisfy it, melted away as attention turned toward Europe and the Middle East.

I didn't know what my next assignment would be, but I suspected something was up when I heard that my mail was being sent to the Rome bureau. Then, in a style typical of the army or the networks, I had marching orders for London. The very name invited chills—Murrow, Shirer, Sevareid, Churchill—a tradition of serious journalism. Visions of commenting, interpreting, and analyzing complicated NATO issues danced in my head. Little did I know.

Once more, I disconnected from Vietnam. This time for good, I vowed. The decade of America's involvement in Southeast Asia may have divided the country, consumed political leaders, disgraced the command, but among journalists, those who passed the test were holding a ticket to success. We left in droves—to forget what we had seen and reach for the stars.

11

OCEANS APART

"Just remember," Bob Mulholland said, "you'd better get along with him. I know what people are saying, but he's a good man. And you'd better make it work."

Bob's routinely pleasant personality, the kind you notice in high school senior class presidents, disappeared as he set his square jaw like a fencer's. It struck me how hard and fast he had been at hiding his ambition. Now, as an executive vice-president, a new harshness had set in. Nothing, not even the Irwin Margolis issue, would screw up his climb to the top. He had opted for power—and backing management's favorite son was part of the package. Margolis had been tapped by Dick Wald, now president of NBC News, to be head of the London bureau. For Mulholland, it was a question of love Dick, love his dog.

Still, he had always been a friend, and I expected at least a few words of encouragement as I headed for my new assignment.

"All right," I replied. "But I've heard some pretty bad stuff about Margolis."

"And what about you? Would you like me to tell you some of the stories I've heard about *your* behavior, like that temper of yours, and pushing people around?"

"Point taken. All right, you have my word I'll give him all the help and cooperation I can."

I was thunderstruck by Mulholland's vehemence and his cold pre-judgment that whatever rumor he heard about me had to be true. I wasn't expecting a golden apple for good service—after all, my low tolerance for fools and my native prickliness had stung a few—but neither was I prepared for a dire warning about "getting along" with the news department's latest and most malevolent hotshot. I had just left the jungles of Cambodia, where the Khmer Rouge had raised guerrilla fighting to an art. The battles to come would be a lot less classy, but no less lethal.

It was the client system in play. Like some ancient Caesar sweeping through the Roman Forum, no American corporate TV mogul would have been caught dead without a cometary tail of clients or hangers-on in the halls of power. Groups of servile yes-men showed you were a man due respect, while a plebeian under the protection of a patrician or patron had an insurance policy. He had to perform certain obeisances—such as cutting the news budget—but by and large he had a free hand. Of course, he could never testify against his master, a law strictly observed in NBC intrigues. Besides, even if your master was fired, you never knew when you might work for him again elsewhere. The system had nothing to do with any such thing as loyalty; survival, not harmony, was the objective.

Dick Wald was a thin-lipped man with transparent skin and a knack for getting good jobs. Had come to NBC from the *Herald Tribune* and was managing editor when the paper folded. He had a smart-aleck approach to broadcasting, as if it were a new hobby. One of his most quoted assertions about TV news was that, with his help, it would become "a wire service of the air," which meant, I supposed, a lean and tough operation with lower profiles for line correspondents. Men like Irwin Margolis were getting aboard to enforce the dictums of a new age.

The halls of 30 Rock resounded with Margolis stories. Gossip abounded about the tall, skinny guy who had worked his way up from the boondocks to become, in Wald's words, "one of the most brilliant men in TV news today." It was not a point of view shared by the rank and file. "He is the most evil man I've ever met"—Don Snyder, a free-lancer based in Northern Ireland, had articulated the general judgment of Margolis, arching his thick black eyebrows in disbelief. Ordered to track down members of the Ulster Freedom Fighters, a murderous right-wing Protestant group, Don had received a death threat—no laughing matter in Irish cowboy country, especially to a Jewish kid from the Bronx. But NBC's guard dog on the Thames nevertheless demanded, "You're not trying hard enough, Don. Find them."

Another chilling tale came from the Rome bureau, which often staffed coverage for Middle East developments. One of their sound men was on duty in Israel when his brother died. A producer phoned London and asked for advice about who should break the news and how fast they could send him home. "Don't tell him a thing," yelled Margolis. "Not until I can get a replacement."

One by one the stories rolled in, proving to be the merest inklings of what was in store for the network's most prestigious bureau, until then a graduate school for the demonstrably able and a showcase for NBC News overseas. Not since King Canute had Londoners seen the like of Irv Margolis, a man who was about to decimate and demoralize network news offices on three continents, and I had the wonderful luck to get there just as he did.

The bureau was already in an uproar when I arrived, pulling up in a taxi at the plaza in fashionable St. James's, where a puzzling sculpture by Henry Moore stood by the entrance. In those days, it was de rigueur that network offices overseas show the flag in high-rent districts only. Thus, our floor in the Economist Building, hard by White's, London's grandest club, steps away from the fruit baskets at Fortnum & Mason and the sachet and sponge shops on Jermyn Street.

Margolis, forever circling the office like a crippled bat, had already pulled his switchblade on the budget and within days of my arrival was busy slashing newspaper and magazine subscriptions to the bone. It was a mark of the new breed of producer-executives, trying to make points with New York by cutting what everyone called "the chickenshit." The correspondents—Garrick Utley, George Montgomery, and myself, plus the radio reporter—of course relied on periodicals to keep up-to-date. But this wunderkind product of local stations lacked not just print experience but also any familiarity with the crafts of reporting and writing and the spirit in which they are practiced. In his mind, pictures meant TV—getting them in the camera, putting them in the right order, and sending them on an electronic signal to New York—"sausage stuffing" one of the staff Brits dubbed it. Productivity made the bureau look good, so what went out was not nearly as important as how much.

Like a jackal hunting up prey for the lions, Margolis would resume his patrol around the floor every morning, trailing about five feet of wire copy. "Here he comes again, playing newsman," observed Montgomery, the first to take his measure.

"Hey, come in here," Margolis would squeak in the cracked cadence of an adolescent's voice about to change. "This is a REALLY great—I mean GREAT story." So we would troop in, and someone would patiently try to explain why it was not a GREAT story, that it was in a country we couldn't get into, that we had done it already, that it was a hype—just for starters. But nothing could stop this morning ritual of walking and shrieking, this outsider's idea of how to conduct the news business.

Margolis had exacted the title of general manager, Europe, as a condition of his London contract. This meant that Africa, the Middle East, and whatever parts of Asia he could ravage like Tamerlane reported to him. A masterful power play. The day-to-day supervision of "Nightly News" coverage was left to the affable Texan, Bob Mac-Farland, who had been a Westfeldt confidant and bar-hopping partner. Stories out of London were sometimes edited in the bureau but more often at the BBC Television Centre, half an hour away in Shepherd's Bush, whence they were satellited to New York. No day was complete without a mad drive to "the Beeb" to make a deadline.

With Margolis came another sign of the new era: a business manager. Money matters had for years been handled by Flo Ferguson, a stylish English lady who doubled as social director, ambassador, and general fixer. Flo's ties into the British landscape and its news sources were deep and wide. But to Margolis she was the past—an echo of Luftwaffe raids when Flo hid under the desk with General Sarnoff. She also had power, in itself reason enough to break her. Her going-away party was held at Claridge's, with Wald flying in to make the good-bye official and to visit his tailor. Flo had a rich husband and wouldn't starve, but her canning was a requiem for earlier times and the transition to a new style of running bureaus and covering news—by ledger, by "manager." Years of forging goodwill in the postwar partnership of two peoples who had beaten the Hun, the friendships of hard times, the memories of graceful hours—were to count for nothing. Even the NBC-owned house in Regent's Park, which traditionally went to the bureau chief, was up for sale.

Margolis's alienation of the British staff—about half of the twenty-strong bureau—was memorable. One woman, another stalwart from an earlier age, who remembered dodging V-ls on the way to the wartime office, was a secondary target. Her whole life had been NBC News. A spinster, she lived alone, had few friends, drank heavily, and led her life vicariously in the glamorous figures passing through from New York. On one of his trips over, Mulholland told her she was finished—"early retirement," as it were—and spent much of the day looking relieved and telling anyone who would listen how "necessary" it was. The woman spent her last few weeks red-eyed and silent in her office.

The two women were replaced by a "business manager"—Al Olsen from Business Affairs in New York, a nice guy in a hit man's job. Enter the bookkeepers, Al their mole. One of his first tasks was to check the taxi accounts. Radio Taxi was a private service made available for anyone who worked late or had a business errand to run, but in reality, it was appropriated by everyone for everything, whether wives who wanted to lunch at the Ritz or staffers who needed more lime after-shave. The bureau production manager, Ed Dyas, admittedly lived much of his day in Radio Taxi backseats. A born operator who had created his own area of influence among the European bureaus and foreign networks, Dyas posed a threat to Margolis. The taxi probe was completely bogus, but when the investigation was over and Margolis had his taxi receipts, he took the matter to his patron. Wald backed his client. Dyas was on his way home. Radio Taxi took him to Heathrow.

Despite his avowed asceticism, Margolis, like most Americans who become automatic Anglophiles, helped himself to the perks of working overseas, and then some. Invitations once meant for the correspondents, the queen's garden party, dinner at the ambassador's house, wound up on his calendar. He even inveigled NBC to pay fees and dues for Les Ambassadeurs, a swank dinner club known for its American membership, especially celebrities. Having a "club" was part of being based in London, not a real English club—no Yank could crack one of those—but a dinner club at least. It went along with the London Life.

I tried to imagine Margolis on the social circuit, gangling in his brown pinstripe suit with vest, complemented by a checked shirt, shiny tie, and black shoes. Addressing butlers and waiters in that high-pitched adolescent voice, conversing with soft-spoken Europeans in that nasal tone, sentences like snorts, nervous energy spilling out as dark designs doodled on menus and tablecloths. Sammy Glick on the Sceptered Isle. Oh yes, they would say, that's the NBC chief in London, that spindly man who prowls the streets in search of discounts on orange juice squeezers no matter how strong the dollar, the man who drinks skim milk and eats water biscuits unless someone is buying lunch. The man whose office is known as "the bordello" since he had it painted purple with a rug to match.

It wasn't long before Margolis was called Genghis Cohen, another savage bon mot from Montgomery. George, a salty Irish-English Protestant, was known for his well-placed harpoons, especially those in the hilarious portraits of English eccentrics he wrote for the evening news. He had been in the country for almost two decades, having worked at Reuters before joining NBC. More than anyone I knew in broadcasting, George looked and talked like a reporter. Straight hair falling in eyes that took in everything, a dirty trench coat, a rain-stained note pad protruding from his pocket. "The way I look at it," he said, "we've repulsed the Hun before in these parts and we can do it again."

Montgomery's loathing of Margolis was total and hard to hide. He courted trouble, especially the night he got drunk while Margolis was out of town and went over to the boss's apartment to make a pass at his wife. Margolis's righteous rage was somewhat diffused by the fact that everybody knew his wife hated him and they would eventually divorce.

Several months later, George was fired. When he asked for a reason, Dick Wald told him, "The quality and quantity of your work has declined." George retreated into the Dubai desert to teach school but never lost track of his old boss. When Margolis himself was finally pushed out, he wrote a note: "Dear Irv, Sorry to hear that, in your case as in mine, the quality and quantity of your work has declined." But George wasn't finished. A few months later, he went to work for Reuters in London and learned that a farewell luncheon was being held for Margolis at a local restaurant. Never missing a chance to commiserate with an old colleague, he fired off a telegram: DEAR IRV, SORRY I CANNOT BE AT YOUR LUNCH. LOVE, GEORGE.

London inspired a certain amount of putting on the dog for the average American. Kept aloft by a sturdy cost-of-living allowance, traveling expenses, and perks beyond their middle-class imaginings, the networks' innocents abroad could partake of the London life without even touching a salary. An American journalist was Someone abroad, not just an inky wretch. What's more, here they called you "Sir."

MacFarland bought a Bentley not long after he arrived, and his tailor came to the office. Visiting brass, often accompanied by a bureau member, religiously checked in at Savile Row and then on to Turnbull & Asser for custom-made shirts. Gucci loafers, not yet ubiquitous, were mailed in from Rome. The finishing touch came at 3:30 P.M. every day when Mary, a sweet old English lady, served tea. All of this seemed like a lot of trouble and expensive trappings just to practice the primitive skill of getting words and pictures to fit two minutes. Sometimes I wondered how anyone could tear himself away long enough to work on a story.

The clubbiness, the largesse, the fact that everyone spoke English made London a prime assignment, especially for American correspondents. But if we were long on life-style, we were short on expertise. Watching the BBC's year-end show, when its correspondents are called in from the field to discuss world affairs, I cringed in the realization that we couldn't compare. The average tour for an American TV reporter or producer was three years, and no language skills were required. Further, the almost routine ignorance of any historical background only invited the patient smirks of our foreign colleagues.

When the Turks fell out with the Greeks over Cyprus in July 1974, we all crashed into Ankara. A government interpreter asked for a letter from the three U.S. networks, formally requesting permission to accompany the invasion. The ABC correspondent volunteered to write it. After it was submitted, an official came over to me and whispered that I had better read it before the minister of information did. My pal, Jay Axelbank of *Newsweek*, who was reading over my shoulder, dissolved in mirth. "Cyprus" was consistently spelled C-y-p-r-e-s-s. The ABC man, based in Europe, went on to a substantial anchor job at another network. I had the distinct feeling that aliens had infiltrated network news.

At NBC London, the people who went out on stories (as distinct from "indoor" staff) did know, however, that there was more to their assignment than Harrods and "Buck House," Yankee shorthand for Buckingham Palace. You only had to meet the generations of unemployed in the north of England, walk in the mean alleys of the impoverished Northern Ireland Catholics, visit a housing project in the West Indian immigrant neighborhoods of Brixton, where racial hatred boiled daily. You had to look for the poor in the U.K., unlike Asia where vast prospects of desperation fill the horizon and the rich stay out of sight. More often than not, when it came down to getting stories on the evening news, the grayness and grime of the United Kingdom often lost out to clichés—the royals at play and quirky Miss Marple types in seedy country houses.

If Margolis and Mulholland exemplified a new breed of steward-ship on the rise—a transition period in TV news management—the European bureaus also found themselves caught in the changing times. The geography of news had already moved away from Asia, but now it was shifting from Europe as well. The Middle East would be a great story throughout the 1970s and well into the 1980s. Third World countries, once lucky to merit a feature if someone happened to be in the area, now found their place in the sun and on the tube. The oil embargo and the Yom Kippur War would point the way, followed by terrorism: hijackings, embassy seizures, car bombs—all images of a new kind of war. London was another place where you got the laundry done and partook of the Life; Rome became a terrorist target but mostly a gateway to the Middle East; Paris, a diplomatic vantage point. But wherever, pictures—not commentary, analysis, words, if you will—assumed primacy in TV news.

My dreams of leaning on the Savoy bar talking gravely about the strategic defense of Europe dissolved in the realization that dodging rubber bullets in Belfast was Britain's hottest story. The rest of it was fireman's work, reacting, getting pictures, writing scripts too short for anything but built-in distortion. The golden, or at least gilded, era of foreign correspondence had given way to cops-and-robbers coverage, mostly out of context. Television reporters skimmed the surface, moved on, and rarely looked back.

Meanwhile in New York, as the news department fought to hang on to second place—even the idea of breaking Cronkite's lead was a laugh—"new ideas" emerged. Some washed up on our shores, such as the "profile" of a famous person that would run on the Sunday evening newscast.

"How about a profile on Graham Greene?" I said, bouncing into Margolis's den.

"Who?" he replied.

"Graham Greene."

No recognition.

"You know, *The Quiet American, The End of the Affair, The Co-medians.*"

He started doodling.

"He's one of the greatest living writers," I pushed on recklessly. "It would be a real beat if he agreed."

"I'll mention it to them," Margolis mumbled, his curled lip telling me how little he thought of the idea. We never discussed the subject again.

While the bureau's contempt for Margolis was virtually unanimous, he nonetheless retained the title of boy wizard, or what one of his detractors called "the oldest child prodigy in TV news." I publicly vowed to give him six months before throwing in my lot with the boys in Sherwood Forest. But he was hard to respect, or even like. I began to suspect that I lacked the essential ingredient for survival in the TV business, the ability to fake it with even the most venal, to flatter, to fawn, to play it with the power side no matter how much you surrendered yourself.

The fishbowl existence of a correspondent had always given me sleepless nights, especially in New York, where the supply line to gossip was much shorter. I never went to bed without feeling anxiety— often sheer panic—over what happened that day and what lay ahead. A catalog of misgivings, things undone, imagined slights, regretted mistakes, looming deadlines, scripts badly written, telephone calls unanswered, enemies in high places, politics not played, betrayals unknown. If fear or failure could have been bottled, I would have had the franchise in the British Isles. The sheer psychic terror of screwing up haunted me and the fear that even if I didn't, the new skills of the business at its worst—infighting, character assassination, dissembling for favors—would do me in.

"Television news is driving in cars," George declared one day, looking out his office window at the gray bubble of London.

The simplicity of his thought filtered out the glamour of my job and spelled the disconnection of the days I spent chasing stories. Driving and driving, past houses with little yellow lights, on a dirt country road, on a highway above a sleeping city, across a bridge linking just one more place to another. And always the little yellow lights in the windows of the houses where other people were living normal lives—dinner with the family, homework with the kids, maybe even watching "us" on the news. Driving in cars, hopping from story to story to feed off somebody else's life for a while. In the end, you had no life of your own.

*   *   *

LONDON in the early seventies still retained the all-male atmosphere of its history, even when it was ruled by queens, a bias not much different from the European countries. There I was in the lap of a big leather chair in a nation run like a men's club, thinking how advanced we were back home on the Women's Question. I never guessed that later in my tour one single event would reverse it all. Out of nowhere, it seemed, Margaret Thatcher won an election to head the Tory party. Everyone recognized that the Old Boys had mucked it up, but no American journalist I knew even dreamed that frustration with the Heath government would overcome traditional male chauvinism. The news stunned Americans. Margaret who? And how? It was difficult to hide a smirk as I realized that the British in 1975 thought enough of a woman to put her in line for prime minister, when only five years earlier—in a country awash with feminists—the president of NBC News was telling an interviewer he wasn't sure that women's voices could be received as authoritative.

But on at least one occasion, good old-fashioned American male supremacy surfaced right in the middle of London. I had been assigned to do a "take-out"—a long status report—on drilling for oil in the North Sea, then heralded as the cure for Britain's economic ills. All the arrangements had been made with the local office of Continental Oil, Conoco, but at the last minute MacFarland discovered that no women were allowed on the rigs. Arguments followed about how treacherous the sea was, how dicey it could get in the helicopter, and so on. To my chagrin, no one in the bureau suggested refusing to do the story if Conoco discriminated. I enlisted our English operator/ receptionist and tracked down Conoco's CEO in the States. He was en route to catch a flight from Kennedy, but within an hour he was on the line from an airport phone booth. I pleaded my case.

"Your men here are telling me I can't go out to the rig because they have a policy about women. I'm asking you to help us."

"Stay where you are," he said reassuringly, "and one of my people will get back to you."

We waited. Sure enough, shortly after he hung up, the company's chief London man telephoned to invite me out to the North Sea.

Sometimes the prejudice worked for you, such as the day we heard the Turks were about to invade Cyprus. Newsmen by the dozen boarded planes for Adana on the coast. When we landed, soldiers detained every American male on the tarmac but ignored me completely, the idea of a newswoman being totally out of their ken. Before

I left the airport I tapped on the glass partition of the guarded waiting room and waved victoriously to Jack Laurence of CBS News.

Northern Ireland could have been the South Bronx, a stop on the international police beat, a running story about how many were killed rather than why. In many ways, television's coverage of "the troubles" resembled the daily reports from Israel's West Bank. Given the time restrictions, after totaling up the body count and writing picture-caption voice-overs to the wild marches of women in curlers or young Palestinians hurling rocks, there was little room left for perspective to frame the story. And as time for documentaries diminished, I became less certain about how far TV news was serving the public's right to know, not just to see.

Montgomery and I alternated the Ulster duty, although he always wound up staying longer. He loved the story and had lived with it for years. I would start counting the days as soon as I got out of the Belfast plane. The Europa Hotel had been bombed so many times, it reminded me of the Caravelle in Saigon. The difference was that charm had eluded it completely (as it had the rest of the Protestant Province) and the architecture was classic Bolshevik modern. The women in curlers (where *were* they all going that night?) terrified me, the children were eight going on eighty, the soldiers searched you wherever you went, and the food defied eating, unless you didn't mind living on soda bread.

Aesthetics aside, there was something philosophically repugnant to me about high-profile Catholic killers. The glorious moment of IRA freedom fighters throwing off British oppression had long ago given way to common thugs robbing banks and accepting arms shipments from Libya to keep it all going.

Beyond political hypocrisy, I found myself uncomfortable, even ashamed, of the world's most compulsive mass-goers identified so closely with bloodshed. Wasn't this the church that asserted the example of Jesus Christ? Even Don Snyder, our resident Belfast maven, confessed to me one day that he had trouble with the idea of Catholic killers. We had become soul mates by that time, ever since we had huddled together in the streets of Londonderry when shooting broke out. After the army pulled back, a group of young toughs heard me do a closer and sign off "Londonderry" instead of "Derry"—a reminder that the British had changed the name of their city. We sped out of there as they tried to overturn our car.

For the American press and networks, it was one of those stories in which we had an invisible stake, translate in some cases "bias." A heavy Irish-American population, open funding of the Catholic cause, public statements by Washington politicians, all tipped the scale. It was no secret that the IRA trusted American newsmen—and used us in the bargain. Still it was no place a network vice-president would visit, not as sexy as Southeast Asia; and then there was the problem of espousing the Irish cause in a bespoke suit. To see the uprising as retaliation for years of persecution was the liberal line, yet not inconsistent with being pro-British.

The fighting had been going on for so long that its special barbarity had faded into the statistics of how many pubs blew on a given day. This systematized terror found highly developed organizations on *both* sides: the Protestant paramilitaries and the IRA. Furthermore, the terrorism existed at the interface of two English-speaking democracies, which, conceptually, should facilitate communication but bred instead a breath-taking mixture of mutual inflammation and ignorance. At night, watching the bonfires against the sky from my window, figures silhouetted against the flames, I could think only of some ancient Druid rites.

Don Snyder maintained good relations with Sinn Fein, the IRA's political organization, as well as the Provisional IRA, aka "Provos," the underground army, so much so that the bureau asked him to set up an interview with David O'Connell, a Provo leader on the run from the police and the British army on both sides of the border. After several months of negotiation, a deal was made, and I left London for a rendezvous in Dublin with the most sought-after fugitive in the British Isles.

O'Connell's bodyguards sneaked him into the underground garage of the Royal Hotel, crouching in the backseat of a car. When we met in one of the rooms, I was struck by his appearance—dark, handsome, tall, and ascetic—like so many priests I had known. He was still carrying shrapnel from his last shootout. The interview went off fine, nothing really new except that a vow to continue the fight from a hunted man clearly ready to die for the cause is big news when he says it in front of a camera.

Afterward, Don and I queried him about visiting an IRA training camp. No newsman we knew had ever seen any, but rumors of their existence persisted. O'Connell made no commitment, but within weeks we had word that we could do the story under two conditions: that they drive us to the location and supply the crew. I balked. They insisted. Margolis agreed. Not the first time cooperation with the Catholics, IRA and otherwise, had led a news organization to a story. Or at least it looked that way at the start.

We left Dublin in the middle of the night with our contact, a reporter from the *Irish Times*. He insisted that we stop twice to change cars, for fear of the agents of a Crown whose powers the Irish rather touchingly exaggerated after more than fifty years of independence. Don arched his bushy eyebrows, always a signal that events had taken a Kafkaesque turn. We knew we were headed west but could get no further information from our host. In the hills just outside Tralee we overnighted at a broken-down shack, proudly billing itself as "The Manhattan Hotel." My attraction for bedbugs was holding; they thrived here, too, so I slept in a squeaky chair. After a breakfast of grease on a plate in a room where the peeling paint fell on your fork, we met our crew in the bar—Dubliners all right, and hung over to prove it. Visibly concerned, our contact shuffled back and forth between his pints and a public telephone. First, he reported that we would be delayed for twenty-four hours.

"We can't do it," I said tartly. The theatrics began to annoy me. "We've come this far on the promise of filming a training camp, not hanging around the countryside."

He returned to the telephone, and Don and I decided that whatever the cuisine at this hotel, things were not kosher in Tralee.

Our contact was back, shaking his head. He swigged his stout and announced, "Well now, you're already here, and so let's all relax and tomorrow morning off we go."

"Why not today?" Don demanded, reaching for my last cigarette.

"Well, you know, just a few complications—a bit of technical stuff, nothing to worry about. It will all be fine for tomorrow."

"What technical stuff?" I asked.

"Yeah, what?" said Don, squinting against the smoke.

"Well, ya see, they have to bring in—uh—the weapons."

"What did you say? Did you say 'bring in the weapons'? If it's a training camp, why aren't the weapons there already?"

"Well, sometimes . . ."

"Is this a setup?" I said, raising my voice sufficiently to move the bartender to ask if it was another round we'd be wanting.

"No, no," the man insisted. "This is exactly how it works, but there isn't any training going on at this particular time, so we thought we'd—you know—just show you how we do it when we do it."

"In other words, you're not really doing it," I said, knowing I was dangerously broaching an exercise in Irish logic.

"In that sense, you might say, well, no, we're not really doing it."

An old English expression came to mind: we had been snookered.

A hefty bar bill was all we could show for two days on the road. We paid it, checked out, and after delivering ourselves of a short lecture to our contact about how "we do it only when it's really being done," headed for Tralee to phone Margolis.

"It was a setup—they're bringing in weapons, the guy admitted it," I told him from a phone booth with no door. Margolis had trouble accepting our version. Perhaps we should wait a day? His main worry was justifying the cost of a crew and not having a story to show for it. He only backed down when we directed the argument to the level of NBC's ethical standards—and perhaps 30 Rock's.

IT is much easier to extract a story from friends, a precept that led us to such gullibility in dealing with the Irish. It was no different in Israel during the Yom Kippur War, only more complicated. There were the obvious ethnic ties with Jewish Americans, of course, a built-in cheering squad. But it was ever so delicate for the newspeople, since a substantial segment of the major U.S. media seemed to be under "Jewish ownership," a datum which the Arabs mined for propaganda purposes. Nevertheless, Arab Americans were invisible at the time, not yet a force in American politics, and therefore at a distinct disadvantage.

Further distortions arose from the primeval notions of the press that still bound the Arab countries. They provided almost no opportunities for correspondents to go into the field. Most information came from government film and communiqués issued from the capitals.

On the Israeli side, many newsmen involved in the coverage both on the scene and stateside were themselves American Jews and often reflected the liberal makeup of that New York–Washington axis which is the backbone of the giant news conglomerates. There was, indeed, a close relationship—an identification with the Zionist dream— among some, and yet it is remarkable how close they held to objectivity, the networks in particular.

"The quickest way to become an anti-Semite is to try to work as a newsman in Israel," one of our Jewish producers muttered, echoing the sentiment of many American Jewish journalists who found the

mocking humor of Israeli officials grating. Their stunning victory in
the Six-Day War a few years earlier had only intensified a native
arrogance. Worst of all was the image-managing—downright censorship—that began the minute I took my seat aboard E1 A1 out of
London.

"Do you want something cold to drink?" a steward asked me.

"Yes," I replied. "I'd like a scotch and soda, please."

"That's not cold, you'll have a ginger ale."

And that was that.

The war played as a Cecil B. De Mille spectacular in which people
actually were killed. Golden deserts, cerulean sky, thousands of tanks
crawling across sand dunes, guns thundering in the near distance, 600
newspeople from more than thirty countries in varying styles of bush
dress, fighting to get to the Sinai or the Golan Heights. The Viet-
namniks soon arrived—Horst Faas and Hugh Mulligan of AP, Bill
Tuohy of the *Los Angeles Times,* Charlie Mohr from *The New York
Times,* Eddie Adams of *Time,* the usual suspects, checking into the Tel
Aviv Hilton. Take away the candlelight and air-raid sirens and it
could have passed for an American Legion convention.

Faas hadn't lost his macabre touch. "If we're lucky today, maybe
we'll get ambushed," he used to say in Vietnam. Now it was, "If your
escort gets killed, that's when you'll get good pictures."

There was full censorship. You drove to the war, covering tank
battles from a Chevrolet. Basically, newsmen played tag with the
fighting forces. Officially, Israeli policy prohibited us from accompanying the troops into battle. For our safety, the command insisted, but
ensuring secrecy for any reason—a decided advantage when a battle
was not going their way. Very far from striking with the "sword of the
Lord and of Gideon" manifest in the devastating Six-Day War, the
Israelis had suffered heavy casualties and lost precious ground on two
fronts in the first few days of this war. American airlifts of supplies and
arms would help turn the tide. After a week of bloody fighting, the
Golan Heights and the Sinai were retaken, and Israeli officials relaxed
their grip on the press.

But New York didn't want aftermath stories, nor did it have much
patience with columns of moving tanks. The pressure was on for
combat pictures, so heavy use was made of film from official Israeli
cameramen traveling with the troops and bringing back scintillating if
selective footage. For foreign newsmen, unless you got lucky and a
Syrian MIG buzzed your position, much of the coverage had a same-
ness about it. An unhappy condition. Puffs of smoke between tanks in

open desert signal a deadliness as great as gunfire in a jungle, but it doesn't translate that way on a living room screen. One day, on the Golan Heights with the Arabs holding the high ground, a British reporter was killed as he sat writing his story in a car. As for the air war, the fighters' speed made it unlikely for a TV news camera to catch a dogfight. Where censorship didn't thwart you, the technology did. It just wasn't a great picture war.

The Israelis made efficient use of a "press bus," to many a euphemism that meant containment and control of the foreign press. To avoid the bus was the first rule—not as a moving press pen but because its size invited enemy artillery. So each reporter relied on his own nerve to decide how far he would drive, always expecting an antitank missile out of nowhere, aware that he was visible to the enemy on the high ground, shivering with the knowledge that although tanks may survive hits, cars (and their occupants) do not.

Every journalist in the field was assigned an escort—not necessarily a soldier—although everyone ranked as military once the Egyptians had stormed the Suez Canal in seven minutes. In fact, one day the Israelis assigned Topol, the Israeli movie star, to our crew. Your guide could stop you if he thought you were lost or onto a military secret, or if he just plain lost his nerve. Making friends with "good escorts"—those, that is, who would lead you into the hot spots—became a full-time guerrilla operation among the reporters. Debates were inevitable. "We're paid to take chances," I snapped to one escort who seemed reticent about advancing toward the Suez Canal.

"Well, Madame, we are not."

Field censorship wasn't the worst part. Once you had your story, official military censors at the station in suburban Herzliyya, the satellite point for all networks, screened every frame of film before it went out. "No, no, no, no, that is not acceptable." The censor's refrain.

Harry Reasoner, then with ABC News, arrived on the scene to much fanfare from the Israelis, experts on the media pecking order. Drew Phillips was there too, having left NBC to work as Harry's producer. They swaggered around, and Phillips allowed as how the army was taking them on a special tour, away from the mass of ordinary journalists. When he returned I saw him at the feed point, looking desperate and brandishing a tiny roll of film. "This is all we have left. They took everything out. Would you believe it? And we have to make air tonight."

They aired a story, but the point was not lost on them or anyone else—you didn't fool around with Israeli censorship. Fifteen networks were covering the war and broadcasting from the feed point. The three American networks alone processed about 10,000 feet of color film each day in a portable developing unit. Still, nothing left the building without an okay from one of the around-the-clock censors.

Certain no-nos were not negotiable, such as anything showing Soviet SAM-6 sites, of intense interest to the United States at the time, especially since this new weapon was knocking out substantial numbers of Israeli aircraft. Most aerial shots, exteriors of military installations, and units going into action such as striking across the Suez Canal, were prime targets for the censor's cut. TV news scripts, newspaper and wire dispatches, all underwent the same scrutiny. The frustration level, coupled with the fatigue—we were sleeping an average of four hours a night, driving through the desert, and filming and editing the rest of the time—wore us down. It was "crash and burn" all the way, battling your way to the deadline, coming up on the satellite with barely seconds to spare. And then all over again as soon as the control room had good-nighted the bird.

Some days, you got nothing on film for all the effort—except maybe shots of camels and their Bedouin masters. On one such expedition, we got stuck in a ditch, and one of the nomadic ghosts tied his camel to our fender to pull us back on the road. New York, leaning on us for material, drove some to desperate moments. One producer laconically related to a particularly irksome network deskman that Prime Minister Golda Meir had visited the Sinai airborne troops and flown with them in a C-130, adding parenthetically that Mrs. Meir's jump had gone off without incident. Silence on the other end. He almost got away with it—the New York man was now asking for a shot list—before bursting into hysterics.

Sometimes New York had its own problems with how the piece played. For example, a story about the longing for peace among Israelis climaxed with a coffee-shop singer, who also happened to work in the NBC bureau, performing a sentimental antiwar ballad. The piece was killed. When I protested, a producer told me the oil companies who sponsored NBC programs were flexing their muscles, disturbed at the lack of coverage from the Arab side and sensing Jewish bias. My piece was too "pro-Israeli." I could never get anyone in management to confirm the tale.

Nevertheless, such tight control inspired much anger—especially among those who had bought Israeli bonds or planted trees. And just to *say* publicly that the material had been censored didn't seem to convey the image-chiseling that was taking place. But this was the era

of Israeli leaders whose names studded the golden days of the "desert
miracle," days when even a hint of division among American Jews
over Israeli policy was unthinkable. Prime Minister Golda Meir, Defense Minister Moshe Dayan, Foreign Minister Abba Eban, Brigadier
General Ezer Weizman—they were the popular heroes and TV celebrities of a dramatic time in Israel's history.

I first saw the prime minister at a news conference in Tel Aviv.
Anticipation rippled through the room as we awaited a meeting with
the lady whose war was going very badly. I had heard all the Jewish
grandmother jokes, so I wasn't prepared for the gray pallor, the chain-
smoking, the lines of worry and maybe even fear. The Israelis had
taken a bad hit: her confidence was shaken, her air force seriously
damaged, her men in Arab prisons. She looked out at the assembled
hundreds and signaled for the first question. Every reporter in the
room was already waving wildly. Getting her attention would take a
miracle, I thought, especially since I was seated well back in the room.
She scanned the crowd and then, raising her hand against the television lights, pointed over the rows of waving arms directly at me.
"Women first," she said firmly.

My colleagues groaned.

But Golda had made her point.

Moshe Dayan was great copy. I interviewed him several times,
usually as he visited desert installations. When the Israeli armored
forces had broken through enemy lines on the northern front, only
thirty-seven miles from the Syrian capital, I asked him whether they
would drive on to the city. Dayan considered the question and said the
offensive was just a reminder to the enemy that "the same road that
leads to Tel Aviv also leads to Damascus."

Dayan was an electric figure, a short man with a monarch's bearing, hands on his hips standing atop a dune in the Sinai, the famous
black patch over one eye, issuing commands in a high-pitched voice,
the embodiment of a small nation determined to endure. A dozen
years later, driving through Galilee, a friend pointed out the small
hillside cemetery in Nahalal where the great commander was buried,
an obscure place just across from the settlement where he was born. I
stood beneath the olive trees shading the modest stone marker. Beside
that simple grave all the images of glory from an earlier time rose up,
only to fade in the haze of an autumn afternoon where a fallen soldier
lay, forgotten, in a silent place of peace.

The Americans, the Soviets, and the United Nations engaged in
a flurry of diplomacy and brinkmanship to end the war. Just as the

cease-fire resolutions began to fall apart, a red flag went up. The United States had placed its military forces around the world on "precautionary alert" in response to reports that Soviet troops were massing for action in the Middle East. We heard the news at night over the car radio, driving down from the Golan Heights, watching the glimmering lights along the Sea of Galilee. There it was—the beginning of World War III, and we wouldn't even have a picture! The crisis passed under the soothing words of Henry Kissinger and the establishment of a UN peace-keeping mission to enforce a cease-fire. By late October, the war was over, but it had brought Middle East affairs back to center stage, where they would continue to attract the roaming spotlight of TV news.

"The Alliance"—a name to which I had never given much thought—assumed a new proportion in the wake of the Middle Eastern war, especially since the administration had moved to counter the perceived Soviet threat without consulting its allies. It seemed whatever glue there was holding the Free World together should be of major interest to an American journalist in Europe, so when I returned to London I asked MacFarland if I could spend some time at NATO headquarters in Brussels to find out how it all worked. Maybe there would be a story in it. Even if not, it seemed obligatory. The idea met with a lukewarm response. Margolis seemed genuinely puzzled, but I did my pain-in-the-ass routine until they were glad to see me go. NATO was not high on the "great picture" list.

When I got back, I had a talk with Montgomery and Utley about what I had learned about the scenario for World War III, wonderful options for the day when Soviet armor bulged through the Fulda Gap. But as usual, we were the only three people who talked news. Margolis and MacFarland, who as editorial people were supposed to be discussing stories, more often concerned themselves with technology: feeds, lines, satellites, line bookings, transshipping, the argot of the new age. If you had a tale to tell, wanted to bounce an idea about something brewing that might make a story, you wandered the halls in search of the other two correspondents or called up a friend from *The Times* of London.

Certain events are "made" for television. Vividness may be the most prized element of a broadcast picture story. Certainly war is vivid enough, along with "live" telecasts of searing events such as the shooting of Lee Harvey Oswald, or even political conventions before the image-makers got into the act. Ceremonial events are heaven-sent, royal weddings the ultimate—controllable, predictable, pretty.

Then there are the stories of scope, breathtaking events, such as space or, at this moment of my London tour, the Sahara Desert. After years of drought, the desert's encroachment on the countries of upper West Africa offered fantastic visuals, epic conflict, and even a measure of philosophy, at least as much as TV news allowed: the desert's inexorable advance pitted human helplessness against the cold impartiality of almighty nature. Was she tired of the human race? It was a story you wanted to hear the end of, and more. So in 1974, I lurched from war as human catastrophe to war as declared by the implacable forces of the earth.

Fred Flamenhaft, the Merlin of "Huntley-Brinkley" film editing and now a producer, came over from New York. Freddie had some names and the phone numbers of a few Peace Corps workers. When we arrived in Mauretania, someone handed us a set of instructions about how to handle the Sahara: "Take along a white flag as a distress signal and two smoke grenades (one red and one black)." For a month we roved the great desert, sending back dozens of studies in vividness. Starving children, hungry camels, French Foreign Legion posts abandoned to their ghosts, rainbows of swirling sand, a U.S. Air Force airlift dropping food into Timbuktu. We traveled light and fast, no second-guessing from the desk. We reported it as we saw it, without any drumbeating in advance. "Nightly News" thought the series was dynamite. This was TV journalism as it was supposed to be.

Best of all, there was no hassle from the bureau. Margolis, steaming that his territory had been invaded by an outsider, opted not to tangle with Flamenhaft, who reported to 30 Rock and didn't care a fig about bureau protocol. Freddie's summation of Margolis was typically succinct: "He's an asshole."

While we immersed ourselves in the graphic flow of life and death in the Third World, a homegrown brand of vividness had gripped American TV news audiences. The Watergate break-in didn't have wounded GIs or starving children, only well-dressed men with deadpan expressions sitting in hearing rooms. They were, however, saying some amazing things. Above it all hovered Richard Nixon, at his best since the Checkers speech, a natural villain for TV news. Europeans, and most of the rest of the world, seemed bemused, wondering what the fuss was all about. "There go those crazy Americans again," was the prevailing attitude. Nixon's popularity overseas remained intact.

Distracted by foreign events, I viewed Watergate through a haze, except when it was shoved into focus by an American expatriate writer I was dating. He was an avowed Nixon-hater who had opted for shabby gentility and socialist views while waiting for his inheritance. "This is it," he said one night in the fall of 1973, just after Nixon had fired the special prosecutor, Archibald Cox. "Nixon has just taken on the real power structure, the ruling class. They'll never let him get away with it."

After the "Saturday Night Massacre," TV news zeroed in on the perception that the president had gone too far. Now the knives were drawn. By August 1974, the revelations of Watergate had roused the moral indignation of a country already battered by an unpopular war and civil strife. Richard Nixon became the first president to resign. Nothing ambiguous about this story, good guys and bad guys, black and white, no gray, no deeper levels: the story's stark simplicity made it a winner.

ABOUT 1820, distilling the judgment of English law, Lord Eldon, high chancellor of England, said: "A corporation is a very dangerous thing. For it has neither a behind to be kicked, nor a soul to be damned." It was unsettling enough having to deal with corporation-think on home plate, 30 Rock, but when the beast left its lair, it became an even more dangerous thing, particularly for anyone on the current hit list. With just such an air of menace did the NBC News overseas "summit" convene in London, late in 1974.

These gatherings had become a sacred rite whereby the president of the department, at least two vice-presidents, and the foreign editor would leave the Rock to meet with assembled bureau chiefs, producers, and correspondents in some designated capital. Places like Belgrade or Lima never made the candidates' list, not without a three-star French restaurant or a Dunhill outlet. That year, the vice-president in charge of financial affairs, Jim White, was along, a sure sign that the news department was being reined in. Jim, a tall Irishman with a soft voice and an ample reserve of tolerance, had nevertheless been pushed to the edge of rage over the latest crisis: Lloyd Dobyns, a correspondent stationed in Paris and a court favorite of Wald, had decided to draw down the petty cash fund—to the tune of $14,000. When confronted, he is reported to have replied: "Just consider it a loan without interest." Dobyns didn't sweat the small stuff. Cases of French wine in his office, a recently acquired French phrase scattered here and there, a silk cravat on occasion. For someone to have "gone Europe" was hardly unique. The petty cash matter was settled quietly, and Dobyns's career continued.

Anticipating the executive arrival, I wrote a jingle to the tune of "Everything's Coming Up Roses," which in the end no one had the nerve to present, so we opted for more docile pursuits, like preparing our Margolis denouncements. By this time, a sizable faction in the bureau wanted him out, but with top brass making it clear from the start that he was still their boy, most of the opposition went underground.

Upon his arrival for the summit, one vice-president, a liberal arts college graduate, careened into my office and asked brightly, "Okay, where are you gonna take me first?"

"How about St. Paul's Cathedral for a look at John Donne's grave?" I replied brightly.

"Who?"

It was that kind of group.

From their lodgings at the deluxe Inn on the Park, management's word vibrated through the Connaught dining room, Claridge's bar, the dance floor of the White Elephant Club, the Ritz tearoom: Tighten your belt. Really? The three-day convocation probably cost 30 Rock the combined salaries of the entire London bureau.

The weekend's most delicious moment came when Ken Bernstein, my old war buddy from Saigon, turned up. Ken, another refugee from print, spoke at least five languages and was at home on most continents, but he didn't fit the new glamour mold. "Dull," was the scuttlebutt. Wald threatened to demote him back to New York, so Ken left NBC and moved to London, roaming the world as a novelist and a travel writer.

As the senior man at the summit, Wald wore his yellow turtleneck sweater for the big speech; at home in London or Scarsdale was the message. Mulholland, still the Dancing Master, yielded to jacket and tie, punctuating his boss's exhortations with tough private talk. A profile in ambition. Everyone got his turn at a separate meeting: mine—a mugging really—took place in Mulholland's hotel room with Margolis in attendance. They read me the riot act, Mulholland stating the general complaint, Margolis coming in for the tight surgical work. "You never do what I tell you to do." A litany of charges, from sowing rebellion in the bureau to not spending enough time on stories.

Strange, I thought, since I had been on the road more than anyone, almost constantly. As for sedition, he had that right. It wasn't in my nature, especially on a story, to suffer the incompetence of another, even the boss's. My mind raced to a night in Belfast—fires raging, young men in the streets looking for targets—and Margolis on the phone from London ordering me to turn on the lights so we could film. The crew had already dug in its heels, but nothing I could say about "creating news with the camera," let alone inciting a riot, could change his mind.

My palms were sweating in the cold room; my usually strong voice squeaked. Every time I tried to defend myself, one of them would hold me for the one-two punch. When it was over, I realized I would be heading home at the end of my tour. No matter. On reflection, they were probably right. I knew I was working in a news department that ceded a great deal of power to people unproven in the field. Still, perhaps it was the way they snarled instead of talked, turning the meeting into verbal gang rape, that made me feel inadequate. On paper, I knew what would turn it around—knuckling under, reining in my temper, suppressing criticism, putting the story second—but I just didn't know how.

Worst of all, I had been naive and plain wrong in understanding human character, investing newspeople by the nature of their calling with more integrity than most mortals acquire in a lifetime. Almost always, the ones I admired were people from print—a small detail that had eluded me in the case of my old friend "Mul." He was pure television. The electronic executive in outlook and perspective, tone and discipline, all handy assets as he rose from news to the giddy levels of top management. As for old friends, what do you say as you wait for a taxi in Rockefeller Center, to someone, once a fellow newsman, getting into his limousine?

Watching Mulholland's cheeks flush with disapproval, I thought back to his arrival in New York just three years earlier, already on the fast track. He was a study in the pathology of television's executive life. He grew up in New Jersey, worked on his high school newspaper, then part-time for the *Stars and Stripes* as an Army clerk-typist in Korea. In 1961 he went to work for WMAQ-TV, the NBC-owned station in Chicago, writing for "The Huntley-Brinkley Report," then only fifteen minutes long. He went on to become a field producer, worked out of London for six months, and then was sent to Washington. The next stop, in 1967, was Los Angeles where he was once again back in local news, but this time as boss. As director of KNBC in Burbank, one of NBC's owned and operated stations, he caught the attention of corporate brass by taking ratings to first place with a two-hour local news broadcast. Tom Brokaw had been one of his anchors.

By the time Mulholland arrived in New York, he had lost his baby fat, traded eyeglasses for contact lenses, and begun to acquire the regulation look of the eastern Establishment. He lost no time in carving out his power base, systematically taking everyone on the show out for lunch or dinner—even the secretaries—to pick their brains. Most expected that he had been brought in to replace Westfeldt, and this in due course actually came about.

"I thought his approach to news didn't fit with mine," one of the program's most respected producers later told me. "He felt that the American people wanted a great variety. I remember him coming up one day from the control room and he said: 'We had twenty-two picture stories on today!' You know, twenty-two picture stories in a twenty-two-minute newscast, and he thought that was the ideal."

Another recalled asking Mulholland why CBS had a story NBC had covered, too, but didn't use. "It had a scratch on it," was his answer. He got hung up on cosmetics a lot. So the long march of style over substance, dazzle over depth, had found another champion, and correspondents were getting the word to say less and show more.

From executive producer, Mulholland had gone on to vice-president in charge of news gathering, which meant that he controlled all correspondents, bureaus, and assignments. Then on to executive vice-president under Wald. In 1976, he would break with news and become executive vice-president in charge of the Moscow Olympics. Six months later he was president of the TV network—sports, entertainment, everything but news—all the while reminding everyone that he had been "a writer in Chicago," a credential which he seemed driven to invoke as he hustled up the corporate ladder. Even then he possessed a wicked self-awareness, a capacity to see himself as a newsman with diamond-hard principles at war with a status-seeking guy on the make. By 1981, he would have it all: president of NBC, second only to Grant Tinker. Life on the 30 Rock Candy Mountain would be very sweet to Bob Mulholland.

To Mulholland—and NBC News—I was clearly dispensable. When the dust settled after my dressing-down, a sense of things disintegrating began to take hold. Chet Huntley died in March 1975, Frank McGee a month later. The old order was passing.

On the other side of the world a new order of a more violent kind was sweeping down the Southeast Asian mainland. Communist forces closed upon Saigon. Hue fell on March 25, Da Nang on March 30. Phnom Penh surrendered to the Khmer Rouge on April 4. On April 30, North Vietnamese tanks rolled into Saigon.

Former Special Forces sergeant Skip Ettinger knew what he had to do: he sent a letter to the White House enclosing his medals.

The networks scrambled to get their staffs out, especially the Vietnamese, who automatically had a price on their heads as agents of the American capitalists. My old friend and cameraman, Vo Huynh, his six-year-old son in his arms, landed in Guam, a refugee. From there, he and his wife and their six children headed to the States. I had always wondered if he felt betrayed after fourteen years of shooting dazzling war footage for American consumption, after living with people who had originally come to stand by the people of South Vietnam. But I had underestimated him. "No, I wasn't surprised," he told me many years later. "I had a feeling for a long time the Americans never intended to win. You know, if they wanted to win it—easy. You know the north, all you have to do is knock over a couple of dikes during the rainy season, and that's it. But they never planned to win that war. That's why I never wanted to buy a house. I knew that someday we were going to get out, one way or the other. No, the Americans never intended to win. Why? To this day, no one can answer that question for me."

As my London assignment drew to a close, I became, happily but warily, engaged to the expatriate writer. We were going back to New York together. I thought the transition might be rocky since he hadn't been home for sixteen years. Still, it took the sting out of the career crisis, that is until I called Mulholland to find out what I would be doing in the States. His answer took my breath away. "Nobody back here wants you," he snapped.

After a transatlantic silence that seemed hours long, I asked him if I could go to the local station. It would at least get me off the road to give marriage a chance, I reasoned silently.

"Network correspondents don't translate well to local stations." It was clear he wanted me out.

"At least, let me try."

"I'll work on it," he said, and clicked off.

A job with WNBC in New York, my old stomping ground from another life, was in the offing. Siberia. A blessing in disguise, I rationalized, trying to ignore the lump in my throat. I felt I had been deserted by my own. And to cap it all, word came that I had won another Emmy and another Overseas Press Club Award, both for the

African drought series. Someone would accept them for me at the ceremonies in New York.

A few weeks later, on a night in June, blue ribbons of light on the Triborough Bridge streaked by the taxi window. Above the great span, still another airplane glided in, its wing lights winking at the red beacon on the Empire State Building. Coming home to New York had always been a chapter marker, a beginning and an end. When the taxi swerved off the ramp onto the narrow East River Drive, I felt at home in the wild waves of traffic surging in all directions, the dark whirl-pools of the river holding their secrets, the low rumble of the city's power. Nothing had changed. Or so it seemed.

12

THE LADY
IN THE
IRON MASK

Like the rest of the country,
New York in 1975 was a drunk coming off an all-night bender.
Through the bloodshot eyes of its hangover, America viewed itself in
a cracked mirror reflecting the legacy of the sixties: riots, marches,
drugs, war, murder. The price for "social progress" had come high, and
now the march of events had wound down to a stumble.

Amid this national disillusionment—all of its vivid images the
stuff of TV news—American astronauts shook hands with Russian
cosmonauts in space, and Richard Nixon's top advisers were sen-
tenced to prison. Japan had reached the inner ring of world economic
power, while New York City—a logo for American power—teetered
on the edge of financial default. No wonder escapist entertainment

dominated television and movie screens. Ever alert to the "pulse of the people," TV news managers took notice.

In the mid-sixties, the difference between local and network news had mainly revolved around content. For both, presentation still demanded sobriety and formality, which underlined objectivity. By the mid-seventies, however, the difference between network and local had become a chasm—a real credibility gap. Network news, with its new assumption of world power, seemed to take itself more seriously, while local news had gone on a show biz binge.

It was no accident that "happy talk" spread like prairie fire through local stations, investing the news programs with determined informality, the esprit de corps of anchors and reporters who championed the nonserious. Unknowing, I was about to be swept into a period of TV news in which serious stuff—politics, accidents, mayhem, the usual run of events—merely challenged the anchor's acting ability to produce studied concern and furrowed brows. "Reporter involvement" had arrived, with reporters shown riding in patrol cars, eating hot dogs, holding babies—getting involved in the story. I dubbed such stories "Watch me type," especially the ones in which the rigors of the newsman's lot were laid out for the audience.

This was the era of "make nice" news, rapprochement with the audience. Consumer news epitomized the new we-are-your-friend-against-hostile-forces approach, formulated to win the audience not just in numbers but in heart. "News you can use" was added to the dictionary of newsroom slogans. Even a "garden spot," featuring a husband-and-wife team prancing among their plants, slithered into the line-up. At one point in the hot pursuit to endear, a seven-year-old boy actor was deployed for a children's news slot.

It was puzzling. The idea of changing one's "pitch" to the public, or having one at all, had never occurred to me. Most of the reporters I knew sat down at their typewriters to get it as straight as they could, not to sell, which is the object of public relations. If anything, whenever I had the audience in mind, it was a kind of midwestern vision, words and ideas aimed at the center of a large land mass—maybe even that little old lady in Dubuque—where millions of people watched and listened. I had no reason to believe they were reading The New Yorker, but I also knew a whole lot of them were smarter than I. It is a very delicate transaction, this engagement with the public. The overbearing, patronizing, or—in the case of what I saw on my return—just plain manipulative, find that audiences are not easily fooled. Almost always, viewers are much more savvy than TV executives know or will admit.

As most local shows stretched to two hours across the country and local news programmers began to be referred to as "profit centers," new kinds of technology roared on the scene. Cameras using videotape instead of film were slowly being tested and put into the field, first in local news. At NBC it was called "E J," for electronic journalism, at the other nets "ENG," short for electronic news gathering. The electrician—the third man on a TV crew—was about to be retired, as management saw it, to save money. The revolution's most pointed message was that better machines meant fewer people and therefore lower costs. Of course, it didn't turn out that way. Maintenance people had to be added just for starters, and middle-level management jobs sprang up like ragweed. When I worked at WNBC in the mid-sixties, the one-hour evening local news program needed five to six camera crews, tops. By 1975, this had jumped to between eighteen and twenty for a two-hour broadcast. "In depth" reporting (which ought to be a redundancy) required long features, went the argument, but actually the lean-and-mean news mentality was being overtaken by the production values of "filmmakers." And as with feature-length films, the staff doubled and then tripled in size—layers of producers, writers, and most of all, anchors.

"Live shots" from the field—"from the scene" as the new lingo went—became the hallmark of local TV journalism. It didn't so much matter if what was expected to happen didn't materialize. For example, if a subway strike was imminent, a live camera on a truck—a "live unit"—would be set up at Penn Station to broadcast pictures of jostling hordes of commuters. If a deal was made at the last moment, the live unit was still *there,* its signal happily bouncing off the World Trade Center tower. That was reason enough to have a reporter broadcast from an almost empty station that a strike had been averted. ("Imagine, dear viewer, if there *had* been a strike!")

Sometimes such units did earn their weight in stories, as on the day a commercial jetliner nose-dived into Kennedy Airport and a mobile unit was, by chance, minutes away. But for the most part, Being There, no matter what the event, became a substitute for the news itself. *"Look, everybody, we're here—and therefore what I'm saying is important."*

Technology also began directing the hunt for "talent"—a term used in contracts to describe on-air reporters, mainly because newsmen belonged to AFTRA, a theatrical union. Now the word was bandied about routinely in local news circles. The invention of the three-quarter-inch videocassette meant that anyone who wanted an on-air job no longer had to fight his way in for an audition. Now, those aspiring to join "talent's" ranks could just send samples of their work on cassette to an agent. Agentry for TV news was turning into an industry, an underground power source that played one net off against the others. By the late seventies agents, headhunters and local news directors were bartering weathermen, sports jocks, pouting blondes, and young men with honeyed voices like pork bellies on the Chicago exchange.

The WNBC news staff was a long-haired travesty of its former button-down self. There comes a classic moment in every foreign correspondent's return when he feels as if he has stepped into a time machine, when he realizes the long leash and footloose habits of an overseas assignment have turned into a noose. But it was more than that. This place bore no relation to the station I had left in 1968. I felt I had been beamed down to an unnamed planet, standing at the newsroom entrance in my London tweeds, like so many foreign correspondents before me who had come home to another world, not the one they remembered. I was a curiosity to most of the staff, many of whom were recent arrivals in TV news but knew me as an overseas type and seemed puzzled about my reasons for being there. There were a few familiar faces, like the gracious and talented Pia Lindstrom, who had become a friend when she worked as a reporter for WCBS in earlier years. Bob Teague was still there, a complete pro and back in the sixties the first black on the air in New York. He had long ago told me: "In this business, Liz, you've got to remember not to sweat the small stuff. Only fight the big ones." And one or two desk men had stayed behind as their colleagues moved up to the network. But for the most part, it seemed a house of mirrors, all reflecting my failure.

Women, most of them in Levi's, accounted for half the staff; intimidated men who gave the ladies wide berth made up the rest. It was quite an amalgam: former housewives with little or no journalistic background answering the call of feminism while their husbands got dinner for the children; professional blacks quick to see racial slights, such as the anchorwoman who refused to believe the looting stories during the 1977 blackout; eager investigative reporters with visions of Watergate aching to be famous; young men untouched by the world, such as the producer who complained about standing in the rain without his galoshes. There was even a Hispanic reporter recruited from a Harlem gang, who came to work carrying a Gucci briefcase and a chip on his shoulder. And across town at WABC, a young advocate, Geraldo Rivera (who sometimes called himself Jerry Rivers), polished his act by forcing his way into places with cameras rolling and declaring that "passion" had come to TV news.

Pushing my confusion to the outer limits was a statuesque white lady producer who specialized, personally and professionally, in black affairs. She delivered a Black Muslim leader to WNBC one day for a live interview, and his knot of bodyguards blocked the news director's path when he tried to get into the studio. Then, as the lady producer wrote her story, the Black Muslims' PR man stood over her typewriter so he could "check the facts." Nobody dared raise an objection.

Perhaps most disorienting of all was trying to understand what everybody was saying amid these grotesqueries. The word "like" polluted sentences with the density of an oil spill, clouding meaning, throwing all specifics—even values—up for grabs. The trick was to leave everything undefined, set no limits, say, or do, "whatever turns you on." As social and sexual mores had crumbled, so too had the language. And what illiteracy hadn't already destroyed, the sociologists and pop psychologists were working on with their banal notions of "relevancy," "getting in touch with your feelings," and "doing your own thing." The only people using the language with precision that year were the North Vietnamese. They renamed Saigon Ho Chi Minh City.

Even the lingo of news was being transformed. Covering a story became "going out on a shoot." Pictures were now almost always "video," and editing copy had been reduced to "reading a script." People talked about "eye contact" and "Q-ratings" that measured one's effect on the audience. "News consultants" had infiltrated enough local stations to convince them that certain tests could guarantee good ratings, everything from sending out questionnaires to monitoring the electrogalvanic impulses of a viewer's skin as he watched Anchor A or Reporter B. Language, facts, whether you were getting it right, had been superseded by the Cult of the Personality, which would eventually suborn the inner sanctums of network news.

If flattery takes its most sincere form as imitation, then its most exquisite expression must be parody. Hilarious send-ups of TV news personalities began to appear around this time, the most trenchant on NBC's own "Saturday Night Live." Gilda Radner's Baba Wah-wah skits were a scathing appraisal of Barbara Walters's talents, her Roseann Roseannadanna character a send-up of a local New York anchorwoman whose Italian-American finesse ranked right up there with Sylvester Stallone's.

"Saturday Night Live" came out of a studio in 30 Rock, and cast members often floated through the building. In fact, one day, hearing that I was a fan and that I "thought he was cute," John Belushi peered into my cubicle. "You were asking about me?" he said, deadpan. Belushi was wearing a brown fedora that fell halfway over his face and a three-sizes-too-large brown overcoat. Next thing I knew, he pulled up a chair, put his feet up on my desk, and began asking questions about the news business. Throughout much of the conversation, I had the feeling he was spacey, focusing off into infinity, talking but not cohering. The mind-expanding exploits associated with the "Saturday Night Live" troupe were well known around 30 Rock. What the production crews didn't put on the in-house grapevine was provided by the makeup artists or by similar close encounters.

If Belushi found my world fascinating, then he was unintentionally a funnier man than anyone thought. Bad enough coming in from the cold, but if you do as a network correspondent, it's usually for bigger and better jobs, not to hit the streets for a local show. The physical closeness of the low-ceilinged work area, the sense of being tied down began to tear at me. The centrifugal force of flying fast on the foreign circuit, a sense of moving with historical events, the freedom of movement—all gone.

More tangible status changes struck me at every turn, such as my cubicle of an office. Gone the quiet and cozy niche overlooking St. James's. Private telephone calls were impossible, expense accounts rare because there was little travel. The crews still included enough old-timers to make me feel somewhat connected, but even they were buckling and retiring under the new tape system. Some made the transition, others simply quit rather than learn a new game. Everyone gave me advice, assuring me the future was local news, but I knew the plunge into the cult of personality and fresh faces was working against a thirty-eight-year-old former foreign correspondent. Besides, people weren't interested in foreign news here, and why should I expect them to be? That I was only made it harder. But, counseled friends and colleagues, you can be a bigger fish in a smaller pond. All right, I determined, let me at least try to apply whatever skills I have to this job and make it work—a thought I carried into a lunch with Earl Ubell, a former science writer and now director of local news in New York. He had a new idea for my career.

"Just think of it," he said. "There you are—standing by a mountain of trash, the refuse of the city that has been ignored by sanitation men and the city fathers—piles of garbage smelling up Manhattan. Every day you are there, on a different street or in an alley or backlot, telling the audience you caught them red-handed."

He stopped in midthought, his nostrils flaring, as though already sniffing the possibilities his imagination conjured. "I know," he said with a maniacal grin. "We'll call you the garbage reporter!"

It wasn't often that local stations had a real live network correspondent, even a former one, to play around with, and Ubell was loving every minute. Watching my face over the avocado salad, he must have picked up the mild frown with which I often camouflaged murderous intent.

"Now I want you to think of the possibilities this beat will have— how much you'll get on the air. Don't let the fact it's garbage allow you to think it's not an important assignment."

My God, I thought, he really means it.

Dejected, I called my old friend Bill Boyle, now on the network side, hoping he would convince me that being a garbage reporter wasn't a bad idea, although I knew it was.

"Oh, no, Liz," he groaned. "Don't let them do this to you. They're trying to ruin you. And even if they're dumb enough to think it will work for the show, it'll destroy everything you've worked to be as a reporter."

The next morning I told Ubell I thought we could come up with some better ideas. He didn't seem surprised. In fact I had a clear impression he was shrugging "nice try." On and on it went. How about the school beat? An investigative unit? Mulholland had been right: network correspondents don't translate well to local. A cameraman friend, aware of my plight, said it even better. "Liz, you're the Lady in the Iron Mask."

As the weeks passed, I occasionally got the routine run of city stories—murders, political infighting, mad bombers, fires. The assignments I dreaded most were "Man in the Street" interviews, a reflex in the drive to buddy up to the public. Standing out in the middle of a sidewalk, putting a loaded question to some unsuspecting or too-polite-to-say-no passerby, was not my idea of news. Nor, by any stretch of credulity, was this random form of interview any indication of public opinion, although executive producers seemed to think it added just the right touch of popular authority. At times while out on a story, I was so ashamed of being associated with the program and its attempts to simulate news, that I would back away from the crew, pretending I was just a curious onlooker.

Hostage taking or "a hostage situation" (the word "situation" was lionized for its wonderful imprecision) by any number of crazies on any given day justified a mobile unit, even if the viewer could see only a few cops in the distance and lots of reporters—well away from the crime—milling in the foreground. Building collapses meant standing in one place for a dozen or so hours. New York tenements tend to go down in winter, so usually it was snowing or raining, and the nearest phone or cup of coffee was three blocks away in a Cuban bodega. Weekend duty—the death shift—was rotated among the reporters, but anchors were exempt, presumably because they were too taxed by all that reading each night. More likely it was because their contracts stipulated they weren't to be subjected to such ignominious duty.

Covering the arrivals and departures of the famous, the accused, the diplomatic, whatever, hurt the most. Unless you were a TV star, you could never get away from airport encounters, the scut work of TV news. These "quick pops," by then a cynical synonym for sound bites or segments of what a person says on camera, were quite likely to make air in New York. The new emphasis on picture and the enormous amount of airtime to fill entailed shooting and using anything that moved.

Of course there were exceptions. Indeed, much later, I came away from one of those dreaded airport arrivals actually feeling I had advanced my understanding of the world. Richard Nixon, long deposed and out of sight, was arriving at Kennedy. Why we were there has long eluded me. But I can still see him about to enter a limousine to depart. We had followed him—filming all the way as he walked from the gate through the terminal and out onto the street—asking questions about his trip and his health and getting polite answers. Suddenly, turning to me and the crew, Nixon asked with genuine curiosity: "Which one are you from?"

I told him, standing curbside (our camera was off), and he launched into a long description of a TV program he had seen on rats—yes, rats: how they lived, how many there were, how they threatened the city. An odd subject for discussion, but there was no trace of the animosity he may have felt for a medium that faithfully recorded his downfall in living color and liked to think it had accelerated it. Indeed, he was friendly, a side of Nixon difficult for most to imagine.

At airports, on the street, in my office, it was a bummer. Chuck Scarborough's office was next to my little alcove. Chuck, an ambitious albino-blond anchorman from Boston with a "voice," reminded some Channel 4 staffers of Ted Baxter, the on-camera newsman featured on TV's "Mary Tyler Moore Show." His office consisted of the usual furniture, a telephone, and a huge blown-up photograph of an airplane's cockpit plastered on the wall. One day, while he was out anchoring, I crept in to inspect his books. There were none, not even a dictionary.

Another anchor, the man among men chosen to do the big six o'clock program, had been imported from California, handpicked by the top brass for his success on the loose-lip circuit. His name was Tom Snyder. In addition to local news anchor duties, he also hosted a late night network talk show, "Tomorrow." Snyder specialized in glibness, clouds of inanity and self-promotion delivered with visibly contrived concern, a passion for local station hyperbole, and an appropriated expertise on just about everything. Editorializing came easy to him. "Saturday Night Live"—again with its surgical eye for the ridiculous— added him to their list. Before NBC finally let him go, he had talked himself within hairspray range of hosting a network news magazine show. If I felt out of place when I returned to Channel 4, my first look at Snyder brought the essential point home: local news and I were not in the same business.

About a month after I arrived, a seven-by-nine-inch envelope with a bulge appeared on my desk, bearing a printed acknowledgment of NBC's appreciation for "Ten Loyal Years of Service." A gold-plated pin in a clear plastic box was accompanied by a note typed on cheap yellow paper.

Liz Trotta

   I came up here personal like to deliver this.
   Had several trumpeters and a man in knee-breeches with a silver salver to carry it on. You missed it all.
   Anyway, three cheers and all that and like they say on other occasionas, wear it in good health.

Dick Wald

My first thought was that it hadn't even been proofread. My second, a combination of rage and despair. I wasn't expecting the royal treatment he gleefully fantasized, but neither did I expect the humiliation of being treated like a joke—ten hard years and the bitter irony of getting a gold-plated pin from the man who had just aborted my career. At the time I judged it deliberately cruel, but it wasn't long before I realized that was how you treated a lady in an iron mask.

Spring was yielding to summer on a warm day in May when I headed for City Hall to cover the latest developments in New York's worsening financial panic. Mayor Abe Beame was threatening to cut city jobs unless the Republicans in Albany and Washington came across. As I stood at the foot of the wide steps on the west side of City Hall Park, I saw another crew approaching, led by a reporter who, even at a distance, cut a figure. Howard Tuckner. We recognized each other at the same instant. He shook his head, smiling with his lips closed, just as I remembered.

"Not exactly Saigon, is it?" he said ruefully, as I noticed the "Channel 11" markings on his crew's gear. Howard had gone local, too. He mumbled the details, but it was clear that this was all he could get. Vietnam and his own vaunting ambition had derailed his career. "Howard Tuckner is Tuckner is Tuckner," Ron Steinman had written in one of many memos to New York. *"The pious hypocrite. I'm tired of him, very tired of him as a person and as someone who works for me. I tried to be fair, to give him my all, to give him all the chance in the world. He blew it and lost me. He doesn't know it yet, but one day he will find out and he will act hurt. Anyway I still use him in the best sense of the tough bureau-chief's world and as long as I can get distance out of him I will. One day he will cry 'uncle'."*

Steinman's memos had been prophetic. Now, behind the unmistakable profile and the air of worldliness, Tuckner was struggling to remain a contender. We promised to call each other for lunch and then faded into the organized confusion of another City Hall news conference. I would never see him again.

For people like Howard, those of a certain age and traditional style, it was a hard time to be working the periphery of TV news. The rules were changing as fast as the audition cassettes came in the mail. Youth, personality, and commercial appeal were the commodities in demand, but many had only old-fashioned news skills to sell. There was a sense of being overtaken by a new order and a vague apprehension that long features and pseudoexposés were being substituted for the pursuit of understanding. Riding herd on the Establishment—a legacy of Watergate—was trumpeted as top priority, but TV news, especially local stations, really didn't have the accumulated knowledge or personnel to carry it off.

For the most part I was operating as the stealth correspondent. When I did get on the air, it was usually with a series, the so-called investigative stuff that was the news fodder of the time. One such, a study of the fast-growing security guard business, did more for the cause of good humor than it did for journalism.

The producer assigned to the series, much to my delight, was Tony Van Witsen, an unconventional, highly intelligent young man who had come up through local stations. He was a cut above the crowd, with unharnessed energy and an almost corny good nature. We learned that the background check for security guard applicants consisted of matching their fingerprints with a computer in Albany to turn up any prior criminal convictions. That was the law, but we had reason to believe it was routinely ignored, so we tested it by getting a man with such a conviction to pose as an applicant. Good old-fashioned tabloid undercover stuff.

If I had gone to Central Casting I couldn't have done as well as I did at the Fortune Society in New York, an association of ex-cons. There he was, Max Rabinowitz, a convicted murderer just "out from nine" in Attica, with the looks of John Garfield and the menacing manner of Richard Widmark. And also smart. Within hours he was hired as a WNBC "consultant." We gave him his instructions and sent him into the field.

Max applied to five security firms, and in no case did he disclose the fact that he was a convicted murderer. A few days later, three of the five firms had hired him, including the Wackenhut Corporation, one of the three largest security companies in the country. Three days after his initial application, he was in uniform, a sedate blue blazer and trousers. He had been given his first job, one of Wackenhut's biggest accounts in New York. On the following Monday, at 7 A.M., Max Rabinowitz, convicted murderer, reported to his client: the offices of NBC at 30 Rockefeller Plaza.

Tony and I hadn't planned it that way, but it couldn't have been better if we had written the script in advance. Now Max was lurking in the hallways. Every so often we would pass him and pretend he was invisible. Later he regaled us with tales of being in charge of security in the VIP booth on election night, and of how he felt pangs of longing when he saw an American Express honcho wearing a diamond pinkie ring.

We got a lot of attention with "Who Guards the Guards?" But after trying mightily to stay out of trouble, I had mixed feelings about sniping at the company again without meaning to. "Look at it this way," said Tony. "We'll both go out with a bang."

As with the security guard story, there were the occasional scandals uncovered—park workers sleeping on the job, numbers parlors in Harlem—and even a one-reporter effort to unravel the city's tangled financial structure. But the political subtleties of the city's workings and a serious examination of how the nation's greatest urban center was buckling under racial and ethnic pressure eluded management's interest and intelligence at the station level.

All across the country large numbers of newly hired on-air staff were pouring in to local stations, wholly ignorant of the terrain. Local TV news was well on its way to being the gypsy universe it has become, with six-figure anchor salaries and better deals making no-mads of newsmen. As though deaf and blind to the world, a succession of local news executives at the New York stations were telling anyone who would listen that "this is the most fascinating news beat in the country"—except they weren't covering it.

As for the "talent" powering the new money machines, one goal emerged above all: to be known. With fame came the authority an audience sought; or to put it another way, being known somehow equated being in the know. "Didja get on?"—the most common ques-tion among correspondents—and "how many times?" now determined your stature. Favored positions went to those who caught on to the personalization of the news. Familiarity and a studied amiability be-came substitutes for understanding, and so the anchor's ability to smile, especially before every commercial and at the end of the broad-cast, established itself as an essential requirement for employment. Fame and familiarity translated into power and prestige.

No serious challenge originated from the print world. Newspapers either folded or blended into chains. Besides, they weren't selling fame. Who knew or cared what James Reston looked like? Print jour-nalists didn't turn heads on the street. Network anchors did. They were the lords of their respective castles, trailed by a host of local minimonarchs who held sway in their own domains.

More and more women were breaking into the business. The same stardust that drew millions of young women to Hollywood in the 1940s beckoned brightly to a new generation of woman TV reporters—most of them equating news with anchoring. The fame machine and the anchor cult joined in glorious symmetry during 1976, when Barbara Walters left NBC for ABC, signing a five-year contract that guaran-teed more than $1 million a year. Third-place ABC News had heeded a news consultant—that enviable vocation by now having infiltrated the network side—and decided it needed a coanchor for Harry Rea-soner on its evening program. So not only did the salary make history, but Walters became the first woman to anchor a network evening newscast. Soon enough the experiment failed, and Walters went off to do what she does best, interviews with the famous. Indeed, the public's perception of interviews as a major component of TV news largely derived from Walters and others who parlayed interviewing into prime time. The idea of reporting—finding the news on the scene, interpreting it, writing it—was largely discounted and replaced by the assumption that anybody could do that, especially a skilled off-camera producer.

"This is a breakthrough for all of us in journalism," Walters told the *Times* when she joined ABC. Newsrooms where straight news was still Holy Writ were troubled. When Walters finally retreated from the anchor chair and no-frills news, feminists saw her as a victim of male chauvinism, especially since the doggedly dour Reasoner made no secret on and off the air of his displeasure. As to why the anchor act failed, one insider implicitly traversed the assumed infallibility of TV executives: "It was a gimmick and the public knew it."

Apart from speculation about whether or not Walters had insisted on a hairdresser, her own press agent, and a full-time limo, there was a more important implication in the transaction: she was now the world's highest-paid newscaster. The breakthrough wasn't in journalism but in the marketplace. Their egos stung, their greed aroused, the news stars moved in for the kill. The million-dollar mark—a barrier crossed only rarely by actors and racehorses—fell like a decayed temple.

The search for someone to replace Walters on NBC's "Today" show rivaled the casting of Scarlett O'Hara. Leaks to the press elicited think pieces and hyperbolic hand-wringing hype. By May even my own name had been thrown into the columns as a possible candidate. It made me laugh. I was still barely hanging on, especially since I was again in trouble, this time over "The Great Gasoline War" series, a sharp five-parter explaining how the cost of a gallon of gasoline is figured, which necessitated research from the wellhead to the pump. Tony Van Witsen, Sid Thiel, and I went at it for three months. Having dealt with oil companies in the past, I knew we had to be extremely careful and that even with a solid story we stood the risk of attack by the oil companies. "There have to be no loopholes," I warned at one meeting. "It has to be airtight, or they'll go for our throats."

The series aired. Within twenty-four hours, messages and telephone calls streamed into the executive suites. Mobil Oil, which had refused to be interviewed, took the point position for the major oil companies. It wanted to buy rebuttal time, charging that we had erred on several counts. NBC refused, and Mobil Oil took out the first of its many ads lambasting the news business. It also embarked on a highly visible underwriting campaign for public television, backing cultural and public programs. Big oil was cleaning up its image.

Full-page ads appeared in the *Times*, the *News* and *The Wall Street Journal*, taking me and the series apart. Entitled, "Whatever Happened to Fair Play?" and using drawings of hatchets, with the words "hatchet job" in boldface, the Mobil flacks took seventeen quotes from the series and then charged we had been wrong on each one. We had aired, said Mobil, "a parade of warmed-over distortions, half-truths, and downright un-truths." Actually, the "errors" were points of interpretation, while some of their new "facts" were in error, but the media blitz was breathtaking.

When you take on Bigness at a network, you often find yourself in the eye of a storm, unbuffeted while those around you leap to the nets. I took no phone calls from Mobil, although it kept trying. I refrained from suing, even though their image-makers had taken their own hatchet to my credibility. Whenever the legal department called to ask me a question, I went up, answered for a few hours, and then returned to my cubicle. Rumors flew. Did I know that Thornton Bradshaw, boss of ARCO (the Atlantic Richfield Corporation) and a director of the RCA board (and later CEO of RCA), had called NBC board chairman Julian Goodman right after the series aired? After all, didn't you know they play golf together and everything? Things can get pretty cozy in the corporate world.

Earl Ubell issued a statement defending the series, but the upshot was that NBC caved in and, in effect, gave Mobil and the other oil companies ninety minutes of air time, "The Great Gasoline Debate," to make their case. I was shocked to read in the *Times* that I was to take part in this network mea culpa. Mobile was licking its chops at the prospect of a reporter being led to the slaughter, pinned down under a barrage of flackery and experts' numbers. Luckily, I ran into Bob Mulholland on the elevator and laid out the situation. Within twenty-four hours, the word had been passed to the station that Trotta was off the oil show.

Mulholland's intervention led me to believe that perhaps I was on my way to redemption, that if I stayed out of trouble and remained in purdah, one day I could go back to the network. I would gladly have taken any assignment, even to one of the world's "armpits." Anything, rather than stay on the amateur hour. Where I lived didn't matter, since by then my personal life was also in tatters. My expatriate fiancé, unable to repatriate, had returned to Europe. Between office and home I realized there were two ways I could look at life: through the tears of a Victorian novel's long-suffering heroine or with the survival skills of Job in drag. I chose the latter.

I started my campaign with Mulholland. He agreed to meet me, and so late one afternoon we turned up Fifth Avenue in search of a place to have a drink. As we walked, I noticed—and he saw that I noticed—a large canvas bag bumping alongside him. "Here they are," he said. "The candidates for the 'Today' job. Cassettes from all over the country. Want to take a look at them with me and tell me what you think?"

A gratuitous remark, perhaps careless, but more likely crafted to inform me that he had become a man of great power and that I wasn't in the running. Funny how he always had a knack for making me feel that I should go back to the drawing board. Later, in a noisy bar, he was still talking about who would replace Walters. When I told him I thought that the future didn't lie with actresses, past or present, he leaned over, his cheeks flushed with irritation: "It's not going to be a news decision. We're giving this one to the entertainment side—and if you ever repeat what I've just said I'll break both your legs."

As it turned out, the job went to a twenty-five-year-old Chicago newscaster with American sweetheart looks, just four years out of college. Jane Pauley would become a role model for women who wanted to go into TV news.

After we had dinner, Mulholland asked if I wanted to see his new co-op, one of those museum-piece luxury apartments on Fifth Avenue, overlooking Central Park. Sure, I said, and he gave me the usual tour, the kind New Yorkers specialize in when they start saying "my place" for "my apartment." Finally, sitting in a chair across from him in the living room, I told him I needed his help.

"It's really pretty awful there, huh?"

"I can't stand it anymore," I said. "I'll take any assignment you've got, anywhere. But I've got to get out of local news."

He looked over his glass with what appeared to be a blend of mild interest and contempt. "Sorry," he said. "I really can't do anything for you. You'll have to go to Wald. He's the president of news, remember?"

I had to admire his single-mindedness. Bob Mulholland was not about to risk his neck for an old pal in news, not from where he sat. I said good-bye with my iron mask intact.

The inevitable appointment with Wald took place with unsurprising results. Sorry, nothing for you at this time. Out of confidence, the fight gone out of me, I sat in his office wondering whose voice I was hearing begging for an assignment. It sounded small and pathetic.

A few months passed, and then as always in news, the band struck up again for musical chairs. Wald was out, replaced by Les Crystal, another old friend from the early days of "Nightly News." In the next few months, with the help of Freddie Flamenhaft, already dying from a brain tumor, I relaunched my campaign to get back to the network, an effort that turned into something of a draft movement as various bureau chiefs, producers, and writers joined the cause. Freddie got Crystal to see me.

Meanwhile, over at "the third network," Roone Arledge, the short, chubby president of ABC Sports, took over the news division with a mandate to make it into a viable competitor, to dig it out of last place with a golden shovel. Like a nouveau riche entrepreneur in need of Picassos by the yard, Arledge opened his wallet, and the talent wars went nuclear. Thus began the first period in TV news when on-air personnel jumped from one network to another like kangaroos. Within a couple of years some correspondents managed to appear on all three. Company loyalty had gone the way of serious journalism.

The Arledge offensive, multiplied by Walters's contract, put enormous pressure on TV news executives to come across or lose their talent. Most caved in, capitulating to astronomical demands for line reporters who had never turned a head, in-house or out. The simple fact that another net wanted one of yours was cause enough to panic managers and overrule accountants. Many lackluster careers were revived. The trick was to be coveted by another net. Management would then give in, first on salary and eventually on airtime, guaranteeing how many times per week some correspondents would appear and how many documentaries they would anchor. Not the finest hour for a dozen or so hard-boiled sophisticates who ran the Big Three.

When Crystal took over, NBC News had been number two for a decade. His background was largely midwestern: out of Duluth, Minnesota, an education at Northwestern University, a copy boy stint for the *Chicago American,* and on to WBBM in Chicago. After local TV jobs in Philadelphia and Altoona, he returned to Chicago in 1963 to join WMAQ, the NBC station. With him in this bunker were Mulholland and Dick Fischer, later to become a vice-president of news under Wald and then Les. It was a small club whose members survived the galloping changes in broadcast news and moved on to become key figures in running NBC.

Now with the Arledge team threatening them, NBC's morning and evening broadcasts—and even worse, from the corporate view- point, the entertainment programs that determine a network's standing—had fallen to third place. Columnists and trade papers won- dered every day what had happened to the venerable peacock. 30 Rock was in turmoil. Walking through the halls one day, Bill Boyle spotted some workmen laying carpet—over the original marble. "Look at that!" he shouted, pointing his finger. "That's just what they're doing with this place, covering up what used to make it work with crap."

True to his promise, Crystal set up an appointment for me to see Dick Fischer before we had our own private chat. A strange tech- nique. Was Fischer a one-man screening committee or a hatchet man before the fact? One dark winter afternoon in late January, I went down to the fifth floor executive suite. I knew that some recent re- modeling had been the subject of ridicule among the Old Guard, but I wasn't prepared for the "Californianization" of NBC: orange pillows piled up on chrome couches, furry beige carpets. The kind of front office chic you find in mirrored skyscrapers where all the receptionists have English accents. I sat outside Fischer's office, my hands clammy against my best tweed skirt, wondering if I looked old.

Fischer, a rangy, sardonic man transplanted from the Burbank office, had a reputation as "one of the boys." Sandy Vanocur later recalled that whenever a male correspondent finished a story, Fischer would exclaim, "Nice set of pipes." Sharp criticism of TV executives rarely surfaced while they were in power, so it wasn't until he was fired that colleagues spoke of him as a man best suited for guard duty at Dachau.

"Come in," he grunted. His thick, black-rimmed eyeglasses did, indeed, lend him the air of a camp commandant. But it was the loud plaid trousers that put me on red alert. I sat down although he didn't invite me to, and watched as he moved to a shelf, picked up a watering can, the kind you see in Miss Muffet drawings, and began watering the base of his desk lamp. *Watering the lamp.* Neither of us spoke while he tipped the can, watching the spray. He emptied the can, returned it to the shelf, sat down, swung his long legs into a cross over the desk, and looked at me without expression. At the same moment, the lamp switched on. By itself.

I must have looked startled because he broke the silence with: "Uh—if you water it, the light stays on. If not, it goes off."

At that moment, I knew my career at NBC News was over.

Without graceful preliminaries he waited for me to state my case, for which he was undoubtedly prepared. I spoke haltingly, noticing the window blinds framing his head. There was something peculiar about them. They were vertical. I had never seen vertical blinds before and, by way of comic relief, said so.

"We've had them in California for years," he said smugly.

Battling the implications of West Coast supremacy, I trudged on, making a timid case for my repatriation.

"I can't hold out any hope," he said, never making it clear why. It was over in five minutes, a curt dismissal.

What chance did I have with Crystal? As I waited for him outside his office, I thought back to when I had worked for him on the network side, holding in awe his sharp intelligence and dedication. The girlish gushing was so obvious, an office joke had it that if you wanted Trotta to do anything, make sure Crystal gives the order. "If he tells her to jump off a cliff, she'll do it."

Five years earlier, just before I left for London, Les had invited me to lunch. As we stood talking by the skating rink in front of 30 Rock, he began summarizing what I had done and where I was going. "After Europe, you'll have had solid experience in a lot of places, national and foreign and on tough stories. Then, frankly, Liz, I think you'll be able to write your own ticket."

It may have been the usual send-off for a foreign correspondent— go out and win one for the front office—but I did believe he was sincere. Now it had come to this, three months before my forty-first birthday, sitting outside his office hoping he would salvage my career, my life.

Suddenly Crystal appeared in the doorway and motioned me into his office with a quick body turn, the on-a-dime kind which usually meant he was going top speed. This was a busy new president. For one thing, his tailor was on the line. Then, someone walked in with what looked like an important piece of paper. Les ran his eye over it sternly, motioning me to a chair. "Read this," he said.

It was an announcement from the NBC public relations department scheduled for release that evening. Fred Silverman was coming to NBC as president and chief executive officer. Silverman, the "man with the golden gut," latest of television's programming ringmasters, specialized in raising networks from last to first place. He was hot. Crystal had a new boss. Of all days, I thought. Why are the gods playing with me?

"Flamenhaft told me about you and local," he said finally.

Then he backed into a monologue, several times broken by distraction that I could only put down to thoughts about the advent of Silverman. The "troublemaker" rap resurfaced from the mists. Yes, he knew it was impossible for me to continue "upstairs." As for the reasons, well, it was out of his department and all that. "But," he went on, looking at me steadily, "I'll give you a six-month audition back on the network side. See how you do and then we'll decide."

"An *audition?*" My tone may have suggested that after thirteen years at NBC not generally misspent, auditioning—trying out, giving samples, walking the runway—seemed at the least unnecessary. I leaned in close to his face, like a cat or a child seeking attention. "Les, it's me. Liz. Remember?" It was more a hello than an admonition. I could see that he didn't like the whole business. And besides, he was probably wondering what Fred Silverman would do to him. "Think it over," he said, shuffling papers on his desk and no longer looking at me.

My choice was simple: an audition at the network where I had made my name, or out.

13

ON BOARD THE ROLLS-ROYCE

"*I*s that the lady from NBC—or is it CBS now?"

The question, attended by a light jab on the shoulder, came from a figure standing on line behind me at a long table spread with food. It was Friday, buffet night at the Tehran Intercontinental.

"Arnett!"

As we jostled each other, laughing, I reminded the room at large that this, after all, must be a big story if the Big A was on it. Peter didn't sweat the small stuff. More than a hundred newsmen in the hotel, all dedicated to finding out about fifty-two Americans held hostage on the other side of town. The line snaked slowly across the polished dance floor, on which no one had danced since Ayatollah Khomeini had come to town. Grim surroundings, but, I reminded myself, at least not lonely ones, not as it had been standing on line at the unemployment office in downtown Manhattan.

Just five months earlier, riding the subway down to Park Place in the shadows of the World Trade Center, I realized how far the TV news business had distanced me from ordinary daily life. Covering stories about people who are in trouble or have little is nothing like being among them day to day. It was disconcerting at first to hear the employment counselor stop in midsentence and look up startled to say: "Why, you're the lady on television!" and then, apologetically, to explain that jobs like mine didn't often cross the desk, but, oh yes, I could certainly collect unemployment insurance, and meanwhile, they would keep their eyes peeled. "But do you think you could just write a little line and sign your name for my daughter who watches you on TV?"

It was a humbling experience, all right, but mitigated by the opportunities for observation. Who were these people on line? The lady in the purple satin parka, the Ivy League–looking guy in the shetland sweater, the black laborer with the distant look in his eyes, the Puerto Rican mother burdened by her screaming infant. As I waited, possible stories unfolded themselves, an occupational hazard.

I don't think I've ever known a reporter who completely lost his reflexes, need them or not. The rough edges stay, and so do the curiosity and skepticism. Quiet weekends and newsless holidays are a drag, so urgent is the need to be "where it's happening." Interpretation and reflection come later, if at all. Now I had more than enough time to reflect, beginning on that frigid winter evening of 1978 when I walked out of Crystal's office and the grand building that had been home—a funny word in retrospect—for thirteen years. By New Year's Eve the notes of "Auld Lang Syne" rang ironically indeed as I tried to figure out what to do with the rest of my life. I had a year and a half to think it all over. As for Crystal, he fell shortly before Christmas came around again, enjoying the briefest term for any NBC News chief in memory: the Pope John Paul I of TV news presidents.

The "CBS Evening News" with Walter Cronkite seemed the natural place to go. It still purred along in first place, the Rolls-Royce among Chevys, as their promoters liked to put it. Oddly enough, I felt a pang or two about talking with this old enemy, so deeply had the NBC competitive reflex been ingrained. To make it worse, when I met Bill Small, the senior vice-president in charge of hard news, to see about a job, it was clear that we didn't click. So disastrous was this meeting that I later recalled the story to David Brinkley when he fell out with Small at NBC.

"Within twelve seconds we knew we hated each other," I told him.

"What took you so long?" shot back Brinkley.

Luckily, John Lane, another CBS News executive and a friend, told me to stand by until the politics of the news department had shifted. I did, and shortly after Small was pushed out of news to the corporate side, the new president of CBS News, Bill Leonard, hired me. He even sent a welcome note to my home. This was, indeed, a first-class operation.

When I arrived at the CBS newsroom on September 4, 1979, I was struck by its chaotic resemblance to the city rooms of old New York newspapers. Real newsrooms have common atmospheres. Batteries of telephones ringing in competition, the staccato of teletypes, wire copy underfoot, wooden desks rimmed with cigarette burns, at least one man in a green eyeshade, and the quiet, tense waiting for something—anything—to happen. The size of the room, forty-eight feet wide by sixty-two feet long, was lost on most because so much was jammed into it. As many as fifty people might be working at once in this news factory—each taking a routine pulse of some aspect of the day's news, a well-drilled company with each member functioning independently yet without missing the purpose of the whole. Surprisingly, even with everyone moving at top speed, collisions were rare. The innards of CBS News were crammed into this space: the foreign and national desks, the New York bureau, the offices of the foreign and national editors, the traffic department, the network radio news staff, a bank of wire service machines, another for telexes, a "flash studio" for breaking news and TV cut-ins, and a studio for network radio hourlies. No color, no new paint, no plants, no vertical blinds; a study in lean and mean. "We do it best with the least," said one executive with Spartan confidence.

If NBC News had been the gentleman's navy of the news forces, then surely CBS was the marines. There was a great deal of pride here, sometimes verging on arrogance—and also continuity. Most of the staff had been with the company for the span of their broadcasting careers. CBS had recruited them young, trained them, and kept them: excellence and team spirit came with the territory. It reminded me of my early days at NBC. I was lucky, getting a chance to do it the traditional way again.

People liked to talk about how CBS founder and chairman William S. Paley viewed his news department as "the jewel in the crown of CBS," or "the great ornament." It made them feel they had an "in" with the boss that no other corporate division enjoyed. Their faith was touching in a way, and even naive in its failure to register that the paternal Paley had won respectability for his network with news, not to mention potent social and political cachet for himself.

The Big Turnover of network jumping proceeded apace, with a dozen or so correspondents and producers already lured away by Arledge, but the CBS ranks were still deep and strong. Of course, the unchanging presences—the technicians, the accountants—hovered overhead, powerful but not august, pervading all the nets like the spirit of the past, their institutional memory. NBC gaffers knew the best Toscanini stories; CBS accountants knew what Dan Rather *really* made. Invisible they might be, but they remained while the on-camera faces faded away.

One of the Cronkite show producers flagged me down on my third day there and handed me a slip of paper. "There's a message here for you to call Walter."

"Okay, okay," I laughed. "So this is the way you test the new kid on the block. Nice try, but I'm not biting."

"Oh, no," he said, almost pleadingly. "It's true, and you'd better call. It's customary around here to do what Walter says."

Reviewing the possibilities, I decided to err on the side of caution and dialed Cronkite's office. His secretary put me on hold, and after a second it sounded as though someone had turned on the evening news. "Hello Liz. And welcome to CBS News." The voice was, of course, big and unmistakable: Uncle Walter, all right. My God, I thought, does he remember Laos? How sassy I was, how I helped throw him in the pool?

No mention of the past. Just a warm conversation about how much he supported my arrival, how he looked forward to having me aboard. It was medicine for an ego that had been badly bruised.

Back in harness, I covered a variety of stories on the general assignment beat, including my own block. In late October, Mohammad Reza Pahlavi, lately shah of Iran, took up residence down the street from my apartment. He had been admitted to the United States for cancer treatment at New York Hospital–Cornell Medical Center. I got the lion's share of the stakeout duty in front of the hospital all day, but it meant getting on the "Evening News" every night. The New York bureau chief, Larry Doyle, was smart and popular, the kind of leader people follow into battle. It was a charge to call him from the scene and find him about three steps ahead of me, working the phones, pulling out the stops to keep CBS and its new correspondent on top of the story.

Meanwhile, just as antishah demonstrations were building up around the country, increasingly hostile protestors, demanding Pahlavi's extradition, were showing up outside the brick walls of the U.S. embassy in Tehran; and after its seizure on November 4, pressure to give him up built to a frenzy on the editorial pages and on the streets of New York. The hostages held in the embassy became the country's most important Americans, their liberty an issue on which depended our very honor. Each night, a somber Cronkite counted the days of their captivity as he signed off.

The furor over the shah increased as the government and a few free-lancers such as Henry Kissinger shopped around for a place to send him. Finally, on December 2, while a dozen reporters, myself included, stood earnestly in the frozen dark outside the hospital, he was spirited out through a series of underground tunnels and flown to Lackland Air Force Base in Texas. I abandoned my sentry post and headed for Tehran.

"I've got a bottle," said Arnett, affecting his best leer. "Let's go to my room." The revolution had outlawed drinking in Iran, a fact driven home to anyone who tried to smuggle in a pint only to have the revolutionary guards pour it over the airport floor, their eyes gleaming with religious fervor. Peter and I sat up most of the night, watching the clock's hands move to 4 A.M. as we relived the Vietnam War. This was followed by a long roll call of "Whatever happened to?" and ringing toasts to everyone we knew from Saigon to Shiraz. It was a valiant effort to make up for the nation's forced abstinence.

More than 300 foreign newsmen had moved in on Tehran, a doleful city of 4 million people dating back to the ninth century, bowed under the ugly assertions of defeated empires. A hodgepodge of mosques, skyscrapers, street carts, high-rises, shacks, palaces, and open sewers. A study in Third World power struggling its way out of the muck. The networks gobbled up most of the Intercontinental Hotel, the CBS office alone occupying three suites. Under the manic direction of David Miller, normally bureau chief in Rome, thirty-four staffers scrambled for stories. The foreign desk in New York lent unstinting support to keep us plugged in on the domestic moves affecting the story. Pressure on all sides. New York rushing to beat the competition. The competition looking for end runs. The Iranian government looking over everyone's shoulder, the militants at the embassy menacing us every day, assorted mullahs and their followers whipping up the explosive anti-American crowds. And over it all, a realization that the American media here were becoming part of the story itself.

Everybody had an angle, a piece of propaganda to sell. And reporting "the other side" usually came up short, as antirevolutionary sentiment was dangerous to well-being. The government saw spies everywhere, especially at the embassy, and considered this sufficient reason to try the wretched hostages, even if the shah had left the United States for Panama. CIA operatives were said to be lurking in every mosque. Meanwhile, the Iranians did a fair amount of lurking themselves. Even home ground at the CBS office wasn't secure. Several times we were beaten by the competition because our hundred-dollar-a-day Iranian translators traded information with their counterparts working for other U.S. news agencies. Many of these translators had studied in the States, where they picked up V-necked cashmeres, gold wristwatches, and a sullen attitude toward their employers. For all we knew, they were working for SAVAK, originally the shah's secret police, now enthusiastically reconstituted by the ayatollah. But we needed them—who spoke Farsi?

Correspondents and crews rotated duty at the embassy's side door where the revolutionary guards congregated. The thousands of feet of tape shot of that famous entrance—which viewers thought to be the main gate—were actually pictures of the building's access to the motor pool. The militants made sure we would be far enough away from their captives. Day after day, in sleet and rain, we stood our watch near where Razmavaran and Taleghani intersected. Main Street, Iran.

Shots of the gate's lock, which became a metaphor for the story, ran into the hundreds. One morning, looking around for a new angle, CBS cameraman Mario Biasetti turned it around, which for some reason—probably the AK-47s in our faces—nobody had tried before. Our piece that night began on a tight close-up of the words "Made in U.S.A." etched on the back of the lock. The embassy itself was a twenty-seven-acre compound of about twenty-five buildings and a small paradise—Persian for "garden"—of trees and lawns, which never looked that way on screen because no one could get a high shot. A helicopter would have been brought down. One resourceful cameraman tried to shoot from the Intercontinental roof. Khomeini's guards arrived to arrest him as a spy, but the hotel's formidable manager barred their entry into the lobby. Mysterious and fearsome as they appeared in their defense of Allah, these young fanatics held tightly to their deepest secret: cowardice.

By the second week we knew the revolutionary guards on sight and even gave them names. My favorite was Mullah Mary, a comely young Persian woman who toted an Uzi submachine gun and a permanent scowl. We kept our eyes on their trigger fingers, yet every morning someone in the bureau would call the "students' office" in the embassy to find out their activities for the day, what new thoughts from the imam had been divined in the night. Off duty at the embassy, sometimes they would drop by the news offices in the hotel, and it was difficult to tell whether we were being threatened or cultivated.

Stakeouts produced little news, except mood pieces, a sense of standing with our people in their need. We longed for shots of hostages waving or sailing out paper airplane notes, but they never came. I had seen my share of flags burned during the Vietnam War and never got hardened to it; now the rabble's daily desecration of the "Great Satan's" flag began to grate. The constant crass hammering of "Death to America," the desperate crybaby mood of the people (many of whom showed up out of mere unemployment) only turned us to our own amusements. This wasn't difficult, given the surreal overlay of the revolutionary frenzy. Who could come away from any of the ayatollahs' harangues without at least clearing one's throat in comic disbelief? Who could watch a rag-wrapped body passed over the heads of a funeral crowd and not toy with the idea that inbreeding had had its day in ancient Persia?

One morning I went down to Qum, usually preceded by the antecedent "holy city of," to cover the wild-eyed Ayatollah Ruholla Khomeini emerging to greet fervent followers camped around his house. We got just close enough to record his remarks, then the crowd turned on us. We ran through the streets, the throngs in mad pursuit. As our driver fumbled for his keys, several of the devout began rocking the old Chevy. Defying a wall of tattered robes and black mustaches, we careened out of that realm of holiness back to the sinful secular world.

The hours were gruelling, the days crazy. Food got ever scarcer, until my diet consisted mainly of Seven-Up and Beluga caviar, one advantage, at least, of being in a country bordering on the Caspian Sea. "Not caviar AGAIN!" echoed loudly through the dining room. The hotel had become an oasis of civility in a Disneyland of screeching crowds and trigger-happy militias. After a hard day crawling through the streets, home was where your colleagues were. Every night I would yell down the hall to an open door, "What are you filing—and are you beating us?"

"Nothing you don't know already, Scoopie. I'll bring my stuff over in a minute." Chris Wren of *The New York Times*, my old journalism school buddy, was sharing his copy with me, just as he had twenty years earlier. It didn't hurt to know what the *Times* was up to; and our agreement was reciprocal, especially when it came to pictures of the hostages, usually shadowy tapes shot by the militants.

The wild negotiating over such instruments catapulted the Iran affair into the murky backwaters of the profession. There was no doubt Khomeini's zealots were staging the demos for our cameras, but we couldn't ignore them. Iranian manipulation of the media became a tricky issue when the militants offered the networks an interview with one of the hostages, William Gallegos. They demanded that it run in prime time and include an unedited propaganda harangue. NBC struck a deal, defending it as "an important public service." Gallegos, a marine corporal, asserted the hostages had not been mistreated, a statement immediately denounced as propaganda and later thoroughly disproved. A gaunt face delivering robotic statements only inflamed the inchoate horrors forming in the country's imagination. It was clear the American networks had chosen to put themselves at the mercy of the "students" as they competed for access to the hostages. Just where did reporting end and manipulation begin?

David Miller directed the CBS coverage with the mad joy of a dervish and the repartee of a stand-up comic. He was a classic TV type, a fixer, crasher, briber par excellence, moving like a locomotive through the foreign scene. Coarse, bullying, loud, he made the Ugly American look like a man of the world. He was also a prize people-mover. What they reported once they got there was immaterial, since no fixer concerns himself with these details. He never left the hotel. Not only was it dangerous out there, but he had a private supply of food stashed in his room. He became even more convinced that invisibility was the answer when the government directed one of the ever-available mobs to march on the hotel in protest against those foreign journalists who trafficked in "imperialist and Zionist distortions."

It was the eve of the Sabbath when he finally ventured forth. Viewing the city for the first time since he got in from the airport weeks earlier, Miller pretended to be awed by the rigors of Islam: "My my, just look at all the nice lights. And all the nice food. And all the nice people out having a good time!" As much a comment on the Iranian revolution as it was on just exactly what American viewers were not seeing on their evening news programs.

Most of the time I operated backed only by a cameraman and sound man—my normal way, but at CBS producers seemed determined to hold their correspondents' hands. Moreover, in Iran the field producers themselves were trying to get on the air. Racing to the car one afternoon to cover still another demo, I had to fend off a producer who insisted there was no more room in the car and that he would handle the story. I convinced him otherwise. Because we were spread so thin, some producers did make air, which only encouraged a belief most of them harbored—that they would be just great on camera. In my enforced sabbatical from TV news, the producer's role had expanded imperially, right over the correspondent's prerogatives.

On big, long-running stories, such as the hostage crisis, the rumor quotient is high. Most, of course, turn out to be false, but they can tie up the phones and imaginations of an entire staff just as exhaustingly as a solid tip. Rumors such as: the hostages had been moved; an American strike force was on its way; the shah was returning; Khomeini lay dying. On and on they came, the usual state of news coverage when a story opens up in a part of the world unfamiliar to most.

As Americans, we were hopelessly ignorant of the forces at work and less inclined to dig too deeply because of the voracious demand for material. How Iran's revolution was sparked, how the ayatollah had kept his hand on the people while in exile, how the superficially modernized state had been capsized by resurgent fundamentalist Islam—all were questions eventually addressed, but not at the outset when the hostage drama eclipsed any interest in the chain of causes. In many ways, we were as ignorant—though perhaps less willfully—as the American government itself, which had ignored the warnings of its own embassy.

Major stories, like soap operas, spin off autonomous themes and characters. A big stage always affords an opportunity for smaller players, and so it was routine to peel off in the middle of the Tehran mayhem to check out unrelated breaking events. A group of disaffected Afghans decided to take over their embassy one morning and held it for five hours. They were protesting the Soviet invasion of their country, a worthy cause, but the raid was so disorganized that I had to stifle a giggle as I filed a radio report to New York via the Afghan ambassador's unguarded telephone. Like campers on a field trip, young men in flying robes darted in and out of doorways, ran upstairs and down, unconcerned that television crews were documenting a certain lack of professionalism in their coup de main.

Or again, local Armenians decided to give the Turkish govern- ment a rush, marching noisily down to the embassy and setting fire to the crescent flag at the mission gate. When I got back to the office, I allowed to Bert Quint as how it was a relief to see someone else's flag get the treatment for a change. "Never a dull moment," cracked Quint, trying to lose himself in Beethoven's Triple Concerto emanat- ing from his tape recorder.

Bert, one of the old-style highly professional line correspondents, had seen his full share of global grief. We had collided as competitors in Cambodia. Now we were part of the same team, especially on that morning we worked on an Iran special anchored by Cronkite. Walter was to ask questions, which Bert and I would take turns to answer. There was no satellite access, so we would broadcast via telephone. The time difference—it was a late-night special—put us on standby very early in the morning. Bert showed up wearing his CBS suit and tapping his pipe. I threw my old trench coat over a flannel nightgown, put on a pair of sunglasses, and padded down to the bureau in a pair of scuffies. We had to share a single telephone, rapidly passing and repassing the receiver. For quality insurance, we had a tiny black rubber cup that fitted over the speaker to filter out extraneous noise and improve transmission. As we passed the telephone, we would also pass the cup. At least that was the plan.

The connection was made, and even from 6,000 miles away the sound of Walter's voice made us automatically sit up to attention. Listening to the intro, I noticed out of the corner of my eye that the Iranian cleaning woman who came in every morning to do the dishes had just arrived. She looked at us and through us, just two more of the strange foreigners. I was sitting in an armchair next to Bert, who was seated at the end of a couch. Knees touching, we were ready to go.

Walter summarized the story to date and then, telling the network audience that Bert and I were on the line, he threw out the first question. Bert took the telephone, holding the rubber filter over the mouthpiece. Then, as Walter began the second question, Bert thrust phone and filter into my hand. At that urgent moment, I muffed the pass. The phone fell to the floor, the filter rolling across the carpet. We dived, Bert scrambling to retrieve the phone, while I was down on all fours in pursuit of the filter, which had disappeared under the couch's upholstery ruffle. Thrashing blindly under the couch, I got tangled in the flannel gown and lost my glasses. Finally, I made a good grab and I was back in my chair, instruments totally in place. But I had missed most of Walter's question. *This is it,* I thought, *down in flames. Oh please God, not on Cronkite's show. This can't be happening!*

The next sound I heard was the smooth, slightly coy sound of my own voice telling the nation and the man they trusted most that the line must have gone bad and would he mind repeating the question. Of course he wouldn't, and, yes, the bad connection was perfectly understandable. But just as Cronkite began again, a hissing sound penetrated the room. Our cleaning lady, in strict fulfillment of her contractual duty, had opened the hot water tap. She was doing the dishes. There was just enough time to make sense of some key words in Walter's question and try to answer before my reply was drowned in a clamor of roaring water and clanging plates.

Bert was signaling wildly to the woman. She stared blankly at us from amidst a cloud of steam, then shrugged her shoulders, adjusted her chadoor, and turned back to her basin. She had both taps on, full blast, all the way to the end of the broadcast. The Iran situation was so tense, we concluded, that New York must have chalked up the sound effects and missed cues to sheer drama. Too bad we weren't on-camera. Liz and Bert would have given Lucy and Desi a run for their ratings.

By New Year's Eve, most of the newspeople were beginning to get cabin fever. We had weathered the strangeness of Christmas, another tussle with the students over pictures of Western clergymen visiting the hostages, and were frankly ready to forget the story for at least a few hours. About six of us, including John Cochran of NBC and Arnett, decided to make a round of the embassy parties. First, the Australians, where costumes seemed the order of the night. Two Aussie officials turned up in drag, expressing reservations about what their ambassador might think—that is, until he arrived dressed as the queen of Sheba.

At the Bangladesh ambassador's residence, beautiful women draped on damask couches eyed our group with suspicion, so the men peeled off to investigate. Meanwhile, the ambassador, smacking his lips, was trying to corral me into an adjoining room. A silent appeal to my compatriots brought swift intervention. We reeled into the Iranian night, daring the ayatollah himself to deny us our boisterous welcome to the New Year.

Before the first week of 1980 ended, the Revolutionary Council was threatening to expel all foreign journalists. By the end of the second week, they ordered all journalists working for American news organizations—more than ninety—to cease sending dispatches by January 15 and to be out of the country by midnight on January 18. We were, they said, guilty of "biased reporting and insults to our Islamic revolution and our religious beliefs." The Orwellian-named Ministry of National Guidance, responsible for controlling the foreign press, issued an explanation: "Unfortunately, Western mass-media reports certain matters that may be factual as far as the occurrence is concerned, but they do not induce to the reader the truth of the matter as it should be." Meanwhile, Iran's revolutionary muscle was being tested by its various non-Persian groups—Kurds, Baluchis. In Tabriz, especially, there had been demonstrations and riots in favor of a rival ayatollah, and it was here that the press had been turning its attention, especially CBS.

A few days before the expulsion order, Miller ordered me north to Tabriz. With me went Steve O'Neill, a British cameraman then based in South Africa for the network. The small, barren city looked quiet under a thin snow. Roaming in different areas of its center were Howard Smith for ABC and NBC's Ike Seamans. Without warning, bands of young men, followers of Ayatollah Kazem Shariat-Madari, went on a tear, breaking windows and looting. Steve was wearing a red handkerchief tied like a headband. "Look for the red, in case you lose me, in case we get separated by the crowd," he shouted over his shoulder as the mob swelled around us on all sides.

We followed them as they rammed into Khomeini's followers. The government militiamen then set fire to the opposition party's headquarters. Steve jumped into the burning building, joining half a dozen silhouetted figures ransacking the files. Finally, the ABC crew arrived. I knew we were exclusive on the rioting, but at the moment I was worrying about Steve and pleaded with the ABC cameraman to help. He disappeared into the building, now fully ablaze. As I waited I could feel my mouth turn to cotton and the icy mountain air begin to stick in my throat. No red headband. Seconds passed, each like a minute, and finally both men emerged blackened and scorched.

We knew the militia would try to take our tapes, so Steve and I left quickly for the airport. The NBC crew stopped to tape a standup with their correspondent in front of the action; the guards arrested them and confiscated their cassettes. ABC had been too late. We were alone on a great story.

But how to get it out? We slipped our cassettes to our driver and guide, a young Kurd who stood about six feet, four inches, instructing him to drive through the mountains back to Tehran in case the militia stopped Steve and me. Then we ran for a phone booth at the airport to call Miller and tell him what we had, but in midcall we spotted armed men running through the airport obviously searching for us. We hit the floor, leaving the phone dangling off its hook, hunched over and listening to our breathing as the militia pounded by the wooden booth.

Once sure they had left, we made a break for the gate, only to find all flights canceled. They were cornering us all right, and they knew what we had. Now, our only way out was to get another car and make the mountain run. We still could get caught, but at least our Kurd, the tapes stuffed into the front of his parka, had more chance of getting through than we did.

Thirteen hours later, having battled mountain passes and a driving snowstorm—with the car heater dead—we pulled up at the Intercon. Bleary-eyed, hungry, cold, but not beaten—at least not until the next day, when CBS New York decided we had to pool the tapes because the other two networks were complaining. Under the "adverse pool"—an arrangement made in hostile environments where networks band together to share material for the greater good—we had to make the story generally available. So the ABC and NBC correspondents recorded their own narrations on our pictures and broadcast what appeared to be their hard-won stories from Tabriz. Small consolation though it was, Miller stood in the middle of the office the next day, holding the cassette on high, bellowing. "If we're gonna get thrown out of here, this is how I wanna go. With Tabriz." It would have been tactless to point out that he had never left the Intercon.

Miller got his wish. It was Yankee-go-home time, although the Iranian authorities were perfectly amenable to anyone who wanted to stay a few extra days to "pay bills" (U.S. dollars were always welcome). As a fitting climax of revolutionary volatility, departure held no terror: no machine guns, no anti-American epithets. When the customs began confiscating Persian carpets, officials honored our protests and rescinded the ban. A bone-weary line of newsmen trudged across the tarmac on expulsion day, bent less under their typewriters than the oriental rugs and caviar they were hauling out on their backs.

WORKING at CBS in these years, one had to look closely to detect any sense that the Cronkite era was drawing to its close. There was certainly no hint that what awaited us would make the Iranian revolution look like Hell Week at Penn State. Walter's retirement, announced in February of 1980, would take place a year later. As for a replacement, after much-publicized finessing between Dan Rather's agent and CBS, Rather aced out Roger Mudd, the odds-on favorite. Pro-Mudd elements may have wrung their hands, but if the troops went misty-eyed about the past or felt uneasy about the future, they kept it hidden under the stiff CBS upper lip. *Time*'s February 25, 1980, cover showed a confident Rather, arms folded over braces, with the words running across his chest: "The $8,000,000 Man. CBS News Explosion." The figure was actually $22 million. Five years later, according to the president of CBS News, it went, as fusion followed fission, to $36 million. "I want to slam things to the edge," Rather told the magazine. "We will have more people, better equipment, more overseas bureaus and better broadcasts." There was no reason to doubt him, not at all. He was replacing Walter Cronkite.

No two men could have been so different, and ostensibly they were in the same profession. Cronkite, America's reassuring uncle, was the classic village explainer, as much a part of the average viewer's day as morning coffee. As CBS's chief anchor since 1962, when he replaced Doug Edwards, Cronkite had become a man of enormous power and even influence. He used his authority as the program's managing editor but rarely branched out into management's turf of hiring, firing, and setting policy. There was always the occasional hotshot who thought it smart to badmouth him (after he stepped down), but I had made up my mind about CBS's "900-pound gorilla" long before, on that day in the Hanoi prison.

I didn't know Rather when I started at CBS, although after chatting with him for a few minutes in the newsroom one day, I was convinced that when charm was handed out he had probably beaten the gods at a hand of five-card stud. I noticed he had a way of fixing you with his eyes and a small, tight smile—engaging at first glance, unsettling at second. Winning, but odd. There was, of course, that business of sassing the president—the famous exchange with Richard Nixon—but I put it in the category of things one wished one hadn't said in the heat of the moment.

I was not looking forward to Cronkite's last program, but Rather's electricity and his solid experience as a reporter, domestic and foreign, certainly augured well for the continuation of the Murrow tradition. If the Old Guard, which included a great many people in the newsroom, felt otherwise, they weren't fools enough to take shots at the new principal anchor. Everyone knew he was no Walter Cronkite, especially after his debut on March 9, 1981, when the camera searched him out—and found nothing.

If Walter Cronkite was the William Allen White of TV news— the genuinely provincial, earnest small-town editor—then Dan Rather was the small-town sorehead who came to the Big City. One could imagine him standing on an East Side co-op balcony, shaking a raised fist, barking into the darkness: "I'm going to beat you yet, New York. I may be from Texas, but I'm tougher than you are."

Watching him on the air, I realized he was a man who lived off his nerve, not any deep understanding of the world's events. Unlike Cronkite, no Olympian depths of authority welled up to hold the viewers. The audience caught on to this in a wink, but not Rather himself.

Some of the CBS News "folk"—a term they loved to use—had a peculiar way of welcoming new employees. Sort of like the welcoming address at marine boot camp on Parris Island. "We have a feeling here that if you haven't done it for CBS News, then you haven't done it. That's really how it works here, Liz." Ed Fouhy, a news vice-president and one of the newsroom macho merchants, was working his old Marine Corps credo, which amused me since Fouhy had abandoned CBS in pique for two years to work at NBC. So much for "Semper Fi." David Buksbaum, Rather's spiritual valet and a producer in the special-events unit, advised me it would take at least two years "before you feel a part of CBS News." What he meant was, before this exclusive club voted me in. All of a sudden, my years at NBC counted for nothing. As far as CBS was concerned, I was still in basic training.

Covering political campaigns, as glamorous as it may sound, is a crucible for newsmen. If the long hours and logistics don't wear you down, the boredom will. It is a good test of a correspondent's mettle, as I had found out in the past and would again in the late winter of 1980. My assignment to George Bush's presidential campaign came just in time for the biting cold of Massachusetts, Michigan, Illinois, Pennsylvania, and Wisconsin. Catching up with the campaign after a short recuperation from Iran proved a lesson in the magic of network agility under the gun. The weekend news wanted a piece out of New England, but the airline schedules offered no way to get me there fast enough. Buksbaum, whose skills in moving people around—which actually takes up most of the time and effort in TV work—talked White House security into letting me hitch a ride on Air Force Two, Vice-President Walter Mondale's plane, at Andrews Air Force Base, Washington, without waiting for the usual clearance—not to cover "Fritz" but to intercept Bush.

Soon after takeoff one of Mondale's press aides said the vice-president heard I had just returned from Iran and was interested in talking to me. I went forward to his private compartment and for forty-five minutes sat listening to Mondale on Iran—that whatever happened, one day we would have to do business there, like it or not. I was fascinated, since not only did he seem quite out of touch with the daily handling of the crisis, but not once did he ask for an eye-witness opinion.

Iran was certainly the top issue that election year, but Bush, I found, played it gingerly, briefly, and sporadically. Overkill would have been dangerous, to be construed as capitalizing on a disaster. Still, on the few occasions Iran did come up in his campaign, the crowds' reaction suggested it was the issue that would blow Jimmy Carter away. Mr. and Mrs. Average American were, to put it in the idiom of the unpublished press, royally pissed off.

Ronald Reagan, also stalking the presidency, sent Bush on the run after winning the New Hampshire primary. Sometimes we hit three states a day, the candidate drawing energy not just from political ambition but from a core of Yankee steel. Bush was an achiever in pure New England terms: shrewd, cautious, persevering, hard-working. Years of doing business in the rugged Odessa-Midlands oil fields of western Texas had not lent more casual rhythms to his speech and manner. One wondered if attempts to "de-prep" the candidate to extend his political appeal might have drowned in blue blood. Watching him on the stump, I vacillated between empathy and irritation as he tried to adjust his words and body language to a dock worker, an auto mechanic, a welfare mother. It just never quite came off. If anything, the sublimation of his rigorous sense of mission only worked against him to create the image of a very accommodating man. On camera it was this apologetic image that flickered across the nation: off-camera, out from under the chameleon needs of the moment, Bush seemed to recover his natural stride, to return to an inborn sense of entitlement and toughness that would one day drive him to the White House.

Charming, even funny, polite to a fault, all that was George Bush, but I had the feeling I wouldn't want to be in the shoes of anyone who tried to cross him, or worse, succeeded. On a personal level, he won over most of us covering his campaign and loosened up as he went along, sometimes baring a strain of humor that bordered on the deadly. It hit me one day at a Ford automobile plant in Detroit. Bush was introducing me to one of the Ford brothers. "And this," he said, "from

CBS News, is Liz Trotta," adding under his breath so only I would hear, "Not exactly a household word."

"I'll get you for that," I promised. He loved it.

It was typical campaign coverage. A press plane hopscotching the electoral target areas through sleet and air pockets, camera crews tripping over everything, producers lugging spare equipment or looking for phones, correspondents wondering where the hell they were, and print reporters talking to one another about the latest polls and analyses. Most of the banter among network people was reduced to where the feed point was and how many times they had made air. In fact, it was on this assignment that I first took notice of how fatuous conversations were getting, how unconnected so many network personnel were to the story. I chalked it up to advancing age, and yet only with the print reporters did I feel engaged in the story itself, not the hardware of its transmission.

To make matters worse, Richard Roth of CBS, who had been with Bush from the very beginning, welcomed my arrival like an advanced case of leprosy. Dedicated to marking off his turf, he had no intention of sharing the story, whatever the national editor laid down, including the aisle seat, which he informed me, was his "usual place."

On most press planes and buses, it is agreed by candidate and media that anything said is automatically and completely off the record. No one can report anything said under this ground rule, not only to protect the candidate but to afford news people a chance to relax from the grind of getting on and off the plane and trailing the candidate from shopping mall to ghetto church. Outsiders—those who dropped in for a few days—were quickly made aware of this rule on the Bush plane if they didn't know it already. Ignoring the custom, one columnist reported a mock wrestling match between an NBC producer and Bush. The columnist was off the plane forthwith. So, in the small smug world of the permanent press corps, the word was passed to watch our words, rule or no rule. Image-makers were the same everywhere, I decided, whether in Iran or on the campaign trail: less concerned with facts than "the truth of the matter as it should be."

As the campaign dragged on and Bush went down to primary defeats in South Carolina, Florida, Alabama, Georgia, Illinois, Wisconsin, and even Texas, newspaper editors and TV producers began to lose interest. Soon, we were to name ourselves chroniclers of the "Stealth Campaign." It was there, but you couldn't see it. A reporter for the *Los Angeles Times* called his office one night, and the desk man put him on hold. He hung on for so long he fell asleep and awoke the next morning with the phone still cradled in his ear, still on hold. Such was the demand for stories about George Bush, clearly not on his way to the White House. Not just yet.

"GRAB one of those Halston numbers—the black one, I think—and come on down for my dinner on Saturday. Everyone's coming, and I'll need a hostess." Craig Spence was on the line from Washington, as usual cooking up a scheme to ensnare the capital's newest movers and shakers. He was noting the Republican advance with relish, getting in on one of the country's periodic binges with wealth. A bull market had served him well. From Tokyo he had watched the new money move in on Wall Street, starting in the sixties. Now the way was clear for a new class of fixers, such as his Korean prototype Tong Sung Park, those who helped people make and move fortunes. Like Craig, they were outsiders who knew their way around the inside: consultants, PR men, information specialists, and lawyers. Red tape–cutters and image-polishers. Spence was a man for the eighties: smart, ruthless, and on the make. He was living on the edge again—just as he had during the war.

For a decade Spence had worked in Tokyo, building up his contacts among the masters of Japan's economic transformation. While most looked to China or even Vietnam as the Asian story of the modern world, Spence had followed his shrewd instinct for spotting comers. Armed with only scant knowledge of the language, but a Yankee's sixth sense for knowing what these determined people could do, he came home.

Washington, D.C., was the natural stage for his talents, and so he bought a lovely old house above Embassy Row, where the high ridge of Kalorama commands the valley of Rock Creek. He never let on, of course, about his ulterior support—he had purchased the house with the backing of a wealthy Japanese Diet member—and fancied himself an heir to the MacArthur mantle, the daimyo, the feudal baron letting the little people in on how profitable democracy could be. What's more, the intense good manners of the Japanese, their nervous attention and deference, fed his sense of being the occupying power. Now he had become adept at attracting the rich, the celebrated, and especially the powerful to his elegant parties: everyone from George Bush to William J. Casey, Rock Hudson, Eric Sevareid, and Ted Koppel.

For me, it was a wonderful retreat, and Craig was always at National Airport to greet me with a limousine, acting his role as the town's hottest rich boy to a tee. But his sense of the finite never left him, and he seemed to be observing himself and his friends in a demonic drama. Perhaps it would be best to say he didn't take any of it seriously. The car was a large toy, the landmark home a playhouse. I often spent weekends and holidays with him. There were no boy-girl demands, and the remote presence of his homosexuality seemed quite unimportant next to the luxury of an old friendship.

So, when the call came, if I wasn't in the clutches of a story, I would hop the shuttle to Washington. The routine was set: you got dressed up for dinner and dressed down for breakfast over the kitchen stove in the morning, gossiping about last night's guests. Often we fell into reminiscence about the good old days in Vietnam, and Craig, ever sensitive to cliché, would affect the stooped posture of an ancient on a cane and hobble around the kitchen mumbling, "By cracky, these young whippersnappers just don't know what it's all about." We dissolved in hysterics until one of us would remind the other "Remember, it's *our* war."

But as casual as our dish sessions might be, Craig's dinner parties were a rigid extension of his preoccupation with the ways and means of power: obsessive concern about the "right" wine, elaborate flower arrangements, the leased limousine, strategic seating, clothes from Britches, the tongue-lashing of his house staff, including a most dignified black retired army sergeant who took it all in silence. Even the *Times* ran a feature about Craig as "something of a mystery man." He was still expert at measuring people's gullibility and stupidity, which skill he used to win contracts from American corporations panting for a foothold in Asia. He had the old dash, but a new hardness had supervened, an awareness that his ability to persuade had acquired a momentum of its own. "Spence doesn't so much drop names as heave them bodily," a reporter wrote. One of the best guessing games in town revolved around what exactly Craig J. Spence did for a living. Was he an agent of "the Company," a term he was now using to allude to alleged CIA friends? The myth was building. And so was the hunger for power and glory that was slowly turning inward and undercutting his judgment.

In early August 1980, Craig phoned me from Washington about another friend from "our" war, Howard Tuckner. Craig had always liked him, as I did, and we joked often about Howard's naked ambition to be a TV network news star. Although he didn't say it, it was plain that Craig felt an identity there, recognizing vulnerability beyond the conceit and posturing. Craig, too, still harbored dreams of "getting back in the game" as he would say, of having his own show on network television. I strongly suspected the money grubbing and influence peddling were at the service of that old desire.

"Have you seen the *Times?*"

"Not yet, I'm still working on yesterday's *Post.*"

"Better get it. Howard Tuckner killed himself."

Like all obituaries, the merciless medley of facts belied the agony of a disintegrating man. Howard had jumped from the window of an apartment building in the Bronx, where his family lived. He was forty-eight years old and had been suffering from depression, said the story, an observation that recalled our meeting five years earlier in front of City Hall. Howard had eventually returned to network news, going to work for ABC in Africa. Then, for some reason, perhaps the death of his wife, he began to retreat within himself. "He put on weight," said a producer who worked with him then. "For days on end, sometimes as long as two weeks, he'd stay in his room."

Perhaps Ron Steinman had got it right all along, especially when he wrote to Reuven Frank from Saigon about Howard's difficulties of enunciation. *"I'm no speech teacher, but I do know that unless a man can hear his own voice he is in trouble. Tuckner doesn't hear himself. He is Narcissus. His mirror image has a prismatic effect that turns in and around itself. And one of the worst problems with him is that he alienates all those he touches. . . . I really don't know what to do with him. I sometimes feel his edge is so thin that the slightest jiggle will split him wide open."*

Vo Huynh, so accustomed to the death of friends, took Tuckner's death with Asian patience. Howard had been his protégé, his war buddy and, for a while, his prototype of an American reporter. "He was a very ambitious guy, you know," said Huynh years later, still radiating the serenity of a sitting Buddha. "For a long time I thought he just wanted to be a reporter—when all the time he really wanted an anchor job. He never told me. But when I heard about his death, I thought about whether he killed himself because of the war, or that the war was part of it. Howard made his name with that war, he was like a rising star. But I told him whatever happens, happens. It's just like a fruit. One day it ripens, you can't force it.

"After he was wounded, the next day he told me he wanted to go back to New York. George Murray had a Vietnam show, and he wanted to anchor it. I was surprised, I thought he was there to cover the war—to be a reporter. The reason I say that Vietnam was a part of why he killed himself? Because it brought him so far—money, women, anything he wanted—he was never happy after the war. Vietnam spoiled him."

IF Tuckner was a victim of history's new events, so too were fifty-two embattled Americans imprisoned in the Tehran embassy. Their plight and a bungled rescue mission demolished Carter's bid for reelection. Not until Ronald Reagan took office were they released—eighteen minutes after he swore the oath. Once more, hundreds of network news people rushed to the scene, namely the American military hospital in Wiesbaden, West Germany, where network trailers and other paraphernalia had been in place for some time. Through one of my old State Department contacts, and with the expertise of Peter Kendall, our London bureau chief, we were able to speak to the only two women—diplomats Elizabeth Ann Swift and Kathryn Koob—who had been held hostage for all those 444 days.

Guided by a series of prearranged signals, we smuggled them away from the hospital in an unmarked van with blackened windows to a hotel outside of town where I interviewed them at length. As the cassettes came off the camera, they were rushed to a satellite point for a CBS exclusive that night. The clear beat took the sting off the network's series of reverses on the hostage story. ABC had often demonstrated its ability to compete with and even beat us. CBS executives in New York hit the warpath. John Lane, a vice-president who inhaled news to stay alive, was reported to have been so angry one night that he picked up a typewriter and threw it. Screaming matches over the Frankfurt–New York telephone line were de rigueur, and at least one correspondent took a producer by the collar and threatened to turn him into German sausage if he didn't stay out of the story's way. I had seen some tense moments among personnel when I worked for NBC News, but this was world-class street fighting. I was not the only one being put to the test.

Even as Cronkite was about to retire, 1981 was shaping up as a bull year for those reporters who liked news as spectacle. A series of budget-breaking extravaganzas kept us on the move. No sooner were the inauguration over and the hostages home, than a deranged young man shot President Reagan and another brought down Pope John Paul II in St. Peter's Square. Both men lived, but the aftermath of these attacks was expensive for hemorrhaging TV news departments, demanding personnel, airtime, and overtime. Reagan recovered soon enough to push for his tax cuts and the defense build-up. He also passed his first Teflon test by breaking the air controllers' strike.

Meanwhile, festering offstage, another social development was inching its way into the headlines. The term *acquired immunodeficiency syndrome* (AIDS) surfaced in medical journals and even the back pages of metropolitan newspapers. Some saw it as the inevitable fallout from the sexual revolution. Some were even ready to greet the deadly virus as God's rod of retribution. But it was not yet a story big or jazzy enough to catch the attention of the networks. They had crossed the gay barrier in a political sense, but gay disease was daunting. When AIDS finally became a running story, once again it was the newspapers that paved the way.

By autumn of that year, it looked as though the international situation might be calming down, that is until the Russians and their Polish client regime decided to bear down on the Solidarity union. The world braced itself.

"There are tanks in the streets of Warsaw," said Lew Allison, threading his way back from the kitchen radio through the crowd in Charlie Osgood's living room while we toasted Christmas, eleven days away. The telephone was ringing as I turned the key in my lock shortly after 1 A.M. It was Peter Larkin, CBS's foreign editor, the familiar sound of a news emergency in his voice. "Martial law has been declared in Poland, and there are large Soviet troop movements on the border. Get out on the first available for London. We can't help you with airplanes. We're too busy moving everybody, but we can deliver some cash by messenger. Go to London and call me." He clicked off, I headed for JFK.

Shortly after I arrived in London, the "Morning News" decided I was to monitor their "listening post" in London, discussing the Polish situation each morning with Charles Kuralt. "Listening" to Warsaw from London meant reading all the international wire copy and phoning around to diplomats, experts, and refugees in an effort to make sense of the rumors coming from all over the Eastern bloc. Everyone thought the worst as stories began to circulate of persecution and mass arrests, executions, and even reopened concentration camps. Basically, I tried to act as a filter against some of the gross distortions and disinformation emanating from all the participants in this upheaval. But quite frankly, although I made air seven days a week, I hardly felt qualified to deliver sage comments about a place where I had never been.

Because of the daily broadcast, I was tied down to going to the studio every morning, just like an anchor. Delightful not to be out in one of Europe's record-breaking winters, wonderful to roll out of bed late and eat lunch in one of the fashionable restaurants around Harrods, right across the street from the bureau. No feet freezing while staked out in the cold on this one, no candy bar lunches, no whining camera crews, no panic to find a telephone. None of that, and you're still on the air every day! So that's how it's done, I thought, sleight-of-hand, reading what you haven't seen or heard or felt. Telling people about something you really don't know much about. There was something to this anchoring business after all. But it rankled, and I began to feel stale, began to long for the all-senses-on-alert feeling I got when arriving on the scene of a breaking story, letting it all wash over me, giving it the eye.

Still, the feedback from New York was good as we munched turkey sandwiches on Christmas Day in the bureau. Once Solidarity had been crushed and a Soviet invasion deterred, the Polish crisis subsided. Come the New Year, we folded down our London listening post and headed home. Warren Lewis, a New York producer, and I sat on the plane wondering out loud about the impending change of command back at the CBS Broadcast Center.

After months of hot speculation about "Whither CBS?" and how Rather would get out of the ratings slump he was in since he took over from Cronkite, two men had been brought in to lead CBS News into a brave new world: Van Gordon Sauter as president, and as vice-president, Edward Joyce. Rumors of what to expect had already filtered into every foreign capital. Accordingly, one of the London producers called the Paris bureau to get a line on the new guys. Invoking a standard CBS directive, he shouted over the line: "Just gimme the headlines please." The answer was startling in its lack of reticence: "Sauter's a phony and Joyce is his hatchet man."

Decks were already being shuffled. Peter Kendall had been called back home, to be secretly told that he was no longer the London bureau chief but would go to Washington as a producer. No reason given. He didn't know it at the time, but Rather, bent on banishing all of Cronkite's men, wanted to get rid of Sandy Socolow as executive producer of the evening news, so Kendall was pushed out of London to make room for Socolow. Sauter and Joyce called it a "prestige bureau"; Sandy knew it was Siberia.

Returning from a long foreign assignment was always pleasant, especially if I had done creditably. On at least three previous occasions, arriving at the Broadcast Center, I had run into one or more of the news brass, who without exception greeted me with a pat on the back. Crossing Fifty-seventh Street on my first day back from London, I was lost in thought until I realized a limousine was bearing down on me. I hopped back onto the curb as the car door flew open to reveal a large man with impressive girth and a fur trapper's beard. He emerged, put a pipe in his mouth, clicked a lighter, and set about firing his tobacco, all the while staring at me through a cloud of smoke and hard breathing in the January air.

Although I had never laid eyes on him, it was clear this must be the new president of CBS News. Not bad timing, I thought, fresh from an important assignment, and here's the new boss ready to greet me. "You must be Van Gordon Sauter," I said, smiling and extending my hand. I identified myself and welcomed him to his new position.

"Ah—yes," he said, puffing on his pipe. "Well, we have lots of work to do."

We fell into step. Without removing the pipe, he was good enough to ask, "How was it over there?" A great story, I replied, and just fine.

"Well," he continued, pipe still in his mouth, "I hope it wasn't too arduous, Christmas and all." I assured him that we enjoyed the work.

Still puffing, he held the door open for me and we entered the Broadcast Center. Then he turned to face me, the pungent fumes of a good tobacco drifting across the Edward R. Murrow plaque on the wall behind me. "Well," he said, "we'll be in touch as we go along."

Standing in the lobby, I watched him disappear into the corridor. Somewhere in my mind a red light went on and a subliminal voice said: "Tread lightly. You were not a hit at the Palladium."

A few days passed, and I decided to drop in on Rather. Here we were with new management, so I thought it was time to take a reading. Besides, my colleagues were making similar forays to find out where they stood.

"Great to see ya," Rather said, the tight smile again radiating a curious imbalance. He was unblinking in his enthusiasm, effusive in his courtly gestures to see me to a chair. Workmen were darting around, still transforming the old Cronkite newsroom into Rather country. In fact, there had been a great deal of guffawing about Walter's chair, which Rather regarded in the same way a vampire looks at garlic. It couldn't have been removed fast enough.

"Well," he began, "we're living in interesting times, as they say, Liz. But we've got the wagons in a circle now, and the good guys are inside. We have a new team, and they've assured me of their cooperation. Now you know and I know the smart money says Dan Rather can't make it, but what do they know? I don't believe them. And maybe I'm a hardheaded fool, but these people who just live and die by those ratings—these naysayers—I'm not going to let them slow me down. I've got to tell you, I know they're whistling Dixie. I know we're going to be number one again and, dammit, I just refuse to believe otherwise."

I cleared my throat. "I just came in really to find out where things are," I said, "and, of course, ready to help, to know what you want me to do for the evening news."

"Well, you have no problem with me, Liz. I don't think there's a woman on this staff who does. We're past all that stuff here at CBS. And I have full confidence in Van. I think he's the right guy to lead us. He has some exciting ideas, new ways to approach a story. And maybe it means a little more, well—uh—personal involvement than we're used to. Like picking up a document to underscore a point during a stand-up, or maybe even a walking stand-up, a little movement. Now I'm not talking about show business, you understand. Don't let anybody tell you Dan Rather is short-cutting news for effect."

"Well, I wasn't so concerned about being a woman, but . . ."

"And you shouldn't be. You know, I realize we live in times when a young, pretty face counts for a lot. But Dan Rather is only interested in first-rate news coverage. Of course, you know there might be some who aren't so—well, you know what I mean . . ." His voice trailed off.

"How do you think Sauter and Joyce stand on that?"

"Well, no, as I said, I think Sauter is good for us, but—by the way, do you have any, uh, any 'past' with Joyce? Did something ever happen between you and him?"

I sat thinking for a few seconds. "You mean something negative?"

"Yeah."

"Dan, the only time I remember encountering Ed Joyce was a good many years back when he was running WCBS. He invited me to lunch and offered me a job. I had just renewed my network contract at NBC and saw no reason to change. But the whole thing was very cordial."

"Are you sure of that?" He was watching me closely.

"Yes, of course. What the heck is going on?"

He hesitated, then leaned back, playing with a pencil, still taking stock.

"I don't know, and I don't want to get you overly concerned, but he's got a thing about you."

"What do you mean a 'thing'?" I said, amazed at the turn this pep talk had taken.

"Look, Liz, I want you to know right up front that you have a supporter in Dan Rather. It's just that Joyce is a question mark. I'm not sure about what he brings to network news."

"What did he say about me, Dan?"

"I don't think he feels you have breakaway capability."

"What was that again?"

"I'm sure it's nothing you can't work on to turn him around," he said, ignoring my question. "This is no cause for alarm, but you might have 'a Joyce problem.' I'm sure it will pass once we get the show on the road. And who knows, as I said, I'm not worried by Van, but if Ed Joyce steps out of line, well then maybe I'll have to . . ."

He didn't finish the sentence. We sat and stared at each other for a few seconds. "Thanks for the fill, Dan," I said finally.

"Give 'em hell, Liz."

On the way back to my office, I ran into a pal from the news desk, a CBS veteran with a reputation for justified cynicism. He had seen me coming out of Rather's office.

"So? What did he say?"

"I don't really know," I replied slowly. "Have you ever heard the phrase 'breakaway capability'?"

He smiled sympathetically. "Welcome to the ranks of the 'Ratherized.' "

14

SEND IN
THE
CLOWNS

It is a shopworn axiom of newsroom bull sessions that "getting the story" usually means being in the right place at the right time. There is seldom mention of its statistical corollary: being in the right place at the wrong time: Miami in August, Paris in January, Bangkok in June. And so it was with Newport in February 1982.

The fabled summer resort, its stately mansions looking to the sea, seemed abandoned by the world as stiff winds skidded over the whitecaps of Narragansett Bay. We arrived, out of season, in unfashionable hordes, to cover the trial of one Claus von Bülow. The story had caught the fancy of the nation, prompting columnists to decry the media's fascination, even as they compounded the interest.

Von Bülow stood accused of trying to kill his wife, Sunny, by injecting her with insulin. She lay in a coma in a New York hospital, unlikely to awaken. Here was tabloid sensation at its juiciest: an autocratic and slightly sinister European socialite of dubious pedigree; a blonde and beautiful woman of wealth and family; two children working to avenge their mother and convict their stepfather; an alert if not snoopy foreign housekeeper; an old Newport mansion; a teary-eyed debutante mistress; and a Columbo-style detective bent on justice.

From the start, the case aroused a fanatic pro-Claus movement (some even wearing "Free Claus" T-shirts) rooting for the faded grandee as the loyal husband victimized by a self-indulgent and alcoholic wife. Very few saw Sunny as a pathetic, drifting middle-aged woman in the clutches of a charming, fortune-hunting rotter. Indeed, the prevailing view of Sunny von Bülow seemed at odds with that feminist defense of women of a certain age. The same factor was very much in play only a year earlier when Jean Harris, former headmistress of the exclusive Madeira School for girls, was tried and convicted for shooting her faithless lover, the Scarsdale diet doctor Herman Tarnower. Feminists rallied to Harris's defense, enshrining her in the tear-stained annals of women scorned by men moving on to greener turf. The fact that she might have committed murder often played a minor role in the debate. Not so with Sunny; Sunny was rich, and that made all the difference. And so it got down to what kind of middle-aged woman you were for: self-made schoolmarm or rich bitch.

The two trials were linked by more than the parable events of tired women and rapacious men. Von Bülow's natty defense attorney, Herald Fahringer, was also handling Jean Harris's appeal. In his manicured hands, with his courtly manner, any woman this side of Lucrezia Borgia would feel safe. Harris had been convicted of second-degree murder, a fact which also brought to light something about how news was covered at CBS. Although I had worked many of the big trials in New York, I was certainly not a trial specialist; good court reporters know the statutes cold, working in a world of judges and lawyers that outsiders, like TV reporters, find difficult to understand. Day to day, I reported the jostle between prosecution and defense, noting Harris's haughty manner and defiance of her own counsel. The jury was charged, but then returned to the courtroom for further clarification of the law from the presiding judge. Usually, the temptation to doze off in such sessions is overpowering, but New York State distinguishes degrees of murder and the shades of intent in ways that held me completely in thrall.

On the day Harris was convicted, I rushed back to the Broadcast Center and began writing. Sandy Socolow, executive producer of the "Evening News," was still on deck in these last days before Rather. I walked into the Fish Bowl, an uninspired term for the tiny room where the program masters made sense of the world. I was always tempted, when entering script in hand, to genuflect to the worried associate producers talking in half sentences on the phone or staring tensely at monitors, waiting for the feeds to come in. In the last hour before Cronkite's "good evening," the Fish Bowl had the air of a Dr. Strangelove war room: a combination of comic dread and frenzied action. It was also deadly serious.

Socolow, a barrel-chested man with a soft voice, possessed a scholarly command of events, kept sharp by his voracious reading of all the daily newspapers before breakfast. If there ever was an "anchor" in TV news it was "Soc." He had come out of the old INS wire school, working as a reporter in the Far East, joined CBS in the late 1950s, and worked closely with Cronkite as a writer. The two former wire service men shared professional and personal bonds that were long and deep. Before coming to New York to run the "Evening News," Sandy had been a vice-president and bureau chief in Washington, guiding CBS coolly through Watergate.

Socolow and Cronkite had a special interest in the Jean Harris story ("a great yarn"). In fact, Cronkite insisted that afternoon on reading my script himself: "Let's have more, more!" Now Socolow was giving it a last read before I recorded the narration. I fidgeted, trying to fathom his expressionless face. He turned over the last page, looked up, and set aside his cigar. "What *is* second-degree murder?"

I had been read by a lot of editors in my career, but this was the first time anyone in TV news had ever asked me to summarize a statute. It was a city editor's question. I took a deep breath and ran down the applicable law, as expounded by the judge just the day before.

Socolow stared at me suspiciously after I finished, as though I had spoiled his day. "Okay, it's a buy."

From that moment on, I looked at Cronkite's protégé in a different way. As the commercial says, he got his job the old-fashioned way: he earned it.

The women who had turned up to cover the Harris trial made no secret of their prejudices, except for Theo Wilson of the *News*, far too much a trial pro to let the defendant get in the way of the story. Diana Trilling, widow of the famous literary critic, was writing a book on

Harris, as was Shana Alexander, and Lally Weymouth, who was free-lancing a piece for *New York* magazine. There were others from smaller news agencies, to a woman identifying all over the place, feeling the fifty-seven-year-old lady's pain, glowering at the recitation of the diet doctor's cruelties. During the recesses, some of the conversation sounded like the minutes of a NOW meeting, or at least a chapter from *Back Street*.

Frankly, their solidarity with Harris struck me as a radical depar-ture from objectivity. The prim schoolmistress may have been dealt a bad hand by a cad, but murder was still against the law. As to miti-gating factors—a crime of passion committed in the heat of the moment—it seemed to me that when a lady buys a gun and drives several hours to a guy's house, she has had ample time to think things through. After firing a burst of shots, her claim that she was trying to kill herself instead of Tarnower had a hollow ring. But, despite my own view—that she should pay the price—I played it straight, leaving justice to judge and jury and feminist outrage to my colleagues.

While a reporter must know how the court system works, there are times when there is no underestimating the merits of a good liberal arts education. Joel Aurnou, Harris's bumbling attorney, unknowingly put this to the test in his summation to the jury, drawing a searing picture of Harris being told by her lover, after fourteen years of intimacy, to "stop bothering me." Pulling out all the stops, the histrionic Aurnou read from the defendant's steamy letters to the cardiologist, ending his summation with an apology for reading "someone else's words." The last excerpt he called "a poem," leaving the impression he was quoting Harris directly. " 'I miss him in the weeping of the rain,' " read Aurnou.

"What do you think?" said Trilling, looking over at me, both arms straddling the back of the wooden benches.

"That sounds awfully familiar," I replied, "but more like Edna St. Vincent Millay than Jean Harris."

"You know, that's a good guess," she said.

During the recess I went to the telephone to call Socolow and fill him in on the morning's doings, including the part about Harris draw-ing upon Millay. After I hung up, an eavesdropping Lally Weymouth, herself an alumna of Madeira, lay in wait for me. She seemed already wary of me, especially since I hadn't known until she told me that her mother owned *The Washington Post*. "Jean wrote that," she said em-phatically, using Harris's first name in obvious tribute to the old school tie.

"If Harris wrote that, then she should be on trial for plagiarism instead of murder," I snapped back.

"You're going to be really sorry if you go with Millay," she said, "Jean Harris wrote those words."

Back at the office, we checked the reference and it was, indeed, Edna St. Vincent Millay, a sonnet from a group entitled "Renascence."

> *Time does not bring relief; you all have lied*
> *Who told me time would ease me of my pain!*
> *I miss him in the weeping of the rain;*
> *I want him at the shrinking of the tide.*
>
>   . . . .
>
> *I say, 'There is no memory of him here!'*
> *And so stand stricken, so remembering him.*

Excerpts of the poem appeared in the *Times* the next morning.

When I arrived in the courtroom, the feminist contingent pretended I wasn't there, except for Trilling. As the judge banged his gavel, she leaned over and whispered: "Nice catch."

If the von Bülow trial was a story made for tabloids, it was also, in these early months of the consulship of Sauter and Joyce, pointing the way for a new CBS News. Deciding to play to the cheap seats, Sauter declared the trial "top priority" and ordered the stops pulled. It was a convenient debut for his theory of "moments" television, a philosophy that wafted through CBS's corridors like a mutant virus. The idea was that every story should contain at least one moment that would grab the viewer's gut, inciting grief, pity, anger, whatever—as long as he "felt" something. What's more, the selection of stories itself depended on their potential for producing these manipulative moments. The era of the "Big Mo" had arrived.

There were plenty of "moments" in the von Bülow affair, hence the queen-size bureau of fourteen people flown in to capture the story. One element in particular certified the coverage's top priority: a camera inside the courtroom, the consequence of a one-year experiment to examine the effects of such an intrusion. Twenty-six states were allowing cameras into their courts, but this case was a surefire test of how—or if—justice would be affected.

Legal experts worried about showboating witnesses and lawyers.

College professors were crawling through the Newport courthouse, taking surveys on what we all thought. The majority opinion among media people was, predictably enough, that cameras should be allowed. My own dissent was based on a suspicion that the courtroom camera could harm our own coverage in unexpected ways. Trial stories, like the court system itself, require equal time for the defense and the prosecution. In a story running around two to two and a half minutes—a hefty amount of network time—the reporter must set the scene, relate the day's news, and if possible explore the ramifications or the next expected development. With a camera in the courtroom, one was duty-bound to include statements—sound bites—from the defense and prosecution from that day. Invariably, they were truncated and, as with so many such fragments, automatically built distortion into the story.

The in-court camera also enforced the basic Dick-and-Jane formula of most TV stories, demanding adherence to the old rule that the words should not fight the picture. Although as time went on, generic pictures, pictures for their own sake—the business calls them "wallpaper"—became the norm, correspondents wondered if anyone was really listening to the words.

If the words counted little enough, the sight of von Bülow in the courtroom listening to the debate on his destiny carried its own dark fascination. He could have been a snapshot for all the movement he showed, his Cartier watch and traces of a hair transplant the subject of countless print stories but barely visible to a camera, which could not capture the aura of malice that seemed to surround him. In casual conversation with him, I felt an unsettling shiver, not unlike the feeling I had interviewing Alger Hiss a year earlier. The emanations were so strong that the *Times* reporter, Dudley Clendinen, was inspired to declare that von Bülow and the proceedings had "no moral center." And so convinced—like the first jury—was he of von Bülow's guilt that he asked his editors not to assign him to the second trial.

Much of the activity in Newport centered around the technological problems of access to the in-court camera tape. The three networks agreed to provide a pool cameraman, rotating each week, who would operate the in-court camera. The feed would go from the courtroom to the Colony House next door, an eighteenth-century statehouse with creaking floors and little heat, which served as press headquarters. Any network or station that wanted the pictures could plug in. Those who couldn't get into the courtroom on crowded days or who needed to stay near the telephones, could cover the trial from here. As the story built to fever pitch, the feed was routed to Providence, where it could be picked up by just about any station in the country. This, of course, involved some rewiring of the old statehouse, for which the nets were only too happy to pay. Sensational as it was, the von Bülow trial was breaking no legal ground, but it was serving as a model for how television could cover major trials.

One day while the jury was out, I got a call in the courthouse press room from another CBS correspondent, Dick Wagner, down in El Salvador. One would have thought that deadly Central American battlefield was a place where "moments" abounded, but Dick was having trouble getting on the air. "What the hell are you guys doing up there?" he shouted. "We have six people down here and there are bad guys shooting at us and we still can't get on."

I suggested he try for Salvadoran reaction to the von Bülow verdict. He was not amused.

Network coverage of the von Bülow trial, in contrast, amounted to overkill. The fourteen of us from the New York office included two producers, three correspondents, three crews, two tape editors, and various gofers and drivers. We set up shop in the Colony House, bringing the number of newspeople on hand to about 140. I got the assignment purely by default when two correspondents before me were called overseas: the first and last time I would work on anything of consequence for the "Evening News" under the new management.

Sauter, Joyce, and Rather were already assigning A and B ratings, and except in cases of extreme emergency, only A listers were eligible to appear regularly on the program. The letter ratings had nothing to do with expertise or experience, since most of the correspondent staff at CBS was seasoned. It had to do with broadcasting personality, what Rather had meant when he reported that Joyce—not he, but Joyce—was wondering about my "breakaway capability." I was catching on to what it meant: the ability to pull away from the pack like a racehorse, or a wide receiver, and become a star. Solid reporting was no longer enough. None of this was stated policy, but, as with most exterminations, the grisly details and numbers come to light long after the deed.

I heard later, when the trial was over, that everyone who had worked the story received a personal thank-you from Howard Stringer, the new executive producer of the Rather broadcast. Sauter and Joyce brought Stringer in to ensure the "moments" coverage, figuring no doubt that his background as a documentary producer would add new dimension to daily news reporting. He was a British subject, a Welshman, and as with so many Brits before him, his Oxford accent worked wonders on the Yanks. But he was a killer, Cassius with charm, enough of it so that even the cunning Laurence Tisch, the billionaire financier who would eventually take over the corporation, fell under his spell. Howard would wind up in charge of it all, president of the CBS Broadcast Group. Tall, beady-eyed, tending to baby fat, a trifle seedy, he pressed his points hard under the cover of "that wonderful English humor." Women on the staff generally disliked him, and he had a reputation for considering them invisible.

His silence on my performance at Newport registered as still another early warning that I was not preferred stock. Cronkite was long gone, and Socolow by this time had been exiled to London as the purge got under way. One by one, all of the CBS Old Guard management, the keepers of the flame, would be extinguished, and the prideful claims that news was the "jewel in the crown" of CBS began to dissolve, insofar as it was subsidized by the other divisions. On the contrary, news was now being seen as a profit center. A new CBS News was under construction, and to accomplish such a transformation it helped to be unburdened by notions about pure news. Broadcasting was the emphasis now, and news was at its service.

Sauter and Joyce. If they sounded like a headline act in vaudeville, it was an amusing and telling coincidence, for in many ways they were the archpractitioners of news as low-budget entertainment. Sauter invested his expertise in the authority of celebrity by pushing for Rather; Joyce made his mark by cutting the budget at a time when the Black Rock M.B.A.s were demanding that the news department make money. Moreover, both men arrived from the world of local stations, an unthinkable résumé in the old days. Network news had been practiced by men and women who came to the job with a certain sense of the world that included Main Street but went beyond the county limits. It was not snobbery, as some station managers would argue, but whether one had spent a career covering fires or the SALT talks. (Indeed, covering fires may be useful preparations for the latter.) It was also the assumption that news was a serious pursuit, not simply a means to ratings and profits. Most important, network news exacted higher standards of reporting and writing than those aspired to by most local TV news operations. As for talent, local stations had long been in the Barbie and Ken business. And a new breed of men was running them. Rootless, hollow, offering amiability for lack of background, and, as they say, "realistic," men who relished nothing more than rubbing polyester with old friends at an affiliates convention.

Joyce's career had been exclusively local until he brought the pettiness and narrow vision of a lifetime to Paley's "jewel." Sauter, once a newspaper reporter, drifted into local TV, managing stations and even trying his hand at anchoring. His network expertise included time in radio and a stint as Paris bureau chief that, by all accounts, consisted mainly of eating his way through the Guide Michelin. As president of CBS Sports, he reveled in the home of spectacle television. Like Bob Mulholland in his early days at NBC, Sauter and Joyce were both known for "turning stations around," that is, making news profitable, the quickest way to get the attention of the corporate side.

Sauter's "style" sent the print press to their word banks for journalistic jazz. There was no end to the myths about him. He had, in one job, kept a parrot in the newsroom; he had a rolltop desk; he spoke in deep phrases; he owned a Jeep. Sauter was great copy—and he knew how to create it.

Under Sauter and Joyce, the word *manager* slid into the parlance of CBS News, along with "setting goals" and creating a "news team"— all the lingo of local news. Sauter especially liked to talk about "compelling television," a phrase immediately picked up by those who dealt into the new regime. News managers were replacing newsmen. Even bureau chiefs were now referred to as bureau managers. By 1985, hardly anyone arched an eyebrow at the realization that all three network news divisions were headed by men whose careers had been made outside TV network journalism: Sauter had gone on to a corporate vice-presidency at Black Rock, leaving Joyce as president of news to guard his legacy; Arledge, offering sports expertise, ran ABC; and Larry Grossman held the fort at NBC. Grossman, however, had been president of the Public Broadcasting System and left NBC after trying to fight off cutbacks in news.

The first time I saw Sauter and Joyce together they were in the CBS cafeteria, a sprawling, no-frills eatery, in keeping with CBS's hard edge. Sauter, big and bearded, stood in line, proffering his tray to the indifferent black behind the hot food counter. Imitating his every move, the slight and smirking Joyce, deferential, trailing at the boss's elbow. Mutt and Jeff, black on black, alpha and omega. Scarcely an eye looked elsewhere as they munched away in the center of the room, pretending not to notice, talking after long intervals like a married couple, team captains at high table.

Joyce was wearing a conventional sport jacket and a straight tie. Sauter, his Ben Franklin glasses perched on his nose, displayed a large bow tie, a worn tweed jacket, and a vest sweater, of the very kind he would dress Dan Rather in a few weeks later. "I don't know," I said to an equally curious colleague. "He looks like the owner of a Greenwich Village bookstore to me, not the president of CBS News." I was missing the point. It was exactly how he wanted to look, just "boho" enough to keep the natives down and arouse the amused attention of the corporate boys. After all, could a man dressed so daringly be without confidence and therefore ability?

In 1982, scenery was moved into place for the upcoming drama. A "shortfall" in the sales department precipitated an economic crisis at CBS; General Westmoreland launched a $120 million libel suit against the network over a documentary which accused him of doctoring assessments of enemy strength in Vietnam; Chairman Paley stepped down. It was more a sign of the times than the weight of his seventy-nine years that Paley, son of a Russian-Jewish immigrant, gave way to a man who had made his name running Jolly Green Giant frozen products for the Pillsbury Corporation, Thomas H. Wyman. A press release preceding the arrival of this handsome WASP reported that as a student at Amherst he had written his major paper on Yeats, a brilliant touch, crafted to disarm the newsies. "Can't be all bad if he reads Yeats," mumbled the conventional lack of wisdom. Wyman set about looking for ways to cut costs, and the team of Sauter and Joyce stood ready for their buck-and-wing. Rather's ratings, perceived by most to be in trouble during the first year of his anchor life, were now reported to be climbing steadily, a conclusion widely circulated by the new management. He would be back in the winner's circle by the end of the year, and in the eyes of Black Rock, that was credential enough for Sauter and Joyce.

Sauter busied himself "fixing" the "Evening News" and endearing himself to Rather with public declarations of support: for example, "The Fish Bowl is more important than the Oval Office." Meanwhile, Joyce took charge of the "Morning News," which was fast becoming the Bermuda Triangle of TV journalism. In the incestuous minuet style of TV news, Shad Northshield, who had been producing both "Sunday Morning" with Charles Kuralt and the "Morning News" (then also with Kuralt), was taken off the program. George Merlis, my old classmate from the Columbia School of Journalism, who had just left ABC as executive producer of "Good Morning America," was recruited to replace Shad on the morning broadcast. Not long after he took over, George told me that I would be assigned to his program full-time. At first, I flattered myself by thinking my old friend wanted me on his staff for my work and our old acquaintance, but when I went to see him, it was clear that Joyce had made the assignment. Years later, I asked George how Sauter and Joyce made these decisions.

"Well, you know, they'd hold an editorial board meeting every day with the key producers from evening and morning news. Because my show was the last one they saw before the meeting, Sauter would often start out by saying, 'Capital broadcast, Brother Merlis.' And it was like a Boys Club, really; they let it all hang out, say everything out in the open. So they told me Rather had a hit list and that you were on it. Joyce also said that you were difficult to deal with. I told him: 'She's a perfectionist.'

"But it was the age thing, of course. They really felt you were too old, you and many of the others, and they came out and said it. Joyce said there was no place at CBS News for these people unless I had a place for them on the 'Morning News.'

"They felt [Richard C.] Hottelet over at the UN was too old, so they gave him to me. And Ray Gandolph—well, Sauter just simply said, 'I'll have no one on who wears a beard,' which I thought kind of strange because, you know, he's sitting there wearing a beard. [Diane] Sawyer they referred to as 'the woman,' and while they didn't come out and say it, they thought Kuralt was too old, too, and that they were replacing him with a guy [Bill Kurtis] who had 'more energy.'

"They were big on the ethnic mix pressure, too. Sauter would say, 'Merlis, go out and find a black for your broadcast.' And there were other times when I'd want to hire someone, and maybe their name ended in -ski, and Sauter would say, 'Sounds too ethnic. Forget it.' They even thought Mort Dean was too 'ethnic.' They were quite a group."

The struggle against age and ethnicity—this militant Californianism—was at the heart of Sauter and Joyce's view of the world, and they immediately imposed their not-so-subtle perceptions on the news operation. They embodied the spirit of "team" journalism, a commedia dell'arte of on-camera stereotypes who would be the network stars, just as they were on local stations around the country: the Interrogator, the Buffoon, the Blonde, the Curmudgeon, the Sophisticate, the Bad Boy, the Vamp, and so on. Correspondents, even B-listers, might sometimes attain these glories if they looked like their beat: hence, the burly Ike Pappas was assigned to labor, the Ivy League Steve Young to New England, and on it went.

As for women, to own something young, good-looking, and

blonde was a vice-president's late-night fantasy. Every TV critic had a shot at the blonde angle, but the fact remained it was a determining factor. Once a joke in local TV news makeup rooms, the peroxide phenomenon now provoked comment even in the Fish Bowl. "Where's your blond wig?" Socolow asked me one day.

In their search for woman anchors, the Sauter-Joyce axis held to the standards set by Miss America panels, arguing that their ingenues coincidentally possessed the intellect of Star Wars physicists. In sweeping Phyllis George out of the sports department to cohost the "Morning News," they finally dispelled any doubt about their affinity for what everyone in TV news called "air-heads." Softly and bitterly, the corridor critics ridiculed the lady for her on-air gaffes, not so much out of snobbery as from a deep sense of shame. She had trouble keeping world leaders straight, for example, volunteering to interview the long-dead Indira Gandhi. The low point came in her interview with convicted rapist Gary Dotson and his accuser, Cathy Webb, who said she had found God and recanted her story. Dotson had done time; Webb was sorry. To affirm this curious partnership, George chirped: "How 'bout a hug?"

Women with hard reporting and writing experience in print were simply not in demand. What's more, the Sauter-Joyce picks even lacked substantial experience in TV news because they were recruited from local stations. The women the dynamic duo brought to CBS—indeed, the women being brought into most of TV news—arrived with two or three years of experience covering local stories. It was not enough. And it began to show. With no expertise to fall back on, they had to assume the appearance of news, to act the news. It wasn't so much discrimination as blotting out serious women journalists in favor of the girl on the locker room door. Sauter, in fact, was widely quoted along the corridors as having said repeatedly that all anchorwomen "should look as though they give good head." Men may have kept their sarcasms to themselves, but they were listening to the silly questions asked in live interviews, to the copy that read like a high school yearbook, and it made them—and me—cringe. Women were hurling themselves back into the Bronze Age.

When I realized the implications of going to the "Morning News," I stubbornly tried to head it off. With no idea at the time of Rather's contribution to my career, I appealed several times to his good friend and keeper, David Buksbaum. In fact, David had become my own confidant since that first week at CBS when he found me wandering past his office, trying to find the newsroom in the labyrinth of hallways. He assured me I had "no Rather problem" and said instead that the one senior woman producer on the "Evening News" was blocking me from the broadcast. How could anyone make such an end run, I asked, when the anchor had clearly preempted management's power? David sighed heavily and assured me that she would be gone in six months and I would be back. Then he switched the subject to his diet doctor. One day at lunch, in a mellow mood after a good bottle of Gavi at his favorite midtown Italian restaurant, he let me in on a secret. As he reached for his wine glass, I noticed a hunk of gold on his wrist, the kind of Rolex watch so popular with Arab sheikhs.

"Some watch," I said.

"Yeah, I know." He pulled back his cuff to reveal further its glittering bulk. "My best friend gave it to me," he said, his voice softening, his eyes misting.

"Who?" No answer. "Rather?" Somehow I could never nerve myself to the forced familiarity of saying "Dan."

"Yep," he said, pulling up his broad shoulders. "And I'll show you something else." He turned the watch over and there were three initials. "Only Dan and I know what they mean—and it goes back some time. It's a secret."

I had heard of male bonding, but this was the limit.

As for Rather, the word was already out that he didn't think much of young women reporters because they hadn't earned their jobs. It was a worthy argument in most cases, I agreed, except it was becoming clear he disliked even more the middle-aged ones who had.

I went to the "Morning News," having been made to see the light not so much by Buksbaum's version of events as by a chance encounter with John Lane one afternoon in Columbus Circle. John, an executive holdover from "the old CBS," was trying valiantly to serve two masters. In all seriousness, and I believe with good intent, he took me by the shoulders and said paternally, "You'd better take the job on the 'Morning News' before this new crowd wakes up one day and discovers you're over forty and not a blonde."

Sauter had already declared at a meeting that no story on the morning program should be longer than ninety seconds, and although that precept was strictly honored, I did manage to do some "long" features (two minutes), but it was bitter medicine. I could have been working in the Elba bureau. Meanwhile, I tried to do as many "Sunday Morning" stories as I could. That was perfectly acceptable because Shad's program, elite and critically acclaimed as it was, had the status of an elephants' graveyard in the minds of the new management.

Gradually, I phased out of the mornings and into Sunday, as a correspondent doing the cover story of the week.

Shad's career had a certain symbolism for those of us relegated to his program: old thoroughbreds retired from the track. He liked to brag about how he had started the show with a band of leftovers, the "Dirty Dozen," and nothing much had changed. Those too old, those with no discernible zip as "broadcasters" were banished to Shad's gang: Robert Pierpoint, George Herman, David Culhane. Who else but Northshield would have let me do a story on AIDS using Camus's *La Peste* (The Plague) as a running theme throughout the script? Shad was all the things Sauter wished to be: the handwoven tweeds he had worn for years, a thorough knowledge of the arts, the documentaries he had made long established as classics. Two big, bluff men: a tough East Coast Jew of culture and education, a wily drifter from Ohio who got lucky. "I wouldn't mind him so much," said Shad, "except that his grammar is so bad."

No crack-of-dawn phone calls, no bullet dodging on this assignment. It was like early retirement, although I loved having twelve to fifteen minutes of air each week to explore a story. Tape editors fought to work on the Sunday show, which demanded a kind of artistry that daily news pieces had no time for. The producers, mainly CBS veterans, simply felt it was the best job they had ever had.

Wise and upscale, "Sunday Morning" offered a cover story as comment on the hard news of the week, but it avoided the trendy in favor of the serious, with a heavy dose of nature essays, profiles, and tearful yarns about visibly noble yet authentic do-gooders. The program's style had its share of satirists, the going joke being that if no one cried on-camera every week we hadn't done our job.

In mid-November 1983 I went in to see Lane about a Beirut assignment. A hard way to rescue my career, but I thought if I could just get back in the foreign field again I might be able to redeem myself. Entering his office, I had a fleeting vision of Gloria Swanson in *Sunset Boulevard*, playing the discarded movie queen trying to make a comeback, whipping out a pistol and plugging her man when he tries to walk ("Nobody leaves a star").

Correspondents were being rotated in and out of Beirut quite haphazardly. Why not let me go for a couple of months, I asked Lane. He parried immediately by saying that it would have to be for four to five months, that I should think this over and get back to him. Meanwhile, he said, he would run it past Ed Joyce. Two weeks later

I returned and said that I couldn't do five months, and why was this the only choice open when other stateside correspondents were waltzing in and out of foreign stories on a weekly basis?

"They work for Dan Rather's program," Lane said, "and they pay for their own people."

"Are any of them volunteering for Beirut?"

"No," he said, his normally short fuse now burning, "but that's the way it is, and that's the way the management wants it."

"What did Joyce say?"

"He doesn't really want a woman there," he said, not looking at me. "No matter how long."

Lane, a daily massgoer, assumed the demeanor of a priest in a confessional. "My daughter," he said, "this is a new game, and we're just going to have to roll with it."

I left, suspecting that Lane didn't want a woman in Beirut either. So I remained stateside, and the assignment spiral was definitely pointing downward. Weekend duty, stakeouts, obits of people not yet dead, oil fires in New Jersey, all of which were "protective," a newsroom euphemism for covering a story that had little chance of making air. At one point, Sam Roberts, the foreign editor, suggested strongly that I see about doing radio hourlies. He didn't say "for career insurance," but the implication was clear.

Three weeks and five days after my meeting with Lane, a truck loaded with explosives rammed into the marine barracks in Beirut, killing 241 servicemen. Three days later, U.S. Marines and army airborne troops invaded Grenada. At first, no one, not even newspeople, knew exactly where to look on a map for this place Grenada. It sounded vaguely like something you drink after dinner. One smartie on the foreign desk wondered aloud how a country with a nutmeg on its flag could be taken seriously.

Ronald Reagan was taking it very seriously, choosing this twelve-mile-wide island in the Windward chain to make a point about America, to redress a string of military setbacks and fiascos: Vietnam, the *Mayaguez*, the USS *Pueblo*, the Iran rescue mission, and now Beirut. America was tired of being humiliated by Third World crazies, turned into a straw giant by gun-shy liberals who resurrected Vietnam every time the Congress voted foreign aid. In the early hours of Oct. 25, 1983, the ghost of Vietnam did not prevail, and America breathed fire again.

The invasion—a "predawn vertical insertion" as the Pentagon

poetically put it—was not only an opportunity to settle old scores with our enemies but with the press itself. The colonels of Vietnam were now the generals running the Pentagon, and many of them were determined not to let the press "lose this one, too." Journalists, barred from the operation, were taken by surprise, as were the thousand or so Cubans on the island. Some journalists who tried to reach the island by boat were blocked by our own destroyers or taken aboard and not allowed to file. Said Vice Admiral Joseph Metcalf III, the fleet commander, to reporters: "I'm down here to take an island. I don't need you running around and getting in the way."

The only pictures of the action were shot by official Defense Department cameramen and a hotel owner who lived just opposite the jump zone. A furor arose, complete with irate network news presidents testifying before Congress and reminders that newsmen had been taken along on military missions even before the Normandy invasion.

In Grenada, the president and his men made their point: they had cured America of the Vietnam syndrome. As for members of the press, they could bloody well wait until the mopping up began before they were allowed on the scene. So, for the first few days, about 400 newspeople lingered on the vacation island of Barbados, 150 miles away, awaiting permission and an airplane ride into what was no longer a war zone.

The Grenada story brought into relief an official attitude toward the press, repaid an old Pentagon debt, and gave the American people a chance to walk tall again; it also revealed the direction of TV news. Local stations, now much less dependent on networks for their coverage and technology, dispatched their own anchormen and star reporters to the scene. Battle reports may have been scarce, but there was no dearth of stylishly coiffed and suited local TV types descending on Barbados, recording stand-uppers at the airport, and shipping them out for their programs even before they went through customs. Many came to the story with Samsonite luggage and coats and ties. War was becoming just another sound bite for a nation with a contracting attention span.

The omnipresent Peter Arnett was, of course, on hand, having abandoned wire service journalism for the wilds of TV news. CNN had snagged him early in its challenge to the Big Three. On one flight into Grenada several days after the initial strike, with the fighting well over, Peter and I sat across from each other in a C-130, not hearing anything above the roar but observing the array of local TV reporters dressed in their new combat clothes. As if in answer to an invisible cue, we locked eyes at 6,000 feet, mutely communicated for a split second, and doubled up.

By the third day, the command started taking in reporters: the networks and the news magazines first, shrewd comment on where newspapers stood in the Pentagon pecking order. Small "pool groups" and then small unilateral groups dutifully trooped in for five-hour escorted tours, but they had to return to Barbados since no telephone or other filing facilities were available. Anyone who chose to stay overnight slept in luxurious oceanfront hotels with no room service but a great view.

When I landed on Grenada, it was clear that a lot of the old Vietnam brass was running the show. One of the PAOs, a friend from Fort Bragg, whispered to me to stay behind with my crew after the press tour left. There was going to be a helicopter assault into the hills where, it was believed, some of the remaining Cuban guerrilla fighters might still be hiding. It seemed hard to believe there could be any hostile forces left, but this was a chance to get exclusive aerial footage, even if it turned out to be a peaceful ride in the country. We landed without incident at a Cuban base in the hills, and there, amid the charred hulks of American choppers, taped a good picture story of what life had been like in the socialist ranks before the American invasion. It wasn't exactly war footage, but it was more than the other nets had and we were elated about getting it back to Barbados for transmission. Meanwhile, both military and civilian sources were letting me in on details of the ragged invasion, the real casualty figures, and what had gone wrong in the first hour of the assault.

We sped to Point Salines and the Cuban-built airport, now a U.S. staging area, to wait for return transport. Another CBS correspondent, a Rather A-lister who had been designated as the "Evening News" man, showed up with another crew. Immediately my crew began bragging about our "great stuff." The new arrivals had very little. "Give me your tapes," the A-lister demanded. He, too, wanted to go back to Barbados, and he intended to take his two-man crew. The long arm of Dan Rather was reaching out across the Caribbean. Since there were only three seats allotted to each net, it meant I would have to stay behind and risk getting stuck without being able to send our story, even if it was only meant for the "Morning News." It seemed ludicrous that he should insist both men return with him, at the expense of a fellow correspondent. It was also apparent he wanted to use my story to bolster what little he had—even though he had not been near where our mission had taken us. It was a tiny detail often winked at in the broadcast news business, voicing over pictures of places you had never been. As for his refusal to let me on the plane, it amounted to screwing your own instead of the competition.

I stood my ground. "No seat, no tapes."

"You are jeopardizing the 'Evening News,' " he said with dire overtones. "We're the next show up and I want your tapes."

I tightened my grip on the cassettes and suggested he perform a solitary act.

As it happened, a C-5A transport turned up minutes after the first group left, and we arrived just behind them on Barbados. By the time I got to the hotel where CBS had improvised a bureau, the A-lister was on the telephone to New York, registering his complaint to the Rather forces. Angry but not cowed, I did the piece for the "Morning News," which ran it as an exclusive. I also briefed a senior producer on the information I had about the botched invasion, especially since I heard that we were doing a late-night special. The producer, a man with long experience in war areas, pitched it directly to Rather's executive producer for the special. The answer was an indifferent thank you.

That night, the pictures of our helicopter assault opened and closed the special. What they meant, where they were taken, what I had learned about the conduct of the mission, all blended into the fog of war. By then, the star correspondents had arrived on Grenada, and they were guided onto the air by their own producers. No scratching for information; it was supplied to them. Stories were not nearly as important as those who aired them.

Three weeks later in New York, my phone rang one morning. It was the Grenada producer who had listened to my invasion briefing and then tried to interest Rather in getting it on the air. "You'd better read *The Wall Street Journal*," he said. "Your story is on the front page."

Sure enough, there it was. No one else ever mentioned it, not even Dan Rather.

The strict division between morning and evening news correspondents was codified by the time Grenada broke. I had dutifully filed radio spots and continued covering the story for the morning program. Not only did I talk to an entirely separate set of people in New York in this slot, but even within the bureau itself there was an obvious ostracism of those not numbered among the Rather disciples. Everything from copy paper to recording booths to desks was parceled out strictly according to caste.

It didn't take an efficiency expert to see the duplication. In this new age of budget awareness, it seemed contradictory that a layer of people had been imposed to serve Rather alone, a fact not lost on a delegation of new observers who arrived one day at the Barbados bureau: the business people. The money managers who tracked expenses sat silently at the news desk, making notes in their ledgers. It was the first time I had ever seen accountants in the field around a breaking story, there to monitor how on- and off-camera stars earned their salaries, especially the new wave of producers, in-house and on the scene.

Producers had become ubiquitous in TV news, for the most part people in their thirties and typical of the video-driven breed spawned by the vivid events of the 1960s. They arrived, not coincidentally, at a time when "underground" filmmakers were coming into their own. Like many of the new correspondent-anchors they served, these field producers had scant writing and reporting backgrounds, but they fit neatly in a business now obsessed with such gimmicks as Chiron machines, which could wipe and move and twist images on the screen, and dramatic pictures that filled Sauter's appetite for "moments."

At CBS particularly, the new producers—often referred to as "video kittens" if they happened to be women—moved in on the correspondents, determining the thrust of a story and often setting out to prove whatever hypothesis they had already formed. In "setting up" a future story, such as a series, the producer did the ground work and thus shaped the story from the start.

There were other forces chipping away at the correspondent. Although white-hot pokers wouldn't make them admit it, most of the producers yearned to be on-camera. Precious few made the jump, so most found compensation in controlling the correspondent's appearance on the screen: the stand-upper. With stars, there was no question of whether their on-camera passages made air, but below that level whether or not the correspondent's face was shown depended almost entirely on the producer in the editing room. In this world, power indeed.

But the new wave of field producers didn't stop there. If a correspondent was to be a star, he had to have daily exposure and usually didn't have time to report the whole story, to be in two places at the same time. Eager to win favor at CBS News, the producers, with management's ready blessing, jumped into the breach, directing the camera crews, doing the interviews, working out a story line, and sometimes even writing the script. Ultimately, the correspondent too often was left with no duties other than to record a narration for his "piece" and establish an on-camera personality. I don't exactly remember when the word *piece* began to mean something other than a story, but the term signaled the triumph of the picture, as though the series of images that connect a story had become an entity above it.

Because I was accustomed to working alone with a crew, the ascendancy of the producer brought me into a series of clashes, often resolved by someone like Lane intervening to tell me that we lived in a new world now (he was kind enough not to say "brave") and that hell-for-leather news coverage had evolved into a kinder and gentler business. Funny to hear him say it, this son of an old-style Chicago newspaper editor, an Irishman who could lose his temper at the drop of a comma. There were others, too, who did not suffer fools. If they were A-listers or anchors, absolution was automatic, such as that accorded Rather the day he stormed off the set when a tennis match cut into his broadcast, leaving the network black for six minutes. Tantrum for tantrum, I couldn't match that.

More worrisome to many of us was the "usage" chart that Joyce, ever the time-and-motion apostle, had created to keep track of the number of times correspondents appeared on the air. But how does a correspondent get on the air when his assignments are not airworthy, when he is covering a "part" of a story that one of the stars will wind up pulling together? It was piecework—strictly assembly line—and that didn't count on the charts. And if a reporter worked on a weekly show such as "Sunday Morning," how could his output be compared with that of the anointed working daily for Rather? Catch-22. Produce, or you're in trouble. But if in trouble, you can't produce.

Even given the best of circumstances—such as a seven-figure salary—most correspondents suffer from varying degrees of paranoia. In fact, there was no lack of real menace in that shark-tank world. So, in 1984, while it was considered important to have a campaign assignment, my persecution index went haywire when I was assigned to cover George McGovern. Surely, it was a symbolic matching of has-beens. Important candidates got important correspondents, unimportant candidates . . . but it was another offer I couldn't refuse. It wasn't enough that I had loathed every position McGovern had taken as the Democratic nominee in 1972, particularly against the war, but now I had to record weeks of his prissy moralizing, his yappy delivery.

"Many said in 1972 I was ahead of my time. Well, I'm back."

In the cold January air of New Hampshire, most thought McGovern's self-resurrection was a desperate last effort to position himself for a job in a Democratic administration. After all, he had lost his senatorial seat in the 1980 Reagan landslide. At sixty-one, he seemed a crass anachronism. Even former devotees were embarrassed, when not simply cynical, at the old maverick trying to raise his army once more.

Most of the time, I was the only reporter on the nostalgia trail. We tramped solitarily through the cold, black mud of Iowa, the soft snows of rural Massachusetts, and the greeting-card villages of New Hampshire. I was struck by McGovern's gentlemanly manner, almost a serenity. Sometimes he carried my luggage, and I knew it wasn't because he thought he would lead the "Evening News." We never discussed Vietnam, although wherever we went the now-middle-aged antiwar kids from the sixties turned out just to get a look at him again. He was part of something they cherished, and knowing that, he needed to reassure their old faith. I grew to like him enormously, admiring his grace and subtle humor, his old-fashioned decency.

It must have been gall for him to see Gary Hart, his 1972 campaign manager, sweep to victory in New Hampshire and pose a serious threat to Walter Mondale. McGovern disliked Hart, despite his gracious public support. At dinner one night he laid it out, saying it was not just Hart's ingratitude but his opportunism: "Gary is simply a very shallow man."

We ran into the Hart forces several times, and while the two candidates shook hands and exchanged polite chatter for the photographers, campaign reporters shared the latest dope. Even then rumors of Hart's philandering kept surfacing, but no one dared, or could verify the hearsay. Still, the tales fitted in with his conscious aping of the Kennedy style—hand in the pocket or pulling at the tie, the studied, distant air, punctuated by boyish grins. Only one detail seemed incongruous yet somehow pulled the picture into focus: his trendy leather boots, more cowboy than Kennedy. Never trust a man who wears boots.

McGovern worked valiantly at trying to regenerate his antiwar stand of the seventies by opposition to American involvement in Lebanon and Central America, but it didn't catch fire. His call for a 25 percent reduction in the military budget set him apart from the other candidates—from the voters, too. His demand for a freeze on nuclear weapons sounded tired. Yet, despite his empty file of issues, McGovern's literacy, ease, and eloquence imparted a tone to the Democratic effort. Whatever it was that drove him—a yearning for respect, a stab at rehabilitation—I had to admire his quiet acceptance of the scant crowds and sarcastic asides, and, most bitter perhaps, the knowledge that his time had passed. Still he clung to his quest. There we were, relics from the wars of the sixties, on a lonely stump across America, trying to find the magic again.

Back on duty at the Broadcast Center, I had a sense of corners rounded, bridges crossed, the clarity and purpose of being a reporter dissolving into the politics and setbacks of a career slowly veering off the track. One truly low point was that afternoon in Venice, California, when I stood surrounded by grunting body builders in Gold's Gym as they offered their monosyllabic thoughts on muscle tension. From foreign affairs to a story on women who pumped iron.

With middle age came a realization of the world slowing down. As the traditional guideposts of career disappeared, so too did the familiar faces of old friends: Jeanie, my old college roommate who ran with the bulls in Spain, had drunk herself to death and was buried in a cemetery outside Madrid on the road to Andalusia; the handsome American expatriate of my London years had also succumbed to red wine, never living to complete his novel. But it was the death of George Barrett that struck the hardest, perhaps because it came not just as the passing of a friend and mentor but as an augury of the times, the solemn portent of a winding down.

The night before he died I stood by his bed at Lenox Hill Hospital as he gasped for air, mercifully unconscious, withered by Parkinson's disease. Visiting him over the months before, I had learned his last lesson in reporting. Not once did I hear him curse the disease or his fate. Instead, he was observing, learning the course of destruction, studying the terrifying effects of the experimental drugs. Even as his body and mind yielded, George remained the consummate reporter: fascinated and humble before what he did not understand.

It is always wrenching to lose a friend, to discover suddenly that one who has been in your corner all along is slipping away, that the coaching and complimenting and, most selfless of all, the listening must have their end. Arriving in airports with no one to say hello, departing from airports with no one to say good-bye—that's what George had said this business was all about seventeen years earlier, seeing me off on my first journey to Vietnam. Now, suddenly, I was preparing to go back. I left for the airport in an April rain, once more living the bitter truth of his words.

15

ENEMIES:
OLD
AND NEW

*T*he Thai Airways 727 pitched and yawed through the heavy skies of the South China Sea. It was monsoon season, and the familiar stacks of bursting clouds evoked memories of countless blind, steep landings and takeoffs when the bad guys were shooting at us and the cover of those clouds was like a mother's arms. Jake's words came back to me like an old prayer from a forgotten missal: "You will always wind up here one way or another, no matter where you go in between. The land of black and gold is like a needle, and you find yourself needing that shot again and again just when you thought the memories had slipped from your mind forever."

The assignment was a fluke, a trade-off, and it had started four months earlier when the foreign editor, Sam Roberts, called me into his broom closet office in the newsroom and closed the door.

"I've gotten you out of some scrapes in the past, and saved your ass a few times, haven't I?"

"Yes," I said, shocked and puzzled. "Look, just tell me what you want me to do."

"We hear you know someone who's very tight with the Vietnamese. Quite frankly, the people from the Cronkite documentary unit have fucked everything up by dealing with the Viets independently, and now the news side is getting shut out. We're in deep trouble on getting visas to cover the anniversary. Can you help me?"

I really thought he was going to cry. Here he was being paid to make Dan Rather look good, and the Cronkiters—that small band of elite outcasts who toiled for the old order—were stealing his thunder. Classic television politics, the territorial imperative.

Even more disheartening, the routine business of keeping in touch with sources—in this case at least knowing who did what in the Vietnamese mission to the UN—had been abandoned. The journalistic basics that you learn as a cub reporter had long ago given way to a preoccupation with the accelerating technology of television and an obsession with on-screen appearance. It was catch-up time. Nobody had been paying any attention to the Vietnamese—and now we needed them. All three networks were planning special coverage for the tenth anniversary of the fall of Saigon, and CBS was getting the runaround on entry permits. In a display of hard-nosed quid pro quo, Roberts told me if I produced visas for the CBS people, I would have a slot on the team.

I picked up the phone fast, which is often how one sets out to chase a story, and learned that NBC News was planning to broadcast live from Ho Chi Minh City, ready to move in with 100 people and equipment enough to refight the war. To make matters worse, a few of the boys at 30 Rock, exiles from CBS, were approaching the assignment with more than usual relish. There were old scores to settle. I had a leaden feeling, but eventually my old contacts came through. So did the visas, and once again I was off to the Far East.

As the cloud cover dissipated, a dozen or so journalists—all veterans of the Southeast Asian wars—pressed their faces to the windows. The deep green velvet foliage and the red dust were still there, and even the bomb craters. It was all a dream. And time had not passed—this was just the next mission in an unending war.

We all had our memories. Bruce Dunning, sitting beside me, could remember boarding the last desperate flight out of Da Nang ten years earlier, when American civilians had to push and kick panicked

South Vietnamese to the ground as they struggled to get on an already overloaded plane. The Communists were coming. And the Americans were leaving. Bruce, then a CBS correspondent, reported and wrote a classic of TV news. But when the new regime took over at CBS, he was a victim, taken off the air and turned into a field producer because the new executive "team" didn't think he sounded masculine enough. And so here we were, two old soldiers who wouldn't fade away.

Hanoi's Gia Lam Airport was a wasteland. There was only one other airplane moving, returning Vietnamese students from a vacation somewhere in the Eastern bloc, the only place they were allowed to go. Nothing else was in motion. The small, shabby terminal was the same one I remembered from another time when haggard and expressionless American fliers lined up to hear their names called, crossing the tarmac to planes that took them out of numbing captivity, some after eight years of torture and isolation.

The customs officials were very young, and I would soon come to realize that only very young, or very old men, cripples, or children, were left in North Vietnam. Generations of war had wiped out most who would be in their twenties, thirties, or forties. Had we really lost? I asked myself. But the thought was checked by the heavy construction machinery dotting the landscape along the bumpy road to the capital. Bridges, railroads, dams, power lines—the Russians were setting up the infrastructure for their beholden client.

Yet something seemed to be getting in the way as I scanned the countryside from our rickety bus. Telephone wires superimposed themselves on the primitive landscape of Tonkin. The modern world was creeping in. Still, unconsciously, I found myself looking for the telltale signs of land mines always coupled in memory with any road in Vietnam. Past and present kept blending.

The Thang Loi Hotel stood on stilts in a marsh at the city's edge. The Cubans had contributed this one-story horror in the name of Communist solidarity. Here the Vietnamese housed all Western guests. It was too far from the city to walk—no taxis, buses, or private cars—so we had to resort to government cars manned by government drivers, accompanied, of course, by two interpreters (or "keepers") from the Ministry of Foreign Affairs: Quan, a gentle, pint-sized bureaucrat, who carried around books by Hemingway and Fitzgerald, and Bich, a beautiful young dragon lady type who wore blue jeans like Cheryl Tiegs and spoke English and Russian like one of James Bond's shady ladies.

The air, thick from charcoal fires, hung like an acrid miasma over the Thang Loi, mixing with the foul odors of swamp rising from beneath the building. Mosquitoes as big as quarters joined the chorus of things that went splash in the night directly below. Apart from the American and European press, several large groups of Russians and East Germans stomped through the dining room, understandably curious about us since they still lived in the shadow of the Berlin Wall.

In the midst of this cultural whirlpool sat a small group of men more noticeable for their silence than their discourse. Five war veterans from the JCRC (Joint Casualty Resolution Commission), assigned to recover missing American servicemen, had flown in with us. This was one of their routine visits, which entailed sitting opposite a battery of Vietnamese officials to request information about MIAs. The usual response: a smile and little else. This time, however, under the eyes of the Western press, the Communist government decided to throw them a tidbit—a visit to a B-52 crash site about fourteen kilometers outside Hanoi. Not unexpectedly, correspondents and photographers were invited, too. The "other side" had not lost its touch for manipulating the media, television in particular; nor had we lost ours for allowing it. Even more humiliating, we were dropping dollars wherever we went. They wanted "green" for everything. Lots of it, from the boys who loaded the TV equipment cases to the Foreign Ministry officials in charge of visiting press. The name of the game was extortion or—in diplomatic parlance—"service fees," and although New York fumed, there was nothing it could do but pay under protest. Hanoi's forces were still winning.

On our second afternoon, a motorcade carrying the three American network teams plus print reporters headed for the hamlet of Yen Thuong, where a B-52 was said to have crashed on the night of December 20, 1972. Our group included the quiet men from the JCRC, who collected names, dates, coordinates, bone fragments, and sightings and interviewed defectors and former POWs—assembling all the pieces that might one day resolve the puzzles of the men who vanished. For them, this was just an outing. There was little they could do without equipment to dig at the site and study soil and debris. In effect, they were being put on parade for us. As far as we were concerned, a trip to a crash site for any reason was a story, however contrived—a point I made in my report.

The Vietnamese had all the major characters at the ready: a woman whose husband and child were said to have been among the eleven villagers killed when the burning airplane fell; an official to say that two of the six-man air crew had parachuted to safety, been taken prisoner, and repatriated under the general release the following year; a man who said that he had seen the crash and, after the fire burned out, what was left in a twenty-six-foot crater: shaving equipment, eyeglasses, and a human arm. I watched as the tall figure of Major John Webb moved through the flower garden that had grown over the unplanned grave. My throat tightened, and I realized time had not absorbed my emotional involvement with this country.

Later that day, we went to the Hanoi airport to ship the story on an outgoing flight. Standing in front of the terminal, George Lewis of NBC News, another old war hand, was listening to his shortwave radio, aiming the aerial into space. Suddenly, he reminded me of the forward air controllers with their field radios. "Hey, George," I yelled out. "Do you think you could manage to call in an air strike?" We both laughed, nervously.

One day in town I managed to slip the keepers and went for a stroll down the old, wide boulevards built by the French. The cracking yellow plaster of the colonial buildings still dominated the view, but here and there an Eastern bloc architectural statement angrily stabbed at the sky. Men in military uniforms seemed to be everywhere, either getting ready to ship out for the Cambodian border or training in one of the hill camps. Military life was still the prime occupation for Vietnamese. Food was pitifully scarce, medicine almost nonexistent, but they had the fourth-largest army in the world.

Nevertheless, Hanoi seemed unchanged, suspended. Nothing was really happening. The slim, hard shape and look of the people told me they were still waiting for the payoff. As in most revolutionary states, political murals adorned the public buildings. On one, painters were in the very act of creating a brightly colored host of implausibly happy workers. As I walked in for a look, an old man in shorts and sandals, leaning on a cane, rose slowly from his chair, his leathery face sheltered by a pith helmet. He smiled with great dignity and deference, this figure from another time, and seemed genuinely pleased to see me. Then, in French, he asked if I would like to sit down or perhaps be shown around. The Communists may have discouraged French as a legacy of imperialism, but all the years of war had not changed his courtliness and manners, formed in the meeting of two formalist cultures. I stayed awhile, and when I finally left, he seemed disappointed, as though the echo of a gentler life he once knew had broken his isolation for just a moment.

We arrived in Ho Chi Minh City, lately Saigon, on the morning of April 20, under a merciless Asian sun. An alumni reunion spirit pervaded the group of some 200 newspeople, many of whom hadn't seen each other since the last helicopter had lifted from the American embassy roof in the final days of the war. By the time I wrote a "scene-setter" for radio in my hotel room, the monsoon had wrapped the city in its cloud of steam. From the very beginning, the Vietnamese were mystified by our pilgrimage. Why were so many Americans interested in coming here to mark their defeat? Resisting the temptation to debate "defeat," most of us would simply say it was a good yarn, that we were journalists first. The American habit of public self-criticism was the point at which we became inscrutable to the Vietnamese mind—and most others, too.

We had returned to Saigon, "that mystical violent state of mind where young reporters learned about the war and themselves." And even as I spoke that line into my tape recorder, there were knocks on the door and calls that actually made it through the hotel's tangled switchboard to make contact again after so long: Peter Arnett, now a CNN correspondent, then a Pulitzer Prize–winning Associated Press reporter; Garrick Utley, my former colleague from NBC in London, who had opened the network's Saigon bureau; Ted Koppel, now a superstar, then a virtually unknown ABC line reporter; Eddie Adams, Time's Pulitzer Prize winner, who had taken the picture of General Loan shooting a Vietcong suspect through the head; Richard Threlkeld, still with CBS; Tim Paige, a British photographer, who carried a steel plate in his head to remind him of the war; Neil Davis of NBC, who three months from this reunion would be killed by tank fire while taking pictures in the streets of Bangkok. Some hadn't been able to return because of other assignments, and then there were those of whom no one spoke but all remembered—the fifty or so dead or missing: Welles Hangen, Sean Flynn, Peter Bellendorf, Howard Tuckner, and the rest.

Tu Do Street was a ghostly sight—a street of dreams, mostly broken, where once green-clad GIs bought girls and trinkets, and the neon lights invited all in to forget the war. Under French rule, it had been the rue Catinat, and some said that after the fall of Dien Bien Phu and the clear ending of their war in Vietnam, French paratroopers had marched down the avenue one last time in the early morning darkness, singing "Je ne regrette rien." A vainglorious tale, perhaps, but so much more dignified than fighting your way onto the last helicopter.

The Silence. It was the silence of the streets and the sullenness of the people that held you, no more the electricity generated by the unpredictable, no more the sense of danger, no more the grace and hope of the Saigonese. Hanoi's southern arm had cleaned up the gutters and moved the beggars out in preparation for our arrival and the big victory parade. But they couldn't hide it all, of course: the former bar girls now working in the souvenir shops along Tu Do Street; the beggar children sneaking back at 3 A.M. to sleep in the doorways; the women—even the hotel chambermaid—whispering as they passed, "Americans stay this time?" Each of us had memories and would search them out. The high-ceilinged room that had been my home at the old Continental Hotel, the dark and cool comfort of the NBC office, the French ladies' shop with the naughty lingerie, the crippled beggar girl in Lam Son Square selling Salem cigarettes from a tray around her neck, the house where the rocket hit. Gone.

Cars, taxis, and motor scooters gone, too, along with the airplanes silhouetted against a turquoise sky and the hollow clapping of the helicopters that went to the pit of your stomach. But there was something wrong with the picture, something else missing: the American Presence. The figures in the painting had disappeared and left only the background.

Three minutes on foot from the Palace Hotel, where CBS was deployed—all five of us—stood the Majestic Hotel, where the hordes of NBC and ABC people had consumed every room. In the old days, the Majestic was an elegant sight perched on the banks of the Saigon River. This year it meant rats. Lots of them. A few of my floormates at the Palace had been visited by the creatures while asleep, but at the Majestic they formed armies of the night. One cameraman was bitten, and rabies vaccine was flown in. I slept with the light on—and a towel stuffed in my door slats.

The Mad Hatter's Tea Party was soon under way, and as technicians busied themselves with setting up their giant satellite dish and overcoming the Viet-American technology gap, the reporters and crews made their story requests. One just didn't run out and start taping in Saigon. All transportation was controlled by the government, except for cyclos—men on bicycles pulling passengers in attached carriages—and these couldn't get you very far.

The most popular requests were for permission to visit the old demilitarized zone that once separated north and south; Tan Son Nhut Airport, once an American military base as well as the main arrivals terminal for civilians; and Cam Ranh Bay, now a Russian naval base. Instead, we were pressed into trips to the war museum, where POW artifacts were a hot item, and an old weapons repair factory run by the Vietcong (right under the Americans' long noses). Officials actively encouraged interviews with "heroes of the people," such as former double agents who had risked life and limb for Uncle Ho. Many of us requested a meeting with General Vo Nguyen Giap, Hanoi's military mastermind, only to be told repeatedly that he was "ill." In fact, Giap had cautioned the regime against its push into Cambodia and consequently become a nonperson. Even in the war museum, one had to look hard to find his only picture.

There was a special irony in the stringent control over our movements. During the war, no censorship had been imposed, and in spite of or perhaps because of that, the American effort took a beating. The majority opinion—that the war was wrong and even immoral—played into the enemy's hands. Now here they were, the "liberators," imposing almost complete censorship simply by restricting our movements, and charging us for it. I could read the confusion in the faces of my fellow newsmen. Telling the truth is difficult when you can't find it.

As for the networks, NBC was busily broadcasting part of its "Today" show live from Vietnam, starring Bryant Gumbel on a platform behind the old presidential palace. The news pickings were so slim for "live coverage" that the mayor of Saigon was a guest one morning. And, of course, interviewing other reporters—a sure sign that all is lost—filled much of the air time. Koppel even did a "Nightline" from Saigon. CBS had settled mainly for think pieces—stories, longer than daily reports, that put events in perspective—first with Cronkite, then with Bob Simon, finally with me. Sam Roberts said that the brass didn't want to "overkill" this strange occasion. CBS was taking the high road. Truly, the tenth anniversary of Saigon's collapse didn't deserve the circus coverage that was designed to promote ratings, but it was more likely that CBS held off for other reasons: a budget about to collapse, a grave delay in getting its act together, and gross miscalculation of the opposition. It was a giggle to watch the executives telling anyone who would listen they had "made the right decision about the Vietnam coverage."

Ours was a beleaguered little band. Bruce Dunning found himself hounded to death by the Vietnamese importunities for money, which they viewed as war reparations, and the technical and logistical demands of coverage. Outmanned we might have been, but determined not to be outdone. So we just did our job. One of our stories centered on the old South Vietnamese military cemetery, its war memorial smashed and countless graves desecrated and looted. Another explained how Western journalists were being force-fed the glories of Communist triumph as they bitched and moaned to roam free. We kept sending our stories, and the "CBS Weekend News" and the "CBS Morning News" kept using them.

As for the Rather people, they said flatly they were interested only in the victory parade. Bruce and I remained philosophical. We were getting very little help from New York. Most of our telexes went unanswered; the few that were came from a desk assistant whose foreign experience seemed to have ended at the Bronx county line. "We're going to make it work," Bruce said. "And we're going to do it alone."

Every day, the rains came—promptly at 3:30 P.M.—just as they always had, usually ruining the shooting schedule if delays in waiting for interpreters and assorted officials hadn't. One morning we were told that we could actually shoot some pictures of Tan Son Nhut Airport. It was pouring by the time the bureaucracy had been un-threaded. I was working on a script for another story, so we agreed that the crew would go off to shoot by itself. Perhaps the tape could be filler for another piece.

Two hours later, Derek Williams returned with one of the most haunting sequences ever taken in Vietnam. The steady beat of rain and the deep grayness of the atmosphere was made yet more melancholy by the acres of American aircraft abandoned in the final days. The difference between a sunny day and a rainy one in Vietnam is like the contrast between Technicolor and black and white; the green and gold are drained into mist. And if some movies succeed only in black and white, this was surely one of them.

"Maybe the anchorman can write a little essay over the pictures in New York," said Derek. The remark was, at best, a put-down and another example of how the power of the imperial anchor pervaded network thinking. It was a weekend, and I had a piece planned already, but I couldn't resist. "Let me give it a try," I said cheerily, as though I had just landed my first job. I sat down and wrote about what was once the world's busiest airport, when you could hear the roar and screech of fighter jets and squint through the downdraft of helicopters. In those days, the air was thick with the smell of firepower and gasoline, and GIs with a dozen accents arrived to begin their time in a terrifying place.

New York gave it a minute—for remembrance.

The last sigh on this sentimental journey was to be the climactic parade, a May Day–type military jamboree along the same route the

North Vietnamese tanks had taken when they entered the doomed city in 1975. This was our guaranteed evening news piece, the one with Dan Rather's chop on it. It was also cut-and-dried, eminently forgettable routine hard news. As it turned out, the Saigonese were still so full of hostility for the North Vietnamese that they refused to cheer, and the parade flopped into spectacular sullenness. That would have made a better story, except that it came as no surprise. The world knew about the boat people.

Before leaving the States, I had talked with Northshield about stories I could do for "Sunday Morning." "Anything you want me to do over there?" I asked, knowing that no one from the executive side would have thought to consult the Kuralt show, a kind of sissy sister to the hard-news boys: precious, but unimportant.

"Yeah," he said, walking away. "Anything that has an American angle. How about Amerasians?"

While the thrust of our activity had been in anticipation of the parade, I was determined to find an Amerasian child. That the audience for "Sunday Morning" was the smallest of any CBS News broadcast concerned me little; it was the best. The trouble was that even talking to Amerasians could get them arrested or sent to a "reeducation camp"; we had to sneak pictures and a few quick interviews with Amerasian children near the old military bases. But how was I going to find *the* one to zero in on? I had submitted a request to meet such a child right from the start—and the answer never came, which meant no, or maybe she'll go away. Then one afternoon, Bruce, the crew, and I drove with our keeper, Mr. Quan, to Cholon, the Chinese quarter of the city, for pictures of market crowds and general atmosphere. While the crew was shooting, I noticed a slim young man with blue eyes and sandy-colored hair staring fixedly at us. He moved with the casual lankiness of an American teenager. Bruce nudged me. "Yeah," I said. "I see him—and he's perfect." I was aching with frustration, knowing one approach would endanger him in a society where Amerasians were already outcasts and nothing escapes the eyes of the party's neighborhood block captains.

But the boy continued to stare, and I decided to risk it. "Look, Quan," I implored our interpreter. "I know the rules about Amerasians, but I just want to talk to him for a bit—without a camera. Please—be a good guy."

Quan swung into the spirit of the moment, as he often did, and from his translation we got the boy's name and address and learned that his Vietnamese mother and American father were in the States.

As we spoke, the boy never took his eyes off us, as though he wanted to say something else, but couldn't right now. The locals began to gather, and Quan was clearly nervous, so we left, telling the boy that we might return.

I was jubilant but brought down to earth by the knowledge that getting anywhere near him with a camera would require official permission. For five solid days I bullied every official within reach, while Bruce did the good-guy routine—easy for him, he had gone to Princeton. The day before we left Vietnam—a Sunday—we got the go signal to interview the boy on camera.

His name was Nguyen Thanh My, the "My" meaning "American." At nineteen, he was working in a small commune, cutting wood for export to the Soviet Union. We shot pictures of him at his job and it was clear everyone involved had been briefed and cleaned up—each worker had a shiny new hard hat and a clean shirt. And My, who had been wearing only dirty trousers and shoes when we met, appeared in a clean white shirt and laundered pants. Then we walked to his aunt's two-room house, where he lived with four young cousins. There, we asked about her sister, My's mother, Hoa, and she showed us some letters Hoa had sent to her from California.

To find Hoa didn't look so difficult at that juncture. Chances of finding the father I rated about minus one on a scale of ten. Like a recovering junkie, I decided to take one day at a time. For the moment, here was Nguyen Thanh My, saying on camera how he longed to see his parents, especially his father—even though his mother did not remember the man's last name. My had applied for a U.S. visa a few years earlier and was still waiting. Above all, he wanted out, wondering—on camera—why his mother had left him behind. "I will find my father when I get to America," he said with heartbreaking certainty.

The story had everything and I knew it. We spent a few more hours taping, talking to relatives, and examining all the documents involved in their application to go to America. Then we packed up. I managed to slip some money to My and his aunt while the various neighborhood spies were distracted, and we said our goodbyes. I'll never forget how My looked. Without saying it, I knew he was telling me that his dreams of leaving, of finding his mother and father, of living in America, all hinged on us. I had a feeling that the end of this story would be long in coming.

As we prepared to leave Saigon, the telex spat forth a message from Sam Roberts, the foreign editor in New York: one of those "Nice work, guys" messages addressed to "all hands," what they call a "hero-gram" in TV news. Bruce and I looked at each other, exhausted from too little sleep, hungry for real food, frazzled from a thousand crises, and now deflated by this. "Is that the best he could do?" I asked sarcastically.

"Let's face it, Liz," Bruce said. "We didn't fail—and this is the payoff."

"No, we didn't fail," I answered, "but that half-assed telex tells me they wish we had." I found myself remembering the old French adage about gratitude being "the memory of the heart." But at the mean and militant court of Dan Rather, favors from the unknighted went un-returned.

Shortly after arriving back in New York, I began the search for My's parents. Northshield was indulgent about "your Amerasian" and not without a modicum of faith as I began the hunt. Locating the mother, Hoa, was not difficult since I had the return address on her letters to the aunt in Saigon. She was working as an inspector in a small electronics plant and living in a sunny house with a swimming pool in Simi Valley, California. It appeared comfortable, but like so many other Vietnamese women, her life had been shaped by violence and separation. Not only was My left behind in Vietnam, but she had two more sons with her in California: a twenty-one-year-old by a Viet-namese husband killed in the war and a twelve-year-old from marriage to an American captain whom she had divorced.

She was forty-four now, her lustrous black hair cut medium length and graying, her black satin pants concealing a fuller but still attrac-tive figure. Over plates of fragrant rice in her kitchen, I asked her about My's father, but like everything else about that country, the story was complicated and tragic. Hoa had worked as a maid for an American couple in Dalat in the early 1960s when the buildup went into high gear. At that point, American officials were allowed to have their wives in-country. The man's name was Dick. His wife left Viet-nam and they eventually divorced, but in the meantime Dick and Hoa lived together, and Hoa became pregnant. Dick was rotated out in 1965, and they said goodbye for what they thought was forever. Ten days later, My was born, one more *bui doi*—child of the dust. Then, when My was three, Hoa went to the States to visit an American captain she had met during the war. They married, and soon her plans to return home to bring My back to the States became academic: Saigon fell.

Only scant evidence of My's father's identity emerged from our long conversations. Over and over I asked her to recall the slightest detail of Dick's appearance or movements, anything to know where to start looking. Little surfaced. His name was Dick, he was tall, he wore glasses, he wore no uniform, he had a beard. It seemed impossible, and indeed it would have been had he been stationed in a larger town, like Saigon. But in Dalat, in the early 1960s (Hoa was uncertain just when), there were just so many American civilians.

I went to Washington and began working the corridors of the State Department, looking for former spooks, advisers, diplomats, anyone who wanted to find ancestry for an Amerasian child. Three weeks went by. I was convinced that I had talked to every contract construction worker who had ever been within 1,000 miles of Southeast Asia. Then, just as determination began to waver, I called a long-retired U.S. adviser now living in Florida. He vaguely remembered a man who might fit the description and offered a partial last name. I made a quick cross-check in the State Department's library and came up with a name that seemed to fit the description: beard, eyeglasses, tall. I asked Hoa if she recognized it; the last name meant nothing to her, nor even the first. Somehow, she had lived more than a decade in this country without realizing Dick and Richard were the same. But it was all I had.

So many government workers retire into the leafy security of the D.C. suburbs that it seemed reasonable that a systematic check of the area codes might yield his name. That didn't lead anywhere, so I tried a different spelling. It worked. Late one evening, I traced him to Maryland, took a deep breath, called him, and told my story, ending, "And she says you're the father."

War requires bravery of men—the kind that is obvious and sometimes glamorous—but to admit to fathering and abandoning a child demands a quiet courage, for which there are no medals. A long pause. A sigh. And then a hoarse voice said, "I probably am."

Now came the hard part, getting him to agree to an interview on camera. After a week's reflection, a few more phone calls, and an honest inducement that the piece could influence the Hanoi government, he agreed. And so on the air went father in semiofficial Maryland, mother in manicured Simi Valley, and son in the dusty alleys of Saigon, a triangle united by blood but blown apart by the storm of time. It was a story told a thousand times, a legacy of scarred innocents and a romance ignited and burned out by the aphrodisiac of war. But we hoped our piece might somehow make a difference once Hoa and Dick were reunited, at least by telephone. As for My, despite

Hoa's and Dick's efforts to cut through the murky depths of foreign policy and Vietnamese intrigue, he remained in Saigon, a young man hanging on to his dream of coming to America.

"Joyce thinks you did a great job, so stop bitching."

That was Buksbaum's advice when I returned from Vietnam and got caught up in negotiations for a new contract. No reward was offered for my work, and even my agent let me know gently we were not dealing from strength without an offer from another network. Middle-aged lady line reporters are not exactly hot commodities in the internecine bidding battles. Still, in the charged atmosphere, it was guaranteed work. I signed.

It didn't take a management consultant to descry that at CBS in 1985, the controlling ethic of the decade—get what you can for yourself—was being zealously pursued by Harvard Business School grads applying new management skills with old-fashioned Sicilian justice. "Keep your friends close and your enemies closer." Just as the Westmoreland libel case wound to its close, raising the question of CBS News's credibility, takeover mania focused on the company, endangering its very solvency. Fairness in Media, a conservative group driven by Senator Jesse Helms of North Carolina, who swore he would become Dan Rather's boss, threatened a proxy fight for seats on the CBS board. The threat collapsed, but turmoil swept through the organization. That wasn't all. The nerveless Ted Turner of CNN, cable TV's Rhett Butler, tendered for the corporation. CBS fought him off and won a Pyrrhic victory with a recapitalization plan that bought back 21 percent of its own stock but loaded the company with a debt of almost $1 billion.

Turbulence in the marketplace struck hard at contracts up for renewal; word was out to hold down all increases to 7 percent—except for the sparkling dozen or so with star status. Ed Joyce later wrote that in those days of going for the gold, management's terror that the stars would defect to another network resulted in "less than twenty per cent of the people who were under contract at CBS News earning more than half of the huge talent payroll."

In hindsight, it is difficult to imagine how so many people adept at analyzing news understood so little about the economic forces determining their careers. For most of us, figuring out where we stood with management was like studying the appearances of the Central Committee to divine Soviet policy. We were watching shadows through a scrim, an executive rite whose sacrifices were human, not economic.

Management did have its reasons to retrench. Audiences for all three networks were falling dramatically; advertising revenue had slowed; cable and independent stations had entered the game; new technology made pictures once controlled by the networks available to all; and local stations didn't really need the big boys anymore to survive. It was time for major surgery, and the free-spending news department was a logical target. The days of Fat City were coming to an end. When it was all over, the million-dollar kids would survive, the rank and file would be gutted—and the ineluctable spirit of corporate greed would wring huge profits in the fray.

Apprehensive about my own future, I had been trying to get a lunch date with Buksbaum, but his schedule seemed busier than ever. Finally, it was set for September 19, with the usual proviso that we would check each other that morning. My phone was ringing as I left for the office. It was Elsie, Buksbaum's secretary, the brassy and wise kind of boss's right hand expected in New York offices B.L. (Before Lib). "He wants you to come to his office," she said, "as soon as you get in."

"Lunch is on then?"

"I don't know. Just come in."

Strange. My innate paranoia leapt to the multiplying rumors of layoffs, but the very day before my agent had told me to cool it. After all, hadn't I just signed a new contract? It made sense in my head but not to the little voice that I listened to on stories when I felt that something was about to give or that somebody was equivocating.

On the way to Buksbaum's office, there in the hallway—an apparition in the dark—loomed the figure of Ed Joyce. "Good morning, Ed," I said brightly, noting the sunken chest under the wide red braces, a vogue which Joyce, like Rather, had in common with the bull-market babies of Wall Street. His eyes skated over me in a millisecond and fastened on the floor. He grunted something as he quickened his pace. What have we here, I wondered? My stomach turned over. Pull yourself together, lady.

Elsie didn't have a chance to announce me; Buksbaum was on his feet gesturing wildly for me to come into his office. He looked ashen; deep lines began at the top of his cheeks and creased down to his mouth.

"What's up? You on for lunch?" I flopped into a chair in front of his desk.

"You're fired," he said.

I said nothing.

"They wanted me to tell you because they know we're—we're—"

"Friends," I said.

Arms outstretched, head tilted, he reminded me of a second-rate lawyer pleading a hopeless case. "I did everything I could to stop it—everything."

"Why?" I said, staring. "Reasons?"

"It's a budget cut. You're one of many."

"And how did I get on the list?"

He dropped his chin and began rubbing his eyes. No answer.

I stood up. "Forget it," I said.

He held out three sheets of paper stapled together. "This explains what your benefits and severance are. They want you to clean your desk out by tonight."

I grabbed the papers and left.

By the time I got to my office the names of the people on the hit list had whizzed through the building. Lew Allison, an old friend from NBC Saigon called, suggesting lunch. "I don't think you should be seen with me," I said, "not in this atmosphere."

"Screw 'em," he said, the roughest language I'd ever heard him use.

That night, I asked a friend to dinner at the "21" Club and charged it to CBS. The next day, the press, already alert with a certain schadenfreude for the first ongoing soap opera *within* a network, called it the most severe cutback ever to strike a news division. Ten percent of the 1,250-person news staff bit the dust to shave $6 million from the budget. Joyce had issued a tough-guy memo to explain the purge, rewritten by one of the old-liners to "make it more human": "This is not a happy day. But I am convinced that by acting as we have today we can avoid similar traumas in the future."

He was wrong; it was only the beginning. Within two years, hundreds more would be forced from the company, including Sauter, Joyce, Wyman, and the rest of the glory boys who had reduced a news institution to just another station.

One small detail emerged as I left CBS, the kind of last-minute touch that bad novelists invent when forced to provide an upbeat ending. The CBS business and legal people had neglected to notice that my four-year contract contained no "cycles"—set intervals at which the company could exercise an option to bow out. An oversight, no doubt, but it wasn't there. They owed me. An old friend rushed to my aid, Raoul Lionel Felder, a combative attorney known for his sensational divorce cases. That's what this was, after all. A painful and petty arbitration followed, and with Raoul at the point of my lance, CBS finally met its obligations. Later, friends told me the "Trotta clause" was being checked carefully in all future CBS contract negotiations. It was the kind of ending Don Corleone himself would have ordered.

Ex-CBSers were still denouncing Joyce when the pit opened under him in the executive jungle three months later. Those who found the body said it bore the toothmarks of a well-known anchorman. I thought back to that conversation with Rather, particularly his impression that I had crossed Joyce long ago. It took a while before a hazy memory surfaced: Chappaquiddick, 1969. The ferretlike skinny guy in the too-big Madras jacket, darting around with his radio mike, was the young Ed Joyce of WCBS radio news in New York, vacationing on the Cape when the story broke. An ambitious Joyce, trying to pass as an old New Englander, stampeded by a flying wedge of network reporters hot on the Kennedy-Kopechne story. Dim visions surfaced of this little man getting the shaft, pushed aside by the TV people, most probably myself included. So that's where it started! I had to laugh. Of course I couldn't be sure, but TV life being what it is at the top—a list of grudges, a pile of old scores, envies burning in a ring of fire—it made sense. Blood oaths of loyalty or revenge are sworn fast and not forgotten.

FROM TV news correspondent to TV news viewer was a brutal transmigration. I sat back and watched like the rest of the nation. A cottage industry of people who cursed TV news as entertainment had already emerged, and although the charge had merit, it was a sobering discovery in my postcorrespondent life. But there was one merciful difference. Unlike old movie stars, my retired colleagues and I were spared the surprise of seeing ourselves on the late show.

Politics and football, Gene McCarthy once said, showcasing his customary nihilism, are in the hands of very similar people, really: "Those who run it are smart enough to understand the game and dumb enough to think it's important." It was withering to think how that remark applied to all of us in TV news who at some time or another surely thought our stories were Holy Writ transmitted. But such self-deceptions common to any profession seemed harmless alongside the pontifical authority with which networks had invested in the anchors.

Deadly serious. Even more surprising was how so many thought networks could detect some special qualities of judgment and insight in
those tapped for fame. It was a subject treated with much throat-
clearing and pompous claims to esoteric knowledge by the decision-
makers. In fact, the selection of talent was made on the basis of such
trade phrases as "gut feelings" and "chemistry" and "believability" and
the usual slogans coughed up by market research. It was a completely
personal—and random—process that nobody within TV news circles
really talked about, especially in public.

The dazzling prestige of these featured players boggled my understanding. Just to be "seen" conferred enough authority to distill the
meaning of the dollar's fluctuations, understand the character of the
French electorate, or read the Kabuki poses of Japanese trade officials.
As a viewer, I followed the barrage of promotion for the stars, their
alleged trustworthiness and uncompromising virtues trotted out for
sale like so many ingredients in a fabric softener. Could it be that
management suspected that fewer and fewer people believed its cre-
ations? Or perhaps they had forgotten that canonization is not expo-
sition. Moving anchors around—to London, to Paris, to a cornfield in
Iowa—certified the importance of a story, at least in the minds of Fish
Bowlers. These unanchored anchors must be where it was happening;
a reporter wasn't enough, went the reasoning. The public wanted their
news stars *at* the story. It was fascinating viewing: three well-dressed
gentlemen running a global steeplechase for the hearts and minds of a
shrinking network TV audience.

How anchors looked—clothes, tone, and pitch—had kept pace
with the world of amusement. Watching old movies from my viewer's
chair, I realized that, like yesterday's film stars, TV reporters prior to
the 1970s bore a shocking resemblance to real people. The good-
natured moon face of a Cronkite, instead of the coast-to-coast square
jaw; the "permed hair" of a few ladies, instead of the lustrous lion's
mane.

Sartorial glamour was now pursued with the earnestness of a Re-
gency fop. For men, the standard blue shirt and dark jacket had given
way to the regulation chic of a pin-striped Washingtonian suit and
Lord Fauntleroy shirt, emphasized with red tie and matching pochette.
Women, like Mesopotamian princesses, tended to gold chokers and
Krugerrand-size earrings sparkling over Armani silk or fussy-sexy frills.
"Where are they going?" I finally asked an old producer friend.

"Not out on stories," he said.

A new blasé, breezy style of news delivery soon evolved into a singsongy, mock-serious rendition of world events. For slaughter in Romanian streets, furrowed brows; for newborn pandas, a smile to show personal warmth or a set of new caps; for Vietnam memory lane stuff, a faintly censorious tilt of the head; for child abuse, fear and loathing in a blank stare. It had been a long journey from covering to vamping the news.

Although Sauter's "moments" TV may have been repudiated by his ouster (the way dictatorship was when Stalin shot the old Bolsheviks), the stardust had settled behind him. Network anchors chatted—live—with their subalterns stationed around the world, these unworthies not daring to face the audience until they invoked the anchor's name. Stories began "Dan" or "Tom" or "Peter," followed by bland chitchat between the far-flung staff and the anchors to establish everyone's "presence." Hard news was dispensed with the depth of a tabloid headline, and a soft feel-good feature closed the program as the anchor smiled good night. It was show and tell.

Cynics may disparage the Golden Age in TV news, but it did exist. Team spirit ran strong, there was fun and glory in the hunt, and a sense of being woven into a tightly knit family that would never come undone. But as the old order passed, for the correspondent especially, a sense of pride was the first to go in a new world of hype and hipness. No longer did management require reporters—network and local—to be well educated, able to write their own material, or capable of reporting a story without a producer's help. Rarer were those who showed any cultural affinity for books, art, language, or good music. Even reading a daily newspaper seemed beyond some. In time, CBS would staff its Moscow bureau with a correspondent who had glided through college and graduate school majoring in journalism and spoke not a word of Russian. Once a serious profession of perception and analysis, TV reporting had become simply a job of going places on a lot of airplanes.

"I moved fifty-two people to the Wall," bragged the NBC foreign editor to me one evening.

"What did they say after they got there?" I asked.

"I don't know," he replied, "that's not my job."

I could see it all from my viewer's chair now, the decade in which TV news, like the corporate culture it adopted, had reincarnated itself in pursuit of cold cash. No longer able to fend off the takeover boys, all three networks succumbed to outsiders: ABC to Capital Cities

Communications, NBC to General Electric, CBS to Laurence Tisch. The age of fatherly giants—the Sarnoffs, the Paleys—was indeed past. High living was over for the rank and file. Even NBC's London bureau had moved from the city's fashionable heart to a grimy industrial suburb. It was time to pull the wagons in a circle and face Indians on all sides: the assertion of "home rule" by local stations that no longer depended editorially or technologically on the networks; CNN, the ubiquitous eye, skimming off viewers, even the president of the United States; competition from myriad cable stations; a flattening population; the avalanche of VCRs; high expectations from stockholders; mushrooming overhead for on-air talent; and a widening credibility gap.

If journalists, not pitchmen, had led the revolution, perhaps the public would have been spared the carny barker's cant employed by news executives to plaster over a leaky set of standards. Defending CBS's decision to "reenact" or "reconstruct" news on "Saturday Night with Connie Chung"—using actors to portray characters in news events—CBS Broadcast Group president Howard Stringer rose to truly evangelical Newspeak: the network needed to "broaden the horizons of nonfiction television, and that includes some experimentation."

From fact to fiction—to pure fantasy.

TV news being what it is—fast money and big egos—few tears are shed in that brass-knuckled world. And yet, when the CBS layoffs hit, many of us discovered we could cry into our pillows with the best of them. Naturally, I felt victimized, a feeling that was reinforced in the winter following my dismissal, when I was strolling along Seventy-second Street and spotted David Buksbaum cringing wordlessly behind his wife's mink coat.

But there were others who did not deny past friendship. Tran Trong Khanh called me shortly after the bloodletting. Khanh was second secretary at the Vietnam mission to the UN. Almost everyone there had fought in the war, Khanh included, and we often traded stories and argued politics. He was an orthodox Communist, to be sure, and while disdainful of his ideology, I admired his discipline and low-budget life-style, refreshing in a diplomat.

"Trotta—this is Khanh. I have called to invite you to lunch at the mission with our new ambassador. Many journalists will be there. You will come then?"

If he had read about my ouster, he was much too polite to let on, and when I told him he seemed mystified by this capitalistic exercise.

I added that since I no longer represented CBS, I couldn't very well attend.

"But you are our friend," he said, fully aware of my politics.

I still didn't go, but a week later he showed up at my door with a delicate sketch of an old pagoda. "May God bless you in the years ahead," he said.

16

GHOSTS

Like a forgotten nightmare of childhood, Vietnam finally emerged into focus. In the last years of the 1980s, Americans had matured enough to look again and this time stare down the Medusa. The cold silence of the postwar years exploded into movies, books, and television dramas. The slogan-worn leftist moralizing was still there and even a peculiar revisionism that served to salve the consciences of those now ambivalent about which side of the barricades they had manned. But Vietnam had come out of the closet: and at some silent cue its own graduates—not the Fondas and the Rambos—began to bear witness.

Old friends of my Southeast Asia days were turning up again. Sooner or later it had to come, the first reunion of war correspondents. The Overseas Press Club in New York announced it, and of course controversy erupted at once. To draw attention to the event, the organizers chose Tom Brokaw as main speaker; no one recalled that he had ever been to Vietnam. David Halberstam, a major figure in the history of the war's reportage, refused to honor the invitation. Many others chimed in, and the speakers' list was amended.

Murmurs of the sixties rose that night as we gathered at the Seventh Regiment Armory. Marching around the entrance, chanting, "Release the prisoners," a band of men who claimed to be veterans demanded (they never ask) that the media work for the liberation of the POWs they believed to be still alive in Southeast Asia.

"Do you get the feeling you've seen all this before?" I asked my date, none other than Colonel Don D'Amico, by then retired and living as a prosperous businessman just outside Denver. D'Amico didn't know if he was ready for this many press people, but after a night of hard drinking, reminiscing, and even rebellion (Robin Moore, who wrote *The Green Berets*, was booed off the dais), he concluded that any group of war correspondents was at least as raucous as a barroom full of fighter pilots. The whole gang was there: Arnett, Faas, Adams, Mulligan, Esper, McArthur, Safer, and the rest, all looking out of place in civilian clothes. Jim Bennett, now a Florida TV news director, once an NBC correspondent in Saigon, surveyed the room, his eyes watering. And Faas, his German accent softening, said, "There will never be another group of extraordinary people like the ones in this room—never."

D'Amico had been in touch regularly since we met that day on the Hanoi airstrip when he was flying out the POWs. His daughter, a baby during the war, had moved to New York, so Don often dropped in, and we would all gather for dinner. Usually the night ended with the two of us in a corner, talking about the old days.

He never told me, although I had wanted to ask so many times, the rest of the story he began that day in the Da Nang Officers' Club. Something about how he looked when the subject arose always stopped me. Still, it was a compulsion, more unfinished business; I simply had to know. One Sunday afternoon—of course it would be a Sunday—the moment came. He was drinking coffee in my study, his gray hair catching a winter sun, leaning back in an easy chair. He was about to be a grandfather; Dora and the kids were fine; life hadn't been so bad since the war.

"Tell me about it again, the rest of it," I said casually. "You know, just for the record. What happened after the airplane blew and you punched out?"

"I don't know," he said. "It's history now, and besides . . ."

Fighter pilots, young or old, never need encouragement to talk about their first love, but losing your airplane, coming *that* close, was another matter. Then he sighed, took off his glasses, and looked into a distance only he could summon. It was October 20, 1968.

"Well—yeah, I passed out. I guess the next thing I remember is hanging from a parachute. And I look down and I can see the flames and the wreckage of my airplane in the water below me. There's a twelve-foot sea because of the typhoon. I'm hanging there and I feel something warm on my neck and chest, so I take off my oxygen mask and it's blood. I could feel the warmth of it on my chest. There's a cut on my chin. And I'm hanging there and the sonofabitches are shooting at me. Every once in a while I'd see something coming up. They knocked out a couple of the panels in my chute.

"I knew the best way to land in water is with your face to the wind so the chute will be above and behind you and it'll drag you on your back. If you're dragged on your face, you'll drown. I know the wind direction because of the fire and smoke. So I'm coming down and manage to hit the water right—on my back, and I roll over and the chute collapsed and sank. But I'm real close to shore. Tiger Island. It was twenty seconds after seven when I hit, because that's when my watch stopped.

"Now I've got to get into the goddamn boat. What a hassle. The boat opens when you eject, so it came down with me, open, and now I'm trying to grab it and push it down between my legs and slide into it. They train you for it, but it doesn't work the way the book says. I'm going up and down in that rough sea and the boat's full of water and I'm exhausted and man, I'm afraid I'm going to drown. Finally I'm in, face down. The chute's underwater acting like a sea anchor. I figure it will keep me from floating onto the beach. They're still shooting and I'm catching my breath. I roll myself over, and I've got to be careful I don't dump myself in again or I've had it. I pull out my radio and call my wingman. He answers: 'I'm down to 4,500 pounds of fuel. I'm leaving.'

"Oh, shit, I say to myself. I've left Tiger Island with 1,000 pounds and gotten home all right. He could have stayed with me, kept me in sight. Then I remembered how the boss—the wing commander—was bitching about the guys coming back low on fuel and the word was out: come back with 2,000 pounds. So I remember seeing him go—and I think that was probably the loneliest moment of my life. My last words to him were, 'Get that chopper in here. I'm getting close to that frappin' island.'

"I was about 100 yards away from Tiger Island, and the winds are pushing me closer, and the boat's going up and down. At the bottom of the crest all I could see was water, and when I got on top I could see the whole world. And I could see two guys shooting at me. One was kneeling. And behind and above them an automatic weapon, maybe a machine gun. I could see it sparkling. You know, I expected it to be like something in the movies, water spraying and bullets whistling past me. And nothing. I thought to myself, Christ, a couple of bad shots.

"I'm sitting there for a while, feeling lonely, thinking about how if I'm captured they're going to drag me up north and I got a broken neck and back. And they're going to wire me. Boy, I'm going to be in bad shape.

"The next thing that happens I see an S-2, an antisubmarine navy plane with a high wing and two-piston engine. This stupid little airplane, and he's only doing about 150 knots and he's flying between me and the island, back and forth, and every time he goes by they stop shooting at me and start shooting at him. So I call this guy. 'Aircraft over Tiger Island. Do you have me in sight?'

" 'Rog, I sure do.'

"It was a real calm and easygoing voice. I said, 'Man, they're shooting the shit out of you.' He says, 'Rog' and keeps flying back and forth, drawing away the fire.

"I'm on my back watching this guy, thinking he's nuts, but I kind of like having him there. You know, company. All of a sudden I hear putt, putt, putt. I look up and here's a stupid chopper, landing in the goddamn water, a Jolly Green, landing right in the water with twelve-foot seas. I look out and in the doorway of the chopper I see the hoist operator, a black guy with horn-rimmed glasses and a white helmet. I remember thinking it was odd because normally they wore camouflage helmets. I throw my left hand out and he grabs me and he's pulling me in. Meantime, I see another guy jump in to help and almost immediately the chopper's going up. He's pulling me in and all of a sudden we take two simultaneous hits, I mean big ones, probably 57-mm. It blew off the chopper's main transmission and the tail section, and I feel this horrible pain in my chest. I had a Mae West on and there's a battery in it, so the concussion pressed me up against the floor of the chopper. The black guy lets go of me. He goes flying back to the far side of the chopper. The chopper rolls. I fall out—and it comes down on top of me.

"Now I'm going down with it. The crew's jumping into the water and I'm tangled in the wreckage. I'm going down deeper and deeper. And it's getting darker and darker. Quieter and quieter. And the motion is getting slower and slower. And I'm pushing water away from my mouth, trying to breathe. And every time I breathe I feel the water going down into my lungs and stomach. It's cold. The water's cold. And I think to myself—I'm dying. And then I saw my four children. They were kind of lined up according to age: Adrienne, Nancy, Donald, J.P.—almost like a picture and they were all kind of smiling. I felt as though I was on my back and they were up above me. And it's getting real quiet, nice and quiet. The churning stops. I know I'm dead. It wasn't a peaceful feeling, but it was a quiet feeling because I was dying and I didn't want to die. And I thought, what a hell of a way to die.

"Then, I don't know how, but I come up like a cork and a hand reaches out and grabs me by the front of my collar—from out of nowhere, but then I see it's the pararescue man. I could have kissed him he was so close. 'Hang on. We've got it made. We've got it made,' he says, holding on to the front of my collar."

D'Amico, only five feet, seven inches, 130 pounds, felt like lead. Now the pararescue was helping him shed the Mae West, extra radio batteries, a .38-caliber pistol loaded with six rounds, plus thirty extra rounds, the rubber G-suit, and other junk in his flight suit—about seventy pounds of gear.

"Man, look at that. Look at that," the pararescue said, watching the incoming fire from Tiger Island. And over it, the little navy plane still trying to distract them from the struggle in the water. "Jesus Christ, they're trying to kill us," said the black guy. He was back, paddling by face-down in a raft, and D'Amico was wondering why the guy still had his helmet and glasses on after everything that had happened. He grabbed on to the raft. Then a second raft came by empty, and he hung on to both of them for a few seconds until the pararescue pushed him onto one of them. By this time he was shaking and going into shock. Meanwhile fighters from the aircraft carrier based offshore at Yankee Station had arrived, backed by D'Amico's own squadron buddies. The war stops when a pilot is down. Everybody concentrates on getting one man out. They were hitting Tiger Island with everything they had. D'Amico had been in the water almost two and a half hours.

" 'Hang in there,' the pararescue guy says to me. 'We've got it made,' and I'm thinking, Look at that, they're knocking the shit out of that island. Now the hoist operator is in one raft and I'm on the other, and the pararescue is in the water holding us both together and loving every minute of it and the sea is really rough. The air force and the North Vietnamese are shooting it out. Bombs, machine gun fire, rockets, artillery. Fourth of July in the South China Sea. And putt, putt, putt, putt—the little navy plane is still flying by taking fire and I'm getting sicker, praying I won't pass out. I knew I'd never make it if I did.

" 'Hey, they're coming in! They're coming in! Get ready!'

"All of a sudden I look back and I see this chopper. As he's coming in, I could see a penetrator coming down, and he's coming closer and closer and then he's right over me, like I was a magnet. The pararescue guy grabs the penetrator and puts it right between my legs and says: 'Hang on.' I'm hanging on and the thing starts going up and I'm thinking 'You better not fall off because if you do they're going to say, "Screw you. Look what you caused." '

"I could hear the chopper shaking in the wind, maybe fifty feet over the water. Oh, God, I thought, here these guys are getting the shit shot out of them because of me, because of one guy down here. I can't fall. I can't fall. I'm coming up face to face to the hoist operator. He turns me around facing in and grabs me, pulling me in and throws me in the back of the chopper. I look up and there's my backseater, Sam Wilburn. He's huddled in back, sees me and gives me the thumbs up signal.

"It was so cold and the chopper was shaking real bad and I thought, Shit, we're going to get it again. We're going to get it again. And the other two guys are coming up on the hoist and one of them—the guy who jumped in the water and held me—comes back and puts his arms around me and says, 'We're going home, we're going home!' "

D'Amico wept, his eyes wide open in old gratitude. I poured him another cup of espresso, trying to control my own tears.

"I better knock this off," he said, rubbing his eyes, blowing his nose.

There was a postscript to the story, the kind that doesn't belong in a tale of courage, endurance, triumph; but, again, this was Vietnam, so it had its own fitness.

D'Amico was taken aboard the hospital ship Repose, *sixty miles off the southern coast, and they cut off his flight suit as he lay on a table in a white*

*room. Through a gauzy veil, cold and shivering, he could hear them, prod-
ding, pressing, asking him if he could feel this pinch, that poke. He could feel
his right foot, but not his left. His body temperature was down to sixty-four
degrees. They gave him a shot, and he went to sleep. When he awoke, he
was lying in a basketlike bed. There was a nurse there, a lieutenant commander, and Sam Wilburn, his backseater, was right across from him.
"You're Catholic, aren't you?"*

"Yes."

*"We don't have a priest here, but if you want, we'll get one off the
beach." It was the first moment—the first instant—D'Amico had thought of
God since they blew him out of the sky.*

"I'm Catholic, I come from an old paisan family. I graduated from
a Catholic university. I go to church and all that. And it strikes me
like that and I started bawling. I've asked the question a million times
over the years, even of my friend Father Murray: why didn't I think
of God? Like everybody he tells me I was too busy, but I can't
accept that. I had a lot of time to think from the time I went into
afterburner until the plane blew up. I had nothing to do but hang on
and yet I still didn't think of God. Remember as a kid in Catholic
school they said if anything ever happens make a quick act of contri-
tion? Remember that? I don't know the answer, and maybe I never
will."

*D'Amico slept deeply, the drugs soothing nerves, countering shock. It was
early evening, still daylight, when the nurse gently brought him around.
"Your colonel is here to see you."*

*D'Amico looked up at the door and there was the boss, Paul Watson,
tall, narrow-eyed, thick white hair. "Isn't that nice?" he thought. "Here's
a wing commander taking time off from his very important job to come out
and see me."*

*He didn't know it then, but Watson had already grilled Wilburn about
Dover Lead's altitude and number of passes over the target. He looked at the
man strapped in the basket, the guy who piloted Dover Lead into the sea. He
didn't ask how his squadron leader felt. "What am I going to tell General
Brown?" Watson drawled. "One of my squadron commanders shot down
up north—strafing. You lost our government a three-and-a-half-million-
dollar Phantom and a million-dollar chopper."*

Still groggy, D'Amico couldn't believe what he heard. He tried to get up

to say something, but the basket's restraining straps held him down. He
dropped back, closed his eyes, and turned away to sleep.

THE audience, mostly young people, sat in silence, rapt in the discussion of a war that was over before they could read. Now, here they were, listening to correspondents soaked in IWT (I Was There) argue about the Tet offensive at a seminar on the events of 1968, the year America went haywire. In that faded world—before laptop computers, VCRs, footprints on the moon, and the singing of whales—any audience would have had its aviaries of hawks and doves hanging from the rafters, with visiting journalists struggling to "maintain their objectivity." Now the tamed and merely curious gathered to hear a battery of newsmen fighting over turf.

"That's bullshit!" Morley Safer roared, his fist crashing down on the table to hammer righteousness into the expletive.

"What's the matter with you, Morley?" I said, struggling to keep reasonable. "North Vietnam's own generals have written books about who really won Tet, what a thrashing they took in the field. Why the whole VC—"

"I don't care what any goddamn general says!" Morley's face flushed down to the collar of an expensive shirt. How dare anyone challenge him on what had happened "out there?" Hadn't a senior CBS producer laid it down that Vietnam was "Morley Safer's War"? Up until then we had thought it was Lyndon Johnson's war, or Ho Chi Minh's.

Perhaps that's why the president got so hot under his equally expensive shirt. Especially after Safer filmed the marines torching Cam Ne village with cigarette lighters, igniting a larger fire under the war-resisters and a generation of TV correspondents now alerted to what kind of story drew the spotlight. The grapevine had it that Lyndon Johnson thought Safer was a security risk; when informed he was not a Communist, just a Canadian, the president barked that he had known all along Safer couldn't have been an American. Make no mistake about it, Morley Safer of "60 Minutes" had his own war—and probably a foreign policy, too—and you better not fool with it.

Whose war was it, anyway? No sooner had Safer and I reduced our debate to scowls than Harrison Salisbury rose to speak. Now we would see whose war it was. But a formidable man from Accuracy in Media was on his feet, stabbing his finger in Salisbury's sightline, recalling the dispatches he had filed from Hanoi, and how he might just as well have been working for the other side. Salisbury voiced a denial as that sore point was touched once more. He had written stories from Hanoi, by most measures unbalanced, about civilian casualties inflicted by American bombing of the north, not naming the source of his information and ultimately missing the Pulitzer Prize in a public controversy. In the eyes of many, Salisbury had taken "was reported" and "was said" beyond journalistic formality to the outer edges of credibility in his initial dispatches. It was a spectacular example of how ideological considerations on both sides had infected coverage of the war. By his fifth dispatch, as an international furor arose, Salisbury finally revealed his sources for casualties and bomb damage: North Vietnamese officials.

It had been quite a coup in 1966 when Salisbury gained entry into the north. Most reporters would have given their souls—and some did—to report from behind enemy lines. The North Vietnamese shrewdly chose the eminent *Times* man to make their case about "indiscriminate bombing," charging that American bombers had struck at the civilian population. Indeed, it later came to light that the man who helped arrange the Salisbury trip was none other than Wilfred Burchett, an Australian-born reporter who made his name "covering" Communist causes.

Burchett had forged his biggest claim to fame during the Korean War when he aided North Korea in "proving" that America was involved in germ warfare. During the Vietnam War, when he wasn't briefing Jane Fonda, he specialized in interviewing American POWs, but only after they had been coerced into agreeing to sit for him. Edited segments seeming to be antiwar in nature were then released by the Communists for distribution. Burchett's propaganda efforts for the Communists didn't seem to bother many Western journalists eager to get into Hanoi. Indeed, so appreciative was Salisbury of his cooperation that he even wrote a glowing introduction to Burchett's memoirs, published in 1983. On this day, twenty-two years later, the charges against the former *Times* man still haunted the war's history.

Now Salisbury stood there, bonily handsome under his thick white hair and mustache. Shaking with rage, he stepped forward to the edge of the stage, defending his role in the war. Both men bellowed at each other until the moderator called a halt.

Gloria Emerson, voguishly bohemian, religiously radical, and almost six feet tall, stood next: a reporter for the *Times* who, by her own admission, had left the paper with an embittered view of her editors' handling of the coverage. The last time I had seen the joyless Gloria, just about the time starving boat people began fleeing Vietnam, she had told me not to worry, that the exodus was no evidence of Communist oppression because "they are all Chinese." Some viewed her as a martyr to the First Amendment, courageously flying truth's banner in the face of hawkish editors, one more casualty of the times (pun intended). Those who tried to maintain some equilibrium in the white-hot climate of war reporting read Gloria's dispatches as something quite other than disinterested. The debutante at war, she smoldered in rage over the sheer awfulness of it all, disgruntled grunts and sad-eyed whores—victims of a corrupt America. It was a great read on the Perrier-with-lime circuit.

One of her more celebrated forays into "committed journalism" (by her own account, in the book she later wrote), unfolded the day she went out with four South Vietnamese "students" on a mission to firebomb an American Jeep in downtown Saigon. There was the *Times* correspondent, waiting for murder to happen on her beat. The attack failed when the sapper unit botched it, and the GI drove away. With such active participation in fighting the war for the other side, it was understandable that Emerson wrote of her Vietnam experience: "I do not expect to recover."

"Do you really believe we could have won that war?" she asked me at a dinner later that evening.

"I certainly do."

"Well, then, of course, you mean we'd have had to go all out on the bombing, and things like that."

"That's right, Gloria," I said, mildly suspecting I was being humored by this elegantly unfocused observation. "Sometimes you have to do that to win a war."

Tom Wicker, *Times* columnist and liberal deity, lingered amid this murmuring of doves. He approached me to say that he admired the "force and grace" with which I had made my argument, and then, his southern drawl suggesting he was still just a good ol' boy, added: "You are aware, of course, how different are our points of view."

It struck me that even after two decades of witnessing the decay of Hanoi's shabby socialist dream, the robotic repression of the south, the bloody rampage of the Khmer Rouge, all these fascinating, immensely likeable people had stuck to their original scripts in this slow-motion tragedy. The old assumptions remained intact. It wasn't their right to their own opinions that appalled but the knowledge that as reporters they had been overtaken by a sense of mission, of righ-

teous proselytizing, of egofeed—all under the banner of "journalism."
To say the war was wrong became a theatrical point of view, a thought
that I doubt reigned uppermost in the minds of those very earnest
people who thought they were offering practical advice.

IT was a season for memory, at first a ripple and then a current of recollection stirring up the past. First there were the professional reunions
and anniversaries, and then the reknitting of personal ties from a war
that had woven us all together. Resolution—reconciliation—would
come none too soon. And it began with a letter from Bill Harben.

My old foreign service friend from Phnom Penh had been writing
speeches and proposals part-time for Craig Spence, the kind of thing
for which the energetic deal-maker had no attention span. An unlikely coupling, but Bill could use the money, and Craig realized the
value of having a former diplomat around to lend a touch of credibility
to Craig J. Spence Associates. Bill had been known to raise a patrician
eyebrow as he watched his employer maneuver through the power-
mad circles of official Washington. In the global village, with fortunes
to be made by a phone call, Craig had emerged as one of the town's
rainmakers—a man who brought people together for a price. He had
long ago decided that only two kinds of people were left in the world:
VIPs and non-VIPs, and now he admitted it with glee: "Why are you
bothering with him? He's nobody."

But slowly and slightly it was all beginning to fray around the
edges. Sudden fits of temper began to cloud his sharp wit. Outbursts in
restaurants at waiters too slow or too fast; a gaunt look, darting eyes,
wild mood swings; tales of drug smuggling in Central America and
inordinate sexual escapades—all of it fed into the rumor mill at the
same time TV news was blaring the arrival of a new epidemic: crack
cocaine.

Bill's letter arrived in early 1988:

*I think you and I would be well advised to distance ourselves from him as
much as possible. It is probably too late, but it would sound better to be able
to say that we had no contact with him recently. . . . I know you have a
maternal desire to help him, but believe me, he heeds no one's good advice.
He is virtually unemployable for more than a few weeks and he must engage
in illegal or unethical schemes to get the money to feed his extraordinary
vanity. He is not sane. I knew it when I saw his face as the uniformed
flunkies of the Madison Hotel bowed low before him, all but giggling to*

themselves, at the order of the proprietor, to whom CJS complained of insufficient deference. It was the face of Caligula before the cheering mob, of Hitler at Compiègne, Mussolini on his balcony. It is incipient schizophrenia, and the use of drugs will exacerbate it.

As summer approached, Craig seemed to get hold of himself again, enough to call his friends for the latest gossip and invite them to a Fourth of July weekend party. But even this invitation hinted at final preparations. He was selling the Kalorama house, for which he had blackmailed a Japanese politician, and buying an apartment in the most distinguished condominium in Washington.

"I refuse to call it a 'condo,' " he announced to me one day. "It sounds so, well, you know . . ."

I suggested he refer it to as "the rooms I've taken at Foxhall," which cheered him and was put to immediate use.

He had come to the condo purchase only after dragging me through the presidential suites of a half-dozen deluxe hotels, toying with the idea of living in one because "the service is full-time." But the Foxhall apartment, which he planned to occupy once he sold his house, was more Bastille than home, as much hospice as refuge. It was becoming plain he expected to die soon, perhaps besieged. He talked about disappearing, even announcing various dates. Friends reached for their copies of *Death in Venice*, counting on his dramatic flair.

He insisted that Skip Ettinger come down for the Fourth of July weekend, too. It would be a kind of reunion for the three of us since the war. "Only the in-group this time—no freeloaders. I'll start rounding up the usual suspects, of course."

Skip still called regularly from assorted phone booths. He was back in the army, stationed at Fort Bragg, home plate for Special Forces, which made him secure. He had returned from Okinawa with two children and a Japanese wife. Karate, now a way of life, had cured him of hard drinking and most of the recurrent nightmares. Having earned the title of *sensei* (teacher) he opened a dojo in Orange Park, Florida, trying to impart Oriental discipline to unruly kids. After ten years, the marriage split and he wound up at Fort Bragg by way of a short tour on the Minnesota tundra. Skip has always had the knack of packing a lot of living into a short furlough.

At Washington's National Airport that bright Saturday morning, heads turned at the hugs and squeals of the teary reunion of two old war buddies after eighteen years. We toured the town, Skip taking pictures of marble generals astride rearing horses, then ended up at the Kalorama house.

Surrounded by solid young men, Craig was holding court in the upstairs study. He had by now invested his bodyguards with code names, cuff mikes, and ear receivers. But in seeking an aura of authority and power, he left the impression of a half-mad dictator clinging to the remnants of a seedy government. My old friend, who once merrily taunted generals and high officials, now never left the house without his muscular coterie.

"What's going on?" I asked.

"You never know," he said grittily. "Someone out there . . ."

What the heck, I decided. With Craig you never did know. It was the game of the week.

The cook and valet were gone, so was the secretary, but Craig had dragooned pals to set the stage with flowers and food. Most of us had already caught on that something was going very wrong. Craig spoke of new deals and contracts, but he seemed to have crossed some invisible line beyond which he really didn't care. He could still nail down a consultant's fee, but the younger Japanese-speaking Americans offering service to Tokyo were acing him out. Even his television schemes—a talk show pilot, a documentary on Korea—had gone awry. Perhaps for dramatic effect at first, and then with regularity, he began quoting Carl Sandburg, asking whether it all mattered "in the dust, in the cool tombs . . ."

His weight loss and rapidly thinning hair were alarming, but most of all the complete absence of the attention span even to finish a sentence. There was an unwholesome, even sinister feeling in the house. He insisted the wooden shutters be closed all the time, left piles of mail unopened on the foyer table; the refrigerator contained nothing but yogurt and cranberry juice. I thought back to a few months earlier when I had visited for the weekend and he had urged me, "Lock your door. You never know who might try to get in." I shuddered. There was nobody else in the house but us. What could he mean? Anyway, I did as I was told, and he tried the door from the outside "just to be sure you're safe."

Craig really threw three kinds of parties: for movers and shakers only, for people he liked, and for his homosexual fraternity. The Fourth of July weekend he had reserved for his friends, although some of the old ones—Eric Sevareid ("a great man") and Ted Koppel ("He's beginning to take himself seriously") had already begun to retreat. His inner circle reeked of Somerset Maugham: a famous Hollywood pro-

ducer, an eminent Mexican psychiatrist, a Catholic law professor, the
son of a Chinese field marshal, a former U.S. attorney for the district,
a retired general, a brilliant Oxford intellectual who dressed like Hi-
laire Belloc, a Texas debutante, a retired La Scala diva.

Long after everyone had mustered on that warm Sunday afternoon, Craig made his entrance at the top of the staircase, a Faustian
figure descending into some unseen abyss. Guests lowered their voices
at his spooky arrival and frail appearance. "Ah, well, here we are," he
said. "Old friends on the nation's birthday." It was actually July 3, but
to Craig, details like this were unimportant. He peered through a pair
of new spectacles that gave him an owlish authority. Soon he was
doing his Howdy Doody–like imitation of Ronald Reagan, followed by
Lyndon Johnson—"Bird, get your ass in here"—and finally, jutting
out his chin, a patrician Franklin Roosevelt waving to the crowds
below.

I looked around the room and realized how far all of these people
had come: Craig had gone from chewing out majors in Saigon to
master of Wyoming Avenue; Skip from pathfinding in Tay Ninh to a
Voltaire chair under a gold mirror; the retired general from pulling
men out of burning choppers in Vietnam to a picture-taking session
under the giant American flag over the main entrance; and Shuja
Nawaz, my Pakistani friend, from the alluvial plains of the Punjab to
explaining Benazir Bhutto beneath the grandfather clock.

Very late that night several of us went on a tour of the White
House, arranged by Craig although he didn't come along. "I can get
in—or get my friends in—any time. They know who I am."

That weekend was drenched in sun, pouring through the now
open shutters and filtering through the French windows, varnishing
the capital with an amber glow. Craig's disintegration, visible though
it was, receded in that golden light, and the ties of the past still held
us innocent in a bond of long friendship. How could we have known?

By summer's end, he was flying out of control, imagining plots
against him, cutting me off after I lambasted him for using drugs. "I'm
tough," he snapped over the telephone. "I can kick it. But I'll go it
alone, like I've done everything else."

I didn't hear from him for months after that. I had joined the list
of people he was, in his words, "resting." Then, on June 29, 1989, *The
Washington Times* published a sensational page one report, naming
Craig as a major client of a sex-for-hire agency servicing the power
elite. Moreover, our late-night tour of the White House, which, reported the *Times*, included two male prostitutes, got top play. From

there the story exploded into a federal grand jury investigation: allegations that at least one of the uniformed Secret Service White House guards had stolen pieces of Truman administration china and given them to Craig, credit card fraud, suspected CIA connections, drug running, the lot. Almost everyone who knew him turned on their answering machines.

As for Craig, he simply changed his unlisted telephone number once again and hunkered down like a pelican in a storm; only a beefy few knew exactly where. Various "sightings" of him were reported like UFOs as the Feds tried to corner him for a subpoena.

A few weeks later my phone rang shortly before midnight. I was up in the Maine woods, in a cabin twenty-five miles from the nearest town. It was Craig.

"I need a friend," he said in a hoarse voice. "Only you. I don't want to see or talk to anyone else."

"Are you sick?" I asked.

"Yeah—I've got it."

"How long do you have?"

"A week, a month, who knows, who cares?"

For the first time in the twenty-three years I had known him, he sounded vulnerable, resigned.

"You know the Secret Service is looking for you?"

"I really don't care."

"But if you talk to them—you'll have a chance of clearing this up. You can't keep running. You—"

"Look, they can't solve the big thing. Besides, I don't want to spend the rest of my life in hearings."

"You're still on drugs, aren't you?"

"What would you do? I'm entitled to under the circumstances."

"But they could find a cure tomorrow. They—"

"No, I'm not going through that. I'm not going into a hospital leaning on someone's arm, suffering from dementia."

"You're tempting fate."

"You believe, you're a Catholic."

"Look, why not play it the way Pascal suggested—a gamble—bet on there being a God. You can't lose."

"I know all about Pascal."

"Then why not? You've been a gambler all your life, always looked for the edge."

"But I don't believe."

He was silent for a few seconds. "We're all going to die, you know."

He kept repeating that, no matter what I said. "I've done it all. Even if I didn't have this, what more is there to do? I feel as though life is repeating itself. Remember Howard Tuckner? A swan dive off a building. Now, there's a possibility."

"Oh stop. Where are you? Do you need anything?"

"I'm in the lap of luxury," he said, sounding lighter, the old charm surfacing. For a while his wit churned the air, mocking the coverage of his escapades in "Memphis on the Potomac." Then he said, "So you're up there writing? Are you going to mention the Christmas piece I did in Saigon? And don't forget the one about how the VC used to hide in the marshes breathing through reeds. Remember?"

Oh yes, I remembered.

Shortly after that conversation, a Secret Service agent phoned "just to tell you to be careful" when I returned to New York. Craig had been arrested after a fight with a call boy in a Manhattan hotel and charged with illegal possession of crack and a loaded 9-mm pistol. He spent three days in jail—where, characteristically, he had won the protection of the burliest dude on the block by providing him with valet services and a salami sandwich—and was released on bail. Meanwhile, the Feds said they hadn't found him.

In early August, back in New York, I heard from him again. He wanted to check out of the Parker Meridien Hotel but had no money. I went over to pay his bill. The Feds had obviously canceled his Amex card. He was high, freakishly tiptoeing across the lobby, whispering into the ears of bellboys. In ill-fitting khakis and a worn polo shirt, he still affected the airs of a crown prince, waving away his lack of credit. A mere oversight.

He insisted on lunching at the Plaza, leaving the table several times to find a telephone and once to kidnap a potted palm from Trader Vic's for our table. The Pierre was next. He crashed a wedding reception, charming his way to the buffet table to wolf down champagne and truffles while engaged in smart conversation with the formally dressed guests. Who *was* this daring man? Finally, after he tripped a waiter carrying a full tray and talked about finding a three-star French restaurant, I left him at Sixtieth and Madison.

He slept in Central Park that night, was robbed, and came pounding on my door at 5 A.M., raving incoherently, demanding a place to sleep. He was haggard, unshaven, and his polo shirt bore the slat marks of a park bench. He fell asleep. By that afternoon, two *Washington Times* reporters, Michael Hedges and Jerry Seper, had traced him to my apartment. He held court for eight hours, spinning filigrees of alleged high intrigue and deals, dropping names, scoring those who had forgotten old favors, not so much granting an interview as dictating an obituary. "How do you think a little faggot like me moved in the circles I did? It's because I had contacts at the highest levels of this government. They'll deny it. I had the world at my house and now they don't know who I am."

Perhaps they didn't know who he was anymore, but Craig knew. More publicist than journalist, he understood very well what demons drove him—what demons drive us all. He returned to Washington, taking on a second life as he made his grand entrances in Georgetown bars and restaurants. He showed no ambivalence about his unsavory reputation; instead, he took on his detractors and talked about suing them. One acquaintance said he was disgruntled that a scandal involving Congressman Barney Frank and a homosexual lover was pushing him off the front page.

After the New York episode, I realized sadly that our friendship, once so strong, could not withstand the combination of AIDS and cocaine. Craig would either be indicted by a grand jury, tried and sent to jail, or sink further into depravity until the disease brought him down.

Early in November, I had a dream in which I saw the mahogany door of the rickety old elevator in the lobby of the Eden Building in Saigon. Craig and I had gone through that door countless times. In my dream it had been sealed with a thick border of concrete, closed forever.

On November 10, Craig J. Spence, dressed in a tuxedo and listening to Mozart, lay down to die on a bed in the Boston Ritz. He had barricaded the door and taken enough booze and pills to carry out the long-promised suicide. Cradled to his ear was a telephone, said the cops, a sign he had been talking to someone. That "someone," they said—perhaps at Spence's request—had tried to warn the hotel switchboard that a guest was in trouble. But there was no way to find out in which room Craig lay dying. He had signed the register "C. S. Kane"—an eerie echo of another haunted man, Orson Welles's portrayal of William Randolph Hearst, Charles Foster Kane.

As for a Viking funeral, he had assembled all the barbaric instruments of his life for the studied perfection of his death. A newspaper clipping lay next to him about efforts to protect CIA agents from testifying before government agencies. A stoic note of resignation to some unnamed "chief" scrawled on the bathroom mirror. A birth certificate, a will, which included a bequest to Mother Teresa, and antidepressant pills were stuffed together into a false ceiling. On a Walkman, a cassette lilted "Eine Kleine Nachtmusik." In a postscript to the note, he apologized to the management for the "inconvenience."

The media gathered for a feast. He was cremated—if indeed it was Spence at all, they imagined gleefully—and a strange man watching the body burn through a furnace window identified himself as from "The Company." The last breath of a man who lived off myths had dissolved into still another. An emblematic story for the eighties, produced, directed, and benighted by CJS: the small-town boy from Kingston, New York, who at last won the front pages that he had coveted for a lifetime. In Vietnam, he had learned the fragility of life and that many men have a price. Meeting that price became his obsession, playing the power game, chasing the sweet life and finally flirting with a modern plague. He was in lockstep with the times all the way.

Skip called. Stunned, like everyone else who had attended the Independence Day weekend party, he replayed it in his mind. For someone used to people dying for a cause, it was difficult for him to fathom why a man who "had everything"—friends, money, a fine house—would set out to destroy himself. I didn't try to explain that it was basically a question of courage, the kind that Craig had so often shown but which had at the last deserted him.

THAT weekend Skip and I had gone to the Vietnam Memorial, twice: the first time after midnight with Skip in uniform, the tilted maroon beret and rows of ribbons—recollecting the medals he had sent back when Saigon fell—gleaming under the lights that illuminated the names carved in black granite panels; then again the next afternoon in a shuffling line of pilgrims, touching the names washed in the bright glow of summer, falling into such silence I could hear the hum of bees.

We walked the war's history of death from 1959 to 1975, descending toward the vertex where the panels meet, deeper and shaded, in a tomb of names and whispers. Then back up the gray path into the sun and a world where Vietnam could still stop a conversation or break a heart. Skip, a fearless young Green Beret at my side in the bush twenty years before, ran his hands across the names, searching for his friends. It was as though he hadn't realized they were gone forever until he felt the ridges in the stone and read the names aloud. "I can't believe it," he whispered, like a child discovering a hidden treasure. "Look here, here he is—look, it's Woody Hunt." Skip's fingers lightly touched the letters: "William S. Hunt." "He was a corporal who came to me from the 173rd Airborne, wanted to join up with my pathfinders. God darn. We operated on two-man teams all over the place. He was a skinny kid, looked like he was just out of high school. He got hit by a sniper just as they were moving off the LZ, ran into a VC battalion. He was carrying the radio and the antenna was sticking out. He was shot in the head. Happened just outside of Dong Tam. Brunowski picked him up and carried him over his shoulder . . ."

He moved a few steps, eyes squinting over the columns of names. "Here's Mixter. He was with us at Kontum, Recon Team Colorado, monitoring the Ho Chi Minh Trail, the classified project. Colorado was so good that in one year of recon they never made contact. David was about six three, a buck sergeant. Why, he could crawl within fifteen meters of an enemy position and they'd never know he was around. So he never got a Combat Infantryman's Badge or a Purple Heart because they never made contact. We were all at the recon club the night before Colorado was inserted, really riding him about it. He looked at us and said, 'I don't want a CIB or a Purple Heart and that's why I run with RT Colorado.' The next morning the tail gunner was sick, so Mixter covered it and he got hit with a B-40 in the chest."

The reading of the dead. Everyone talked about how the names cut into the Wall had power, but not until that moment did I understand. And yet, just as sad as the memory of these young men were the inglorious names of those driven by a pain you cannot see, who had died not on the battlefields but inside, long after they had left the war—Frank Donghi, Howard Tuckner, and soon, Craig Spence. Vietnam hadn't killed them outright—no mortar fragments, no sniper's bullet; it had merely persuaded them they were invincible. Skip and I stood there, survivors, doing what survivors have always done: visiting monuments, blowing taps, flying flags. Not just remembering the dead but celebrating the living.

There were others who had survived. Peter Arnett ("By all logic I should be dead") was covering national affairs for CNN and living in Arlington, Virginia, not far from "Little Saigon," where we met one day for a bowl of pho and listened to the familiar singsong chatter of our old allies. He and his North Vietnamese wife had separated; his daughter, a Harvard honors grad, was on her way to becoming, naturally, a reporter. Horst Faas, after buying up every available piece of porcelain this side of the Mekong, was running AP's European photo operation from London. Speedy Gaspard, my defeated "soldier in the rain," was, at sixty-two, a general in the South Carolina National Guard and on his fourth marriage. Vo Huynh, near retirement, had gone from the jungle's waist-deep muck to the red carpets of the White House, where he was NBC's camerman for the Reagan years.

Of all those I knew, perhaps Barbara Gluck, Saigon's Perle Mesta, had pursued survival by the most original route. She had divorced her husband, Joe, and moved to Santa Fe, still taking her marvelous pictures. By 1985 she was moving "into the spirit realm" and started the Global Light Network. I left a message for her on an answering machine tape that played temple gongs, and when we met some months later, she talked about her path from war photographer to "spiritual facilitator." Barbara, too, had left the war with its ghosts.

"Vietnam sent me on a spiritual quest," she told me. "It was really one experience that did it, at the scene of a plane crash. Joe and I were supposed to go to Ban Me Thuot on Monday, but on the previous Friday, I woke up and knew that I couldn't go that day, so I changed our Air Vietnam tickets to Sunday. That Monday, the plane blew up in mid-air.

"I got to the scene within forty-five minutes of the crash and it was beyond nightmares. I started taking pictures and the camera protected me, but when I put it down, suddenly, right there in the middle of the jungle, it was so quiet, but I was experiencing profound chaos. That chaos led me to the work in consciousness and sent me to meditation.

"Why did I feel chaos? Because all the people who died there violently and suddenly were unprepared and their souls were hanging around the place. There was such confusion because death had not been an issue for anyone on that plane. So I believe I was sent back to the establishment world in order to lead people back to consciousness, to help them find a dimension within themselves."

There would be yet another survivor. Although I didn't know it then. Nguyen Thanh My, the blue-eyed Amerasian boy I had found in the streets of Saigon, finally arrived in the United States at Los Angeles Airport in the fall of 1990. He was met by his mother, Hoa, who had not seen him for twenty-two years. Her determination to get him out had never wavered, and Dick, the father My had never seen, the man I located while reporting the story, had also pitched in to help bring him over. My spoke not a word of English, but insisted on getting on the telephone to thank me, to laugh, and to remember.

It was a time for long thoughts, that afternoon at the Wall. In the distance, three bronze figures held Skip and me in their gaze. We walked across the Mall to a small island of shrubs and flowers where they stood, wary and unafraid, as though searching for a phantom comrade. We circled the burnished men, discovering that it was not only the Wall they faced but a tree line in the middle distance, the kind grunts ran into on patrol, alert for friend or foe hidden behind the brilliant green—green, in all shades, traveling across time from the flat rice fields and carpeted valleys of Vietnam to this patch of remembrance. The moving pictures still burned, but years had washed the vividness to a paler tone, a lighter green, and a cooler sun that made silver transparencies of the leaves around us.

America's longest war—a decade of TV images—had shaped not just how we saw it but ourselves. Khe Sanh, Con Thien, An Loc, Song Be, Ia Drang, A Shau, My Tho, Dak Tho—once newspaper type, now places in the heart. As young reporters, young soldiers, we had set our course by the war, honed our skills, tested our commitment to fairness or to victory, found, or didn't find, the "fire in the belly" to see it through. If we dreaded failure, the thought of success was sometimes worse. At best, with a little luck and a measure of sacrifice you would come home as a reporter or a Pentagon colonel and later—much later—admit to a close friend that Vietnam had made you a person, too. The fierce drive to "make it," the struggle to get it right, the Hail Marys to stay alive, the faithless loves that almost kill, the pals who lost their lives or their way, the tears shed in the night—all of it had left a mark. For those who had fought the war, for those who had reported it, unburied memories would stretch to the horizon as they had for everyone from Shiloh to Anzio.

The statues and the wall they guarded cast their spell, turning the clock back farther yet, rewinding the images of a career—a life. I remembered a little girl standing in a railway station crowd in 1945, waiting for an uncle she barely remembered to come home from Normandy; that same girl skating in the park, her father keeping a sharp eye out for thin ice; and later, a nervous young woman in blue reading her script in a dark studio. From there, she and many others like her had set their course by one fixed measure: a dedication to news. Not for entertainment—war as Greek tragedy, civil strife as morality play, politics as sport—but for its own sake. It was that simple, the way we perceived and reported news, that classic and impersonal. Reporting was a calling, a vocation, something you knew you had to do for reasons you couldn't quite explain. Perhaps we believed, but were ashamed to admit, that there was something worthy about coming as close as possible to the truth. All you had to watch out for was that nothing, like a swollen ego or a quarterly report, got in the way of that. Regrettably, it didn't last, and the reporter as chronicler, a shadow on the sidewalk, went the way of silent movies.

Still I counted myself among the survivors with memories of people and places that would never fade, imprints of the mind. They came flooding back that afternoon: Singapore, Belfast, Kabul, Tehran. I had seen my share and reported it all. But Vietnam was where it began and ended, this war that had divided and bound us—from battle cry to epitaph, from nightmare to nostalgia, from symbol to souvenir.

The columns of visitors were thinning now, heads bowed as they disappeared amid the trees. Off to one side, a reporter and his television crew had been taping a story on the crowds drawn to the Wall. Now Skip and I watched as they wrapped up their gear and lugged it across the grass at a clip, bolting for the evening news, no doubt.

I smiled in salute. And then—at last—we headed home.

AFTERWORD
to the
paperback
edition

All reporters worth the name are brick-throwers deep inside. That is why when the revolution began in television news, those who manned the ramparts found resistance native to their blood. Restlessness and ferment preceded the struggle as the portentous man in the 1930s trench coat was slowly replaced by a earnest anchor given to smiling. The profession itself, feeling old in this moment of crisis, was as stunned as everyone else.

It was an irrevocable sense of loss that drove me to write this book. The term *broadcast journalist* had come to take in everyone from talk-show host to disc jockey, and that, it seemed to me, cried out for comment. Looking back to the publication of *Fighting for Air* three years ago, I suspect that when some enterprising filmmaker documents the history of television news, images of these years will be run at top speed, as in a Chaplin movie where characters bob and weave and events overlap in a blur of motion. For during this brief time, new tastes and wondrous technologies relegated the once-venerable Big Three to relic status. Like ancient cities sliding into the sand, they, too, are fighting for air, beset by modern competitors and stripped of their deep-voiced authority.

Cable networks, interactive television, fiber optics, and computers have hurled "electronic journalism"—a phrase that once seemed oxymoronic—into an orbit of instant communication that broaches fantasy: a young Chinese faces down a tank, the Russian parliament burns, a Bosnian mother cradles her dying child, all in real time.

It took two hundred years for newspapers to go from highly partisan rags to the broad-gauge of news, from war diaries to daily combat correspondence. But carried by science and imagination, television journalism burst out of its narrow range of wars, fires, and politics to an ever-expanding field of coverage in a mere fifteen years. In a moment, in the twinkling of an eye, television news became omnipresent and godlike.

Even as television news recorded the dismantling of the Berlin Wall, its own oligarchy was disintegrating. Indeed, the withering away of the Soviet state and the decentralization of big network power had much in common. Powerful economic forces helped finish off both Leninist tyranny and networkism. Self-importance crumbled in the free marketplace.

Political muscle and impenetrable mystique had kept both institutions on top of the heap. In the fifties, at the height of the Cold War, both powers lived off the discouragement of competition and flexed their legal muscle to remain indispensable. In the sixties, war and dissent afforded American network news a golden age, and the communists a victory in southeast Asia. In the seventies, a warning gun went off when entertainment found a home in local news. The ground shook and the false front of invincibility began to crack. In the late eighties, rear-guard actions were still raging. By the last decade of this century, even that game was up.

Television news has come a long way from a spring day in 1965 when *The New York Times* rebuked me for chasing an evasive politician on camera. Such persistent tactics are now de rigueur. With the old news world falling apart, so too disappeared the need to keep up respectability, the starched-collar formality that impelled the networks to mimic the Old Gray Lady. Now, the personnel recruited for television news, and unhappily the *Times* itself, are more often in the service of social experiment than the disinterested pursuit of truth. Tone and weight have been drowned out by a frantic concern for diversity over substance and user-friendliness over probity—all this a natural consequence of feverish consumer choice. The disease of the week has replaced analysis of foreign affairs, and there is little time left over after the multiculturalists and sex activists have had their time. Serious television journalism is not threatened. It is absent.

Even the quixotic Dan Rather was finally driven to developing a news conscience when he declared that the profession should be "ashamed" of what it had become. Mr. Rather made public his concern not long after they had paired him with the obligatory news "companion," an anchorwoman, and his ratings went south. It is difficult to imagine any current anchor being touted for a U.S. senate seat as Chet Huntley was, or for vice-president of the United States, as was Walter Cronkite. It is, at best, uncomfortable to suppose that holding political office should be a natural outgrowth of reporting, but the mere suggestion reflected the authority of these news eminences.

The era of the classical anchor was already over when, after forty years with NBC News, John Chancellor retired and hardly anyone noticed. The realization that no torch would pass came with the death of Eric Sevareid, an international icon and the last practitioner of authentic broadcast commentary. That generation of men, hardened by a big war and energized by American optimism, has all but faded.

Network news, having lost its ability to awe, is being usurped by different constituencies. Radio, repeatedly pronounced dead, has reincarnated itself in a nationwide cacophony of personalities and interviewers. Some of the best tables at Le Cirque can now be reserved for Larry King and Rush Limbaugh. The hot-money shows are the electronic tabloids—heavy on scandal and three-handkerchief tales. With their slightly seedy personnel and intimations of doom, they constitute para-news, not quite journalism and allegedly not only entertainment. Nevertheless, they cover a certain type of breaking news, from the perils of Lady Di to the hobbies of Michael Jackson. Most extraordinary, although maddening to most people over thirty, is the steady beat of MTV. Spewing shock images, this perfect liaison of sex and rock rams home a cultural statement that is a logical extension of the quest for pure amusement. That established, they even tacked on news.

Out of all this arises the paradox of modern TV journalism. While there is more of it than ever before as cameras cross once-closed borders and get to stories faster than ever before, television coverage has not kept up with the technology. The world may be far more complicated than it was thirty years ago, but you would guess the reverse from the trivialized reporting of complicated events. Consider that for all its heroic proportions—and the ability to transmit on-scene—war in the Persian Gulf became a horrorless drama that could have been called "Gone with the Sand."

War coverage itself is a series of frenzied landings in some savaged backwater after real action is over. The command, having vowed never again to suffer the burn of Vietnam-brand reportage, has vigilantly kept television journalists away from grim realities. Gone is the open coverage of war that put TV news on the map and set my own course. Instead, reporting from the enemy's camp is now a tempting alternative. It follows then that just like so many made-for-television stories, our wars are now as tentative as the public's attention span.

All of this hardly encourages young people. Many of them—eager to be next to the center of things, to go places, to be on-camera—have asked for advice. My only reply is that to cover world events is more than ever a splendid calling, because there is more than ever to tell. The trick is finding a middle ground between authority and entertainment.

Thirty years ago I entered the profession knowing that television news had not yet came into its own, that as the age of American innocence receded the ripening of serious reporting was just beyond the horizon. It was, and it can be again. Broadcast news is going to be remade in the next ten years. For this to happen, it must be reclaimed from its triviality; this will call for an advance on a very broad front and an understanding of how to orchestrate the staggering proliferation of channels and news sites. More people will be needed—not the few dozen operating out of Manhattan who invented TV news as they went along in the fifties and sixties—but thousands. Nor will it be the personal business it was in those years, defined by an astonishingly small group of executives, entrepreneurs, and on-screen people who all knew one another.

There is so much more to coverage than a summary of what the president said in the Rose Garden, and, as the market dictates more specialization, the challenge will be to get behind and above the giant figures and facades. There is, indeed, a brave new world and it will demand disciplined professional cadres to make it work. The future can—and must be—dare I say, an age of enlightenment, a recasting of broadcast journalism's original principles as the world is rewired for news.

It has been a long time since the drone of Luftwaffe bombers over London conjured up pictures for Ed Murrow's words. Television, with its early weak images, contracted the imagination, distanced most events from the viewer, and was pronounced a cool medium. A new generation of serious professionals must reach back to its deepest traditions and look ahead to its new strengths to fashion tomorrow's planetary news. And every reporter worth the name should keep those bricks handy.

I began this book with a quote from Tennyson, and it seems fitting to let him end it:

> Tis not too late to seek a newer world . . .
> Though much is taken, much abides; and though
> We are not now that strength which in old days
> Moved heaven and earth, that which we are, we are . . .

New York, 1993

Acknowledgments

When you have an idea for a story—a long one—there is no end to the number of people who urge you to write a book. Some get off the bandwagon right away, many more in midstream, and in the end, only precious few remain with patience and humor enough to see you through. Happily, I was blessed with a sturdy cheering squad of friends and colleagues who stood the course.

Among those on the "atta girl" list are: Jim Aspbury, Jim Benenson, Dudley Clendinen, Raoul Lionel Felder, Liz Frank, Professor Richard Gordon, Madeleine Lejwa, Stan Losak, Helen Muller, Amos Perlmutter, Andrew Salter, Kate Skattebol, Sandy Socolow, Susan Whelan, and Lois Zuckerman.

On the operational side, Tony Van Witsen, an intrepid factfinder, doubled as old pal and scholar in digging out research material. David Meyer of the NBC legal staff refreshed my memory on several key points. And my agent, Tom Wallace, brought his literacy and good counsel to every stage of a work in progress.

My editors were lavish in their efforts to make me look good. Fred Hills, who saw the possibilities from the beginning, sent me in the right direction, keeping a firm but artistic hand on the manuscript, and exercising a ready wit that so often pulled me over the rough spots. Burton Beals, a master of continuity and clarity, sculpted the masses of prose and always understood what I was trying to say. Daphne Bien, smart and sunny, made me feel welcome even while juggling a half dozen other authors, some of them waiting on hold.

Much is made of where writers write, and again I was blessed. From 1989–90, I was a fellow at the Gannett Foundation Media Center at Columbia University. Everette E. Dennis, executive director, and godfather to journalists far and wide, always had his door open when I sought advice.

At the Vanderbilt University Television News Archives in Nashville, Tennessee, I found a treasure of news broadcasting history, thanks to the enthusiastic help of Jacklyn Freeman and her staff. And on many a day, the New York Society Library, with its old-world poise and rich collections, was a harbor of serenity.

Lastly, deepest appreciation to Timothy Dickinson, who pulled the story out of me with relentless questioning, shrewd advice, occasional scolding and a unique respect for the language.

As a postscript, my compliments to "the lions"—a pair of Siamese attack cats who kept me company and never danced on the Macintosh before I hit the "save" button.

INDEX

ABC, 26, 27, 55, 95–96, 126, 188, 233, 246, 277, 295, 304, 305, 319, 338, 339, 351–52
ABC News, 65, 91, 98, 102, 121, 180, 255, 277
ABC Sports, 281
Abel, Elie, 77
Accuracy in Media (AIM), 361–62
acquired immunodeficiency syndrome (AIDS), 306, 324, 368, 370
Adams, Eddie, 254, 338, 355
"adverse pool," 297
Agency for International Development, U.S. (USAID), 89, 124
Agnew, Spiro, 42, 155

media assailed by, 187–89
Air Vietnam, 81
air war, 137–39, 148
Albee, Edward, 22
Alexander, Shana, 314
Alger, Horatio, 28
Allison, Lew, 186, 306, 348
Alpha Company, 112, 115, 117, 119
Alsop, Joseph W., 44–45
  Arnett and, 161–62
Americal Division, U.S., 209
American Federation of Television and Radio Artists (AFTRA), 50, 76, 268
antiwar protests, see peace movement

Apocalypse Now (film), 123
Apollo 8, 165
Apollo 11, 180, 184
Archangel, Colonel, 220–21
Arena, Dominick, 180
Arkin, Alan, 22
Arledge, Roone, 281, 282, 287, 319
Arlen, Michael, 156
Army-McCarthy hearings, 16
Arndt, Detlev, 116
Arnett, Nina, 234
Arnett, Peter, 97, 285, 338, 355
    Alsop and, 161–62
    described, 96
    post-Vietnam experience of, 372–373
    Trotta and, 234, 286, 289, 295, 326–27
Associated Press (AP), 21, 25, 46, 69, 114, 117, 125, 144, 192, 254, 338
    correspondents of, 96–97
    Saigon bureau of, 96
Auricon camera, 62–63, 112
Aurnou, Joel, 314
Avnet, Sy, 29, 30
Axelbank, Jay, 246
Ayeen (Trotta's amah), 227

"Backstage Wife," 314
Baez, Joan, 68, 72, 231
Bandaranaike, Sirimavo, 195
Bangladesh, 199, 212
    Kennedy's visit to, 216–18
    Trotta in, 211–16
Barbieri, Luisa, *see* Mazzacane, Luisa Barbieri
Barrett, David, 82, 127
Barrett, George, 17, 20, 57, 127
    career of, 81–82
    death of, 332
Bartlett's Familiar Quotations, 55
Bay of Pigs, 15
BBC, 215, 230
    correspondents of, 246
BBC Television Centre, 243
Beame, Abe, 34, 275
Beat Generation, 19
Beatles, 56, 204
Beatty, Warren, 68

Beirut barracks bombing, 325
Bell, Jack, 69
Bell, Steve, 219
Bellendorf, Peter, 120–21, 338
Belushi, John, 271
Benewah, USS, 158
Bennett, Jim, 355
Berle, A. A., 18
Bernstein, Ken, 87–88, 128, 261
    Corrigan correspondence of, 103
Bernstein, Leonard, 92
Bhutto, Benazir, 214, 367
Bhutto, Zulfikar Ali, 213–15
Biasetti, Mario, 290
Bich (interpreter), 335
black market, 93, 94, 135
Black Panthers, 92, 198
Blair, Frank, 53, 205–6
boat people, 342, 363
Boccaccio, Giovanni, 70
"boiler room girls," 192–93
Borneo Bulletin, 222
Bourgholtzer, Frank, 174
Boyle, Bill, 29, 272, 282
    Hurley incident and, 47–48
    nicknames bestowed by, 33
Boyle, James A., 192, 194
Bradley, Omar, 83
Bradshaw, Thornton, 279
Brady, Phil, 235–36
breakaway capability, 310, 317
Brelis, Dean, 53, 95
Breslin, Jimmy, 177–78
Brewster, Kingman, Jr., 198
Brinkley, David, 25, 27, 33, 43, 53, 114, 172, 186, 207
    Huntley's retirement and, 204–5
    Johnson and, 173
    Trotta and, 287
Brokaw, Tom, 355
Brooklyn Eagle, 67
Browder, Earl, 110
Brown, Harvey, 210
Brunowski (U.S. soldier), 372
Bucher, Lloyd, 164–65
Buckley, Pat, 35
Buckley, William F., 34–35
Buksbaum, David, 299, 322–23, 346–48, 352
    Trotta fired by, 348
Bunker, Ellsworth, 161–62, 232

Burchett, Wilfred, 362
Burke, David, 180, 183
Burn, Jake, 78, 105, 145, 228, 230, 234, 333
  Steinman replaced by, 185
  Trotta's relationship with, 105, 165–66, 185–86, 233
Burnett, Carol, 22
Burrows, Larry, 97
Bush, George, 299–302
  personality of, 300–301

Calley, William Laws, Jr., 208–10
Cambodia, 93, 142, 210, 226, 229, 294, 340
  U.S. invasion of, 196–98
Cambridge, Godfrey, 201
"Camel News Caravan," 16
cameramen, 37–38, 40, 180
Camus, Albert, 324
Capital Cities Communications, 351–52
"Capital Parade," 45
Carey, Hugh, 180
Carter, Jimmy, 300, 305
Caruso, Enrico, 37
Casey, William J., 302
Catholics and Catholicism, 16, 18, 70–71, 360
CBS, 10, 11, 18, 27, 43, 55, 119, 126, 170, 188, 233, 236, 263, 289, 290, 292, 293, 296, 307, 313, 317, 321, 322, 323, 327, 328
  attempted takeovers of, 346
  competitiveness of, 25–26
  correspondents of, 95–96
  financial difficulties of, 346–47, 351–53
  Iran hostage exclusive by, 305
  as "producer's network," 44
  Vietnam War and hiring practice of, 95–96
  Westmoreland's suit against, 320, 346
CBS Broadcast Group, 318
"CBS Evening News," 286, 288, 313, 317, 323, 328
  Fish Bowl room of, 313
"CBS Morning News," 306, 320, 321, 322, 323, 327, 328, 341

CBS News, 11, 17, 66, 180, 210, 250, 298, 299, 300–301, 308, 342, 346
  duplicated divisions of, 328–29
  field producers of, 329–30
  Huntley's retirement and, 204–5
  "managers" at, 319
  NBC News contrasted with, 287
  newsroom of, 287
  Old Guard ousted from, 318
  von Bülow trial and, 315
  women anchors and, 320–21
"CBS plus thirty," 45
CBS Sports, 319
CBS-TV, 25
"CBS Weekend News," 341
censorship:
  Israeli, 254–57
  in Vietnam, 340
Central Intelligence Agency (CIA), 90, 214, 290, 370–71
Century Club, 208
Cercle Sportif, 91, 92
Chambers, Al, 230, 231, 236
Chancellor, John, 25, 53, 108, 205
  Trotta's confrontations with, 174–75, 207
  women's movement and, 207–8
Chappaquiddick incident, 10, 178–184, 216, 349
  inquest of, 183–84, 191–95
  Kennedy's account of, 182–83
Chappaquiddick Press Club, 192
Charley O's, 78
Chiang Kai-shek, Mme., 56
Chicago American, 281
Chicago *Sun-Times*, 108
Chicago Tribune, 20–21, 28
China, Peoples Republic of, 16, 174, 211
Choudhoury, Abu Sayeed, 215
Chou En-lai, 226
Chung, Connie, 352
Churchill, Winston, 239
Clausewitz, Carl von, 98
Clendinen, Dudley, 316
clichés, 33, 110
client system, 241
CNN, 326, 338, 346, 352, 372
Cochran, John, 295
Cogley, John, 70, 73

College of New Rochelle, 70–72
Collingwood, Charles, 95
collusion theory, 187–88
Colombo, Joseph A., Sr., 200–202
Columbia School of Journalism, 15, 44, 60, 320
Coma (film), 14
Comedians, The (Greene), 247
"committed journalism," 363
Communist party, U.S., 110
Congress, U.S., 45, 186, 325, 326
Congress of Racial Equality (CORE), 42
Connery, Sean, 22–23
Conservative party, U.S., 34
Continental Palace Hotel, 86, 89, 104, 339
Cordelia, Mother, 71
Corelli, Franco, 22
correspondents, 130
    of AP, 96–97
    of BBC, 246
    British and American contrasted, 246
    of CBS, 95–96
    combat pay of, 132
    fatalities of, 120–21
    field producers and, 293, 329–30
    fishbowl existence of, 248
    local news and, 277
    of NBC, 95
    psychiatric screening of, 83
    reunion of, 354–55
    at Tet seminar, 361–64
    tours of, 174, 175, 231
    see also journalism; networks; television news; Vietnam press corps
Corrigan, Bill, 57, 76–77, 81, 83, 125, 135, 176, 219, 222
    Bernstein's correspondence with, 103
    Donghi fired by, 156
    nickname of, 34
    Steinman's correspondence with, 6, 123
    Trotta lectured by, 181
Cox, Archibald, 260
"credibility gap," 188
Cronkite, Walter, 25, 75, 96, 172,

    204, 247, 286, 289, 299, 305, 307, 313, 318, 334, 340, 350
    attempted blackmail of, 236–37
    chair of, 308
    Harris story and, 313
    professionalism of, 238–39
    Rather compared to, 299
    retirement of, 298
    Trotta's introduction to, 236
    Trotta's Iran broadcast and, 294–295
    Trotta welcomed by, 288
    Vietnam pullout statement of, 65
Crystal, Les, 34, 81, 286
    background of, 281–82
    Mulholland and, 281–82
    Trotta's interview with, 283–84
Cu Chi Regiment, 112–13
Culhane, David, 324
Cyprus, 246, 249

D'Amico, Adrienne, 358
D'Amico, Don, 137, 139, 146, 166, 173–74, 213, 238–39, 355
    background of, 138
    crash and rescue of, 356–61
    fateful mission of, 147–54
D'Amico, Donald, 358
D'Amico, Dora, 138
D'Amico, J. P., 358
D'Amico, Nancy, 358
Damone, Vic, 201
Damore, Leo, 195
Davis, Bette, 40
Davis, Gary, 19
Davis, Neil, 338
Day, Doris, 24
Dayan, Moshe, 257
Dean, Morton, 321
Decameron (Boccaccio), 70
Defense Department, U.S., 325–26
De Mille, Cecil B., 121, 254
Democratic party, U.S., 34, 35, 36, 65, 331
Denton, Jeremiah, 235
Dewey, Thomas E., 36
Dick (My's father), 344–46, 373
Dickerson, Nancy, 27, 53, 56, 205
Dien Bien Phu, 97, 125, 338
Dinis, Edmund, 193, 194

Dobyns, Lloyd, 260
Domino Theory, 105
Donaldson, Sam, 65–66
Donghi, Diane, 120
Donghi, Frank, 77, 80, 85, 98, 102, 123, 128, 137, 145, 372
  Corrigan's firing of, 156
  death of, 170
  personal problems of, 119–20, 168–69
  Steinman on, 86, 156
Donne, John, 261
Dotson, Gary, 322
Downs, Hugh, 52
Doyle, Larry, 288–89
Drayne, Dick, 180, 183
Dunning, Bruce, 334–35, 340, 341, 342, 344
Duvalier, François, 197
Dyas, Ed, 244
Dylan, Bob, 20

"E and E" briefing, 142
Eban, Abba, 257
Edwards, Doug, 298
Eldon, John Scott, Lord, 260
electronic journalism (EJ), 268
electronic news gathering (ENG), 268
Ellsberg, Daniel, 210, 232
Elsie (secretary), 347
El Salvador, 317
Emerson, Gloria, 362–63
Emmy award, 170, 264–65
End of the Affair, The (Greene), 247
English Usage (Fowler), 109
Enterprise, 214
Eshkol, Levi, 195
Esper (correspondent), 355
Ettinger, Pearle Chauncey, Jr. (Skip), 166, 213, 367
  calls to Trotta by, 176–77, 189–190
  fourth Vietnam tour of, 208–9
  medals returned by, 264
  as pathfinder scout, 159–61
  postwar experience of, 228, 365–366
  Vietnam Memorial visited by, 371–72, 374–75
executive producers, 41

Faas, Horst, 96–97, 125, 162, 234, 254, 355, 373
Fahringer, Herald, 312
Fairness in Media, 346
Farrar, John, 193
Federal Bureau of Investigation (FBI), 120
Federal Communications Commission (FCC), 18
Feinsinger, Nathan, 55
Felder, Raoul Lionel, 349
Feminine Mystique, The (Friedan), 196
Ferguson, Flo, 243
field producers, 63, 293, 329–30
"Firebase Sandy," 132
Fire Support Base "Julie," 157
First Infantry Division, U.S., 83
Fischer, Dick, 282
  Trotta's interview with, 282–83
Fish Bowl, 313, 320, 322
Fitzgerald, F. Scott, 335
516th Vietcong Battalion, 158
Flamenhaft, Fred, 107–8, 110, 111, 281, 284
  on Margolis, 259
  Northshield and, 109
Flick, Bob, 104–5, 116, 156
Flynn, Errol, 118
Flynn, Sean, 118, 338
Fonda, Jane, 68, 231, 362
Forche Caudine, Le, 36–37
Fortune Society, 276
Fouhy, Ed, 299
Fourth Infantry Division, U.S., 82
Fowler, Henry W., 109
Francis, Connie, 201
Frank, Barney, 370
Frank, Reuven, 33, 53, 60, 66, 188, 211, 216
  bizarre memo of, 101–2
  career of, 110–11
  on Donghi, 170
  personality of, 111
  Steinman's correspondence with, 123, 145–46, 304
  Tuckner and, 100, 101
Frederick, Pauline, 27, 53, 56, 175, 205
  Trotta advised by, 174

Friedan, Betty, 196
Fulbright, William, 186

Gallegos, William, 292
Gallup Poll, 186
Gandhi, Indira, 195, 221–22, 322
Gandolph, Ray, 321
Garfield, John, 276
Gargan, Joseph, 179–80, 183, 195
Gaskill, Nemo, 180, 181
Gaspard, George, 89–90, 373
Gazzara, Ben, 22
Gelinas, Rick, 72
General Electric, 352
George, Phyllis, 322
Gifford, Alec, 51–52
Gish, Lillian, 22
Global Light Network, 373
Gluck, Barbara, 88, 373
Goad, Rex, 38
God and Man at Yale (Buckley), 35
Goldberg, Arthur J., 203
Goodman, Julian, 279
"Good Morning America," 320
Grable, Betty, 67
Grant, Cary, 204
"Great Gasoline War" news series, 278–79
Green Berets, The (film), 145
Green Berets, The (Moore), 89, 355
Greene, Graham, 86, 247
Grenada, 325
  media and, 326–27
Grossman, Larry, 319
Gumbel, Bryant, 340
"Gunsmoke," 224
Guthrie, Andy, 104, 105, 146
Guys and Dolls, 109

Halberstam, David, 355
Hamilton, George, 58
Hangen, Pat, 163
Hangen, Welles, 95, 163, 338
Hanoi Hannah, 132
"happy talk," 267
Harben, Bill, 364–65
Harriman, W. Averell, 18, 102
Harris, Jean, 312
  women's identification with, 313–14

Harsch, Joseph C. (correspondent), 53
Hart, Gary, 57, 331
Hayden, Tom, 232
Hearst, William Randolph, 370
Heath, Edward R., 249
Hedges, Michael, 310
Helms, Jesse, 346
Hemingway, Ernest, 20, 41, 47, 108, 233, 335
Herman, George, 324
Hesse, Hermann, 184
Heston, Charlton, 165
Higgins, Marguerite, 57
Hillman Periodicals, 15
Himmelfarb, Ida, 28
Hiss, Alger, 316
Hoa (My's mother) 343–46, 373
Ho Chi Minh, 99, 119, 185, 226, 361
Ho Chi Minh Trail, 89, 372
Hoffman, Abbie, 198–99
Homecoming, Operation, 234–35
Hong Kong, 145, 163
Hope, Bob, 231
Hottelet, Richard, 321
Hudson, Rock, 302
Huet, Henri, 97
Huk guerrillas, 220
Humbert, King of Italy, 36
Humphrey, Hubert, 65, 68, 69, 79, 122
Hunt, Richard, 172
Hunt, William S., 372
Huntley, Chet, 25, 27, 33, 41, 43, 53, 114, 127–28, 172
  Agnew's media assault and, 188
  death of, 263
  Perkins memo of, 192
  retirement of, 204–5
  Socolow on, 204–5
  Trotta and, 49–50, 132, 171, 205
Huntley, Tippy, 49–50
"Huntley-Brinkley Report, The," 60, 62, 63, 75, 81, 103, 170–171, 173, 262
  "Mafia Women" on, 200
  Mekong Delta piece on, 161
  Tay Ninh battle on, 127
  Thuong Duc story on, 144–45
  unheard voices of, 107–9
Hurley, Cornelius (Connie), 192

Hurley, Old Man, 47
Hurley's bar, 47–48, 50
Huston, John, 22
Huynh, Vo, see Vo Huynh

I Corps, U.S., 130, 132
in-court camera, 315–17
India-Pakistan War, 211–15
INS, 46, 313
Inter-Catholic Press Agency, 16
International Control Commission
   (ICC), 231
interviews, 25
   local news and, 278
   "Man in the Street," 272–73
   subjects of, 40–41
   tricks of, 224–25
Iran hostage crisis, 10, 285, 289–
   297, 300
   American media and, 290
   embassy parties during, 295
   failed rescue mission and, 305,
   325
   hostage release in, 305–6
   journalists' expulsion and, 295–
   297
   media manipulation in, 292
   non-Persian groups and, 296
   protests during, 293–94
   rumors and, 293
   staged demonstrations in, 292
Ireland, 250
Irish Republican Army (IRA), 250–
   251
Irish Times, 252
Iron Curtain, 16
Israel, 250, 253
   military censorship by, 254–57
Italian-American Civil Rights
   League, 200

Javits, Jacob, 56
Jayavarmaparameçvara, Khmer
   king, 231
Jefferson, Thomas, 233
Johanson, Andrew, 170
John Paul I, Pope, 286
John Paul II, Pope, 305
Johnson, Lynda Bird, 58
Johnson, Lyndon B., 56, 122, 137,
   138, 172, 186, 361, 367

Brinkley and, 173
death of, 232
presidential race abandoned by, 65
Johnson, Mac, 52, 126–27, 211
Joint Casualty Resolution Commission (JCRC), 336
Jones, Jim, 104
journalism, 15–16
   as allegory, 179
   "committed," 363
   drinking and, 46–48
   electronic, 268
   Joyce-Sauter practice of, 318
   "team," 321
   see also correspondents; networks;
   television news; Vietnam press
   corps
Joyce, Edward, 307, 309, 310, 315,
   324–25, 347, 348
   career of, 319
   Chappaquiddick story and, 349
   decision making by, 321–22
   dress of, 319–20
   journalism as practiced by, 318
   ratings assigned by, 317
   "usage" chart of, 330
Justice Department, U.S., 200

Kalischer, Peter, 95
Kamm, Henry, 221
Kardisch, Van, 66, 67–68, 199,
   205, 206
Kendall, Peter, 305, 307
Kennedy, Edward M. (Ted), 178,
   179, 180–85, 349
   Bangladesh visit of, 216–18
   Chappaquiddick account of, 182–
   183
   inquest and, 191–95
   Trotta's confrontation with, 182
Kennedy, Ethel, 179
Kennedy, Jackie, 45
Kennedy, Joan, 180, 216, 217
Kennedy, John F., 15, 172, 178,
   180, 182, 217, 331
Kennedy, Robert, 10, 65, 67, 68,
   101, 177, 178–79, 180, 192
   assassination of, 78
   at Charley O's, 78–79
   Presidential campaign, 74
   Trotta and, 56

Kennedy, Rose, 183
Kennedy family, 179, 193
Kennedy-Nixon debate, 19
Kennerly, David Hume, 229–30, 237
Kent State incident, 197
Kerr, Jean, 71
Khomeini, Ayatollah Ruholla, 285, 290, 291, 292, 293, 296
Khoo, Terry, 228
Khrushchev, Nikita, 15
Kiker, Douglas, 174
Kimball, Penn, 18
King, Martin Luther, Jr., 65
Kintner, Robert, 29
  background and personality of, 44–45
  Trotta memos of, 45, 48
Kirkpatrick, Clayton, 21
Kissinger, Henry, 211, 232, 258, 289
KNBC, 262
Koob, Kathryn, 305
Kopechne, Joseph, 195
Kopechne, Mary Jo, 178, 179, 181–184, 191–94, 216, 349
Koppel, Ted, 224, 302, 338, 340, 366
Korean War, 17, 137, 139, 362
Kravitz, Sy, 200–202
Kuralt, Charles, 306, 320, 321, 342
Kurtis, Bill, 321
Kutzleb, Dick, 14, 29, 54, 56–57

Lalo (Trotta's uncle), 83–84
Lane, John, 287, 305, 323, 324–325, 330
Laos, 97, 142, 210, 226, 229, 234
Larkin, Peter, 306
"Laugh-In," 118
Laurence, Jack, 250
Lebanon, 325
Lee Kuan Yew, 226
Leonard, Bill, 287
Levine, Irving R., 174
Lewis, Anthony, 18
Lewis, George, 337
Lewis, Warren, 307
"licking the lollipop," 223
Liebling, A. J., 32
Life, 97, 193

Lindbergh, Anne Morrow, 71
Lindbergh, Charles, 136
Lindsay, John V., 34, 35
  interviewed by Trotta, 29–31
  reelection of, 178
  transit strike and, 54
Lindstrom, Pia, 269
Loan, General, 338
Lodge, Henry Cabot, 232
Long, Mr. (driver), 85, 120, 166
Long Island Press, 16
Look, Christopher, 193
"loop," 63
Loren, Sophia, 56
Los Angeles Times, 175, 254, 301–2
Luce, Henry, 162

McAndrew, Bill, 31, 44, 55, 60
MacArthur, Douglas, 92, 234, 302
MacArthur, George, 97, 355
McCarthy, Abigail, 69
McCarthy, Bob, 30, 46
McCarthy, Eugene, 60, 62, 65, 67, 232
  Catholicism of, 70–71
  character of, 69–70, 73–74
  Chicago riots and, 73–74
  eccentric demeanor of, 73–74
  on Pat Nixon, 70
  on politics, 349
  set speech of, 68–69
  Trotta's introduction to, 66
McCarthy campaign, 61–78, 177
  Newman and, 68
  results of, 76
McCormick, Robert R., 21
MacFarland, Bob, 243, 246, 249, 258
  Westfeldt and, 243
McGee, Frank, 25, 53, 205, 207, 263
McGovern, George, 230, 232, 330–332
Mackin, Cassie, 196
MacLaine, Shirley, 68
McMahon, Ed, 201
McNamara, Robert, 210, 232
MacNeil, Robert (Robin), 29
  backward film episode and, 38–39
Madeleine, Mother, 72
Mafia, 199–201

"Mafia Women," 200
Mailer, Norman, 177–78
"make nice" news, 267
male chauvinism, 37, 57–58, 98,
  196, 205–7
Manila Times, 219
Manson, Charles, 185
Mao Tse-tung, 16, 226
Marcos, Ferdinand, 218, 220, 221
Marcos, Imelda, 97, 220
Margolis, Irwin, 34, 240–45, 248,
  252, 253
  Flamenhaft on, 259
  gossip about, 241–42
  Montgomery's loathing of, 245
  morning patrol of, 243
  Trotta and, 247, 260–62
  Wald on, 242
marijuana, 185
Markham, Paul, 179–80, 183
Martin, Joel, 131
Marx, Karl, 120
Mary (tea server), 246
"Mary Tyler Moore Show," 274
Mathur, Vishnu, 219, 222
Maugham, Somerset, 366
Maxine (Trotta's friend), 20
Mayaguez, 325
Mazzacane, Giorgio (grandfather),
  ˙36–37
Mazzacane, Lillian Theresa, *see*
  Trotta, Lillian Theresa Mazza-
  cane
Mazzacane, Luisa Barbieri (grand-
  mother), 36
Meany, Don, 58–59
"Meet the Press," 216, 220
Meir, Golda, 195, 256, 257
"Memphis on the Potomac," 369
Merlis, George, 320–21
Merron, Rich, 97, 118
Mesta, Perle, 373
Metcalf, Joseph, III, 326
MIAs, 336
Mid-West Regional Republican
  Committee, 187
Military Assistance Command Viet-
  nam (MACV), 88, 155
Millay, Edna St. Vincent, 314–15
Miller, David, 289, 292–93, 296,
  297

Millis, Walter, 170
Millstein, Gilbert, 109–10, 111
Milton, John, 55
Minh the Tailor, 122
Minnelli, Liza, 22
Minow, Newton, 18–19
Missouri, 126
Mixter, David, 372
Mobile Riverine Force, 157
Mobil Oil, 278–79
Mohr, Charles, 135, 254
"moments," theory of, 315
Mondale, Walter, 299–300, 331
Monde, Le, 188
Montelegre, Felicia, 92
Montgomery, George, 242–43, 246,
  258
  Margolis loathed by, 245
  Wald and, 245
moon landing, 180
Moore, Henry, 242
Moore, Robin, 89, 355
Moorehead, Agnes, 22
Moses, Robert, 42
Mother Wore Tights (film), 67
Movietone News, 37
Mudd, Roger, 96, 298
Mukti Bahini, 217
Mulholland, Bob, 244, 247, 272, 319
  career of, 33–34, 262–63
  Crystal and, 281–82
  Trotta and, 240–41, 261–62,
    264, 279–80
Mullah Mary, 291
Muller, Bobby, 197
Mulligan, Hugh, 97–98, 254, 355
"Murderer's Row," 53–54
Murray, Father, 360
Murray, George, 304
Murrow, Edward R., 25, 27, 239,
  298, 308
My, Nguyen Thanh, *see* Nguyen
  Thanh My
My Lai massacre, 197, 208–9

Nash, Max, 114, 117
Nashville *Tennessean*, 172
National Aeronautics and Space
  Administration (NASA), 178
National Organization for Women
  (NOW), 205, 208, 314

Nawaz, Shuja, 213–14, 367
NBC, 25–26, 29, 30, 38, 48, 49,
    52, 63, 66, 74, 93, 94, 108,
    111, 115, 127, 131, 158, 165,
    181, 188, 199, 204, 205, 216,
    235–36, 242, 244, 263, 268,
    270, 274, 277, 287, 295, 296,
    299, 319, 338, 339, 340, 352
  Big Picture and, 156–57
  "Californiazation" of, 282
  client system and, 241
  as "correspondents network,"
    44
  correspondents of, 95
  correspondent "tours" at, 174,
    175, 231
  hiring standards of, 27–28
  Iran deal of, 292
  Mobil Oil and, 278–79
  psychiatrist rule of, 83
  Pueblo incident and, 164
  Saigon bureau of, 99, 101, 102,
    104, 145
  television news and, 27
  transit strike scoop by, 55
  women and, 27–28
NBC News, 43, 60, 66, 75, 81, 98,
    102, 109, 126, 170, 171, 181,
    184, 185, 212, 227–28, 240,
    244, 249, 263, 281, 283, 286,
    305, 334, 337
  budget crunch at, 211
  CBS News contrasted with, 287
  growth of, 108
  Huntley's retirement from, 204–5
  Hurley incident and, 47–48
  "Murderer's Row" of, 53–54
  nicknames at, 33–34
  Saigon bureau of, 96
  "summit" of, 260–61
NBC News Overseas, 242
"NBC Nightly News," 205, 209,
    227, 243, 259
NBC Symphony Orchestra, 29
Nehru, Jawaharlal, 195
networks:
  anchors of, 350–51
  campaign ground rule of, 301
  financial problems of, 347, 351–
    352
  local news and, 267, 318

news vs. entertainment on, 18–
    19
  POW coverage by, 234–35
  Real Air War of, 232–33
  rivalry between, 25–26
  selection of talent by, 349–50
  Vietnam anniversary broadcasts
    of, 340
  von Bülow trial coverage by,
    317–18
  White House intimidation of,
    188–89
  see also correspondents; journal-
    ism; television news; Vietnam
    press corps
Newark Evening News, 110
New Haven Register, 21
New Jersey, 139–40
"New Journalism," 177
Newman, Edwin, 25, 43, 53
Newman, Paul, 56, 68
Newman Club, 72
New Republic, 18
news, see correspondents; journal-
    ism; networks; television news;
    television news, local
Newsday, 14, 21, 22, 23, 26, 28,
    29, 42
Newsweek, 246
New York, 177, 314
New York Daily News, 25, 28, 46,
    193, 205, 279, 313
New Yorker, 156, 267
New York Herald Tribune, 28, 31,
    44, 51, 126
New York Mets, 185
New York Post, 28, 67, 304
New York Times, 16, 17, 19, 24,
    26, 28, 81–82, 88, 99, 109,
    135, 145, 170, 185, 201, 210,
    221, 234, 254, 279, 292, 304,
    315, 362, 363
New York World-Telegram, 24, 28,
    39
New York World-Telegram and Sun,
    28
Nghia (cameraman), 140, 142–43
Nguyen Thanh My, 343–46, 373
Nha Trang, 154
nicknames, 33–34
"Nightline," 340

Ninth Infantry Division, U.S., 157, 186
Ninth Marine Expeditionary Brigade, U.S., 76
Nixon, Pat, 70
Nixon, Richard M., 36, 65, 79, 122, 135, 155, 175, 176, 184, 196, 259, 266, 272, 273, 298
    media's conflict with, 186–89
    reelection of, 230
    resignation of, 260
    silent majority speech of, 186
North Atlantic Treaty Organization (NATO), 239
Nixon-Kennedy debate, 19
North Korea, 164, 362
Northshield, Shad, 107–8, 110, 111, 320, 323–24, 342, 344
    Flamenhaft and, 109
    Westfeldt's replacement of, 171–172

O'Connell, David, 251
O'Connor, Norman J., 72
Olsen, Al, 244
101st Airborne Division, U.S., 97, 112, 117, 131
O'Neill, Steve, 296–97
173rd Airborne Division, U.S., 372
"On His Blindness" (Milton), 55
"Ora Italiana, L'," 37
Operation Homecoming, 234–35
Operation Tiger Claw, 158
Osgood, Charles, 306
Oswald, Lee Harvey, 29, 202, 258
Overseas Press Club, 354
Overseas Press Club Award, 186, 264–65

Pahlavi, Mohammad Reza, Shah of Iran, 288–89, 290
Paige, Tim, 338
Pakistan-India War, 211–15
Pakistan People's Party, 214
Paley, William S., 288, 319, 320, 352
Palm Tree Prophet, 119
Pappas, Ike, 321
Paris Match, 125
Paris peace talks, 102, 132, 139, 155, 165, 185, 229, 231

Park, Tong Sung, 302
Parnell, Charles S., 47
Patterson, Alicia, 21–22
Pauley, Jane, 280
Paul VI, Pope, 42
Peace Corps, 233, 259
peace movement, 11, 59, 65, 122
    Christmas bombing and, 230
    extent of, 176
    hard-hats vs., 198
    media as perceived by, 188
    North Vietnamese exploitation of, 138, 189
Pentagon Papers, 210–11
People's Action Party, 226
Peoples Temple, 104
Perkins, Jack, 59, 191–92, 234, 235
Philippines, 218–19
Phillips, Drew, 39, 193, 194, 255
Pierpont, Robert, 324
Pinza, Ezio, 84
Plague, The (Camus), 324
Podell, Jules, 202
Poland, 306–7
Pond, Geoffrey, 178
"pool reporting," 232–33
Powell, Adam Clayton, Jr., 45
Power, Tyrone, 211
Presley, Elvis, 71
"press bus," 255
Pressman, Gabe, 24, 54
Prince, Buck, 48
print media, 15–16, 17, 25, 28–29, 43–44, 95, 135–36, 137
prisoners of war (POWs), 230, 336, 355, 362
    network coverage of, 234–35
    release of, 238–39
    Trotta's encounter with, 237–38
producers, 41, 63, 188, 293, 329–330
psychiatrists, 82–83
Public Broadcasting System (PBS), 29, 319
Pueblo, 105, 164–65, 325
Pulitzer Prize, 16, 50, 57, 96–97, 338, 362

"Q-ratings," 270
Quan (interpreter), 335, 342–43
Quarles, Norma, 196

"quick pops," 273
Quiet American, The (Greene), 86, 247
Quill, Mike, 54
Quint, Bert, 294–95

Rabinowitz, Max, 276
race riots, 59–60, 65
radical chic, 92, 192
Radner, Gilda, 270
Rahman, Mujibur, 215
Raphael, Father, 16
Rather, Dan, 81, 96, 288, 307, 313, 318, 320, 322–23, 325, 327, 334, 341, 342, 344, 346, 347, 349
    Cronkite compared to, 299
    debut of, 298–99
    duplicated news division and, 328–29
    hit list of, 321
    ratings assigned by, 317
    tennis match episode of, 330
    on Time cover, 298
    Trotta's meeting with, 308–10
Ray (Trotta's uncle), 83
Razor's Edge, 72
RCA, 26, 29, 47, 211, 279
Reagan, Ronald, 10, 204, 300, 325, 367
    attempted assassination of, 305–6
Real Air War, 232–33
Reasoner, Harry, 255, 277–78
reenactments, 352
"Renascence" (Millay), 315
"reporter involvement," 267
Repose, 359
Republican party, U.S., 34, 35, 65, 275, 302
Reston, James, 277
Reuters, 245
Revolutionary Council, Iranian, 295
Reynolds, Jack, 165
Rivera, Geraldo, 270
Robards, Jason, 47
Robb, Charles, 58
Robbins, Al, 171, 207
Roberts, Sam, 325, 333–34, 340, 343
Robinson, Doug, 145

Rockefeller, Nelson, 24, 65, 203
    interviewed by Trotta, 16
    philandering of, 56–57
"rocket belt," 86
Rogers, Kenny, 173
Rolling Stones, 56
Rolling Thunder program, 137
Roosevelt, Franklin D., 367
Rosenthal, A. M., 82
Rosenthal, Edwin M., 164–65
Rosholt, Jerry, 209
Roth, Richard, 301
Ruby, Jack, 202
Rusk, Dean, 232
Russell, Jack, 116

Saarinen, Aline, 196, 205–6, 207
Safer, Morley, 355, 361
Salisbury, Harrison, 361–62
Sandburg, Carl, 366
Sannio Club, 36
Sarnoff, David, 29, 49, 243, 352
Sarnoff, Robert W., 211
"Saturday Night Live," 270–71, 274
"Saturday Night Massacre," 260
"Saturday Night with Connie Chung," 352
Sauter, Van Gordon, 307, 309, 310, 320, 348
    on anchorwomen, 322
    decision making by, 321–22
    journalism as practiced by, 318
    "moments" theory of, 315, 329, 351
    ratings assigned by, 317
    story length limited by, 323
    "style" of, 319
    Trotta's first meeting with, 308
    von Bülow trial and, 315
SAVAK, 290
Sawyer, Diane, 321
Scarborough, Chuck, 273–74
Schulberg, Stuart, 206–7
Schwartz, Lou, 23–24
Seale, Bobby, 198–99
Seamans, Ike, 296
Senate, U.S., 56, 73
Seper, Jerry, 310
Sevareid, Eric, 72, 239, 302, 366
Shafer, Bob, 58–59

Shariat-Madari, Ayatollah Kazem, 296
Sheppard, Sam, 193
Sherman, William T., 94
Shirer, William, 239
Shor, Toots, 49
Shoumacher, David, 66
Sidey, Hugh, 179
"silent majority," 186, 187
Silverman, Fred, 283–84
Simon, Bob, 340
Sinatra, Frank, 56, 201
Singapore, 225–26
Sinn Fein, 251
Sirhan, Sirhan, 185
Six-Day War, 93, 254
"Sixth Hour News, The," 29, 31, 48, 99
"60 Minutes," 361
Slote, Leslie, 56–57
Small, Bill, 286–87
Smith, Howard, 296
Snyder, Don, 242, 250–52
Snyder, Tom, 274
Socolow, Sandy, 307, 314, 318, 322
  career of, 313
  on Huntley, 204–5
Soldier's Medal, 176
Solidarity, 306, 307
"Some Enchanted Evening," 84
South Pacific, 84
Soviet Union, 257–58, 293
Spence, Craig J., 91–93, 189–90, 228
  decline and death of, 365–71, 372
  in Harben's letter, 364–65
  personality of, 92
  Washington life style of, 302–4
Spivak, Lawrence, 216
Stalin, Joseph, 351
Stallone, Sylvester, 271
stand-uppers, 41, 223–24, 329
Stars and Stripes, 105, 146, 262
"Star-Spangled Banner, The," 230
State Department, U.S., 164, 222, 305, 345
"Stealth Campaign," 301
Steinbeck, John, Jr., 119
Steinman, Ron, 57, 77, 99, 100

on Big Picture approach, 157
Burn's replacement of, 185
Corrigan correspondence of, 86, 123
on Donghi, 86, 156
Frank correspondence of, 123, 145–146, 304
on Tuckner, 99, 100, 101, 275, 304
Sterba, Jim, 234
Stern, Carl, 174
Stern, Isaac, 185
Stewart, Jimmy, 204
Stone, Dana, 118
Stringer, Howard, 317–18, 352
Students for a Democratic Society (SDS), 60, 120
Studies and Observation Group (SOG), 89
Sulzberger, Arthur Hays, 162
"Sunday Morning," 320, 323, 324, 330, 342
Sunset Boulevard (film), 324
Swanson, Gloria, 324
Swayze, John Cameron, 16
Swift, Elizabeth Ann, 305

Tabriz, rioting in, 296–97
Tarnower, Herman, 312
Tate, Sharon, 185
Taylor, Telford, 231
Tay Ninh battle, 122–28
Teague, Bob, 269
television news, 11, 155, 221
  ad-libbing and, 41
  "adverse pool" and, 297
  Agnew's assault on, 187–89
  air war neglected by, 136–37
  anchors and, 350–51
  Arlen on, 156
  in Asia, 222–23
  big stories and, 75–76
  campaign ground rule of, 301
  clichés and, 33, 110
  collusion theory and, 187–88
  daily life and, 286
  declining quality of, 349–51
  double standard and, 37, 57–58
  drinking and, 46–48
  early days of, 227
  events "made" for, 258–59

television news (*cont.*)
  executive producers of, 41
  field producers and, 63, 293,
    329–30
  filming of, 62–63
  Golden Age of, 351
  Grenada invasion and, 326–27
  in-court camera and, 315–16
  Israeli censorship of, 254–57
  JFK assassination and, 26–27
  junior producers and, 188
  Moses on, 42
  NBC and, 27
  network entertainment and, 18–19
  news desk and, 67
  nicknames and, 33–34
  Nixon and, 187–89
  Pentagon Papers and, 211
  pilots and, 148
  print media and, 15–16, 17, 25,
    28–29, 43–44, 95, 135–36, 137
  reenactments on, 352
  slanting of, 175
  story processing by, 102, 103–4
  talent selection in, 349–50
  technology and, 32–33, 37–38,
    42, 62–64, 170–71, 268–69,
    334
  theory of "moments" and, 315
  underground press and, 118–19
  unpopularity of, 186–89
  Vietnam War and, 95, 98, 156
  women anchors and, 321–22
  women and, 27–28, 29, 165–66,
    175–76
  see also correspondents; journal-
    ism; networks; Vietnam press
    corps
television news, local, 40, 44, 266–
    284
  company loyalty and, 281
  correspondents and, 277
  Grenada invasion and, 326
  growth of, 268
  "happy talk" on, 267
  interviews as perceived by, 278
  network news and, 267, 318
  new lingo of, 268–70, 319
  "reporter involvement" and, 267
  routine coverage by, 272–73
  shortcomings of, 275, 277

  technology and, 268–69
  women and, 277–78
Tennyson, Alfred, Lord, 6
Teresa, Mother, 228, 371
terrorism, 251
Tet offensive, 59, 65, 76, 98, 100,
    101, 103, 108, 115, 165, 166
  Saigon affected by, 90–91
  seminar on, 361–64
Thatcher, Margaret, 249
Theodore, Bill, 156
theory of "moments," 315
Thiel, Sid, 278
"thousand-yard stare," 113
366th Tactical Fighter Wing, U.S., 136
Threlkeld, Richard, 338
Thuong Duc, 140–45
Tiegs, Cheryl, 335
Tiger Claw, Operation, 158
Time, 18, 179, 254, 338
  Rather on cover of, 298
Times (London), 162, 258
Tinker, Grant, 263
Tisch, Laurence, 318, 352
"Today" show, 27, 69, 186, 205–7,
    279–80
  Trotta and, 51–52, 235
  Vietnam broadcasts of, 340
  women on, 205–7
Tokyo Rose, 132
"Tomorrow" show, 274
"Tonight" show, 47, 201
Tontons Macoutes, 197
Topol, 255
Toscanini, Arturo, 29, 288
Townsend, Dallas, 17–18
Trang Bang, 104, 105, 111–17
Transit Workers Union, 54
Tran Trong Khanh, 352–53
Treaster, Joe, 88
Trilling, Diane, 313–14, 315
Trotta, Thomas (Gaetano; father),
    35, 143
Trotta, Lillian Theresa Mazzacane
    (mother), 35
Trotta, Liz:
  African drought covered by, 259,
    265
  Amerasian story of, 342–46, 373
  awards won by, 170, 186, 201–2,
    264–65

bag of tricks of, 224–25
CBS firing of, 348
celebrity status of, 56–57, 74–75
childhood memories of, 83–84
crash site visit of, 336–37
dysentery of, 229–30
early career of, 12–15, 16, 20–24, 29–31, 39–40
education of, 15–17, 28, 70–72
embarrassing moments of, 45–46, 51–52
family background of, 35–37
first blooper of, 54–55
first combat experience of, 111–116
first interview by, 29–31
first live television appearance of, 45–46
Grenada invasion covered by, 327–28
"groupie" incident and, 203–4
"hair problem" of, 45
ID card of, 88–89
in-court camera disfavored by, 316
"Joyce problem" of, 309–10, 349
letters of, 80–81, 105–6
McCarthy campaign assignment of, 60
McGovern campaign and, 330–332
male chauvinism and, 37, 57–58, 98, 205–7
in Mekong Delta, 157–61
nearsightedness of, 223
nicknames of, 16, 34
physical hardships endured by, 144
Polish crisis covered by, 306–7
press center's view of, 131–32
psychiatrist and, 82–83
rocket attack and, 87
second Vietnam tour of, 186, 189
sexual harassment encountered by, 66
"shoot" incident of, 130–31
Singapore bureau assignment of, 217
Tabriz rioting and, 296–97
at Tay Ninh battle, 122–27

Thuong Duc experience of, 140–145
Times Square series by, 24, 29
unemployed, 286
VA story of, 197–98
Vietnam arrival of, 85
Vietnam assignment of, 77–78
Wald's gift to, 274–75
women's rights stories by, 196
"Trotta clause," 349
Troup Junior High School, 28
Troup Trumpet, 84
Tuckner, Howard, 338, 369, 372
career of, 99–101
death of, 303–4
Frank and, 100, 101
Huynh and, 100
Steinman on, 99, 100, 101, 275, 304
Trotta's New York meeting with, 275
on Tuckner, 304–5
wounded, 59
Tuohy, Bill, 254
Turner, Ted, 346
Twain, Mark, 25
25th Army, Japanese, 233
Twenty-fifth Infantry Division, U.S., 112–13

U.S. News & World Report, 227
Ubell, Earl, 271–72, 279
Ullman family, 35
Ulster Freedom Fighters, 242
"Ulysses" (Tennyson), 6
underground press, 118–19
United Nations, 15, 27, 164, 174, 257, 321, 334
United Press International (UPI), 46, 126
United States, 102, 186, 238
air war policy of, 137–38
Cambodia invaded by, 196–98
Middle East and, 257–58
Pueblo incident and, 164–65
Vietnam pullout of, 186
Utley, Garrick, 53, 242, 258, 338

VA hospitals, 197–98
Vale, Jerry, 201

Van Ess, Hugh, 112, 115
Vanocur, Sander, 25, 44, 282
Van Witsen, Tony, 276, 278
"vast wasteland," 18–19
Victoria, Queen of England, 222
"video kittens," 329
Vietcong, 86, 92, 112–13, 119,
    131, 135, 160, 197
Vietminh, 98
Vietnam, Democratic Republic of
    (North), 59, 102, 136, 137,
    146, 186, 189
  air war and, 137–38
  antiwar sentiment exploited by,
    138, 189
Vietnam, Republic of (South), 59
  National Assembly of, 86
Vietnam, united, 335–41
"Vietnamization," 186, 189
Vietnam Memorial, 371–72, 374–
    375
Vietnam press corps:
  army view of, 131
  black humor of, 97–98
  defeatism in, 98, 134–35
  estrangement of, 136
  grunts as viewed by, 136
  life style of, 93–95
  male domination of, 95
  see also correspondents; journal-
    ism; networks; television news
Vietnam Veterans of America, 198
Vietnam War, 19, 53, 57, 76, 320,
    325, 354–55, 374
  air war strategy in, 137–39, 148
  civilian casualties in, 160
  ideology and coverage of, 362
  peace agreement in, 232
  rumors in, 155
  sounds of, 87
  television news and, 95, 98, 156
  Tet seminar and, 361–64
  Trotta influenced by, 9–11
  U.S. pullout from, 186
  veteran correspondents in, 95–96
  World War II contrasted with,
    135
  see also Tet offensive
Vi Giac, 157
VIZNEWS, 199
Vo Huynh, 98, 104, 112–15, 122,

    125–26, 127, 128, 154, 166,
    190
  postwar life of, 373
  as refugee, 264
  on Tuckner, 304–5
  Tuckner and, 100
von Bülow, Claus, 311–12, 315–18
  described, 316
von Bülow, Sunny, 311–12
Vo Nguyen Giap, 340

WABC, 270
Wagner, Dick, 317
Wagner, Robert F., 34
Wald, Richard, 34, 217, 240, 243,
    260, 261, 263, 280–81
  on Margolis, 242
  Montgomery and, 245
  Trotta's gift from, 274–75
Wallace, Jim, 227
Wall Street Journal, 279, 328
Walters, Barbara, 27, 206, 270, 280
  contract of, 277–78, 281
war:
  men and women in, 133–34
  seductiveness of, 133
Washington Post, 14, 314
Washington Times, 367, 370
Watergate affair, 195, 210–11, 259–
    260, 269, 275
Watson, Paul, 360
Watts, Cliff, 213
Wayne, John, 89, 133, 145, 204
WBBM, 281
WBZ, 181, 182
WCBS, 309
WCBS News, 29
WCBS radio, 349
WDSU, 51
Weathermen, 120
Webb, Cathy, 322
Webb, John, 337
Weizman, Ezer, 257
WELI, 37
Welles, Orson, 370
Westfeldt, Wallace, 173, 196, 207,
    215, 236, 263
  Agnew's media assault and, 187,
    188
  MacFarland and, 243
  Northshield replaced by, 171–72

Westmoreland, William, 92, 232
  CBS suit of, 320, 346
Weymouth, Lally, 314–15
Wharton, Edith, 72
White, Bob, 51
White, Jim, 260
White, William Allen, 299
White House Scholars, 50
Wicker, Tom, 363
Widmark, Richard, 276
Wilburn, Sam, 149, 151, 153, 359, 360
Williams, Derek, 341
Wilson, Theo, 193, 313
Winters, Jonathan, 47
WMAQ, 262, 281
WNBC, 14, 24, 29, 32, 37, 49, 99, 165, 169, 264, 268
  security guard story of, 276
  staff of, 269–70
"Women in Prison," 207
women's issues, 11, 175, 195–96, 269
  Chancellor and, 207–8
  Harris trial and, 313–14

"Today" show and, 205–8
Women's Wear Daily, 58
Woodstock festival, 20, 184–85
World Citizen, 19
World's Fair (1964–65), 41–42
World War II, 17, 21, 25, 82, 119, 233
  Vietnam contrasted with, 135
Wren, Christopher, 16, 292
Wyman, Thomas H., 302, 348

Xuan Tuy, 102, 189

Yale University, 35, 198
Yamashita, Tomoyuki, 233
Yashiro (sound man), 140, 142, 143, 213
Yasuda, Yunichi, 157, 159, 213
Yates, Ted, 93
Yeats, William Butler, 320
Yom Kippur War, 247, 253
Young, Steve, 321
Young Americans for Freedom, 19

Ziegfeld, Flo, 174